# PROGRAMMING LOGIC AND DESIGN
## INTRODUCTORY
### THIRD EDITION

Joyce Farrell

William Rainey Harper College

## Programming Logic and Design, Introductory, Third Edition

by Joyce Farrell

**Managing Editor:**
Jennifer Muroff

**Acquisitions Editor:**
Roberts Apse

**Product Manager:**
Tricia Boyle

**Development Editor:**
Lisa Ruffolo

**Marketing Manager:**
Brian Berkeley

**Editorial Assistant:**
Amanda Piantedosi

**Production Editor:**
Christine Gatliffe

**Cover Designer:**
Nancy Goulet

**Interior Designer:**
Betsy Young

**Compositor:**
GEX Publishing Services

**Manufacturing Coordinator:**
Laura Burns

# ◾◾◾◾ BRIEF CONTENTS

PREFACE                                                                     xi

CHAPTER ONE
An Overview of Computers and Logic                                           1

CHAPTER TWO
Understanding Structure                                                     35

CHAPTER THREE
Modules, Hierarchy Charts, and Documentation                               73

CHAPTER FOUR
Writing and Designing a Complete Program                                  113

CHAPTER FIVE
Making Decisions                                                          149

CHAPTER SIX
Looping                                                                   203

CHAPTER SEVEN
Control Breaks                                                            245

CHAPTER EIGHT
Arrays                                                                    285

APPENDIX A
Solving Difficult Structuring Problems                                    A-1

APPENDIX B
Understanding Numbering Systems and Computer Codes                        B-1

APPENDIX C
Using a Large Decision Table                                              C-1

GLOSSARY                                                                  G-1

INDEX                                                                     I-1

# TABLE OF CONTENTS

PREFACE        xi

## CHAPTER ONE

**An Overview of Computers and Logic**       1

    Understanding Computer Components and Operations    2
    Understanding the Programming Process    5
        Understand the Problem    6
        Plan the Logic    6
        Code the Program    7
        Translate the Program into Machine Language    7
        Test the Program    8
        Put the Program into Production    9
    Understanding the Data Hierarchy    10
    Using Flowchart Symbols and Pseudocode Statements    12
    Using and Naming Variables    16
    Ending a Program by Using Sentinel Values    18
    Using the Connector    20
    Assigning Values to Variables    21
    Understanding Data Types    22
    Understanding the Evolution of Programming Techniques    24
    Chapter Summary    26
    Key Terms    26
    Review Questions    29
    Exercises    32

## CHAPTER TWO

**Understanding Structure**       35

    Understanding Unstructured Spaghetti Code    36
    Understanding the Three Basic Structures    37
    Using the Priming Read    44
    Understanding the Reasons for Structure    50
    Recognizing Structure    52
    Two Special Structures—Case and Do Until    59
        The Case Structure    59
        The Do Until Loop    60
    Chapter Summary    64
    Key Terms    64
    Review Questions    65
    Exercises    68

## CHAPTER THREE

### Modules, Hierarchy Charts, and Documentation    73

Modules, Subroutines, Procedures, Functions, or Methods    74
    Modularization Provides Abstraction    74
    Modularization Allows Multiple Programmers to Work on a Problem    75
    Modularization Allows You to Reuse Your Work    75
    Modularization Makes it Easier to Identify Structures    76
Modularizing a Program    77
Modules Calling Other Modules    81
Declaring Variables    82
Creating Hierarchy Charts    84
Understanding Documentation    86
Output Documentation    87
Input Documentation    94
Completing the Documentation    99
Chapter Summary    101
Key Terms    101
Review Questions    103
Exercises    106

## CHAPTER FOUR

### Writing and Designing a Complete Program    113

Understanding the Mainline Logical Flow Through a Program    114
Housekeeping Tasks    118
    Declaring Variables    118
    Opening Files    123
    A One-Time-Only Task—Printing Headings    124
    Reading the First Input Record    124
Writing the Main Loop    129
Performing End-Of-Job Tasks    132
Understanding the Need for Good Program Design    134
Storing Program Components in Separate Files    135
Selecting Variable and Module Names    137
Designing Clear Module Statements    138
    Avoiding Confusing Line Breaks    138
    Using Temporary Variables to Clarify Long Statements    139
    Using Constants Where Appropriate    139
Maintaining Good Programming Habits    140
Chapter Summary    141
Key Terms    141

Review Questions                                                                142
Exercises                                                                      145

## CHAPTER FIVE

# Making Decisions                                                             **149**
Evaluating Boolean Expressions to Make Comparisons                             150
Using the Logical Comparison Operators                                         152
Understanding AND Logic                                                        156
   Writing Nested AND Decisions for Efficiency                                 161
   Combining Decisions in an AND Selection                                     163
   Avoiding Common Errors in an AND Selection                                  164
Understanding OR Logic                                                         166
   Avoiding Common Errors in an OR Selection                                   167
   Writing OR Decisions for Efficiency                                         170
   Combining Decisions in an OR Selection                                      172
Using Selections within Ranges                                                 174
   Common Errors Using Range Checks                                            176
Understanding Precedence When Combining AND and OR Selections                  178
Understanding the Case Structure                                               180
Using Decision Tables                                                          182
Chapter Summary                                                               190
Key Terms                                                                     191
Review Questions                                                              192
Exercises                                                                    196

## CHAPTER SIX

# Looping                                                                     **203**
Understanding the Advantages of Looping                                       204
Using a While Loop with a Loop Control Variable                               204
Using a Counter to Control Looping                                            207
Looping with a Variable Sentinel Value                                        211
Looping by Decrementing                                                       213
Avoiding Common Loop Mistakes                                                 214
   Neglecting to Initialize the Loop Control Variable                         214
   Neglecting to Alter the Loop Control Variable                              214
   Using the Wrong Comparison with the Loop Control Variable                  215
   Including Statements Inside the Loop that Belong Outside the Loop          215
   Initializing a Variable That Does Not Require Initialization               216
Using the For Loop                                                            217
Using the Do Until Loop                                                       219
Recognizing the Characteristics Shared by All Loops                          223

Nesting Loops 224

Using a Loop to Accumulate Totals 230

Chapter Summary 233

Key Terms 233

Review Questions 234

Exercises 239

## CHAPTER SEVEN

## Control Breaks 245

Understanding Control Break Logic 246

Performing a Single-Level Control Break to Start a New Page 246

Using Control Data within a Heading in a Control Break Module 252

Using Control Data within a Footer in a Control Break Module 254

Performing Control Breaks with Totals 256

Performing Multiple-Level Control Breaks 261

Performing Page Breaks 267

Chapter Summary 273

Key Terms 274

Review Questions 275

Exercises 280

## CHAPTER EIGHT

## Arrays 285

Understanding Arrays 286

How Arrays Occupy Computer Memory 286

Manipulating an Array to Replace Nested Decisions 287

Array Declaration and Initialization 297

Run-Time and Compile-Time Arrays 299

Loading an Array from a File 302

Searching for an Exact Match in an Array 304

Using Parallel Arrays 306

Remaining within Array Bounds 310

Improving Search Efficiency Using an Early Exit 312

Searching an Array for a Range Match 314

Chapter Summary 318

Key Terms 318

Review Questions 319

Exercises 323

## APPENDIX A                                        A-1
Solving Difficult Structuring Problems

## APPENDIX B                                        B-1
Understanding Numbering Systems and Computer Codes

## APPENDIX C                                        C-1
Using a Large Decision Table

## GLOSSARY                                           G-1

## INDEX                                              I-1

# ■ ■ ■ ■ PREFACE

*Programming Logic and Design, Introductory, Third Edition* provides the beginning programmer with a guide to developing structured program logic. This textbook assumes no programming language experience. The writing is nontechnical and emphasizes good programming practices. The examples are business examples; they do not assume mathematical background beyond high school business math. Additionally, the examples illustrate one or two major points; they do not contain so many features that students become lost following irrelevant and extraneous details.

The examples in *Programming Logic and Design* have been created to provide students with a sound background in logic no matter what programming languages they eventually use to write programs. This book can be used in a standalone logic course that students take as a prerequisite to a programming course, or as a companion book to an introductory programming text using any programming language.

## Organization and Coverage

*Programming Logic and Design, Introductory, Third Edition* introduces students to programming concepts and enforces good style and logical thinking. General programming concepts are introduced in Chapter 1. Chapter 2 discusses the key concepts of structure, including what structure is, how to recognize it, and, most importantly, the advantages to writing structured programs. Chapter 3 extends the information on structured programming to the area of modules. By Chapter 4 students can write complete, structured business programs. Chapters 5 and 6 explore the intricacies of decision making and looping. Students learn to develop sophisticated programs that use control breaks and arrays in Chapters 7 and 8. Three appendices allow students to gain extra experience with structuring large unstructured programs, using the binary numbering system, and working with large decision tables.

*Programming Logic and Design* combines text explanation with flowcharts and pseudocode examples to provide students with alternative means of expressing structured logic. Numerous detailed, full-program exercises at the end of each chapter illustrate the concepts explained within the chapter, and reinforce understanding and retention of the material presented.

*Programming Logic and Design* distinguishes itself from other programming logic books in the following ways:

- It is written and designed to be non-language specific. The logic used in this book can be applied to any programming language.
- The examples are everyday business examples; no special knowledge of mathematics, accounting, or other disciplines is assumed.
- The concept of structure is covered earlier than in many other texts. Students are exposed to structure naturally, so they will automatically create properly designed programs.
- Text explanation is interspersed with both flowcharts and pseudocode so students can become comfortable with both logic development tools and understand their interrelationship.
- Complex programs are built through the use of complete business examples. Students see how an application is built from start to finish instead of studying only segments of programs.

## Features of the Text

New to this edition of the text is the addition of pseudocode to complement virtually every flowchart diagram, and the addition of flowcharts to complement almost all pseudocode examples. Another new feature in this edition is that every chapter illustrates at least one complete program. Program modules are still discussed in easily digested segments, but are then coordinated into one full program so that the student can view all the modules from beginning to end to comprehend and appreciate their relationships.

To improve students' comprehension of the looping process, `endwhile` has been added to the pseudocode in all looping examples in this edition; this mirrors the use of `endif` in all decision examples, as in the following sample:

---

PSEUDOCODE EXAMPLE USING `endwhile`

```
while not eof
     perform mainLoop()
endwhile
```

---

To assist the student, each chapter now lists key terms and their definitions; the list appears in the order the terms are encountered in the chapter. Along with the chapter summary, the list of key terms provides a snapshot overview of a chapter's main ideas. A glossary has also been added to the end of the book, listing all the key terms in alphabetical order along with working definitions.

Also new to this edition, 20 multiple-choice review questions appear at the end of every chapter to allow students to test their comprehension of the major ideas and techniques presented. Additional end-of-chapter flowcharting and pseudocoding exercises are included so students have more opportunities to practice concepts as they learn them.

*Programming Logic and Design* is a superior textbook because it includes the following features:

*New!*     ■ Microsoft® Office Visio® Professional 2003, trial version: This text now includes Visio 2003, a diagramming program that helps users create flowcharts and diagrams easily while working through the text, enabling them to visualize concepts and learn more effectively.

*New!*     ■ Interior design: New to the third edition—a highly visual, full-color interior presents material in a way that is engaging and appealing to the reader.

       ■ Objectives: Each chapter begins with a list of objectives so the student knows the topics that will be presented in the chapter. In addition to providing a quick reference to topics covered, this feature provides a useful study aid.

       ■ Flowcharts: This book has plenty of figures and illustrations, including flowcharts, which provide the reader with a visual learning experience, rather than one that involves simply studying text. You can see an example of a flowchart in the sample page shown in this Preface.

       ■ Pseudocode: This book also includes numerous examples of pseudocode, which illustrate correct usage of the programming logic and design concepts being taught. You can see an example of pseudocode in the sample page shown in this Preface.

       ■ Tips: These notes provide additional information—for example, another location in the book that expands on a topic, or a common error to watch out for. You can see an example of a tip in the sample page shown in this Preface.

■ Chapter summaries: Following each chapter is a summary that recaps the programming concepts and techniques covered in the chapter. This feature provides a concise means for students to review and check their understanding of the main points in each chapter.

*New!*     ■ Key terms: New to the third edition—chapters end with a collection of all the key terms found throughout the chapter, as shown in the following sample. Definitions are also included in sentence format and in the order in which they appear in the chapter.

---

SAMPLE LIST OF END-OF-CHAPTER KEY TERMS

### KEY TERMS

The **mainline logic** of a program is the overall logic of the main program from beginning to end.

A **housekeeping** module includes steps you must perform at the beginning of a program, to get ready for the rest of the program.

The **main loop** of a program contains the steps that are repeated for every record.

---

*New!*     ■ Review questions: New to the third edition—20 review questions at the end of each chapter reinforce the main ideas introduced in the chapter, as shown in the following sample. Successfully answering these questions demonstrates mastery of the concepts and information presented.

---

SAMPLE REVIEW QUESTIONS

### REVIEW QUESTIONS

1.  **Input records usually contain _____.**
    a.  less data than an application needs
    b.  more data than an application needs
    c.  exactly the amount of data an application needs
    d.  none of the data an application needs

2.  **A program in which one operation follows another from the beginning until the end is a _____ program.**
    a.  modular
    b.  functional
    c.  procedural
    d.  object-oriented

---

■ Exercises: Each chapter concludes with meaningful programming exercises that provide students with additional practice of the skills and concepts they have learned. These exercises increase in difficulty and are designed to allow students to explore logical programming concepts. Each exercise can be completed using flowcharts, pseudocode, or both. In addition, instructors can choose to assign the exercises as programming problems to be coded and executed in a programming language.

The figure below shows an example of our new, highly visual design, including an example of the numbered lists, tips, flowcharts, and pseudocode seen throughout the text.

SAMPLE PAGE SHOWING KEY ELEMENTS FOUND IN THE TEXT

Understanding the Mainline Logical Flow Through a Program   **117**

follows another from the beginning until the end. You write the entire set of instructions for a procedural program, and when the program executes, instructions take place one at a time, following your program's logic. The overall logic, or **mainline logic**, of almost every procedural computer program can follow a general structure that consists of three distinct parts:

1. Performing housekeeping, or initialization tasks. **Housekeeping** includes steps you must perform at the beginning of a program to get ready for the rest of the program.
2. Performing the main loop repeatedly within the program. The **main loop** contains the instructions that are executed for every record until you reach the end of the input of records, or `eof`.
3. Performing the end-of-job routine. The **end-of-job routine** holds the steps you take at the end of the program to finish the application.

**TIP** □ □ □ □ | Not all programs are procedural; some are object-oriented. A distinguishing feature of many (but not all) object-oriented programs is that they are event-driven; often the user determines the timing of events in the main loop of the program by using an input device such as a mouse. As you advance in your knowledge of programming, you will learn more about object-oriented techniques.

You can write any procedural program as one long series of programming language statements, but most programmers prefer to break their programs into at least three parts. The main program can call the three major modules, as shown in the flowchart and pseudocode in Figure 4-6. The module or subroutine names, of course, are entirely up to the programmer.

**TIP** □ □ □ □ | Reducing a large program into more manageable modules is sometimes called **functional decomposition**.

**FIGURE 4-6:** FLOWCHART AND PSEUDOCODE OF MAINLINE LOGIC

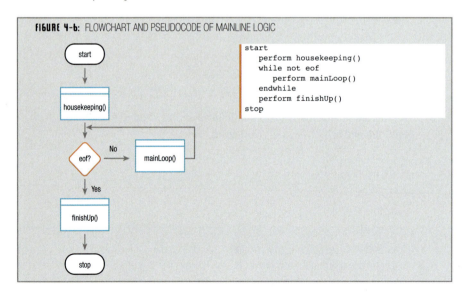

```
start
    perform housekeeping()
    while not eof
        perform mainLoop()
    endwhile
    perform finishUp()
stop
```

## Teaching Tools

The following supplemental materials are available when this book is used in a classroom setting. All of the teaching tools available with this book are provided to the instructor on a single CD-ROM.

**Electronic Instructor's Manual**. The Instructor's Manual that accompanies this textbook provides additional instructional material to assist in class preparation, including Sample Syllabi, Chapter Outlines, Technical Notes, Lecture Notes, Quick Quizzes, Teaching Tips, Discussion Topics, and Key Terms.

**ExamView®**. This textbook is accompanied by ExamView, a powerful testing software package that allows instructors to create and administer printed, computer (LAN-based), and Internet exams. ExamView includes hundreds of questions that correspond to the topics covered in this text, enabling students to generate detailed study guides that include page references for further review. The computer-based and Internet testing components allow students to take exams at their computers, and also save the instructor time by grading each exam automatically.

**PowerPoint Presentations**. This book comes with Microsoft PowerPoint slides for each chapter. These are included as a teaching aid for classroom presentation, to make available to students on the network for chapter review, or to be printed for classroom distribution. Instructors can add their own slides for additional topics they introduce to the class.

**Solutions**. Solutions to Review Questions and Exercises are provided on the Teaching Tools CD-ROM and may also be found on the Course Technology Web site at **www.course.com**. The solutions are password protected.

**Distance Learning**. Course Technology is proud to present online courses in WebCT and Blackboard to provide the most complete and dynamic learning experience possible. When you add online content to one of your courses, you're adding a lot: Topic Reviews, Practice Tests, Review Questions, Assignments, PowerPoint presentations, and, most of all, a gateway to the 21st century's most important information resource. We hope you will make the most of your course, both online and offline. For more information on how to bring distance learning to your course, contact your local Course Technology sales representative.

## Acknowledgments

I would like to thank all of the people who helped to make this book a reality, especially Lisa Ruffolo, Development Editor, whose hard work, attention to detail, sense of humor, and perceptive appreciation of the methodology required to teach this subject matter have made this a quality textbook. Thank you, Lisa, for making my job easier. Thanks also to Tricia Boyle, Product Manager; Jennifer Muroff, Managing Editor; Christine Gatliffe, Production Editor; and Beverly Jackson, Technical Editor. I am grateful to be able to work with so many fine people who are dedicated to producing quality instructional materials.

I am grateful to the many reviewers who provided helpful and insightful comments during the development of this book, including Karen Allen, Community College of Rhode Island; Nelson Capaz, Pasco-Hernando Community College; R. Scott Cost, University of Maryland–Baltimore County; Bob Husson, Craven Community College; Jerome Patchen, Community College of Baltimore County–Essex; Herbert Rebhun, University of Houston–Downtown; Pamela Silvers, Asheville-Buncombe Technical Community College.

Thanks, too, to my husband, Geoff, who acts as friend and advisor in the book-writing process. This book is, as were its previous editions, dedicated to him and to my daughters, Andrea and Audrey.

–Joyce Farrell

# 1

# AN OVERVIEW OF COMPUTERS AND LOGIC

### After studying Chapter 1, you should be able to:

- ☐ Understand computer components and operations
- ☐ Describe the steps involved in the programming process
- ☐ Describe the data hierarchy
- ☐ Understand how to use flowchart symbols and pseudocode statements
- ☐ Use and name variables
- ☐ Use a sentinel, or dummy value, to end a program
- ☐ Use a connector symbol
- ☐ Assign values to variables
- ☐ Recognize the proper format of assignment statements
- ☐ Describe data types
- ☐ Understand the evolution of programming techniques

## UNDERSTANDING COMPUTER COMPONENTS AND OPERATIONS

The two major components of any computer system are its hardware and its software. **Hardware** is the equipment, or the devices, associated with a computer. For a computer to be useful, however, it needs more than equipment; a computer needs to be given instructions. The instructions that tell the computer what to do are called **software**, or programs, and are written by programmers. This book focuses on the process of writing these instructions.

**TIP** □ □ □ □ | Software can be classified as application software or system software. Application software comprises all the programs you apply to a task—word-processing programs, spreadsheets, payroll and inventory programs, and even games. System software comprises the programs that you use to manage your computer—operating systems, such as Windows or Unix. This book focuses on the logic used to write application software programs, although many of the concepts apply to both types of software.

Together, computer hardware and software accomplish four major operations:

1. Input
2. Processing
3. Output
4. Storage

Hardware devices that perform **input** include keyboards and mice. Through these devices, **data**, or facts, enter the computer system. **Processing** data items may involve organizing them, checking them for accuracy, or performing mathematical operations on them. The piece of hardware that performs these sorts of tasks is the **central processing unit**, or **CPU**. After data items have been processed, the resulting information is sent to a printer, monitor, or some other **output** device so people can view, interpret, and use the results. Often, you also want to store the output information on storage hardware, such as magnetic disks, tapes, or compact discs. Computer software consists of all the instructions that control how and when the data are input, how they are processed, and the form in which they are output or stored.

Computer hardware by itself is useless without a programmer's instructions or software, just as your stereo equipment doesn't do much until you provide music on a CD or tape. You can buy prewritten software that is stored on a disk, or you can write your own software instructions. You can enter instructions into a computer system through any of the hardware devices you use for data; most often, you type your instructions using a keyboard and store them on a device such as a disk or CD.

You write computer instructions in a computer **programming language**, such as Visual Basic, Pascal, COBOL, RPG, C#, C++, Java, or Fortran. Just as some people speak English and others speak Japanese, programmers also write programs in different languages. Some programmers work exclusively in one language, whereas others know several and use the one that seems most appropriate for the task at hand.

No matter which programming language a computer programmer uses, the language has rules governing its word usage and punctuation. These rules are called the language's **syntax**. If you ask, "How the get to store do I?" in English, most people can figure out what you probably mean, even though you have not used proper English syntax. However, computers are not nearly as smart as most people; with a computer, you might as well have asked, "Xpu mxv ot dodnm cadf B?" Unless the syntax is perfect, the computer cannot interpret the programming language instruction at all.

Every computer operates on circuitry that consists of millions of on-off switches. Each programming language uses a piece of software to translate the specific programming language into the computer's on-off circuitry language, or **machine language**. The language translation software is called a **compiler** or **interpreter**, and it tells you if you have used a programming language incorrectly. Therefore, syntax errors are relatively easy to locate and correct—the compiler or interpreter you use highlights every syntax error. If you write a computer program using a language such as C++, but spell one of its words incorrectly or reverse the proper order of two words, the translator lets you know it found a mistake by displaying an error message as soon as you try to run the program.

Although there are differences in how compilers and interpreters work, their basic function is the same—to translate your programming statements into code the computer can use. When you use a compiler, an entire program is translated before it can execute; when you use an interpreter, each instruction is translated just prior to execution. You do not choose which type of translation to use—it depends on the programming language.

For a program to work properly, you must give the instructions to the computer in a specific sequence, you must not leave any instructions out, and you must not add extraneous instructions. By doing this, you are developing the **logic** of the computer program. Suppose you instruct someone to make a cake as follows:

```
Stir
Add two eggs
Add a gallon of gasoline
Bake at 350 degrees for 45 minutes
Add three cups of flour
```

Even though you have used the English language syntax correctly, the instructions are out of sequence, some instructions are missing, and some instructions belong to procedures other than baking a cake. If you follow these instructions, you are not going to end up with an edible cake, and you may end up with a disaster. Logical errors are much more difficult to locate than syntax errors; it is easier for you to determine whether "eggs" is spelled incorrectly in a recipe than it is for you to tell if there are too many eggs or if they are added too soon.

Just as baking directions can be given correctly in French, German, or Spanish, the same logic of a program can be expressed in any number of programming languages. This book is almost exclusively concerned with the logic development process. Because this book is not concerned with any specific language, the programming examples could have been written in Japanese, C++, or Java. The logic is the same in any language. For convenience, the book uses English!

Once instructions have been input to the computer and translated into machine language, a program can be **run**, or **executed**. You can write a program that takes a number (an input step), doubles it (processing), and tells you the answer (output) in a programming language such as Java or C++, but if you were to write it using English-like statements, it would look like this:

```
Get inputNumber.
Compute calculatedAnswer as inputNumber times 2.
Print calculatedAnswer.
```

**TIP** ◻ ◻ ◻ ◻ | You will learn about the odd elimination of the space between words like "input" and "Number" and "calculated" and "Answer" in the next few pages.

The instruction to `Get inputNumber` is an example of an input operation. When the computer interprets this instruction, it knows to look to an input device to obtain a number. Computers often have several input devices, perhaps a keyboard, a mouse, a CD drive, and two or more disk drives. When you learn a specific programming language, you learn how to tell the computer which of those input devices to access for input. Logically, however, it doesn't really matter which hardware device is used, as long as the computer knows to look for a number. The logic of the input operation—that the computer must obtain a number for input, and that the computer must obtain it before multiplying it by two—remains the same regardless of any specific input hardware device. The same is true in your daily life—if you follow the instruction "Get eggs from store," it does not really matter if you are following a handwritten instruction from a list or a voice mail instruction left on your cell phone—the process of getting the eggs, and the result of doing so, are the same.

**TIP** ◻ ◻ ◻ ◻ | Many computer professionals categorize disk drives and CD drives as storage devices rather than input devices. Such devices actually can be used for input, storage, and output.

Processing is the step that occurs when the mathematics is performed to double the `inputNumber`; the statement `Compute calculatedAnswer as inputNumber times 2` represents processing. Mathematical operations are not the only kind of processing, but they are very typical. After you write a program, the program can be used on computers of different brand names, sizes, and speeds. Whether you use an IBM, Macintosh, Linux, or Unix operating system, and whether you use a personal computer that sits on your desk or a mainframe that costs hundreds of thousands of dollars and resides in a special building in a university, multiplying by 2 is the same process. The hardware is not important; the processing will be the same.

In the number-doubling program, the `Print calculatedAnswer` statement represents output. Within a particular program, this statement could cause the output to appear on the monitor (which might be a flat panel screen or a cathode-ray tube), or the output could go to a printer (which could be laser or inkjet), or the output could be written to a disk or CD. The logic of the process called "Print" is the same no matter what hardware device you use.

Besides input, processing, and output, the fourth operation in any computer system is storage. Storage comes in two broad categories. All computers have **internal storage**, probably referred to more often as **memory**, **main memory**, or **primary memory**. This storage is inside the machine and is the type of storage most often discussed in this book. Computers also have **external storage**, which is permanent storage outside the main memory of the machine, on a device such as a floppy disk, hard disk, or magnetic tape. In other words, external storage is outside of the main memory, not necessarily outside the computer. Both programs and data sometimes are stored on each of these kinds of media.

To use computer programs, you must first load them into memory. You might type a program into memory from the keyboard, or you might use a program that has already been written and stored on a disk. Either way, a copy of the instructions must be placed in memory before the program can be run.

A computer system needs both internal memory and external storage. Internal memory is needed to run the programs, but internal memory is **volatile**—that is, its contents are lost every time the computer loses power. Therefore, if you are going to use a program more than once, you must store it, or **save** it, on some nonvolatile medium. Otherwise, the program in main memory is lost forever when the computer is turned off. External storage (usually disks or tape) provides a nonvolatile medium.

TIP □ □ □ □ | Even though a hard disk drive is located inside your computer, the hard disk is not main, internal memory. Internal memory is temporary and volatile; a hard drive is permanent, nonvolatile storage. After one or two "tragedies" of losing several pages of a typed computer program due to a power failure or other hardware problem, most programmers learn to periodically save the programs they are in the process of writing, using a nonvolatile medium, such as a disk.

Once you have a copy of a program in main memory, you want to execute or run the program. To do so, you must also place any data that the program requires into memory. For example, after you place the following program into memory and start to run it, you need to provide an actual `inputNumber`—for example, 8—that you also place in main memory.

```
Get inputNumber.
Compute calculatedAnswer as inputNumber times 2.
Print calculatedAnswer.
```

The `inputNumber` is placed in memory in a specific memory location that the program will call `inputNumber`. Then, and only then, can the `calculatedAnswer`, in this case 16, be calculated and printed.

TIP □ □ □ □ | Computer memory consists of millions of numbered locations where data can be stored. The memory location of `inputNumber` has a specific numeric address, for example, 48604. Your program associates `inputNumber` with that address. Every time you refer to `inputNumber` within a program, the computer retrieves the value at the associated memory location. When you write programs, you seldom need to be concerned with the value of the memory address; instead, you simply use the easy-to-remember name you created.

TIP □ □ □ □ | Computer programmers often refer to memory addresses using hexadecimal notation, or base 16. Using this system, they might use a value like 42FF01A to refer to a memory address. Despite the use of letters, such an address is still a number. When you use the hexadecimal numbering system, the letters A through F stand for the values 10 through 15.

## UNDERSTANDING THE PROGRAMMING PROCESS

A programmer's job involves writing instructions (such as the three instructions in the doubling program in the preceding section), but a professional programmer usually does not just sit down at a computer keyboard and start typing. The programmer's job can be broken down into six programming steps:

1. Understand the problem.
2. Plan the logic.
3. Code the program.
4. Translate the program into machine language.

5. Test the program.

6. Put the program into production.

## UNDERSTAND THE PROBLEM

Professional computer programmers write programs to satisfy the needs of others. For example: the Human Resources Department that needs a printed list of all employees, the Billing Department that wants a list of clients who are 30 or more days overdue in their payments, and the office manager who wants to be notified when specific supplies reach the reorder point. Because programmers are providing a service to these users, programmers must first understand what it is the users want.

Suppose the director of human resources says to a programmer, "Our department needs a list of all employees who have been here over five years, because we want to invite them to a special thank-you dinner." On the surface, this seems like a simple enough request. An experienced programmer, however, will know that he or she may not yet understand the whole problem. Does the director want a list of full-time employees only, or a list of full- and part-time employees together? Does she want people who have worked for the company on a month-to-month contractual basis over the past five years, or only regular, permanent employees? Do the listed employees need to have worked for the organization for five years as of today, as of the date of the dinner, or as of some other cutoff date? What about an employee who worked three years, took a two-year leave of absence, and has been back for three years? Does he or she qualify? The programmer cannot make any of these decisions; the user is the one who must address these questions.

More decisions still might be required. For example, what does the user want the report of five-year employees to look like? Should it contain both first and last names? Social Security numbers? Phone numbers? Addresses? Is all this data available? Several pieces of documentation are often provided to help the programmer understand the problem. This documentation includes print layout charts and file specifications, which you will learn about in Chapter 3.

Really understanding the problem may be one of the most difficult aspects of programming. On any job, the description of what the user needs may be vague—worse yet, the user may not even really know what he or she wants, and users who think they know what they want frequently change their minds after seeing sample output. A good programmer is often part counselor, part detective!

## PLAN THE LOGIC

The heart of the programming process lies in planning the program's logic. During this phase of the programming process, the programmer plans the steps to the program, deciding what steps to include and how to order them. You can plan the solution to a problem in many ways. The two most common tools are flowcharts and pseudocode. Both tools involve writing the steps of the program in English, much as you would plan a trip on paper before getting into the car, or plan a party theme before going shopping for food and favors.

 You may hear programmers refer to planning a program as "developing an algorithm." An **algorithm** is the sequence of steps necessary to solve any problem. You will learn more about flowcharts and pseudocode later in this chapter.

The programmer doesn't worry about the syntax of any particular language at this point, just about figuring out what sequence of events will lead from the available input to the desired output. You will learn more about planning the logic later; in fact, this book focuses on this crucial step almost exclusively.

## CODE THE PROGRAM

Once the programmer has developed the logic of a program, only then can he or she write the program in one of more than 400 programming languages. Programmers choose a particular language because some languages have built-in capabilities that make them more efficient than others at handling certain types of operations. Despite their differences, programming languages are quite alike—each can handle input operations, arithmetic processing, output operations, and other standard functions. The logic developed to solve a programming problem can be executed using any number of languages. It is only after a language is chosen that the programmer must worry about each command being spelled correctly and all of the punctuation getting into the right spots—in other words, using the correct *syntax*.

Some very experienced programmers can successfully combine the logic planning and the actual instruction writing, or **coding** of the program, in one step. This may work for planning and writing a very simple program, just as you can plan and write a postcard to a friend using one step. A good term paper or a Hollywood screenplay, however, needs planning before writing, and so do most programs.

Which step is harder, planning the logic or coding the program? Right now, it may seem to you that writing in a programming language is a very difficult task, considering all the spelling and grammar rules you must learn. However, the planning step is actually more difficult. Which is more difficult: thinking up the twists and turns to the plot of a best-selling mystery novel, or writing a translation of an already written novel from English to Spanish? And who do you think gets paid more, the writer who creates the plot or the translator? (Try asking friends to name any famous translator!)

## TRANSLATE THE PROGRAM INTO MACHINE LANGUAGE

Even though there are many programming languages, each computer knows only one language, its machine language, which consists of many 1s and 0s. Computers understand machine language because computers themselves are made up of thousands of tiny electrical switches, each of which can be set in either the on or off state, which is represented by a 1 or 0, respectively.

Languages like Java or Visual Basic are available for programmers to use because someone has written a translator program (a compiler or interpreter) that changes the English-like **high-level programming language** in which the programmer writes into the **low-level machine language** that the computer understands. If you write a programming language statement incorrectly (for example, by misspelling a word, using a word that doesn't exist in the language, or using "illegal" grammar), the translator program doesn't know what to do and issues an error message identifying a **syntax error**, or misuse of a language's grammar rules. You receive the same response when you speak nonsense to a human language translator. Imagine trying to look up a list of words in a Spanish-English dictionary if some of the listed words are misspelled—you can't complete the task until the words are spelled correctly. Although making errors is never desirable, syntax errors are not a major concern to programmers, because the compiler or interpreter catches every syntax error, and the computer will not execute a program that contains them.

A computer program must be free of syntax errors before you can execute it. Typically, a programmer develops a program's logic, writes the code, and then compiles the program, receiving a list of syntax errors. The programmer then corrects the syntax errors, and compiles the program again. Correcting the first set of errors frequently reveals a new set of errors that originally were not apparent to the compiler. For example, if you could use an English compiler and submit the sentence `The grl go to school`, the compiler at first would point out only one syntax error to you. The second word, `grl`, is illegal because it is not part of the English language. Only after you corrected the word `girl` would the compiler find another syntax error on the third word, `go`, because it is the wrong verb form for the subject `girl`. This doesn't mean `go` is necessarily the wrong word. Maybe `girl` is wrong; perhaps the subject should be `girls`, in which case `go` is right. Compilers don't always know exactly what you mean, nor do they know what the proper correction should be, but they do know when something is wrong with your syntax.

When writing a program, a programmer might need to recompile the code several times. An executable program is created only when the code is free of syntax errors. When you run an executable program, it typically also might require input data. Figure 1-1 shows a diagram of this entire process.

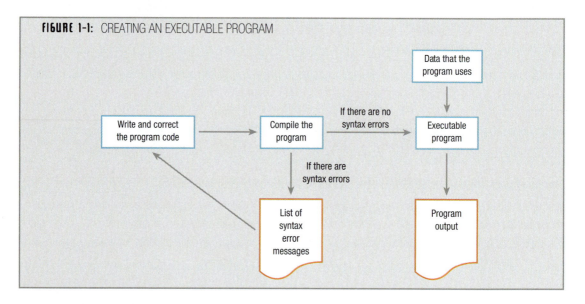

**FIGURE 1-1:** CREATING AN EXECUTABLE PROGRAM

## TEST THE PROGRAM

A program that is free of syntax errors is not necessarily free of **logical errors**. For example, the sentence `The girl goes to school`, although syntactically perfect, is not logically correct if the girl is a baby or a dropout.

Once a program is free from syntax errors, the programmer can test it—that is, execute it with some sample data to see whether the results are logically correct. Recall the number-doubling program:

```
Get inputNumber.
Compute calculatedAnswer as inputNumber times 2.
Print calculatedAnswer.
```

If you provide the value 2 as input to the program and the answer 4 prints out, you have executed one successful test run of the program.

However, if the answer 40 prints out, maybe it's because the program contains a logical error. Maybe the second line of code was mistyped with an extra zero, so that the program reads:

```
Get inputNumber.
Compute calculatedAnswer as inputNumber times 20.
Print calculatedAnswer.
```

The error of placing 20 instead of 2 in the multiplication statement caused a logical error. Notice that nothing is syntactically wrong with this second program—it is just as reasonable to multiply a number by 20 as by 2—but if the programmer intends only to double the `inputNumber`, then a logical error has occurred.

Programs should be tested with many sets of data. For example, if you write the program to double a number and enter 2 and get an output value of 4, that doesn't necessarily mean you have a correct program. Perhaps you have typed this program by mistake:

```
Get inputNumber.
Compute calculatedAnswer as inputNumber plus 2.
Print calculatedAnswer.
```

An input of 2 results in an answer of 4, but that doesn't mean your program doubles numbers—it actually only adds 2 to them. If you test your program with additional data and get the wrong answer—for example, if you use a 3 and get an answer of 5—you know there is a problem with your code.

Selecting test data is somewhat of an art in itself, and it should be done carefully. If the Human Resources Department wants a list of the names of five-year employees, it would be a mistake to test the program with a small sample file of only long-term employees. If no newer employees are part of the data being used for testing, you don't really know if the program would have eliminated them from the five-year list. Many companies don't know that their software has a problem until an unusual circumstance occurs—for example, the first time an employee has more than nine dependents, the first time a customer orders more than 999 items at a time, or when (in an example that was well-documented in the popular press) a new century begins.

## PUT THE PROGRAM INTO PRODUCTION

Once the program is tested adequately, it is ready for the organization to use. Putting the program into production might mean simply running the program once, if it was written to satisfy a user's request for a special list. However, the process might take months if the program will be run on a regular basis, or if it is one of a large system of programs being developed. Perhaps data entry people must be trained to prepare the input for the new program, users must be trained to understand the output, or existing data in the company must be changed to an entirely new format to accommodate this program. **Conversion**, the entire set of actions an organization must take to switch over to using a new program or set of programs, can sometimes take months or years to accomplish.

You might consider maintaining programs as a seventh step in the programming process. After programs are put into production, making required changes is called maintenance. Maintenance is necessary for many reasons: for example, new tax rates are legislated, the format of an input file is altered, or the end user requires additional information not included in the original output specifications. You might consider retiring the program as the eighth and final step in the programming process. A program is retired when it is no longer needed by an organization—usually when a new program is in the process of being put into production.

## UNDERSTANDING THE DATA HIERARCHY

Some very simple programs require very simple data. For example, the number-doubling program requires just one value as input. Most business programs, however, use much more data—inventory files list thousands of items, personnel and customer files list thousands of people. When data are stored for use on computer systems, they are often stored in what is known as a **data hierarchy**, where the smallest usable unit of data is the character. **Characters** are letters, numbers, and special symbols, such as "A", "7", and "$". Anything you can type from the keyboard in one keystroke (including a space or a tab) is a character. Characters are made up of smaller elements called bits, but just as most human beings can use a pencil without caring whether atoms are flying around inside it, most computer users can store characters without caring about these bits.

Computers also recognize characters you cannot enter from the keyboard, such as foreign alphabet characters like φ or Σ.

Characters are grouped together to form a field. A **field** is a single data item, such as `lastName`, `streetAddress`, or `annualSalary`. For most of us, an "S", an "m", an "i", a "t", and an "h" don't have much meaning individually, but if the combination of characters makes up your last name, "Smith", then as a group, the characters have useful meaning.

Related fields are often grouped together to form a record. **Records** are groups of fields that go together for some logical reason. A random name, address, and salary aren't very useful, but if they're your name, your address, and your salary, then that's your record. An inventory record might contain fields for item number, color, size, and price; a student record might contain ID number, grade point average, and major.

Related records, in turn, are grouped together to form a file. **Files** are groups of records that go together for some logical reason. The individual records of each student in your class might go together in a file called CLASS. Records of each person at your company might be in a file called PERSONNEL. Items you sell might be in an INVENTORY file.

Some files can have just a few records; others, such as the file of credit card holders for a major department store chain or policyholders of an insurance company, can contain thousands or even millions of records.

Finally, many organizations use database software to organize many files. A **database** holds a group of files, often called **tables**, that together serve the information needs of an organization. Database software establishes and maintains relationships between fields in these tables, so that users can write questions called **queries**. Queries pull related data items together in a format that allows businesspeople to make managerial decisions efficiently. Chapter 16 of the Comprehensive version of this text covers database creation.

In summary, you can picture the data hierarchy, as shown in Figure 1-2.

**FIGURE 1-2:** THE DATA HIERARCHY

```
Database
    File
          Record
                Field
                      Character
```

A database contains many files. A file contains many records. Each record in a file has the same fields. Each record's fields contain different data items that consist of one or more stored characters in each field.

As an example, you can picture a file as a set of index cards, as shown in Figure 1-3. The stack of cards is the EMPLOYEE file, in which each card represents one employee record. On each card, each line holds one field—`name`, `address`, or `salary`. Almost all the program examples in this book use files that are organized in this way.

**FIGURE 1-3:** EMPLOYEE FILE REPRESENTED AS A STACK OF INDEX CARDS

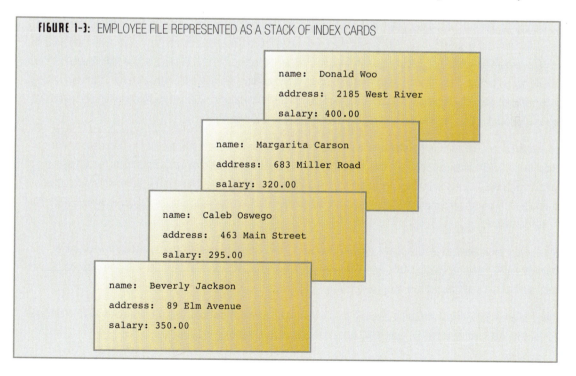

## USING FLOWCHART SYMBOLS AND PSEUDOCODE STATEMENTS

When programmers plan the logic for a solution to a programming problem, they often use one of two tools, **flowcharts** or **pseudocode** (pronounced "sue-doe-code"). A flowchart is a pictorial representation of the logical steps it takes to solve a problem. Pseudocode is an English-like representation of the same thing. *Pseudo* is a prefix that means "false," and to *code* a program means to put it in a programming language; therefore, *pseudocode* simply means "false code," or sentences that appear to have been written in a computer programming language but don't necessarily follow all the syntax rules of any specific language.

You have already seen examples of statements that represent pseudocode earlier in this chapter, and there is nothing mysterious about them. The following five statements constitute a pseudocode representation of a number-doubling problem:

```
start
    get inputNumber
    compute calculatedAnswer as inputNumber times 2
    print calculatedAnswer
stop
```

Using pseudocode involves writing down all the steps you will use in a program. Usually, programmers preface their pseudocode statements with a beginning statement like "start" and end them with a terminating statement like "stop". The statements between "start" and "stop" look like English and are indented slightly so that "start" and "stop" stand out. Most programmers do not bother with punctuation such as periods at the end of pseudocode statements, although it would not be wrong to use them if you prefer that style. Similarly, there is no need to capitalize the first word in a sentence, although you might choose to do so. This book follows the conventions of using lowercase letters for verbs that begin pseudocode statements and omitting periods at the end of statements.

Some professional programmers prefer writing pseudocode to drawing flowcharts, because using pseudocode is more similar to writing the final statements in the programming language. Others prefer drawing flowcharts to represent the logical flow, because flowcharts allow programmers to visualize more easily how the program statements will connect. Especially for beginning programmers, flowcharts are an excellent tool to help visualize how the statements in a program are interrelated.

Almost every program involves the steps of input, processing, and output. Therefore, most flowcharts need some graphical way to separate these three steps. When you create a flowchart, you draw geometric shapes around the individual statements and connect them with arrows.

When you draw a flowchart, you use a parallelogram to represent an **input symbol**, which indicates an input operation. You write an input statement, in English, inside the parallelogram, as shown in Figure 1-4.

**FIGURE 1-4:** INPUT SYMBOL

TIP □ □ □ □ | When you want to represent entering two or more values in a program, you can use one or multiple flowchart symbols or pseudocode statements—whichever seems more reasonable and clear to you. For example, the pseudocode to input a user's name and address might be written as:

```
get inputName
get inputAddress
```

or as:

```
get inputName,inputAddress
```

The first version implies two separate input operations, whereas the second implies a single input operation retrieving two data items. The end result is the same in both cases—after the statements have executed, `inputName` and `inputAddress` will have received values from an input device.

Arithmetic operation statements are examples of processing. In a flowchart, you use a rectangle as the **processing symbol** that contains a processing statement, as shown in Figure 1-5.

**FIGURE 1-5:** PROCESSING SYMBOL

```
compute calculatedAnswer
as inputNumber times 2
```

To represent an output statement, you use the same symbol as for input statements—the **output symbol** is a parallelogram, as shown in Figure 1-6.

**FIGURE 1-6:** OUTPUT SYMBOL

```
print
calculatedAnswer
```

TIP □ □ □ □ | As with input, output statements can be organized in whatever way seems most reasonable. A program that prints the length and width of a room might use the statement:

```
print length
print width
```

or:

```
print length, width
```

In some programming languages, using two print statements places the output values on two separate lines on the monitor or printer, whereas using a single print statement places the values next to each other on the same line. This book follows the convention of using one print statement per line of output.

To show the correct sequence of these statements, you use arrows, or **flowlines**, to connect the steps. Whenever possible, most of a flowchart should read from top to bottom or from left to right on a page. That's the way we read English, so when flowcharts follow this convention, they are easier for us to understand.

To be complete, a flowchart should include two more elements: a **terminal symbol**, or start/stop symbol, at each end. Often, you place a word like "start" or "begin" in the first terminal symbol and a word like "end" or "stop" in the other. The standard terminal symbol is shaped like a racetrack; many programmers refer to this shape as a **lozenge**, because it resembles the shape of a medicated candy lozenge you might use to soothe a sore throat. Figure 1-7 shows a complete flowchart for the program that doubles a number, and the pseudocode for the same problem.

**FIGURE 1-7:** FLOWCHART AND PSEUDOCODE OF PROGRAM THAT DOUBLES A NUMBER

```
start
get inputNumber
compute calculatedAnswer as
        inputNumber times 2
print calculatedAnswer
stop
```

**TIP**  ▫ ▫ ▫ ▫    Programmers seldom create both pseudocode and a flowchart for the same problem. You usually use one or the other.

The logic for the program represented by the flowchart and pseudocode in Figure 1-7 is correct no matter what programming language the programmer eventually uses to write the corresponding code. Just as the same statements could be translated into Italian or Chinese without losing their meaning, they also can be coded in C#, Java, or any other programming language.

After the flowchart or pseudocode has been developed, the programmer only needs to: (1) buy a computer, (2) buy a language compiler, (3) learn a programming language, (4) code the program, (5) attempt to compile it, (6) fix the syntax errors, (7) compile it again, (8) test it with several sets of data, and (9) put it into production.

"Whoa!" you are probably saying to yourself. "This is simply not worth it! All that work to create a flowchart or pseudocode, and *then* all those other steps? For five dollars, I can buy a pocket calculator that will double any number for me instantly!" You are absolutely right. If this were a real computer program, and all it did was double the value of a number, it simply would not be worth all the effort. Writing a computer program would be worth the effort only if you had many—let's say 10,000—numbers to double in a limited amount of time—let's say the next two minutes. Then, it would be worth your while to create a computer program.

Unfortunately, the number-doubling program represented in Figure 1-7 does not double 10,000 numbers; it doubles only one. You could execute the program 10,000 times, of course, but that would require you to sit at the computer telling it to run the program over and over again. You would be better off with a program that could process 10,000 numbers, one after the other.

One solution is to write the program as shown in Figure 1-8 and execute the same steps 10,000 times. Of course, writing this program would be very time-consuming; you might as well buy the calculator.

---

**FIGURE 1-8:** INEFFICIENT PSEUDOCODE FOR PROGRAM THAT DOUBLES 10,000 NUMBERS

```
start
     get inputNumber
     compute calculatedAnswer as inputNumber times 2
     print calculatedAnswer
     get inputNumber
     compute calculatedAnswer as inputNumber times 2
     print calculatedAnswer
     get inputNumber
     compute calculatedAnswer as inputNumber times 2
     print calculatedAnswer
     . . . and so on
```

---

A better solution is to have the computer execute the same set of three instructions over and over again, as shown in Figure 1-9. With this approach, the computer gets a number, doubles it, prints out the answer, and then starts over again with the first instruction. The same spot in memory, called `inputNumber`, is reused for the second number and for any subsequent numbers. The spot in memory named `calculatedAnswer` is reused each time to store the result of the multiplication operation. The logic illustrated in the flowchart shown in Figure 1-9 contains a major problem—the sequence of instructions never ends. You will learn to handle this problem later in this chapter.

---

**FIGURE 1-9:** FLOWCHART OF INFINITE NUMBER-DOUBLING PROGRAM

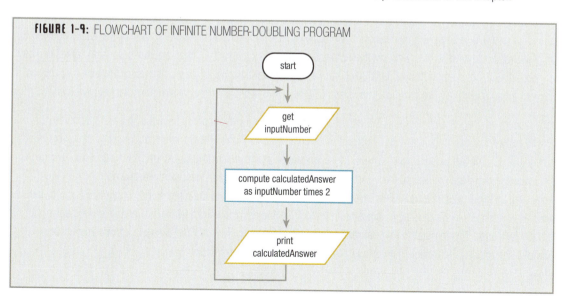

## USING AND NAMING VARIABLES

Programmers commonly refer to the locations in memory called `inputNumber` and `calculatedAnswer` as variables. **Variables** are memory locations, whose contents can vary or differ over time. Sometimes, `inputNumber` can hold a 2 and `calculatedAnswer` will hold a 4; at other times, `inputNumber` can hold a 6 and `calculatedAnswer` will hold a 12. It is the ability of memory variables to change in value that makes computers and programming worthwhile. Because one memory location can be used over and over again with different values, you can write program instructions once and then use them for thousands of separate calculations. *One* set of payroll instructions at your company produces each individual's paycheck, and *one* set of instructions at your electric company produces each household's bill.

The number-doubling example requires two variables, `inputNumber` and `calculatedAnswer`. These can just as well be named `userEntry` and `programSolution`, or `inputValue` and `twiceTheValue`. As a programmer, you choose reasonable names for your variables. The language interpreter then associates the names you choose with specific memory addresses.

A variable name is also called an **identifier**. Every computer programming language has its own set of rules for naming identifiers. Most languages allow both letters and digits within variable names. Some languages allow hyphens in variable names, for example `hourly-wage`. Others allow underscores, as in `hourly_wage`. Still others allow neither. Some languages allow dollar signs or other special characters in variable names, for example `hourly$`; others allow foreign alphabet characters, such as $\pi$ or $\Omega$.

TIP ▫ ▫ ▫ ▫ | You also can refer to a variable name as a **mnemonic**. In everyday language, a mnemonic is a memory device, like the sentence "Every good boy does fine," which makes it easier to remember the notes on the musical scale. In programming, a variable name is a device that makes it easier to reference a memory address.

Different languages put different limits on the length of variable names, although in general, newer languages allow longer names. For example, in some very old versions of BASIC, a variable name could consist of only one or two letters and one or two digits. You could have some cryptic variable names like `hw` or `a3` or `re02`. In other languages, variable names can be very long. COBOL, for example, allows up to 30 characters in its variable names, so names like `AMOUNT-OF-SALE` and `TOTAL-FOR-JANUARY` are common. In addition, COBOL allows hyphens in its variable names for better readability.

Many modern languages, such as C++, C#, and Java, allow more than two hundred characters in a variable name. Variable names in these languages usually consist of lowercase letters, don't allow hyphens, but do allow underscores, so you can use a name like `price_of_item`. These languages are case sensitive, so `HOURLYWAGE`, `hourlywage`, and `hourlyWage` are considered three separate variable names, although the last example, in which the new word begins with an uppercase letter, is easiest to read. Most programmers who use the more modern languages employ the format in which multiple-word variable names are run together, and each new word within the variable name begins with an uppercase letter. This format is called **camel casing**, because such variable names, like `hourlyWage`, have a "hump" in the middle. The variable names in this text are shown using camel casing.

Even though every language has its own rules for naming variables, when designing the logic of a computer program, you should not concern yourself with the specific syntax of any particular computer language. The logic, after all, works with any language. The variable names used throughout this book follow only two rules:

1. *Variable names must be one word*. The name can contain letters, digits, hyphens, underscores, or any other characters you choose, with the exception of *spaces*. Therefore, `r` is a legal variable name, as is `rate`, as is `interestRate`. The variable name `interest rate` is not allowed because of the space. No programming language allows spaces within a variable name. If you see a name such as `interest rate` in a flowchart or pseudocode, you should assume that the programmer is discussing two variables, `interest` and `rate`, each of which individually would be a fine variable name.

**TIP** ☐ ☐ ☐ ☐ | As a convention, this book begins variable names with a lowercase letter.

**TIP** ☐ ☐ ☐ ☐ | When you write a program, your compiler may show variable names in a different color from the rest of the program. This visual aid helps your variable names stand out from words that are part of the programming language.

2. *Variable names should have some appropriate meaning*. This is not a rule of any programming language. When computing an interest rate in a program, the computer does not care if you call the variable `g`, `u84`, or `fred`. As long as the correct numeric result is placed in the variable, its actual name doesn't really matter. However, it's much easier to follow the logic of a program with a statement in it like `compute finalBalance as equal to initialInvestment times interestRate` than one with a statement in it like `compute someBanana as equal to j89 times myFriendLinda`. You might think you will remember how you intended to use a cryptic variable name within a program, but several months or years later when a program requires changes, you, and other programmers working with you, will appreciate clear, descriptive variable names.

Notice that the flowchart in Figure 1-9 follows these two rules for variables: both variable names, `inputNumber` and `calculatedAnswer`, are one word, and they have appropriate meanings. Some programmers have fun with their variable names by naming them after friends or creating puns with them, but such behavior is unprofessional and marks those programmers as amateurs. Table 1-1 lists some possible variable names that might be used to hold an employee's last name and provides a rationale for the appropriateness of each one.

**TIP** ☐ ☐ ☐ ☐ | Another general rule in all programming languages is that variable names may not begin with a digit, although usually they may contain digits. Thus, in most languages budget2013 is a legal variable name, but 2013Budget is not.

**TABLE 1-1:** VALID AND INVALID VARIABLE NAMES FOR AN EMPLOYEE'S LAST NAME

| Suggested variable names for employee's last name | Comments |
|---|---|
| employeeLastName | Good |
| employeeLast | Good—most people would interpret Last as meaning Last Name |
| empLast | Good—emp is short for employee |
| emlstnam | Legal—but cryptic |
| lastNameOfTheEmployeeInQuestion | Legal—but awkward |
| last name | Not legal—embedded space |
| employeelastname | Legal—but hard to read without camel casing |

## ENDING A PROGRAM BY USING SENTINEL VALUES

Recall that the logic in the flowchart for doubling numbers, shown in Figure 1-9, has a major flaw—the program never ends. This programming situation is known as an **infinite loop**—a repeating flow of logic with no end. If, for example, the input numbers are being entered at the keyboard, the program will keep accepting numbers and printing out doubles forever. Of course, the user could refuse to type in any more numbers. But the computer is very patient, and if you refuse to give it any more numbers, it will sit and wait forever. When you finally type in a number, the program will double it, print the result, and wait for another. The program cannot progress any further while it is waiting for input; meanwhile, the program is occupying computer memory and tying up operating system resources. Refusing to enter any more numbers is not a practical solution. Another way to end the program is simply to turn the computer off! But again, that's neither the best nor an elegant way to bring the program to an end.

A superior way to end the program is to set a predetermined value for `inputNumber` that means "Stop the program!" For example, the programmer and the user could agree that the user will never need to know the double of 0 (zero), so the user could enter a 0 when he or she wants to stop. The program could then test any incoming value for `inputNumber` and, if it is a 0, stop the program. Testing a value is also called making a **decision**.

You represent a decision in a flowchart by drawing a **decision symbol**, which is shaped like a diamond. The diamond usually contains a question, the answer to which is one of two mutually exclusive options—often yes or no. All good computer questions have only two mutually exclusive answers, such as yes and no, true and false, or less than and not less than. For example, "What day of the year is your birthday?" is not a good computer question because there are 366 possible answers. But "Is your birthday June 24?" *is* a good computer question because, for everyone in the world, the answer is either yes or no.

**TIP** ☐ ☐ ☐ ☐    A yes-or-no decision is called a **binary decision**, because there are two possible outcomes.

The question to stop the doubling program should be "Is the `inputNumber` just entered equal to 0?" or "`inputNumber` = 0?" for short. The complete flowchart will now look like the one shown in Figure 1-10.

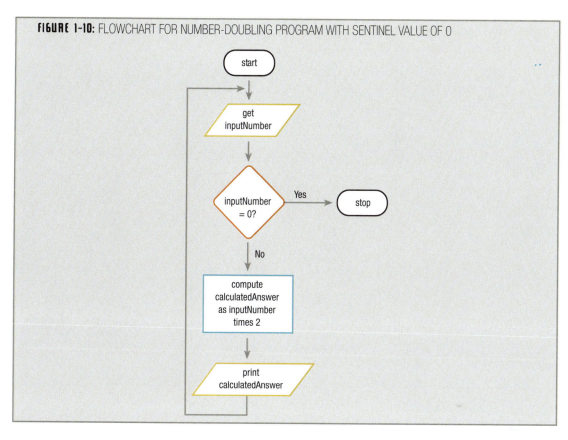

**FIGURE 1-10:** FLOWCHART FOR NUMBER-DOUBLING PROGRAM WITH SENTINEL VALUE OF 0

One drawback to using 0 to stop a program, of course, is that it won't work if the user *does* need to find the double of 0. In that case, some other data entry value that the user never will need, such as 999 or −1, could be selected to signal that the program should end. A preselected value that stops the execution of a program is often called a **dummy value** because it does not represent real data, but just a signal to stop. Sometimes, such a value is called a **sentinel value** because it represents an entry or exit point, like a sentinel who guards a fortress.

Not all programs rely on user data entry from a keyboard; many read data from an input device, such as a disk or tape drive. When organizations store data on a disk or tape, they do not commonly use a dummy value to signal the end of the file. For one thing, an input record might have hundreds of fields, and if you store a dummy record in every file, you are wasting a large quantity of storage on "non-data." Additionally, it is often difficult to choose sentinel values for fields in a company's data files. Any `balanceDue`, even a zero or a negative number, can be a legitimate value, and any `customerName`, even "ZZ" could be someone's name. Fortunately, programming languages can recognize the end of data in a file automatically, through a code that is stored at the end of the data. Many programming languages use the term **eof** (for "end of file") to talk about this marker that automatically acts as a sentinel. This book, therefore, uses `eof` to indicate the end of data, regardless of whether the code is a special disk marker or a dummy value such as 0 that comes from the keyboard. Therefore, the flowchart and pseudocode can look like the examples shown in Figure 1-11.

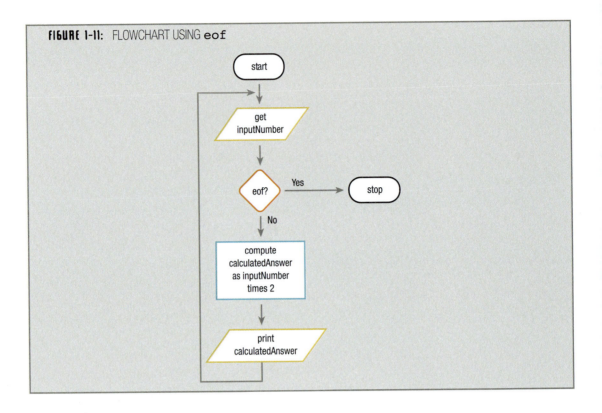

**FIGURE 1-11:** FLOWCHART USING eof

## USING THE CONNECTOR

By using just the input, processing, output, decision, and terminal symbols, you can represent the flowcharting logic for many diverse applications. When drawing a flowchart segment, you might use only one other symbol, the **connector**. You can use a connector when limited page size forces you to continue a flowchart in an unconnected location or on another page. If a flowchart has six processing steps and a page provides room for only three, you might represent the logic as shown in Figure 1-12.

By convention, programmers use a circle as an on-page connector symbol, and a symbol that looks like a square with a pointed bottom as an off-page connector symbol. The on-page connector at the bottom of the left column in Figure 1-10 tells someone reading the flowchart that there is more to the flowchart. The circle should contain a number or letter that can then be matched to another number or letter somewhere else, in this case on the right. If a large flowchart needed more connectors, new numbers or letters would be assigned in sequence (1, 2, 3... or A, B, C...) to each successive pair of connectors. The off-page connector at the bottom of the right column in Figure 1-10 tells a reader that there is more to the flowchart on another page.

When you are creating your own flowcharts, you should avoid using any connectors, if at all possible; flowcharts are more difficult to follow when their segments do not fit together on a page. Many programmers would even say that if a flowchart must connect to another page, it is a sign of poor design. Your instructor or future programming supervisor may require that long flowcharts be redrawn so you don't need to use the connector symbol. However, when continuing on a new location or page is unavoidable, the connector provides the means.

**FIGURE 1-12:** FLOWCHART USING THE CONNECTOR

## ASSIGNING VALUES TO VARIABLES

When you create a flowchart or pseudocode for a program that doubles numbers, you can include the statement `compute calculatedAnswer as inputNumber times 2`. This statement incorporates two actions. First, the computer computes the arithmetic value of `inputNumber` times 2. Second, the computed value is stored in the `calculatedAnswer` memory location. Most programming languages allow a shorthand expression for **assignment statements** such as `compute calculatedAnswer as inputNumber times 2`. The shorthand takes the form `calculatedAnswer = inputNumber * 2`. The equal sign is the **assignment operator**; it always requires the name of a memory location on its left side—the name of the location where the result will be stored.

**TIP** ☐ ☐ ☐ ☐    In Pascal, the same expression is calculatedAnswer := inputNumber * 2. You type a colon followed by an equal sign to create the assignment symbol. Java, C++, C#, Visual Basic, and many other languages all use the equal sign for assignment.

**TIP** ☐ ☐ ☐ ☐    Most programmers use the asterisk (*) to represent multiplication. When you write pseudocode, you can use an X or a dot for multiplication (as most mathematicians do), but you will be using an unconventional format. This book will always use an asterisk to represent multiplication.

According to the rules of algebra, a statement like `calculatedAnswer = inputNumber * 2` should be exactly equivalent to the statement `inputNumber * 2 = calculatedAnswer`. That's because in algebra, the equal sign always represents equivalency. To most programmers, however, the equal sign represents assignment, and `calculatedAnswer = inputNumber * 2` means "multiply `inputNumber` by 2 and store the result in the variable called `calculatedAnswer`." Whatever operation is performed to the right of the equal sign results in a value that is placed in the memory location to the left of the equal sign. Therefore, the incorrect statement `inputNumber * 2 = calculatedAnswer` means to attempt to take the value of `calculatedAnswer` and store it in a location called `inputNumber * 2,` but there can't be a location called `inputNumber * 2`. For one thing, `inputNumber * 2` can't be a variable because it has spaces in it. For another, a location can't be multiplied. Its contents can be multiplied, but the location itself cannot be. The backwards statement `inputNumber * 2 = calculatedAnswer` contains a syntax error, no matter what programming language you use; a program with such a statement will not execute.

**TIP** ▫ ▫ ▫ ▫ When you create an assignment statement, it may help to imagine the word "let" in front of the statement. Thus, you can read the statement calculatedAnswer = inputNumber * 2 as "Let calculatedAnswer equal inputNumber times two." The BASIC programming language allows you to use the word "let" in such statements.

Computer memory is made up of millions of distinct locations, each of which has an address. Fifty or sixty years ago, programmers had to deal with these addresses and had to remember, for instance, that they had stored a salary in location 6428 of their computer. Today, we are very fortunate that high-level computer languages allow us to pick a reasonable "English" name for a memory address and let the computer keep track of where it is. Just as it is easier for you to remember that the president lives in the White House than at 1600 Pennsylvania Avenue, Washington, D.C., it is also easier for you to remember that your salary is in a variable called `mySalary` than at memory location 6428104.

Similarly, it does not usually make sense to perform mathematical operations on names given to memory addresses, but it does make sense to perform mathematical operations on the *contents* of memory addresses. If you live in `blueSplitLevelOnTheCorner`, adding 1 to that would be meaningless, but you certainly can add 1 person to the number of people already in that house. For our purposes, then, the statement `calculatedAnswer = inputNumber * 2` means exactly the same thing as the statement `calculate inputNumber * 2 and store the result in the memory location named calculatedAnswer`.

**TIP** ▫ ▫ ▫ ▫ Many programming languages allow you to create named constants. A named constant is a named memory location, similar to a variable, except its value never changes during the execution of a program. If you are working with a programming language that allows it, you might create a constant for a value like pi = 3.14 or countySalesTaxRate = .06.

## UNDERSTANDING DATA TYPES

Computers deal with two basic types of data—character and numeric. When you use a specific numeric value, such as 43, within a program, you write it using the digits and no quotation marks. A specific numeric value is often called a

**numeric constant**, because it does not change—a 43 always has the value 43. When you use a specific character value, or **string** of characters, such as "Chris", you enclose the string, or **character constant**, within quotation marks.

TIP ▫ ▫ ▫ ▫ | Some languages require single quotation marks surrounding character constants, whereas others require double quotation marks. Many languages, including C++, C#, Java, and Pascal, reserve single quotes for a single character such as 'C', and double quotes for a character string such as "Chris".

Similarly, most computer languages allow at least two distinct types of variables. One type of variable can hold a number, and is often called a **numeric variable**. In the statement `calculatedAnswer = inputNumber * 2`, both `calculatedAnswer` and `inputNumber` are numeric variables; that is, their intended contents are numeric values, such as 6 and 3, 150 and 75, or –18 and –9.

Most programming languages have a separate type of variable that can hold letters of the alphabet and other special characters such as punctuation marks. Depending on the language, these variables are called **character**, **text**, or **string variables**. If a working program contains the statement `lastName = "Lincoln"`, then `lastName` is a character or string variable.

Programmers must distinguish between numeric and character variables, because computers handle the two types of data differently. Therefore, means are provided within the syntax rules of computer programming languages to tell the computer which type of data to expect. How this is done is different in every language; some languages have different rules for naming the variables, but with others you must include a simple statement (called a **declaration**) telling the computer which type of data to expect.

Some languages allow for several types of numeric data. Languages such as Pascal, C++, C#, and Java distinguish between **integer** (whole number) numeric variables and **floating-point** (fractional) numeric variables that contain a decimal point. Thus, in some languages, the numbers 4 and 4.3 would have to be stored in different types of variables.

Some programming languages allow even more specific variable types, but the character versus numeric distinction is universal. For the programs you develop in this book, assume that each variable is one of the two broad types. If a variable called `taxRate` is supposed to hold a value of 2.5, assume that it is a numeric variable. If a variable called `inventoryItem` is supposed to hold a value of "monitor," assume that it is a character variable.

TIP ▫ ▫ ▫ ▫ | Values such as "monitor" and 2.5 are called constants or literal constants because they never change. A variable value *can* change. Thus, inventoryItem can hold "monitor" at one moment during the execution of a program, and later you can change its value to "modem".

By convention, this book encloses character data like "monitor" within quotation marks to distinguish the characters from yet another variable name. Also, by convention, numeric data values are not enclosed within quotation marks. According to these conventions, then, `taxRate = 2.5` and `inventoryItem = "monitor"` are both valid statements. The statement `inventoryItem = monitor` is a valid statement only if `monitor` is also a character variable. In other words, if `monitor ="color"`, and subsequently `inventoryItem = monitor`, then the end result is that the memory address named `inventoryItem` contains the string of characters "color".

Every computer handles text or character data differently from the way it handles numeric data. You may have experienced these differences if you have used application software such as spreadsheets or database programs. For example, in a spreadsheet, you cannot sum a column of words. Similarly, every programming language requires that you distinguish variables as to their correct type, and that you use each type of variable appropriately. Identifying your variables correctly as numeric or character is one of the first steps you have to take when writing programs in any programming language. Table 1-2 provides you with a few examples of legal and illegal variable assignment statements.

**TIP** ▫ ▫ ▫ ▫  The process of naming program variables and assigning a type to them is called **making declarations**, or **declaring variables**. You will learn how to declare variables in Chapter 4.

**TABLE 1-2:** SOME EXAMPLES OF LEGAL AND ILLEGAL ASSIGNMENTS

*Assume lastName and firstName are character variables.*

*Assume quizScore and homeworkScore are numeric variables.*

| Examples of valid assignments | Examples of invalid assignments |
|---|---|
| lastName = "Parker" | lastName = Parker |
| firstName = "Laura" | "Parker" = lastName |
| lastName = firstName | lastName = quizScore |
| quizScore = 86 | homeworkScore = firstName |
| homeworkScore = quizScore | homeworkScore = "92" |
| homeworkScore = 92 | quizScore = "zero" |
| quizScore = homeworkScore + 25 | firstName = 23 |
| homeworkScore = 3 * 10 | 100 = homeworkScore |

## UNDERSTANDING THE EVOLUTION OF PROGRAMMING TECHNIQUES

People have been writing computer programs since the 1940s. The oldest programming languages required programmers to work with memory addresses and to memorize awkward codes associated with machine languages. Newer programming languages look much more like natural language and are easier for programmers to use. Part of the reason it is easier to use newer programming languages is that they allow programmers to name variables instead of using awkward memory addresses. Another reason is that newer programming languages provide programmers with the means to create self-contained modules or program segments that can be pieced together in a variety of ways. The oldest computer programs were written in one piece, from start to finish; modern programs are rarely written that way—they are created by teams of programmers, each developing his or her own reusable and connectable program procedures. Writing several small modules is easier than writing one large program, and most large tasks are easier when you break the work into units and get other workers to help with some of the units.

**TIP** ▢ ▢ ▢ ▢  You will learn to create program modules in Chapter 3.

Currently, there are two major techniques used to develop programs and their procedures. One technique, called **procedural programming**, focuses on the procedures that programmers create. That is, procedural programmers focus on the actions that are carried out—for example, getting input data for an employee and writing the calculations needed to produce a paycheck from the data. Procedural programmers would approach the job of producing a paycheck by breaking down the paycheck-producing process into manageable subtasks.

The other popular programming technique, called **object-oriented programming**, focuses on objects, or "things," and describes their features, or attributes, and their behaviors. For example, object-oriented programmers might design a payroll application by thinking about employees and paychecks, and describing their attributes (such as last name or check amount) and behaviors (such as the calculations that result in the check amount).

With either approach, procedural or object-oriented, you can produce a correct paycheck, and both techniques employ reusable program modules. The major difference lies in the focus the programmer takes during the earliest planning stages of a project. Object-oriented programming employs a large vocabulary; you can learn this terminology in Chapter 13 of the Comprehensive version of this book. For now, this book focuses on procedural programming techniques. The skills you gain in programming procedurally—declaring variables, accepting input, making decisions, producing output, and so on—will serve you well whether you eventually write programs in a procedural or object-oriented fashion, or in both.

## CHAPTER SUMMARY

☐ Together, computer hardware (equipment) and software (instructions) accomplish four major operations: input, processing, output, and storage. You write computer instructions in a computer programming language that requires specific syntax; the instructions are translated into machine language by a compiler or interpreter. When both the syntax and logic of a program are correct, you can run, or execute, the program to produce the desired results.

☐ A programmer's job involves understanding the problem, planning the logic, coding the program, translating the program into machine language, testing the program, and putting the program into production.

☐ When data are stored for use on computer systems, they are stored in a data hierarchy of character, field, record, file, and database.

☐ When programmers plan the logic for a solution to a programming problem, they often use flowcharts or pseudocode. When you draw a flowchart, you use parallelograms to represent input and output operations, and rectangles to represent processing.

☐ Variables are named memory locations, the contents of which can vary. As a programmer, you choose reasonable names for your variables. Every computer programming language has its own set of rules for naming variables; however, all variable names must be written as one word without embedded spaces, and should have appropriate meaning.

☐ Testing a value involves making a decision. You represent a decision in a flowchart by drawing a diamond-shaped decision symbol containing a question, the answer to which is either yes or no. You can stop a program's execution by using a decision to test for a sentinel value.

☐ A connector symbol is used to continue a flowchart that does not fit together on a page, or must continue on an additional page.

☐ Most programming languages use the equal sign to assign values to variables. Assignment always takes place from right to left.

☐ Programmers must distinguish between numeric and character variables, because computers handle the two types of data differently. A variable declaration tells the computer which type of data to expect. By convention, character data values are included within quotation marks.

☐ Procedural and object-oriented programmers approach program problems differently. Procedural programmers concentrate on the actions performed with data. Object-oriented programmers focus on objects and their behaviors and attributes.

## KEY TERMS

**Hardware** is the equipment of a computer system.

**Software**, or programs, are written by programmers and tell the computer what to do.

**Input** devices include keyboards and mice; through these devices, data enter the computer system. Data can also enter a system from storage devices such as magnetic disks and CDs.

**Data** are facts.

**Processing** data items may involve organizing them, checking them for accuracy, or performing mathematical operations on them.

The **central processing unit**, or **CPU**, is the piece of hardware that processes data.

Information is sent to a printer, monitor, or some other **output** device so people can view, interpret, and work with the results.

**Programming languages**, such as Visual Basic, Pascal, COBOL, RPG, C#, C++, Java, or Fortran, are used to write programs.

The **syntax** of a language consists of its rules.

**Machine language** is a computer's on-off circuitry language.

A **compiler** or **interpreter** translates a high-level language into machine language and tells you if you have used a programming language incorrectly.

You develop the **logic** of the computer program when you give instructions to the computer in a specific sequence, without leaving any instructions out or adding extraneous instructions.

The **running**, or **executing**, of a program occurs when the computer actually uses the written and compiled program.

**Internal storage** is called **memory**, **main memory**, or **primary memory**.

**External storage** is permanent storage outside the main memory of the machine, on a device such as a floppy disk, hard disk, or magnetic tape.

Internal memory is **volatile**—that is, its contents are lost every time the computer loses power.

You **save** a program on some nonvolatile medium.

An **algorithm** is the sequence of steps necessary to solve any problem.

**Coding** a program means writing the statements in a programming language.

**High-level programming languages** are English-like.

**Machine language** is the **low-level** language made up of 1s and 0s that the computer understands.

A **syntax error** is an error in language or grammar.

**Logical errors** occur when incorrect instructions are performed, or when instructions are performed in the wrong order.

**Conversion** is the entire set of actions an organization must take to switch over to using a new program or set of programs.

The **data hierarchy** represents the relationship of databases, files, records, fields, and characters.

**Characters** are letters, numbers, and special symbols such as "A", "7", and "$".

A **field** is a single data item, such as `lastName`, `streetAddress`, or `annualSalary`.

**Records** are groups of fields that go together for some logical reason.

**Files** are groups of records that go together for some logical reason.

A **database** holds a group of files, often called **tables**, that together serve the information needs of an organization.

**Queries** are questions that pull related data items together from a database in a format that enhances efficient management decision making.

A **flowchart** is a pictorial representation of the logical steps it takes to solve a problem.

**Pseudocode** is an English-like representation of the logical steps it takes to solve a problem.

**Input symbols** are represented as parallelograms in flowcharts.

**Processing symbols** are represented as rectangles in flowcharts.

**Output symbols** are represented as parallelograms in flowcharts.

**Flowlines**, or arrows, connect the steps in a flowchart.

A **terminal symbol**, or start/stop symbol, is used at each end of a flowchart. Its shape is a **lozenge**.

**Variables** are memory locations, whose contents can vary, or differ, over time.

A variable name is also called an **identifier**.

A **mnemonic** is a memory device; variable identifiers act as mnemonics for hard-to-remember memory addresses.

**Camel casing** is the format for naming variables in which multiple-word variable names are run together, and each new word within the variable name begins with an uppercase letter.

An **infinite loop** is a repeating flow of logic without an ending.

Testing a value is also called making a **decision**.

You represent a decision in a flowchart by drawing a **decision symbol**, which is shaped like a diamond.

A yes-or-no decision is called a **binary decision**, because there are two possible outcomes.

A **dummy value** is a preselected value that stops the execution of a program. Such a value is sometimes called a **sentinel value** because it represents an entry or exit point, like a sentinel who guards a fortress.

Many programming languages use the term **eof** (for "end of file") to talk about an end-of-data file marker.

A **connector** is a flowchart symbol used when limited page size forces you to continue the flowchart on the same or following page.

An **assignment statement** stores the result of any calculation performed on its right side to the named location on its left side.

The equal sign is the **assignment operator**; it always requires the name of a memory location on its left side.

A **numeric constant** is a specific numeric value.

A **string constant**, or **character constant**, is enclosed within quotation marks.

**Numeric variables** hold numeric values.

**Character**, **text**, or **string variables** hold character values. If a working program contains the statement `lastName = "Lincoln"`, then `lastName` is a character or string variable.

A **declaration** is a statement that names a variable and tells the computer which type of data to expect.

**Integer** values are whole number, numeric variables.

**Floating-point** values are fractional, numeric variables that contain a decimal point.

The process of naming program variables and assigning a type to them is called **making declarations**, or **declaring variables**.

The technique known as **procedural programming** focuses on the procedures that programmers create.

The technique known as **object-oriented programming** focuses on objects, or "things," and describes their features, or attributes, and their behaviors.

## REVIEW QUESTIONS

1. **The two major components of any computer system are its _____.**

    a. input and output
    b. data and programs
    c. hardware and software
    d. memory and disk drives

2. **The major computer operations include _____.**

    a. hardware and software
    b. input, processing, output, and storage
    c. sequence and looping
    d. spreadsheets, word processing, and data communications

3. **Another term meaning "computer instructions" is _____.**

    a. hardware
    b. software
    c. queries
    d. data

4. **Visual Basic, C++, and Java are all examples of computer _____.**

    a. operating systems
    b. hardware
    c. machine languages
    d. programming languages

5. **A programming language's rules are its _____.**

    a. syntax
    b. logic
    c. format
    d. options

6. **The most important task of a compiler or interpreter is to _____.**

    a. create the rules for a programming language
    b. translate English statements into a language such as Java
    c. translate programming language statements into machine language
    d. execute machine language programs to perform useful tasks

**7.** **Which of the following is a typical input instruction?**

    a. `get accountNumber`

    b. `calculate balanceDue`

    c. `print customerIdentificationNumber`

    d. `total = janPurchase + febPurchase`

**8.** **Which of the following is a typical processing instruction?**

    a. `print answer`

    b. `get userName`

    c. `pctCorrect = rightAnswers / allAnswers`

    d. `print calculatedPercentage`

**9.** **Which of the following is not associated with internal storage?**

    a. main memory

    b. hard disk

    c. primary memory

    d. volatile

**10.** **Which of the following pairs of steps in the programming process is in the correct order?**

    a. code the program, plan the logic

    b. test the program, translate it into machine language

    c. put the program into production, understand the problem

    d. code the program, translate it into machine language

**11.** **The two most commonly used tools for planning a program's logic are _____.**

    a. flowcharts and pseudocode

    b. ASCII and EBCDIC

    c. Java and Visual Basic

    d. word processors and spreadsheets

**12.** **The most important thing a programmer must do before planning the logic to a program is _____.**

    a. decide which programming language to use

    b. code the problem

    c. train the users of the program

    d. understand the problem

**13.** **Writing a program in a language such as C++ or Java is known as _____ the program.**

    a. translating

    b. coding

    c. interpreting

    d. compiling

14. **A compiler would find all of the following programming errors except _____.**

   a. the misspelled word "prrint" in a language that includes the word "print"

   b. the use of an "X" for multiplication in a language that requires an asterisk

   c. a `newBalanceDue` calculated by adding a `customerPayment` to an `oldBalanceDue` instead of subtracting it

   d. an arithmetic statement written as `regularSales + discountedSales = totalSales`

15. **Which of the following is true regarding the data hierarchy?**

   a. files contain records

   b. characters contain fields

   c. fields contain files

   d. fields contain records

16. **The parallelogram is the flowcharting symbol representing _____.**

   a. input

   b. output

   c. both a and b

   d. none of the above

17. **Which of the following is not a legal variable name in any programming language?**

   a. `semester grade`

   b. `fall2005_grade`

   c. `GradeInCIS100`

   d. `MY_GRADE`

18. **In flowcharts, the decision symbol is a _____.**

   a. parallelogram

   b. rectangle

   c. lozenge

   d. diamond

19. **The term "eof" represents _____.**

   a. a standard input device

   b. a generic sentinel value

   c. a condition in which no more memory is available for storage

   d. the logical flow in a program

20. **The two most broad types of data are _____.**

   a. internal and external

   b. volatile and constant

   c. character and numeric

   d. permanent and temporary

### EXERCISES

1. **Match the definition with the appropriate term.**

   1. Computer system equipment     a. compiler
   2. Another word for programs       b. syntax
   3. Language rules                  c. logic
   4. Order of instructions          d. hardware
   5. Language translator           e. software

2. **In your own words, describe the steps to writing a computer program.**

3. **Consider a student file that contains the following data:**

   | LAST NAME | FIRST NAME | MAJOR | GRADE POINT AVERAGE |
   | --- | --- | --- | --- |
   | Andrews | David | Psychology | 3.4 |
   | Broederdorf | Melissa | Computer Science | 4.0 |
   | Brogan | Lindsey | Biology | 3.8 |
   | Carson | Joshua | Computer Science | 2.8 |
   | Eisfelder | Katie | Mathematics | 3.5 |
   | Faris | Natalie | Biology | 2.8 |
   | Fredricks | Zachary | Psychology | 2.0 |
   | Gonzales | Eduardo | Biology | 3.1 |

   **Would this set of data be suitable and sufficient to use to test each of the following programs? Explain why or why not.**

   a. a program that prints a list of Psychology majors
   b. a program that prints a list of Art majors
   c. a program that prints a list of students on academic probation—those with a grade point average under 2.0
   d. a program that prints a list of students on the dean's list
   e. a program that prints a list of students from Wisconsin
   f. a program that prints a list of female students

4. **Suggest a good set of test data to use for a program that gives an employee a $50 bonus check if the employee has produced more than 1,000 items in a week.**

5. **Suggest a good set of test data for a program that computes gross paychecks (that is, before any taxes or other deductions) based on hours worked and rate of pay. The program computes gross as hours times rate, unless hours are over 40. Then, the program computes gross as regular rate of pay for 40 hours, plus one and a half times the rate of pay for the hours over 40.**

6. **Suggest a good set of test data for a program that is intended to output a student's grade point average based on letter grades (A, B, C, D, or F) in five courses.**

7. **Suggest a good set of test data for a program for an automobile insurance company that wants to increase its premiums by $50 per month for every ticket a driver receives in a three-year period.**

8. **Assume that a grocery store keeps a file for inventory, where each grocery item has its own record. Two fields within each record are the name of the manufacturer and the weight of the item. Name**

at least six more fields that might be stored for each record. Provide an example of the data for one record. For example, for one product the manufacturer is DelMonte, and the weight is 12 ounces.

9.    Assume that a library keeps a file with data about its collection, one record for each item the library lends out. Name at least eight fields that might be stored for each record. Provide an example of the data for one record.

10.    Match the term with the appropriate shape.

1. Input                    A.

2. Processing               B.

3. Decision                 C.

4. Terminal                 D.

5. Connector                E.

11.    Which of the following names seem like good variable names to you? If a name doesn't seem like a good variable name, explain why not.

a.  c

b.  cost

c.  costAmount

d.  cost amount

e.  cstofdngbsns

f.  costOfDoingBusinessThisFiscalYear

g.  cost2004

12.   **If myAge and yourRate are numeric variables, and departmentCode is a character variable, which of the following statements are valid assignments? If a statement is not valid, explain why not.**

   a.   myAge = 23
   b.   myAge = yourRate
   c.   myAge = departmentCode
   d.   myAge = "departmentCode"
   e.   42 = myAge
   f.   yourRate = 3.5
   g.   yourRate = myAge
   h.   yourRate = departmentCode
   i.   6.91 = yourRate
   j.   departmentCode = Personnel
   k.   departmentCode = "Personnel"
   l.   departmentCode = 413
   m.   departmentCode = "413"
   n.   departmentCode = myAge
   o.   departmentCode = yourRate
   p.   413 = departmentCode
   q.   "413" = departmentCode

13.   **Complete the following tasks:**

   a.   Draw a flowchart to represent the logic of a program that allows the user to enter a value. The program multiplies the value by 10 and prints out the result.
   b.   Write pseudocode for the same problem.

14.   **Complete the following tasks:**

   a.   Draw a flowchart to represent the logic of a program that allows the user to enter a value that represents the radius of a circle. The program calculates the diameter (by multiplying the radius by 2), and then calculates the circumference (by multiplying the diameter by 3.14). The program prints both the diameter and the circumference.
   b.   Write pseudocode for the same problem.

15.   **Complete the following tasks:**

   a.   Draw a flowchart to represent the logic of a program that allows the user to enter two values. The program prints the sum of the two values.
   b.   Write pseudocode for the same problem.

16.   **Complete the following tasks:**

   a.   Draw a flowchart to represent the logic of a program that allows the user to enter three values. The first value represents hourly pay rate, the second represents the number of hours worked this pay period, and the third represents the percentage of gross salary that is withheld. The program multiplies the hourly pay rate by the number of hours worked, giving the gross pay; then, it multiplies the gross pay by the withholding percentage, giving the withholding amount. Finally, it subtracts the withholding amount from the gross pay, giving the net pay after taxes. The program prints the net pay.
   b.   Write pseudocode for the same problem.

# 2 UNDERSTANDING STRUCTURE

## After studying Chapter 2, you should be able to:

- [ ] Describe the features of unstructured spaghetti code
- [ ] Describe the three basic structures of sequence, selection, and loop
- [ ] Use a priming read
- [ ] Appreciate the need for structure
- [ ] Recognize structure
- [ ] Describe two special structures—case and do until

## UNDERSTANDING UNSTRUCTURED SPAGHETTI CODE

Professional computer programs usually get far more complicated than the number-doubling program from Chapter 1, shown in Figure 2-1.

**FIGURE 2-1:** NUMBER-DOUBLING PROGRAM

```
get inputNumber
calculatedAnswer = inputNumber * 2
print calculatedAnswer
```

Imagine the number of instructions in the computer program that NASA uses to calculate the launch angle of a space shuttle, or in the program the IRS uses to audit your income tax return. Even the program that produces a paycheck for you on your job contains many, many instructions. Designing the logic for such a program can be a time-consuming task. When you add several thousand instructions to a program, including several hundred decisions, it is easy to create a complicated mess. The popular name for snarled program statements is **spaghetti code**. The reason for the name should be obvious—the code is as confusing to read as following one noodle through a plate of spaghetti.

For example, suppose you are in charge of admissions at a college, and you've decided you will admit prospective students based on the following criteria:

- You will admit students who score 90 or better on the admissions test your college gives, as long as they are in the upper 75 percent of their high-school graduating class. (These are smart students who score well on the admissions test. Maybe they didn't do so well in high school because it was a tough school, or maybe they have matured.)

- You will admit students who score at least 80 on the admissions test if they are in the upper 50 percent of their high-school graduating class. (These students score fairly well on the test, and do fairly well in school.)

- You will admit students who score as low as 70 on your test if they are in the top 25 percent of their class. (Maybe these students don't take tests well, but obviously they are achievers.)

Table 2-1 summarizes the admission requirements.

**TABLE 2-1:** ADMISSION REQUIREMENTS

| Test score | High-school rank (%) |
|---|---|
| 90–100 | 25–100 |
| 80–89 | 50–100 |
| 70–79 | 75–100 |

The flowchart for this program could look like the one in Figure 2-2. This kind of flowchart is an example of spaghetti code. Many computer programs (especially older computer programs) bear a striking resemblance to the flowchart in

Figure 2-2. Such programs might "work"—that is, they might produce correct results—but they are very difficult to read and maintain, and their logic is difficult to follow.

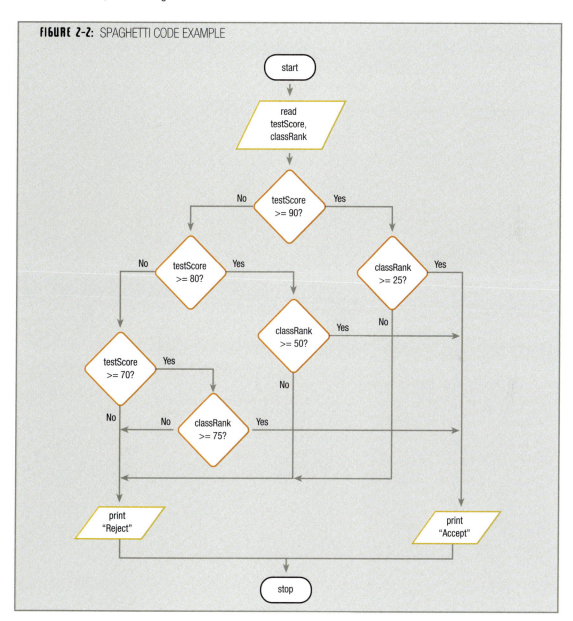

**FIGURE 2-2:** SPAGHETTI CODE EXAMPLE

## UNDERSTANDING THE THREE BASIC STRUCTURES

In the mid-1960s, mathematicians proved that any program, no matter how complicated, can be constructed using only three sets of flowcharting shapes or structures. A **structure** is a basic unit of programming logic; each structure is a sequence, selection, or loop. With these three structures alone, you can diagram any event, from doubling a number to performing brain surgery.

The first of these structures is a sequence, as shown in Figure 2-3. With a **sequence structure**, you perform an action or event, and then you perform the next action, in order. A sequence can contain any number of events, but there is no chance to branch off and skip any of the events. Once you start a series of events in a sequence, you must continue step-by-step until the sequence ends.

**FIGURE 2-3:** SEQUENCE STRUCTURE

The second structure is called a **selection structure** or **decision structure**, as shown in Figure 2-4. With this structure, you ask a question, and, depending on the answer, you take one of two courses of action. Then, no matter which path you follow, you continue with the next event.

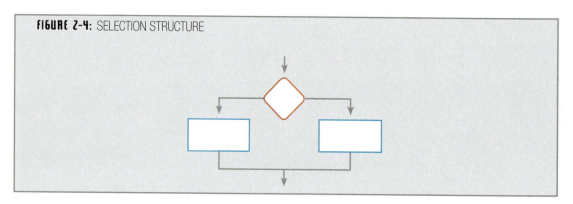

**FIGURE 2-4:** SELECTION STRUCTURE

Some people call the selection structure an **if-then-else** because it fits the following statement:

```
if someCondition is true then
    do oneProcess
else
    do theOtherProcess
```

For example, while cooking you may decide the following:

```
if we have brownSugar then
    use brownSugar
else
    use whiteSugar
```

Similarly, a payroll program might include a statement such as:

```
if hoursWorked is more than 40 then
    calculate overtimePay
else
    calculate regularPay
```

The previous examples can also be called **dual-alternative ifs**, because they contain two alternatives—the action taken when the tested condition is true and the action taken when it is false. Note that it is perfectly correct for one branch of the selection to be a "do nothing" branch. For example:

```
if it is raining then
    take anUmbrella
```

or

```
if employee belongs to dentalPlan then
    deduct $40 from employeeGrossPay
```

The previous examples are **single-alternative ifs**, and a diagram of their structure is shown in Figure 2-5. In these cases, you don't take any special action if it is not raining or if the employee does not belong to the dental plan. The case where nothing is done is often called the **null case**.

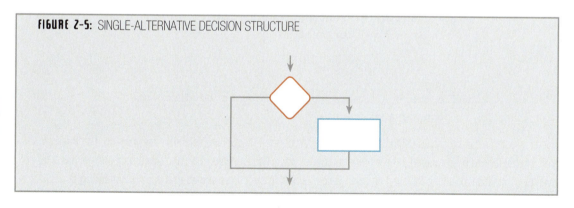

**FIGURE 2-5:** SINGLE-ALTERNATIVE DECISION STRUCTURE

The third structure, shown in Figure 2-6, is a loop. In a **loop structure**, you ask a question; if the answer requires an action, you perform the action and ask the original question again. If the answer requires that the action be taken again, you take the action and then ask the original question again. This continues until the answer to the question is such that the action is no longer required; then you exit the structure. You may hear programmers refer to looping as **repetition** or **iteration**.

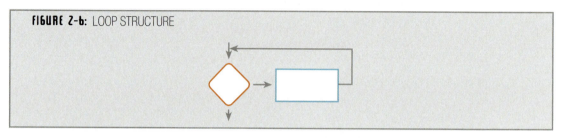

**FIGURE 2-6:** LOOP STRUCTURE

Some programmers call this structure a **do while** because it fits the following statement:

```
while testCondition continues to be true,
    do someProcess
```

You encounter examples of looping every day, as in:

```
while you continue to beHungry
    take anotherBiteOfFood
```

or

```
while unreadPages remain in the readingAssignment
    read another unreadPage
```

In a business program, you might write:

```
while quantityInInventory remains low
    continue to orderItems
```

or

```
while there are more retailPrices to be discounted
    compute a discount
```

All logic problems can be solved using only these three structures—sequence, selection, and looping. The three structures, of course, can be combined in an infinite number of ways. For example, you can have a sequence of steps followed by a selection, or a loop followed by a sequence. Attaching structures end-to-end is called **stacking** structures. For example, Figure 2-7 shows a structured flowchart achieved by stacking structures, and also shows pseudocode that might follow that flowchart logic.

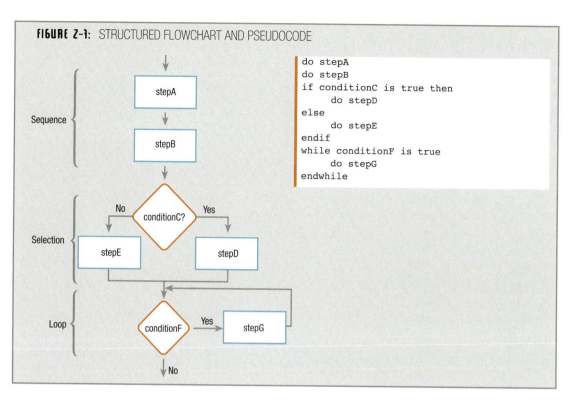

**FIGURE 2-7:** STRUCTURED FLOWCHART AND PSEUDOCODE

```
do stepA
do stepB
if conditionC is true then
     do stepD
else
     do stepE
endif
while conditionF is true
     do stepG
endwhile
```

The pseudocode in Figure 2-7 shows two end-structure statements—`endif` and `endwhile`. You can use an `endif` statement to clearly show where the actions that depend on a decision end. The instruction that follows `if` occurs when its tested condition is true, the instruction that follows `else` occurs when the tested condition is false, and the instruction that follows the `endif` occurs in either case—it is not dependent on the `if` statement at all. In other words, statements beyond the `endif` statement are "outside" the decision structure. Similarly, you use an `endwhile` statement to show where a loop structure ends. In Figure 2-7, while `conditionF` continues to be true, `stepG` continues to execute. If any statements followed the `endwhile` statement, they would be outside of, and not a part of, the loop.

Besides stacking structures, you can replace any individual steps in a structured flowchart diagram or pseudocode segment with additional structures. In other words, any sequence, selection, or loop can contain other sequences, selections, or loops. For example, you can have a sequence of three steps on one side of a selection, as shown in Figure 2-8. Placing a structure within another structure is called **nesting** the structures.

**FIGURE 2-8:** FLOWCHART AND PSEUDOCODE SHOWING A SEQUENCE NESTED WITHIN A SELECTION

```
if conditionA is true then
     do stepE
else
     do stepB
     do stepC
     do stepD
endif
```

When you write the pseudocode for the logic shown in Figure 2-8, the convention is to indent all statements that depend on one branch of the decision, as shown in the pseudocode. The indentation and the `endif` statement both show that all three statements (`do stepB`, `stepC`, and `stepD`) must execute if `conditionA` is not true. The three statements constitute a **block**, or group of statements that executes as a single unit.

In place of one of the steps in the sequence in Figure 2-8, you can insert a selection. In Figure 2-9, the process named `stepC` has been replaced with a selection structure that begins with a test of the condition named `conditionF`.

**FIGURE 2-9:** SELECTION IN A SEQUENCE WITHIN A SELECTION

```
if conditionA is true then
     do stepE
else
     do stepB
     if conditionF is true then
          do stepH
     else
          do stepG
     endif
     do stepD
endif
```

In the pseudocode shown in Figure 2-9, notice that `do stepB`, `if conditionF is true then`, `else`, and `do stepD` all align vertically with each other. This shows that they are all "on the same level." If you look at the same problem flowcharted in Figure 2-9, you see that you could draw a vertical line through the symbols containing `stepB`, `conditionF`, and `stepD`. The flowchart and the pseudocode represent exactly the same logic. The `stepH` and `stepG` processes, on the other hand, are one level "down"; they are dependent on the answer to the `conditionF` question. Therefore, the `do stepH` and `do stepG` statements are indented one additional level in the pseudocode.

Also notice that the pseudocode in Figure 2-9 has two `endif` statements. Each is aligned to correspond to an `if`. An `endif` always partners with the most recent `if` that does not already have an `endif` partner, and an `endif` should always align vertically with its `if` partner.

In place of `do stepH` on one side of the new selection in Figure 2-9, you can insert a loop. This loop, based on `conditionI`, appears inside the selection that is within the sequence that constitutes the "No" side of the original `conditionA` selection. In the pseudocode in Figure 2-10, notice that the `while` aligns with the `endwhile`, and that the entire `while` structure is indented within the true half of the `if` structure that begins with the decision based on `conditionF`. The indentation used in the pseudocode reflects the logic you can see laid out graphically in the flowchart.

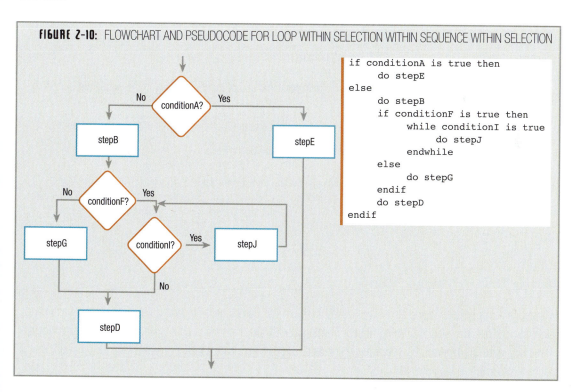

**FIGURE 2-10:** FLOWCHART AND PSEUDOCODE FOR LOOP WITHIN SELECTION WITHIN SEQUENCE WITHIN SELECTION

```
if conditionA is true then
        do stepE
else
        do stepB
        if conditionF is true then
                while conditionI is true
                        do stepJ
                endwhile
        else
                do stepG
        endif
        do stepD
endif
```

The combinations are endless, but each of a structured program's segments is a sequence, a selection, or a loop. The three structures are shown together in Figure 2-11. Notice that each structure has one entry and one exit point. One structure can attach to another only at one of these entry or exit points.

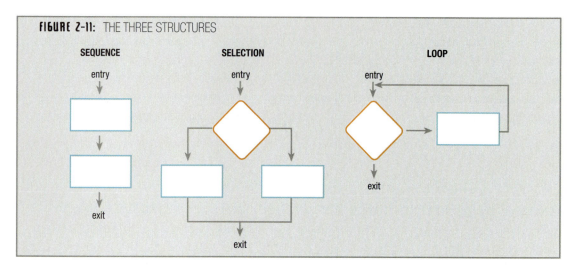

**FIGURE 2-11:** THE THREE STRUCTURES

In summary, a structured program has the following characteristics:

- A structured program includes only combinations of the three structures—sequence, selection, and loop.
- Structures can be stacked or connected to one another only at their entrance or exit points.
- Any structure can be nested within another structure.

## USING THE PRIMING READ

For a program to be structured and also work the way you want it to, sometimes you need to add extra steps. The priming read is one kind of added step. A **priming read** or **priming input** is the first read or data input statement in a program. If a program will read 100 data records, you read the first data record in a statement that is separate from the other 99. You must do this to keep the program structured.

At the end of Chapter 1, you read about a program like the one in Figure 2-12. The program gets a number and checks for end of file. If it is not end of file, then the number is doubled, the answer is printed, and the next number is input.

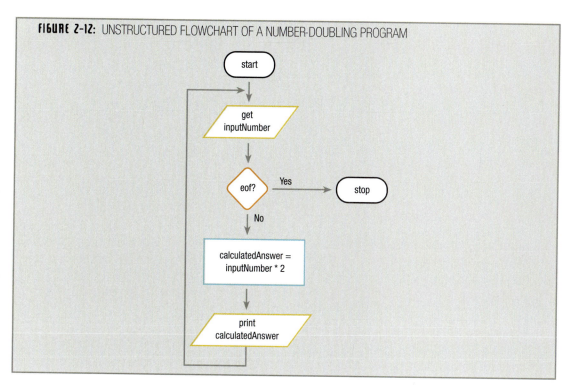

**FIGURE 2-12:** UNSTRUCTURED FLOWCHART OF A NUMBER-DOUBLING PROGRAM

Is the program represented by Figure 2-12 structured? At first, it might be hard to tell. The three allowed structures were illustrated in Figure 2-11.

The flowchart in Figure 2-12 does not look exactly like any of the three shapes shown in Figure 2-11. However, because you may stack and nest structures while retaining overall structure, it might be difficult to determine whether a flowchart as a whole is structured. It's easiest to analyze the flowchart in Figure 2-12 one step at a time. The beginning of the flowchart looks like Figure 2-13.

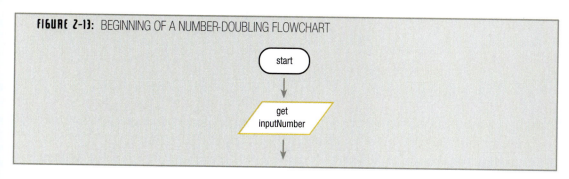

**FIGURE 2-13:** BEGINNING OF A NUMBER-DOUBLING FLOWCHART

Is this portion of the flowchart structured? Yes, it's a sequence. Adding the next step of the flowchart looks like Figure 2-14.

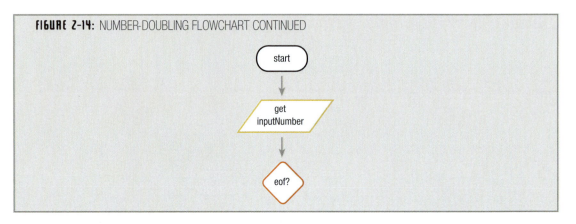

**FIGURE 2-14:** NUMBER-DOUBLING FLOWCHART CONTINUED

The sequence is finished; either a selection or a loop is starting. You might not know which one, but you do know the sequence is not continuing, because sequences can't contain questions. With a sequence, each step must follow without any opportunity to branch off. Therefore, which type of structure starts with the question in Figure 2-14? Is it a selection or a loop?

With a selection structure, the logic goes in one of two directions after the question, and then the flow comes back together; the question is not asked a second time. However, in a loop, if the answer to the question results in the loop being entered and the loop statements executing, then the logic returns to the question that started the loop; when the body of a loop executes, the question that controls the loop is always asked again.

In the doubling problem in the original Figure 2-12, if it is not `eof` (that is, if the end-of-file condition is not met), some math is done, an answer is printed, a new number is obtained, and the `eof` question is asked again. In other words, while the answer to the `eof` question continues to be *no*, eventually the logic will return to the `eof` question. (Another way to phrase this is that while it continues to be true that `eof` has not yet been reached, the logic keeps returning to the same question.) Therefore, the doubling problem contains a structure beginning with the `eof` question that is more like the beginning of a loop than it is like a selection.

The doubling problem *does* contain a loop, but it's not a structured loop. In a structured loop, the rules are:

1. You ask a question.
2. If the answer indicates you should perform a procedure, you do so.
3. If you perform the procedure, then you must go right back to repeat the question.

The flowchart in Figure 2-12 asks a question; if the answer is *no* (that is, while it is true that the `eof` condition has not been met), the program performs two tasks: it does the arithmetic and it prints the results. Doing two things is acceptable because two steps constitute a sequence, and it is fine to nest a structure within another structure. However, when the sequence ends, the logic doesn't flow right back to the question. Instead, it goes *above* the question to get another number. For the loop in Figure 2-12 to be a structured loop, the logic must return to the `eof` question when the sequence ends.

The flowchart in Figure 2-15 shows the flow of logic returning to the `eof` immediately after the sequence. Figure 2-15 shows a structured flowchart, but the flowchart has one major flaw—it doesn't do the job of continuously doubling numbers.

**FIGURE 2-15:** STRUCTURED, BUT NONFUNCTIONAL, FLOWCHART OF NUMBER-DOUBLING PROBLEM

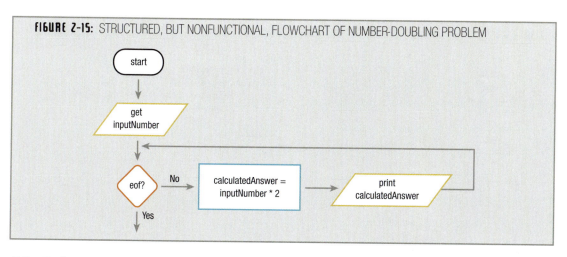

Follow the flowchart in Figure 2-15 through a typical program run. Suppose when the program starts, the user enters a 9 for the value of `inputNumber`. That's not `eof`, so the number doubles, and 18 prints out as the `calculatedAnswer`. Then the question `eof?` is asked again. It can't be `eof` because a new value representing the sentinel (ending) value can't be entered. The logic never returns to the `get inputNumber` step, so the value of `inputNumber` never changes. Therefore, 9 doubles again and the answer 18 prints again. It's still not `eof`, so the same steps are repeated. This goes on *forever*, with the answer 18 printing repeatedly. The program logic shown in Figure 2-15 is structured, but it doesn't work; the program in Figure 2-16 works, but it isn't structured!

**TIP** ▢ ▢ ▢ ▢  The loop in Figure 2-16 is not structured because in a structured loop, after the steps that execute within the loop, the flow of logic must return directly to the loop-controlling question. In Figure 2-16, the logic does not return to the loop-controlling question; instead it goes "too high" outside the loop to repeat the `get inputNumber` step.

**FIGURE 2-16:** FUNCTIONAL BUT NONSTRUCTURED FLOWCHART

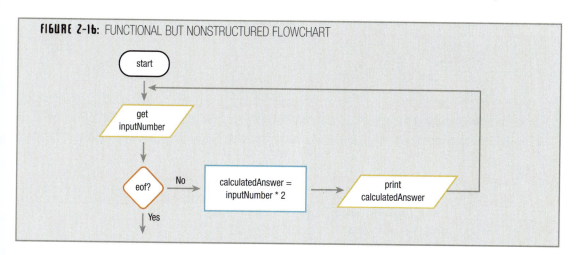

How can the number-doubling problem be both structured and work? Often, for a program to be structured, you must add something extra. In this case, it's an extra `get inputNumber` step. Consider the solution in Figure 2-17; it's structured, *and* it does what it's supposed to do! The program logic illustrated in Figure 2-17 contains a sequence and a loop. The loop contains another sequence.

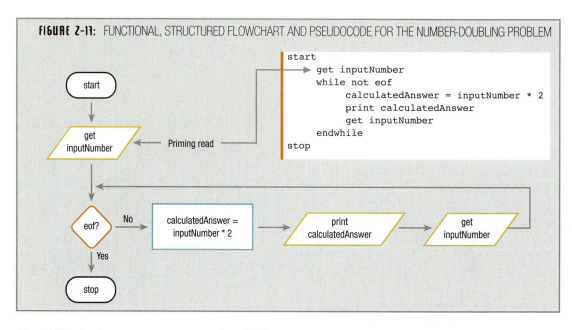

**FIGURE 2-17:** FUNCTIONAL, STRUCTURED FLOWCHART AND PSEUDOCODE FOR THE NUMBER-DOUBLING PROBLEM

```
start
    get inputNumber
    while not eof
        calculatedAnswer = inputNumber * 2
        print calculatedAnswer
        get inputNumber
    endwhile
stop
```

The additional `get inputNumber` step is typical in structured programs. The first of the two input steps is the priming input, or priming read. The term *priming* comes from the fact that the read is first, or *primary* (what gets the process going, as in "priming the pump"). The purpose of the priming read step is to control the upcoming loop that begins with the `eof` question. The last element within the structured loop gets the next, and all subsequent, input values. This is also typical in structured loops—the last step executed within the loop alters the condition tested in the question that begins the loop, which in this case is the `eof` question.

As an additional way to determine whether a flowchart segment is structured, you can try to write pseudocode for it. Examine the unstructured flowchart in Figure 2-12 again. To write pseudocode for it, you would begin with the following:

```
start
    get inputNumber
```

When you encounter the `eof` question in the flowchart, you know that either a selection or looping structure should begin. Because you return to a location higher in the flowchart when the answer to the `eof` question is *no* (that is, while the `not eof` condition continues to be *true*), you know that a loop is beginning. So you continue to write the pseudocode as follows:

```
start
    get inputNumber
    while not eof
        calculatedAnswer = inputNumber * 2
        print calculatedAnswer
```

Continuing, the step after `print calculatedAnswer` is `get inputNumber`. This ends the `while` loop that began with the `eof` question. So the pseudocode becomes:

```
start
     get inputNumber
     while not eof
          calculatedAnswer = inputNumber * 2
          print calculatedAnswer
          get inputNumber
     endwhile
stop
```

This pseudocode is identical to the pseudocode in Figure 2-17, and now matches the flowchart in the same figure. Creating the pseudocode requires you to repeat the `get inputNumber` statement. The structured pseudocode makes use of a priming read and forces the logic to become structured—a sequence followed by a loop that contains a sequence of three statements.

**TIP** ▫ ▫ ▫ ▫ | Years ago, programmers could avoid using structure by inserting a "go to" statement into their pseudocode. A "go to" statement would say something like "after print answer, go to the first get number box", and would be the equivalent of drawing an arrow starting after "print answer" and pointing directly to the first "get number" box in the flowchart. Because "go to" statements cause spaghetti code, they are not allowed in structured programming.

Figure 2-18 shows another way you might attempt to draw the logic for the number-doubling program. At first glance, the figure might seem to show an acceptable solution to the problem—it is structured, containing a single loop with a sequence of three steps within it, and it appears to eliminate the need for the priming input statement. When the program starts, the question `eof?` is asked. The answer is *no*, so the program gets an input number, doubles, and prints it. Then, if it is still not `eof`, the program gets another number, doubles it, and prints it. The program continues until `eof` is encountered when getting input. The last time the `get inputNumber` statement executes, it encounters `eof`, but the program does not stop—instead it calculates and prints one last time. This last output is extraneous—the `eof` value should not be doubled and printed. As a general rule, an `eof` question should always come immediately after an input statement. Therefore, the best solution to the number-doubling problem remains the one shown in Figure 2-17—the solution containing the priming input statement.

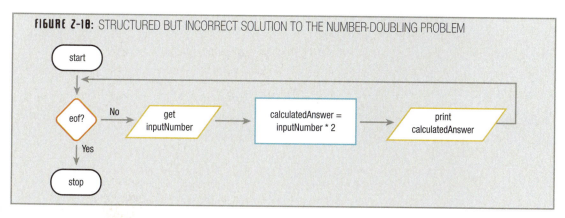

**FIGURE 2-18:** STRUCTURED BUT INCORRECT SOLUTION TO THE NUMBER-DOUBLING PROBLEM

A few languages do not require the priming read. For example, programs written using the Visual Basic programming language can "look ahead" to determine if the end of file will be reached on the next input record. However, most programming languages cannot predict the end of file until an actual read operation is performed, and they require a priming read to properly handle file data.

## UNDERSTANDING THE REASONS FOR STRUCTURE

At this point, you may very well be saying, "I liked the original doubling program just fine. I could follow it. Also, the first program had one less step in it, so it was less work. Who cares if a program is structured?"

Until you have some programming experience, it is difficult to appreciate the reasons for using only the three structures—sequence, selection, and loop. However, staying with these three structures is better for the following reasons:

- *Clarity*—The doubling program is a small program. As programs get bigger, they get more confusing if they're not structured.

- *Professionalism*—All other programmers (and programming teachers you might encounter) expect your programs to be structured. It's the way things are done professionally.

- *Efficiency*—Most newer computer languages are structured languages with syntax that lets you deal efficiently with sequence, selection, and looping. Older languages, such as assembly languages, COBOL, and RPG, were developed before the principles of structured programming were discovered. However, even programs that use those older languages can be written in a structured form, and structured programming is expected on the job today. Newer languages such as C#, C++, and Java enforce structure by their syntax.

- *Maintenance*—You, as well as other programmers, will find it easier to modify and maintain structured programs as changes are required in the future.

- *Modularity*—Structured programs can be easily broken into routines that can be assigned to any number of programmers. The routines are then pieced back together like modular furniture at each routine's single entry or exit point. Additionally, often a module can be used in multiple programs, saving development time in the new project.

Most programs that you purchase are huge, consisting of thousands or millions of statements. If you've worked with a word-processing program or spreadsheet, think of the number of menu options and keystroke combinations available to the user. Such programs are not the work of one programmer. The modular nature of structured programs means that work can be divided among many programmers; then the modules can be connected, and a large program can be developed much more quickly. Money is often a motivating factor—the more quickly you write a program and make it available for use, the sooner it begins making money for the developer.

Consider the college admissions program from the beginning of the chapter. It has been rewritten in structured form in Figure 2-19, and is easier to follow now. Figure 2-19 also shows structured pseudocode for the same problem.

Don't be alarmed if it is difficult for you to follow the many nested ifs within the pseudocode in Figure 2-19. After you study the selection process in more detail, reading this type of pseudocode will become much easier for you.

**FIGURE 2-19:** FLOWCHART AND PSEUDOCODE OF STRUCTURED COLLEGE ADMISSION PROGRAM

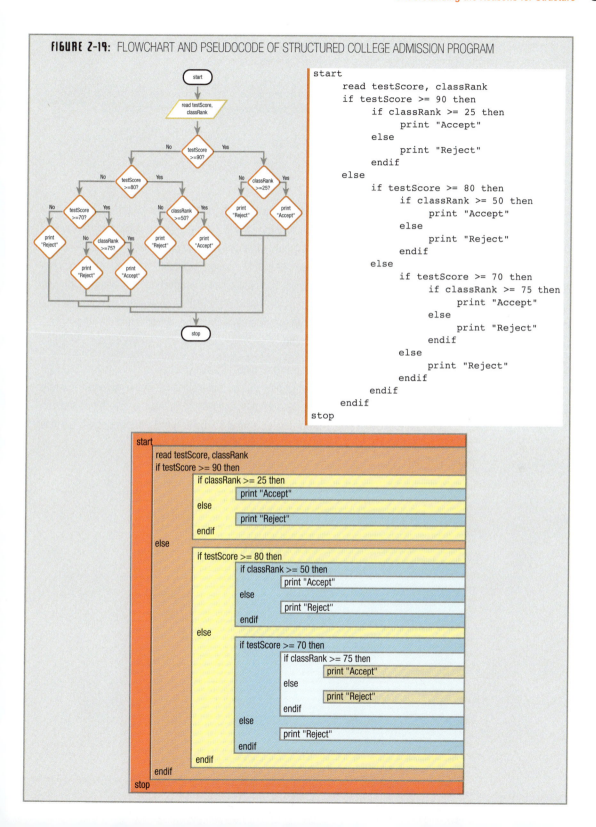

```
start
    read testScore, classRank
    if testScore >= 90 then
        if classRank >= 25 then
            print "Accept"
        else
            print "Reject"
        endif
    else
        if testScore >= 80 then
            if classRank >= 50 then
                print "Accept"
            else
                print "Reject"
            endif
        else
            if testScore >= 70 then
                if classRank >= 75 then
                    print "Accept"
                else
                    print "Reject"
                endif
            else
                print "Reject"
            endif
        endif
    endif
stop
```

In the lower portion of Figure 2-19, the pseudocode is repeated using colored backgrounds to help you identify the indentations that match, distinguishing the different levels of the nested structures.

**TIP** □ □ □ □ | As you examine Figure 2-19, notice that the bottoms of the three `testScore` decision structures join at the bottom of the diagram. These three joinings correspond to the last three `endif` statements in the pseudocode.

## RECOGNIZING STRUCTURE

Any set of instructions can be expressed in a structured format. If you can teach someone how to perform any ordinary activity, then you can express it in a structured way. For example, suppose you wanted to teach a child how to play Rock, Paper, Scissors. In this game, two players simultaneously show each other one hand, in one of three positions—clenched in a fist, representing a rock; flat, representing a piece of paper; or with two fingers extended in a V, representing scissors. The goal is to guess which hand your opponent might show, so that you can show the hand that beats it. The rules are that a flat hand beats a fist (because a piece of paper can cover a rock), a fist beats a hand with two extended fingers (because a rock can smash a pair of scissors), and a hand with two extended fingers beats a flat hand (because scissors can cut paper). Figure 2-20 shows the pseudocode for the game.

Figure 2-20 shows a fairly complicated set of statements. Its purpose is not to teach you how to play a game (although you could learn how to play by following the logic), but rather to convince you that any task to which you can apply rules can be expressed logically using only combinations of sequence, selection, and looping. In this example, a game continues while a friend agrees to play, and within that loop, several decisions must be made in order to determine the winner.

**FIGURE 2-20**: PSEUDOCODE FOR THE ROCK, PAPER, SCISSORS GAME

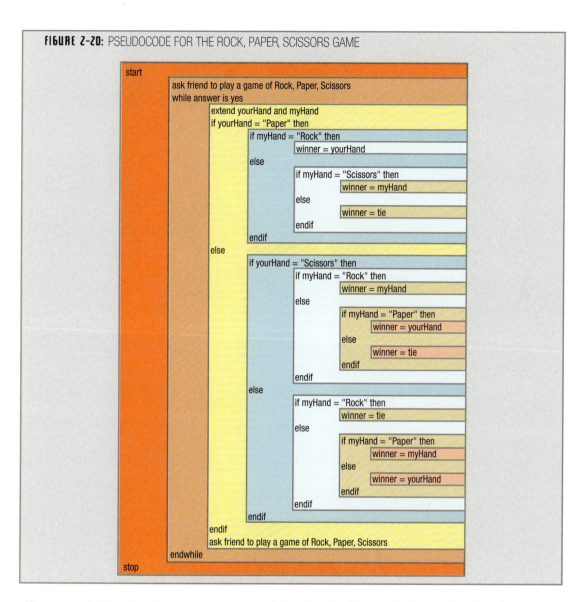

```
start
    ask friend to play a game of Rock, Paper, Scissors
    while answer is yes
        extend yourHand and myHand
        if yourHand = "Paper" then
            if myHand = "Rock" then
                winner = yourHand
            else
                if myHand = "Scissors" then
                    winner = myHand
                else
                    winner = tie
                endif
            endif
        else
            if yourHand = "Scissors" then
                if myHand = "Rock" then
                    winner = myHand
                else
                    if myHand = "Paper" then
                        winner = yourHand
                    else
                        winner = tie
                    endif
                endif
            else
                if myHand = "Rock" then
                    winner = tie
                else
                    if myHand = "Paper" then
                        winner = myHand
                    else
                        winner = yourHand
                    endif
                endif
            endif
        endif
        ask friend to play a game of Rock, Paper, Scissors
    endwhile
stop
```

When you are just learning about structured program design, it is difficult to detect whether a flowchart of a program's logic is structured. For example, is the flowchart segment in Figure 2-21 structured?

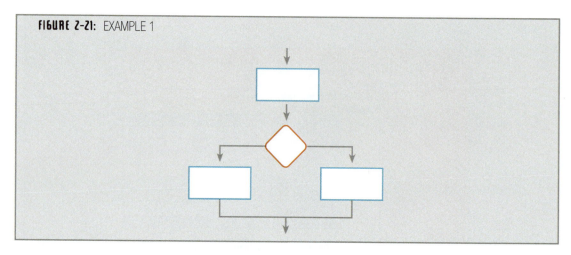

**FIGURE 2-21:** EXAMPLE 1

Yes, it is. It has a sequence and a selection structure.

Is the flowchart segment in Figure 2-22 structured?

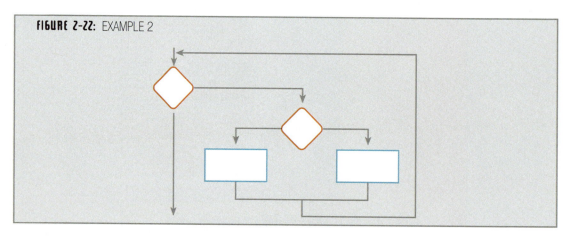

**FIGURE 2-22:** EXAMPLE 2

Yes, it is. It has a loop, and within the loop is a selection.

Is the flowchart segment in Figure 2-23 structured? (The symbols are lettered so you can better follow the discussion.)

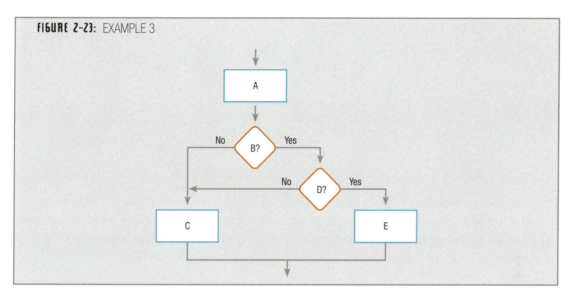

**FIGURE 2-23:** EXAMPLE 3

No, it isn't; it is not constructed from the three basic structures. One way to straighten out a flowchart segment that isn't structured is to use what you can call the "spaghetti bowl" method; that is, picture the flowchart as a bowl of spaghetti that you must untangle. Imagine you can grab one piece of pasta at the top of the bowl, and start pulling. As you "pull" each symbol out of the tangled mess, you can untangle the separate paths until the entire segment is structured. For example, with the diagram in Figure 2-23, if you start pulling at the top, you encounter a procedure box, labeled A. (See Figure 2-24.)

**FIGURE 2-24:** UNTANGLING EXAMPLE 3, FIRST STEP

A single process like A is part of an acceptable structure—it constitutes at least the beginning of a sequence structure. Imagine you continue pulling symbols from the tangled segment. The next item in the flowchart is a question that tests a condition labeled B, as you can see in Figure 2-25.

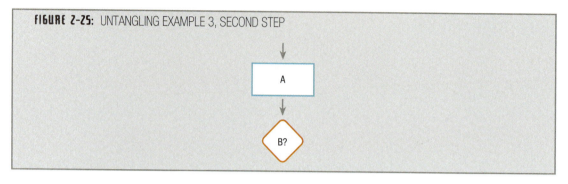

**FIGURE 2-25:** UNTANGLING EXAMPLE 3, SECOND STEP

At this point, you know the sequence that started with A has ended. Sequences never have decisions in them, so the sequence is finished; either a selection or a loop is beginning. A loop must return to the question at some later point. You can see from the original logic in Figure 2-23 that whether the answer to B is yes or no, the logic never returns to B. Therefore, B begins a selection structure, not a loop structure.

To continue detangling the logic, you pull up on the flowline that emerges from the left side (the "No" side) of Question B. You encounter C, as shown in Figure 2-26. When you continue beyond C, you reach the end of the flowchart.

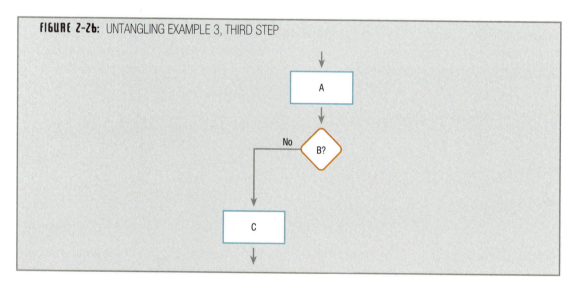

**FIGURE 2-26:** UNTANGLING EXAMPLE 3, THIRD STEP

Now you can turn your attention to the "Yes" side (the right side) of the condition tested in B. When you pull up on the right side, you encounter Question D. (See Figure 2-27.)

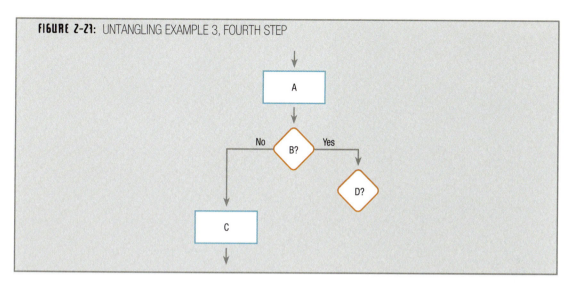

FIGURE 2-27: UNTANGLING EXAMPLE 3, FOURTH STEP

Follow the line on the left side of Question D. If the line is attached somewhere else, as it is (to Step C) in Figure 2-23, just untangle it by repeating the step that is tangled. (In this example, you repeat Step C to untangle it from the other usage of C.) Continue pulling on the flowline that emerges from Step C, and you reach the end of the program segment, as shown in Figure 2-28.

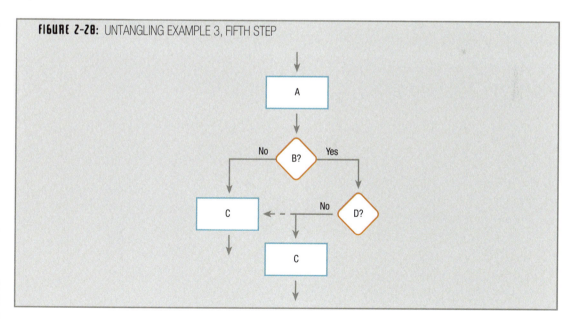

FIGURE 2-28: UNTANGLING EXAMPLE 3, FIFTH STEP

Now pull on the right side of Question D. Process E pops up, as shown in Figure 2-29; then you reach the end.

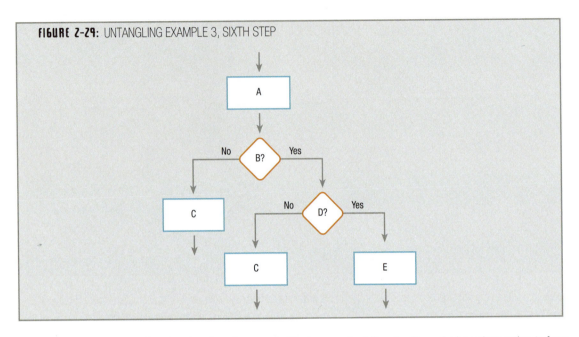

**FIGURE 2-29:** UNTANGLING EXAMPLE 3, SIXTH STEP

At this point, the untangled flowchart has three loose ends. The loose ends of Question D can be brought together to form a selection structure, then the loose ends of Question B can be brought together to form another selection structure. The result is the flowchart shown in Figure 2-30. The entire flowchart segment is structured—it has a sequence (A) followed by a selection inside a selection.

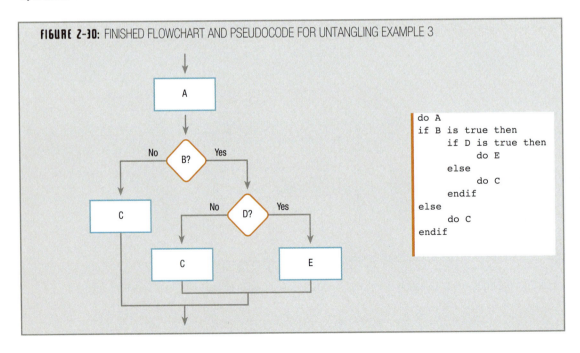

**FIGURE 2-30:** FINISHED FLOWCHART AND PSEUDOCODE FOR UNTANGLING EXAMPLE 3

```
do A
if B is true then
        if D is true then
                do E
        else
                do C
        endif
else
        do C
endif
```

TIP □ □ □ □ If you want to try structuring a very difficult example of an unstructured program, see Appendix A.

## TWO SPECIAL STRUCTURES—CASE AND DO UNTIL

TIP □ □ □ □ You can skip this section for now without any loss in continuity. Your instructor may prefer to discuss the case structure with the Decision chapter, and the do until loop with the Looping chapter.

You can solve any logic problem you might encounter using only the three structures: sequence, selection, and loop. However, many programming languages allow two more structures: the case structure and the do until loop. These structures are never *needed* to solve any problem—you can always use a series of selections instead of the case structure, and you can always use a sequence plus a do while loop in place of the do until loop. However, sometimes these two additional structures—the case and the do until—are convenient. Programmers consider them both to be acceptable, legal structures.

### THE CASE STRUCTURE

You can use the **case structure** when there are several distinct possible values for a single variable you are testing, and each value requires a different course of action. Suppose you administer a school at which tuition is $75, $50, $30, or $10 per credit hour, depending on whether a student is a freshman, sophomore, junior, or senior. The structured flowchart in Figure 2-31 shows a series of decisions that assigns the correct tuition to a student.

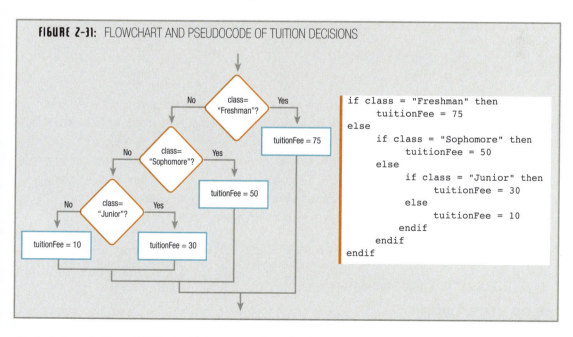

**FIGURE 2-31:** FLOWCHART AND PSEUDOCODE OF TUITION DECISIONS

```
if class = "Freshman" then
      tuitionFee = 75
else
      if class = "Sophomore" then
            tuitionFee = 50
      else
            if class = "Junior" then
                  tuitionFee = 30
            else
                  tuitionFee = 10
            endif
      endif
endif
```

The logic shown in Figure 2-31 is absolutely correct and completely structured. The `class="Junior"` selection structure is contained within the `class="Sophomore"` structure, which is contained within the `class="Freshman"` structure. Note that there is no need to ask if a student is a senior, because if a student is not a freshman, sophomore, or junior, it is assumed the student is a senior.

Even though the program segments in Figure 2-31 are correct and structured, many programming languages permit using a case structure, as shown in Figure 2-32. When using the case structure, you test a variable against a series of values, taking appropriate action based on the variable's value. To many, such programs seem easier to read, and the case structure is allowed because the same results *could* be achieved with a series of structured selections (thus making the program structured). That is, if the first program is structured and the second one reflects the first one point by point, then the second one must be structured also.

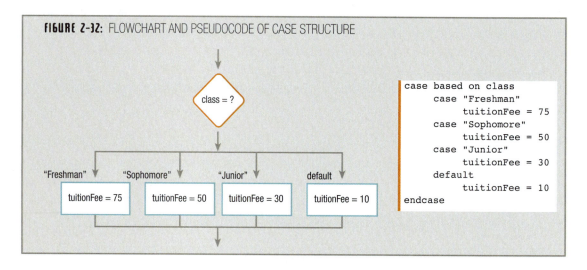

**FIGURE 2-32:** FLOWCHART AND PSEUDOCODE OF CASE STRUCTURE

```
case based on class
    case "Freshman"
        tuitionFee = 75
    case "Sophomore"
        tuitionFee = 50
    case "Junior"
        tuitionFee = 30
    default
        tuitionFee = 10
endcase
```

**TIP** □ □ □ □  The term "default" used in Figure 2-32 means "if none of the other cases were true." Each programming language you learn may use a different syntax for the default case.

Even though a programming language permits you to use the case structure, you should understand that the case structure is just a convenience that might make a flowchart, pseudocode, or actual program code easier to understand at first glance. When you write a series of decisions using the case structure, the computer still makes a series of individual decisions, just as though you had used many if-then-else combinations. In other words, you might prefer looking at the diagram in Figure 2-32 to understand the tuition fees charged by a school, but a computer actually makes the decisions as shown in Figure 2-31—one at a time. When you write your own programs, it is always acceptable to express a complicated decision-making process as a series of individual selections.

**TIP** □ □ □ □  You usually use the case structure only when a series of decisions is based on different values stored in a single variable. If multiple variables are tested, then most programmers use a series of decisions.

## THE DO UNTIL LOOP

Recall that a structured loop (often called a do while) looks like Figure 2-33. A special case loop called a do until loop looks like Figure 2-34.

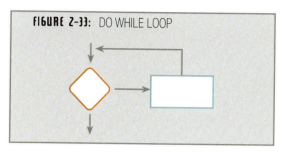

**FIGURE 2-33:** DO WHILE LOOP

**FIGURE 2-34:** DO UNTIL LOOP

An important difference exists between these two structures. In a do while loop, you ask a question and, depending on the answer, you might or might not enter the loop to execute the loop's procedure. Conversely, in a **do until loop**, you ensure that the procedure executes at least once; then, depending on the answer to the controlling question, the loop may or may not execute additional times.

**TIP** ☐ ☐ ☐ ☐ | In a do while loop, the question that controls a loop comes at the beginning, or "top," of the loop body. In a do until loop, the question that controls the loop comes at the end, or "bottom," of the loop body.

You encounter examples of do until looping every day. For example:

```
do
        pay bills
until all bills are paid
```

and

```
do
        wash dishes
until all dishes are washed
```

In these examples, the activity (paying bills or washing dishes) must occur at least one time. You ask the question that determines whether you continue only after the activity has been executed at least one time.

You can duplicate the same series of events generated by any do until loop by creating a sequence followed by a do while loop. For example:

```
pay bills
while there are more bills to pay
        pay bills
endwhile
```

Consider the flowcharts and pseudocode in Figures 2-35 and 2-36.

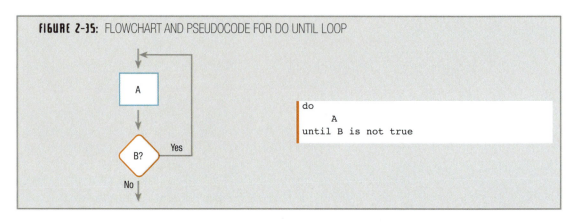

**FIGURE 2-35:** FLOWCHART AND PSEUDOCODE FOR DO UNTIL LOOP

```
do
    A
until B is not true
```

**FIGURE 2-36:** FLOWCHART AND PSEUDOCODE FOR SEQUENCE FOLLOWED BY DO WHILE LOOP

```
do A
while B is true
    do A
endwhile
```

In Figure 2-35, A is done, and then B is asked. If B is yes, then A is done and B is asked again. In Figure 2-36, A is done, and then B is asked. If B is yes, then A is done and B is asked again. In other words, both flowcharts and pseudocode segments do exactly the same thing.

Because programmers understand that a do until can be expressed with a sequence followed by a do while, most languages allow the do until. Again, you are never required to use a do until; you can always accomplish the same events with a sequence followed by a do while.

Figure 2-37 shows an unstructured loop. It is neither a do while loop (that begins with a decision and, after an action, returns to the decision), nor a do until loop (that begins with an action and ends with a decision that might repeat the action). Instead, it begins like a do until, with a process followed by a decision, but one branch of the decision does not repeat the initial process; instead, it performs an additional new action before repeating the initial process. If you need to use the logic shown in Figure 2-37—performing a task, asking a question, and perhaps performing an additional task before looping back to the first process—then the way to make the logic structured is to repeat the initial process within the loop, at the end of the loop. Figure 2-38 shows the same logic as Figure 2-37, but now it is structured logic, with a sequence of two actions occurring within the loop. Does this diagram look familiar to you? It uses the same technique of repeating a needed step that you saw earlier in this chapter, when you learned the rationale for the priming read.

**FIGURE 2-37**: UNSTRUCTURED LOOP

**FIGURE 2-38**: SEQUENCE AND STRUCTURED LOOP THAT ACCOMPLISH THE SAME TASKS AS FIGURE 2-37

**TIP** ▫ ▫ ▫ ▫ | It is difficult for beginning programmers to distinguish between do while and do until loops. You can think of a do while loop as one that continues to execute while a condition remains true—for example, `while not end of file is true, process records`, or `while hungry is true, eat food`. On the other hand, a do until loop continues until some condition becomes false—for example, `address envelopes until there are no more envelopes`. When you use a do until loop, at least one performance of the action always occurs.

## CHAPTER SUMMARY

- ☐ The popular name for snarled program statements is spaghetti code.

- ☐ Clearer programs can be constructed using only three basic structures: sequence, selection, and loop. These three structures can be combined in an infinite number of ways by stacking and nesting them. Each structure has one entry and one exit point; one structure can attach to another only at one of these entry or exit points.

- ☐ A priming read or priming input is the first read or data input statement prior to beginning a structured loop. The last step within the loop gets the next, and all subsequent, input values.

- ☐ You use structured techniques to promote clarity, professionalism, efficiency, and modularity.

- ☐ One way to straighten a flowchart segment that isn't structured is to imagine the flowchart as a bowl of spaghetti that you must untangle.

- ☐ You can use a case structure when there are several distinct possible values for a variable you are testing. When you write a series of decisions using the case structure, the computer still makes a series of individual decisions.

- ☐ In a do while loop, you ask a question and, depending on the answer, you might never enter the loop to execute the loop's procedure. In a do until loop, you ensure that the procedure executes at least once. You can duplicate the same series of events generated by any do until loop by creating a sequence followed by a do while loop.

## KEY TERMS

**Spaghetti code** is snarled, unstructured program logic.

A **structure** is a basic unit of programming logic; each structure is a sequence, selection, or loop.

With a **sequence structure**, you perform an action or event, and then you perform the next action, in order. A sequence can contain any number of events, but there is no chance to branch off and skip any of the events.

With a **selection**, or **decision**, **structure**, you ask a question, and, depending on the answer, you take one of two courses of action. Then, no matter which path you follow, you continue with the next event.

An **if-then-else** is another name for a selection structure.

**Dual-alternative ifs** define one action to be taken when the tested condition is true, and another action to be taken when it is false.

**Single-alternative ifs** take action on just one branch of the decision.

The **null case** is the branch of a decision in which no action is taken.

With a **loop structure**, you ask a question; if the answer requires an action, you perform the action and ask the original question again.

**Repetition** and **iteration** are alternate names for a loop structure.

A do while is a loop in which a process continues while some condition continues to be true.

Attaching structures end-to-end is called stacking structures.

Placing a structure within another structure is called nesting the structures.

A block is a group of statements that execute as a single unit.

A priming read or priming input is the first read or data input statement in a program.

You can use the case structure when there are several distinct possible values for a single variable you are testing, and each requires a different course of action.

In a do until loop, you ensure that a procedure executes at least once; then, depending on the answer to the controlling question, the loop may or may not execute additional times.

## REVIEW QUESTIONS

1. **Snarled program logic is called _____ code.**

   a. snake
   b. spaghetti
   c. string
   d. gnarly

2. **A sequence structure can contain _____.**

   a. only one event
   b. exactly three events
   c. no more than three events
   d. any number of events

3. **Which of the following is *not* another term for a selection structure?**

   a. decision structure
   b. if-then-else structure
   c. loop structure
   d. dual-alternative if structure

4. **The structure in which you ask a question, and, depending on the answer, take some action, then ask the question again can be called all of the following except _____.**

   a. if-then-else
   b. loop
   c. repetition
   d. iteration

5. **Placing a structure within another structure is called _____ the structures.**

   a. stacking
   b. nesting
   c. building
   d. untangling

6. **Attaching structures end-to-end is called _____.**
   a. stacking
   b. nesting
   c. building
   d. untangling

7. **The statement** `if age >= 65 then seniorDiscount = "yes"` **is an example of a**
   _____.
   a. single-alternative if
   b. loop
   c. dual-alternative if
   d. sequence

8. **The statement** `while temperature remains below 60, leave the furnace on` **is an example of a _____.**
   a. single-alternative if
   b. loop
   c. dual-alternative if
   d. sequence

9. **The statement** `if age < 13 then movieTicket = 4.00 else movieTicket = 8.50` **is an example of a _____.**
   a. single-alternative if
   b. loop
   c. dual-alternative if
   d. sequence

10. **Which of the following attributes do all three basic structures share?**
    a. Their flowcharts all contain exactly three processing symbols.
    b. They all contain a decision.
    c. They all begin with a process.
    d. They all have one entry and one exit point.

11. **The first input statement in a program _____.**
    a. is called a priming input
    b. cannot result in `eof`
    c. is the only part of a program allowed to be unstructured
    d. executes hundreds or even thousands of times in most business programs

12. **A group of statements that execute as a unit is a _____.**
    a. cohort
    b. family
    c. sequence
    d. block

13. **Which of the following is acceptable in a structured program?**
    a. placing a sequence within the true half of a dual-alternative decision
    b. placing a decision within a loop

c. placing a loop within one of the steps in a sequence

d. All of these are acceptable.

14. **Which of the following is *not* a reason for enforcing structure rules in computer programs?**

a. Structured programs are clearer to understand than unstructured ones.

b. Other professional programmers will expect programs to be structured.

c. Structured programs can be broken into modules easily.

d. Structured programs usually are shorter than unstructured ones.

15. **Which of the following is *not* a benefit of modularizing programs?**

a. Modular programs are easier to read and understand than nonmodular ones.

b. Modular components are reusable in other programs.

c. If you use modules, you can ignore the rules of structure.

d. Multiple programmers can work on different modules at the same time.

16. **Which of the following is true of structured logic?**

a. Any task can be described using the three structures.

b. You can use structured logic with newer programming languages, such as Java and C#, but not with older ones.

c. Structured programs require that you break the code into easy-to-handle modules.

d. All of these are true.

17. **The structure that you can use when you must make a decision with several possible outcomes, depending on the value of a single variable, is the _____.**

a. multiple-alternative if structure

b. case structure

c. do while structure

d. do until structure

18. **Which type of loop ensures that an action will take place at least one time?**

a. a do until loop

b. a do while loop

c. a do over loop

d. any structured loop

19. **A do until loop can always be converted to _____.**

a. a do while followed by a sequence

b. a sequence followed by a do while

c. a case structure

d. a selection followed by a do while

20. **Which of the following is never required by any program?**

a. a do while

b. a do until

c. a selection

d. a sequence

## EXERCISES

1. **Match the term with the structure diagram. (Because the structures go by more than one name, there are more terms than diagrams.)**

   1. sequence      5. decision
   2. selection     6. if-then-else
   3. loop          7. iteration
   4. do while

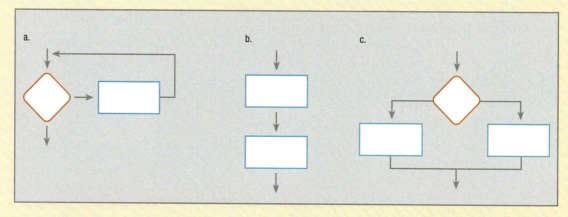

2. **Match the term with the pseudocode segment. (Because the structures go by more than one name, there are more terms than pseudocode segments.)**

   1. sequence      4. decision
   2. selection     5. if-then-else
   3. loop          6. iteration

   ```
   a. while not eof
          print theAnswer
      endwhile
   b. if inventoryQuantity  >  0 then
          do fillOrderProcess
      else
          do backOrderNotification
      endif
   c. do localTaxCalculation
      do stateTaxCalculation
      do federalTaxCalculation
   ```

3.  **Is each of the following segments structured, or unstructured? If unstructured, redraw it so that it does the same thing but is structured.**

c.

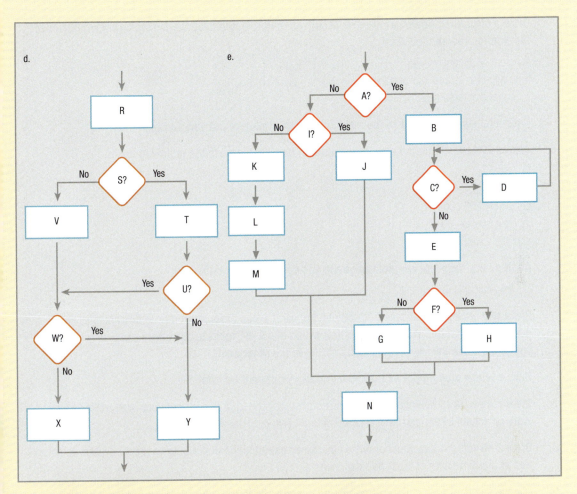

4.    Write pseudocode for each example (a through e) in Exercise 3.

5.    Assume you have created a mechanical arm that can hold a pen. The arm can perform the follow-ing tasks:

☐ Lower the pen to a piece of paper.
☐ Raise the pen from the paper.
☐ Move the pen one inch along a straight line. (If the pen is lowered, this action draws a one-inch line from left to right; if the pen is raised, this action just repositions the pen one inch to the right.)
☐ Turn 90 degrees to the right.
☐ Draw a circle that is one inch in diameter.

Draw a structured flowchart or write pseudocode that would describe the logic that would cause the arm to draw the following:

a.  a one-inch square
b.  a two-inch by one-inch rectangle
c.  a string of three beads

Have a fellow student act as the mechanical arm and carry out your instructions.

6.  Assume you have created a mechanical robot that can perform the following tasks:

☐ Stand up.
☐ Sit down.
☐ Turn left 90 degrees.
☐ Turn right 90 degrees.
☐ Take a step.

Additionally, the robot can determine the answer to one test condition:

☐ Am I touching something?

Place two chairs 20 feet apart, directly facing each other. Draw a structured flowchart or write pseudocode that describes the logic that would allow the robot to start from a sitting position in one chair, cross the room, and end up sitting in the other chair.

Have a fellow student act as the robot and carry out your instructions.

7.  Draw a structured flowchart or write structured pseudocode describing your preparation to go to work or school in the morning. Include at least two decisions and two loops.

8.  Draw a structured flowchart or write structured pseudocode describing your preparation to go to bed at night. Include at least two decisions and two loops.

9.  Choose a very simple children's game and describe its logic, using a structured flowchart or pseudocode. For example, you might try to explain Musical Chairs; Duck, Duck, Goose; the card game War; or the elimination game Eenie, Meenie, Minie, Moe.

10. Draw a structured flowchart or write structured pseudocode describing how your paycheck is calculated. Include at least two decisions.

11. Draw a structured flowchart or write structured pseudocode describing the steps a retail store employee should follow to process a customer purchase. Include at least two decisions.

# 3

# MODULES, HIERARCHY CHARTS, AND DOCUMENTATION

## After studying Chapter 3, you should be able to:

- ☐ Describe the advantages of modularization
- ☐ Modularize a program
- ☐ Understand how a module can call another module
- ☐ Explain how to declare variables
- ☐ Create hierarchy charts
- ☐ Understand documentation
- ☐ Create print charts
- ☐ Interpret file descriptions
- ☐ Understand the attributes of complete documentation

## MODULES, SUBROUTINES, PROCEDURES, FUNCTIONS, OR METHODS

Programmers seldom write programs as one long series of steps. Instead, they break the programming problem down into reasonable units, and tackle one small task at a time. These reasonable units are called **modules**. Programmers also refer to them as **subroutines**, **procedures**, **functions**, or **methods**.

TIP ▫ ▫ ▫ ▫ | The name that programmers use for their modules usually reflects the programming language they use. COBOL, RPG, and BASIC programmers are most likely to use "subroutine." Pascal and Visual Basic programmers use "procedure" (or "subprocedure"). C and C++ programmers call their modules "functions," whereas C#, Java, and other object-oriented language programmers are more likely to use "method."

The process of breaking a large program into modules is called **modularization**. You are never required to break a large program into modules, but there are at least four reasons for doing so:

- Modularization provides abstraction.
- Modularization allows multiple programmers to work on a problem.
- Modularization allows you to reuse your work.
- Modularization makes it easier to identify structures.

### MODULARIZATION PROVIDES ABSTRACTION

One reason modularized programs are easier to understand is that they enable a programmer to see the big picture. **Abstraction** is the process of paying attention to important properties while ignoring nonessential details. Abstraction is selective ignorance. Life would be tedious without abstraction. For example, you can create a list of things to accomplish today:

```
Do laundry
Call Aunt Nan
Start term paper
```

Without abstraction, the list of chores would begin:

```
Pick up laundry basket
Put laundry basket in car
Drive to laundromat
Get out of car with basket
Walk into laundromat
Set basket down
Find quarters for washing machine
. . .and so on.
```

You might list a dozen more steps before you finish the laundry and move on to the second chore on your original list. If you had to consider every small, **low-level** detail of every task in your day, you would probably never make it out of bed in the morning. Using a higher-level, more abstract list makes your day manageable. Abstraction makes complex tasks look simple.

**TIP** ☐ ☐ ☐ ☐ | Abstract artists create paintings in which they see only the "big picture"—color and form—and ignore the details. Abstraction has a similar meaning among programmers.

Likewise, some level of abstraction occurs in every computer program. Fifty years ago, a programmer had to understand the low-level circuitry instructions the computer used. But now, newer **high-level** programming languages allow you to use English-like vocabulary in which one broad statement corresponds to dozens of machine instructions. No matter which high-level programming language you use, if you display a message on the monitor, you are never required to understand how a monitor works to create each pixel on the screen. You write an instruction like `print message` and the details of the hardware operations are handled for you.

Modules or subroutines provide another way to achieve abstraction. For example, a payroll program can call a module named `computeFederalWithholdingTax`. You can write the mathematical details of the function later, someone else can write them, or you can purchase them from an outside source. When you plan your main payroll program, your only concern is that a federal withholding tax will have to be calculated; you save the details for later.

## MODULARIZATION ALLOWS MULTIPLE PROGRAMMERS TO WORK ON A PROBLEM

When you dissect any large task into modules, you gain the ability to divide the task among various people. Rarely does a single programmer write a commercial program that you buy off the shelf. Consider any word-processing, spreadsheet, or database program you have used. Each program has so many options, and responds to user selections in so many possible ways, that it would take years for a single programmer to write all the instructions. Professional software developers can write new programs in weeks or months, instead of years, by dividing large programs into modules and assigning each module to an individual programmer or programming team.

## MODULARIZATION ALLOWS YOU TO REUSE YOUR WORK

If a subroutine or function is useful and well-written, you may want to use it more than once within a program or in other programs. For example, a routine that checks the current month to make sure it is valid (not lower than 1 or higher than 12) is useful in many programs written for a business. A program that uses a personnel file containing each employee's birth date, hire date, last promotion date, and termination date can use the month-validation module four times with each employee record. Other programs in an organization can also use the module; these include programs that ship customer orders, plan employees' birthday parties, and calculate when loan payments should be made. If you write the month-checking instructions so they are entangled with other statements in a program, they are difficult to extract and reuse. On the other hand, if you place the instructions in their own module, the unit is easy-to-use and portable to other applications.

You can find many real-world examples of **reusability**. When you build a house, you don't invent plumbing and heating systems; you incorporate systems with proven designs. This certainly reduces the time and effort it takes to build a house. Assuming the plumbing and electrical systems you choose are also in service in other houses, they also improve the **reliability** of your house's systems—they have been tested under a variety of circumstances and have been proven to function correctly. Similarly, software that is reusable is more reliable, yet saves time and money. If you create the functional components of your programs as stand-alone modules and test them in your current programs, much of the work will already be done when you use the modules in future applications.

## MODULARIZATION MAKES IT EASIER TO IDENTIFY STRUCTURES

When you combine several programming tasks into modules, it may be easier for you to identify structures. For example, you learned in Chapter 2 that the selection structure looks like Figure 3-1.

When you work with a program segment that looks like Figure 3-2, you may question whether it is structured. If you can modularize some of the statements and give them a more abstract group name, as in Figure 3-3, it is easier to see that the program involves a major selection and that the program segment is structured.

**FIGURE 3-1:** SELECTION STRUCTURE

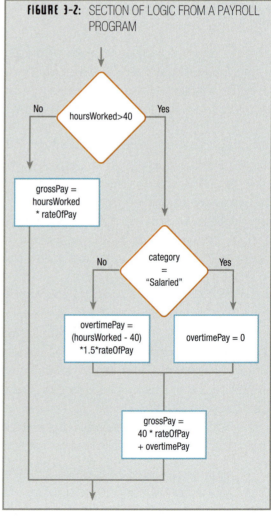

**FIGURE 3-2:** SECTION OF LOGIC FROM A PAYROLL PROGRAM

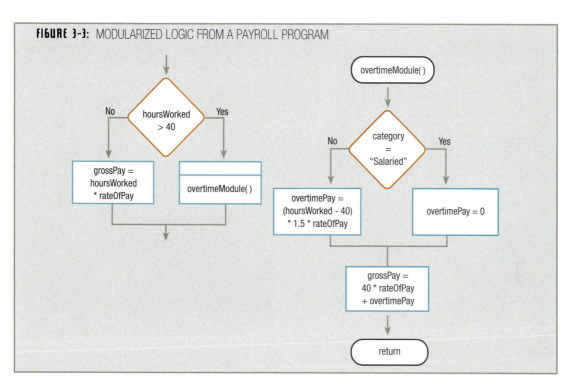

**FIGURE 3-3:** MODULARIZED LOGIC FROM A PAYROLL PROGRAM

The single program segment shown in Figure 3-2 accomplishes the same steps as the two program segments shown together in Figure 3-3; both program segments are structured. The structure may be more obvious in the program segments in Figure 3-3 because you can see two distinct parts—a decision structure calls a subroutine named `overtimeModule()`, and that module contains another decision structure, which is followed by a sequence. Neither of the program segments shown in Figures 3-2 and 3-3 is superior to the other in terms of functionality, but you may prefer to modularize to help you identify structures.

**TIP** ▫ ▫ ▫ ▫  A professional programmer will never modularize simply to *identify* whether a program is structured—he or she modularizes for reasons of abstraction, ease of dividing the work, and reusability. However, for a beginning programmer, being able to see and identify structure is important.

## MODULARIZING A PROGRAM

When you create a module or subroutine, you give it a name. The rules for naming modules are different in every programming language, but they often are similar to the language's rules for variable names. In this text, module names follow the same two rules used for variable names:

- Module names must be one word.
- Module names should have some meaning.

Additionally, in this text, module names are followed by a set of parentheses. This will help you distinguish module names from variable names. This style corresponds to the way modules are named in many programming languages, such as Java, C++, C#, and Pascal.

Table 3-1 lists some possible module names for a module that calculates an employee's gross pay, and provides a rationale for the appropriateness of each one.

**TABLE 3-1:** VALID AND INVALID MODULE NAMES FOR A MODULE THAT CALCULATES AN EMPLOYEE'S GROSS PAY

| Suggested module names for a module that calculates an employee's gross pay | Comments |
| --- | --- |
| calculateGrossPay() | Good |
| calculateGross() | Good—most people would interpret "Gross" to be short for "Gross pay" |
| calGrPy() | Legal, but cryptic |
| calculateGrossPayForOneEmployee() | Legal, but awkward |
| calculate gross() | Not legal—embedded space |
| calculategrosspay() | Legal, but hard to read without camel casing |

**TIP** □ □ □ □ As you learn more about modules in specific programming languages, you will find that you sometimes place variable names within the parentheses of module names. Any variables enclosed in the parentheses contain information you want to send to the module. For now, the parentheses we use at the end of module names will be empty.

**TIP** □ □ □ □ Most programming languages require that module names begin with an alphabetic character. This text follows that convention.

**TIP** □ □ □ □ Although it is not a requirement of any programming language, it frequently makes sense to use a verb as all or part of a module's name, because modules perform some action. Typical module names begin with words such as get, compute, and print. When you program in visual languages that use screen components such as buttons and text boxes, the module names frequently contain verbs representing user actions, such as click and drag.

When a program uses a module, you can refer to the main program as the **calling program**, because it "calls" the module's name when it wants to use the module. The flowchart symbol used to call a subroutine is a rectangle with a bar across the top. You place the name of the module you are calling inside the rectangle.

**TIP** □ □ □ □ Instead of placing only the name of the module they are calling in the flowchart, many programmers insert an appropriate verb, such as "perform" or "do," before the module name.

**TIP** □ □ □ □ A module can call another module, and the called module can call another. The number of chained calls is limited only by the amount of memory available on your computer.

You draw each module separately with its own sentinel symbols. The symbol that is the equivalent of the `start` symbol in a program contains the name of the module. This name must be identical to the name used in the calling program. The symbol that is the equivalent of the `stop` symbol in a program does not contain "stop"; after all, the program is not ending. Instead, the module ends with a "gentler," less final term, such as `exit` or `return`. These words correctly indicate that when the module ends, the logical progression of statements will return to the calling program.

A flowchart and pseudocode for a program that calculates the arithmetic average of two numbers a user enters can look like Figure 3-4. Here the **main program**, or program that runs from start to stop and calls other modules, calls three modules named `getInput()`, `calculateAverage()`, and `printResult()`.

The logic of the program in Figure 3-4 proceeds as follows:

1. The main program starts.
2. The main program calls the `getInput()` module.
3. Within the `getInput()` module, the prompt "Enter a number" appears. A **prompt** is a message that is displayed on a monitor, asking the user for a response.
4. Within the `getInput()` module, the program accepts a value into the `firstNumber` variable.
5. Within the `getInput()` module, the prompt "Enter another number" appears.
6. Within the `getInput()` module, the program accepts a value into the `secondNumber` variable.
7. The `getInput()` module ends, and control returns to the main calling program.
8. The main program calls the `calculateAverage()` module.
9. Within the `calculateAverage()` module, a value for the variable `average` is calculated.
10. The `calculateAverage()` module ends, and control returns to the main calling program.
11. The main program calls the `printResult()` module.
12. Within the `printResult()` module, the value of `average` is displayed.
13. Within the `printResult()` module, a thank-you message is displayed.
14. The `printResult()` module ends, and control returns to the main calling program.
15. The main program ends.

Whenever a main program calls a module, the logic transfers to the module. When the module ends, the logical flow transfers back to the main calling program and resumes where it left off.

**TIP** □ □ □ □ | The computer keeps track of the correct memory address to which it should return after executing a module by recording the memory address in a location known as the *stack*.

**FIGURE 3-4:** FLOWCHART AND PSEUDOCODE FOR AVERAGING PROGRAM WITH MODULES

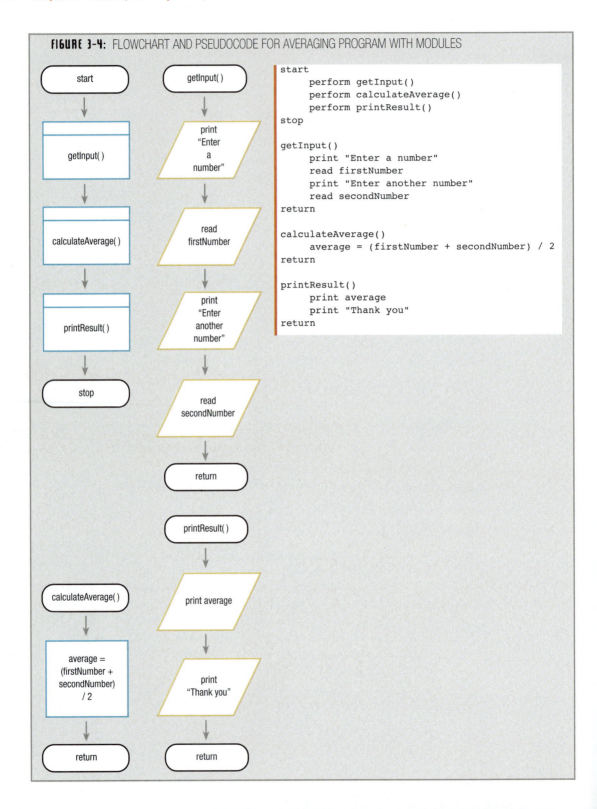

```
start
     perform getInput()
     perform calculateAverage()
     perform printResult()
stop

getInput()
     print "Enter a number"
     read firstNumber
     print "Enter another number"
     read secondNumber
return

calculateAverage()
     average = (firstNumber + secondNumber) / 2
return

printResult()
     print average
     print "Thank you"
return
```

## MODULES CALLING OTHER MODULES

Just as a program can call a module or subroutine, any module can call another module. For example, the program illustrated in Figure 3-4 can be broken down further, as shown in Figure 3-5.

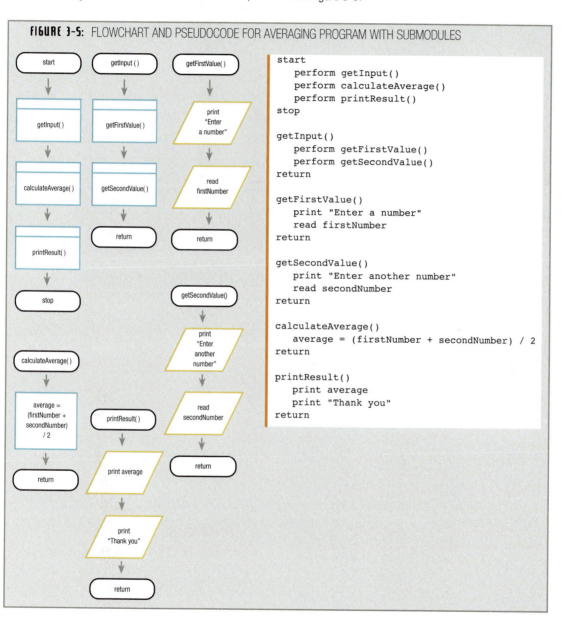

**FIGURE 3-5:** FLOWCHART AND PSEUDOCODE FOR AVERAGING PROGRAM WITH SUBMODULES

```
start
    perform getInput()
    perform calculateAverage()
    perform printResult()
stop

getInput()
    perform getFirstValue()
    perform getSecondValue()
return

getFirstValue()
    print "Enter a number"
    read firstNumber
return

getSecondValue()
    print "Enter another number"
    read secondNumber
return

calculateAverage()
    average = (firstNumber + secondNumber) / 2
return

printResult()
    print average
    print "Thank you"
return
```

After the program in Figure 3-5 begins:

1. The main program calls the `getInput()` module, and the logical flow transfers to that module.
2. From there, the `getInput()` module calls the `getFirstValue()` module, and the logical flow immediately transfers to the `getFirstValue()` module.
3. The `getFirstValue()` module displays a prompt and reads a number. When `getFirstValue()` ends, control passes back to `getInput()`, where `getSecondValue()` is called.
4. Control passes to `getSecondValue()`, which displays a prompt and retrieves a second value from the user. When this module ends, control passes back to the `getInput() module`.
5. When the `getInput()` module ends, control returns to the main program.
6. Then, `calculateAverage()` and `printResult()` execute as before.

Determining when to break down any particular module further into its own subroutines or submodules is an art. Programmers do follow some guidelines when deciding how far to break down subroutines, or how much to put in them. Some companies may have arbitrary rules, such as "a subroutine should never take more than a page," or "a module should never have more than 30 statements in it," or "never have a method or function with only one statement in it."

Rather than use such arbitrary rules, a better policy is to place together statements that contribute to one specific task. The more the statements contribute to the same job, the greater the **functional cohesion** of the module. A routine that checks the validity of a `month` variable's value, or one that prompts a user and allows the user to type in a value, are considered cohesive. A routine that checks date validity, deducts insurance premiums, and computes federal withholding tax for an employee would be less cohesive.

## DECLARING VARIABLES

The primary work of most modules in most programs you write is to manipulate data—for example, to calculate the figures needed for a paycheck, customer bill, or sales report. You store your program data in variables.

Many program languages require you to declare all variables before you use them. **Declaring a variable** involves providing a name for the memory location where the computer will store the variable value, and notifying the computer of what type of data to expect. Every programming language requires that you follow specific rules when declaring variables, but all the rules involve identifying at least two attributes for every variable:

- You must declare a data type.
- You must give the variable a name.

You learned in Chapter 1 that different programming languages provide different variable types, but that all allow at least the distinction between character and numeric data. The rest of this book uses just two data types—`num`, which holds number values, and `char`, which holds all other values, including those that contain letters and combinations of letters and numbers.

Remember, you also learned in Chapter 1 that variable names must not contain spaces, so this book uses statements such as `char lastName` and `num weeklySalary` to declare two variables of different types.

**TIP** ☐ ☐ ☐ ☐ | Although it is not a requirement of any programming language, it usually makes sense to give a variable a name that is a noun, because it represents a thing.

Some programming languages, such as Visual Basic, BASIC, and RPG, do not require you to name any variable until the first time you use it. However, other languages, including COBOL, C++, C#, Java, and Pascal, require that you declare variables with a name and a type. Some languages require that you declare all variables at the beginning of a program, before you write any executable statements; others allow you to declare variables at any point, but require the declaration before you can use the variable. For our purposes, this book follows the convention of declaring all variables at the beginning of a program.

In many modern programming languages, variables typically are declared within each module that uses them. Such variables are known as **local variables**. As you continue your study of programming logic, you will learn how to use local variables and understand their advantages. For now, this text will use **global variables**—variables that are given a type and name once, and then used in all modules of the program.

For example, to complete the averaging program shown in Figure 3-5 so that its variables are declared, you can redraw the main program flowchart to look like the one shown in Figure 3-6. Three variables are required: `firstNumber`, `secondNumber`, and `average`. The variables are declared as the first step in the program, before you use any of them, and each is correctly identified as numeric. They appear to the side of the "declare variables" step in an **annotation symbol** or **annotation box**, which is simply an attached box containing notes. You can use an annotation symbol any time you have more to write than you can conveniently fit within a flowchart symbol.

**TIP** ☐ ☐ ☐ ☐ | Many programming languages support more specific numeric types with names like int (for integers or whole numbers), float or single (for single-precision, floating-point values; that is, values that contain one or more decimal-place digits), and double (for double-precision, floating-point values, which means more memory space is reserved). Many languages distinguish even more precisely. For example, in addition to whole-number integers, C++, C#, and Java allow short integers and long integers, which require less and more memory, respectively.
Many programming languages support more specific character types. Often, programming languages provide a distinction between single-character variables (such as an initial or a grade in a class) and string variables (such as a last name), which hold multiple characters.

Figure 3-6 also shows pseudocode for the same program. Because pseudocode is written and not drawn, you might choose to list the variable names below the `declare variables` statement, as shown.

Programmers sometimes create a **data dictionary**, which is a list of every variable name used in a program, along with its type, size, and description. When a data dictionary is created, it becomes part of the program documentation.

**TIP** ☐ ☐ ☐ ☐ | After you name a variable, you must use that exact name every time you refer to the variable within your program. In many programming languages, even the case matters, so a variable name like `firstNumber` represents a different memory location than `firstnumber` or `FirstNumber`.

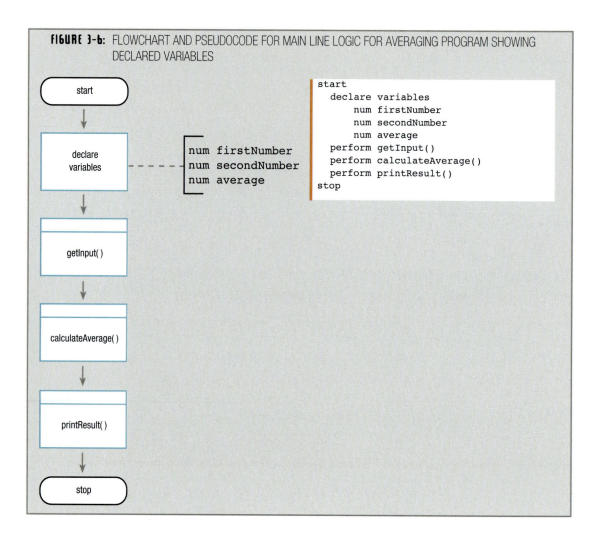

**FIGURE 3-6:** FLOWCHART AND PSEUDOCODE FOR MAIN LINE LOGIC FOR AVERAGING PROGRAM SHOWING DECLARED VARIABLES

```
start
    declare variables
        num firstNumber
        num secondNumber
        num average
    perform getInput()
    perform calculateAverage()
    perform printResult()
stop
```

## CREATING HIERARCHY CHARTS

When a program has several modules calling other modules, programmers often use a tool besides flowcharts or pseudocode to show the overall picture of how these modules are related to one another. You can use a **hierarchy chart** to illustrate modules' relationships. A hierarchy chart does not tell you what tasks are to be performed within a module; it doesn't tell you *when* or *how* a module executes. It tells you only which routines exist within a program and which routines call which other routines.

The hierarchy chart for the last version of the number-averaging program looks like Figure 3-7, and shows which modules call which others. You don't know *when* the modules are called or *why* they are called; that information is in the flowchart or pseudocode. A hierarchy chart just tells you *which* modules are called by other modules.

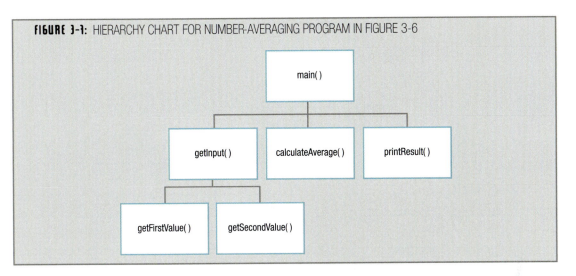

**FIGURE 3-7:** HIERARCHY CHART FOR NUMBER-AVERAGING PROGRAM IN FIGURE 3-6

You may have seen hierarchy charts for organizations, such as the one in Figure 3-8. The chart shows who reports to whom, not when or how often they report. Program hierarchy charts operate in an identical manner.

**FIGURE 3-8:** AN ORGANIZATIONAL HIERARCHY CHART

Figure 3-9 shows an example of a hierarchy chart for the billing program of a mail-order company. The hierarchy chart supplies module names only; it provides a general overview of the tasks to be performed, without specifying any details.

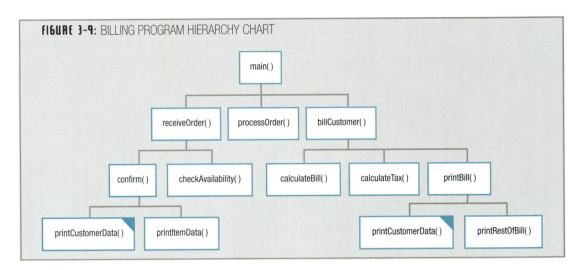

**FIGURE 3-9:** BILLING PROGRAM HIERARCHY CHART

Because program modules are reusable, a specific module may be called from several locations within a program. For example, in the billing program hierarchy chart in Figure 3-9, you can see that the `printCustomerData()` module is used twice. By convention, you blacken a corner of each box representing a module used more than once. This action alerts readers that any change to this module will affect more than one location.

The hierarchy chart can be a useful tool when a program must be modified months or years after the original writing. For example, if a tax law changes, a programmer might be asked to rewrite the `calculateTax()` module in the billing program diagrammed in Figure 3-9. As the programmer changes the `calculateTax()` routine, the hierarchy chart shows what other dependent routines might be affected. If a change is made to `printCustomerData()`, the programmer is alerted that changes will occur in multiple locations. A hierarchy chart is useful for "getting the big picture" in a complex program.

## UNDERSTANDING DOCUMENTATION

**Documentation** refers to all of the supporting material that goes with a program. Two broad categories of documentation are the documentation intended for users and the documentation intended for programmers. People who use computer programs are called **end users**, or **users** for short. Most likely, you have been the end user of an application such as a word-processing program or a game. When you purchase software that other programmers have written, you appreciate clearly written instructions on how to install and use the software. These instructions constitute user documentation. In a small organization, programmers may write user documentation, but in most organizations, systems analysts or technical writers produce end-user instructions. These instructions may take the form of a printed manual, or may be presented online through a Web site or on a compact disc.

When programmers begin to plan the logic of a computer program, they require instructions known as **program documentation**. End users never see program documentation; rather, programmers use it when planning or modifying programs.

Program documentation falls into two categories: internal and external. **Internal program documentation** consists of **program comments**, or nonexecuting statements that programmers place within their code to explain program statements in English. The method for inserting comments within a program differs in each programming language, but every method provides a means for inserting clarifying comments that do not affect the running of a program. You will learn how to insert comments when you learn a specific programming language.

TIP ☐ ☐ ☐ ☐  In the BASIC programming language, program comments begin with the letters REM (for REMark). In C++, C#, and Java, comments can begin with two forward slashes (//). An RPG program indicates that a line is a comment if there is an asterisk (*) in the sixth typed position in the line.

TIP ☐ ☐ ☐ ☐  Some newer programming language such as C# and Java provide a tool that automatically converts the programmer's internal comments to external documentation.

**External program documentation** includes all the supporting paperwork that programmers develop before they write a program. Because most programs have input, processing, and output, usually there is documentation for all these functions.

## OUTPUT DOCUMENTATION

Output documentation is usually the first to be written. This may seem backwards, but if you're planning a trip, which do you decide first: how to get to your destination or where you're going?

Most requests for programs arise because a user needs particular information to be output, so the planning of program output is usually done in consultation with the person or persons who will be using it. Only after the desired output is known can the programmer hope to plan the processes needed to produce the output.

Often the programmer does not design the output. Instead, the user who requests the output presents the programmer (or programming team) with an example or sketch of the desired result. Then the programmer might work with the user to refine the request, suggest improvements in the design, or clarify the user's needs. If you don't determine precisely what the user wants or needs at this point, you will write a program that the user soon wants redesigned and rewritten.

A very common type of output is a printed report. You can design a printed report on a **printer spacing chart**, which is also referred to as a **print chart** or a **print layout**. Figure 3-10 shows a printer spacing chart, which basically looks like graph paper. The chart has many boxes, and in each box the designer places one character that will be printed.

**FIGURE 3-10:** PRINTER SPACING CHART

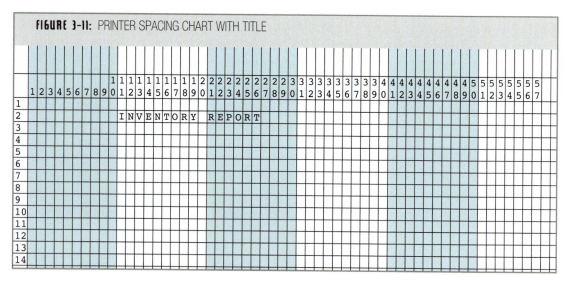

**TIP** □ □ □ □ Besides using handwritten print charts, you can design report layouts on a computer using a word-processing program or other design software.

For example, if you want to create a printed report with the title INVENTORY REPORT, and you decide that the title looks best 11 spaces over from the left of the page and one line down, you would begin to create the printer spacing chart shown in Figure 3-11.

**FIGURE 3-11:** PRINTER SPACING CHART WITH TITLE

You might want to skip a line and print the column headings ITEM NAME, PRICE, and QUANTITY IN STOCK, so the printer spacing chart would evolve into the one in Figure 3-12.

**FIGURE 3-12:** PRINTER SPACING CHART WITH TITLE AND COLUMN HEADINGS

```
          1 1 1 1 1 1 1 1 1 1 2 2 2 2 2 2 2 2 2 2 3 3 3 3 3 3 3 3 3 3 4 4 4 4 4 4 4 4 4 4 5 5 5 5 5 5 5 5
 1 2 3 4 5 6 7 8 9 0 1 2 3 4 5 6 7 8 9 0 1 2 3 4 5 6 7 8 9 0 1 2 3 4 5 6 7 8 9 0 1 2 3 4 5 6 7 8 9 0 1 2 3 4 5 6 7
 1
 2              I N V E N T O R Y   R E P O R T
 3
 4      I T E M   N A M E           P R I C E         Q U A N T I T Y   I N   S T O C K
 5
 6
 7
 8
 9
10
11
12
13
14
```

The title and column headings' values will be **constant**, or unchanging, on every page of the report. In other words, in this example, the title and column headings will not change based on the date, the number of pages that print, any input data, or any other conditions. Therefore, the title and column headings are written on the print chart exactly as they will appear on the report. The exact spacing and the use of upper- or lowercase characters make a difference. Notice that the constants used within a report do not need to follow the same rules as variable names. Within a report, constants like INVENTORY REPORT and ITEM NAME can contain spaces. These headings exist to help readers understand the information presented in the report—not for a computer to interpret.

A print layout typically shows how the variable data will appear on the report. Of course, the data will probably be different every time the report is run. Thus, instead of writing in actual item names and prices, the users and programmers usually use Xs to represent generic variable character data and 9s to represent generic variable numeric data. (Some programmers use Xs for both character and numeric data.) For example, Figure 3-13 shows how some data will look in the print chart.

Each line containing Xs and 9s representing data is a **detail line**, or a line that displays the data details. Detail lines typically appear many times per page, as opposed to **heading lines**, which contain the title and any column headings, and usually appear only once per page.

Even though an actual inventory report might eventually go on for hundreds or thousands of detail lines, writing two or three rows of Xs and 9s is sufficient to show how the data will appear. For example, if a report contains employee names and salaries, those data items will occupy the same print positions on output for line after line, whether the output eventually contains 10 employees or 10,000. A few rows of identically positioned Xs and 9s are sufficient to establish the pattern.

In any report layout, then, you write in constant data (such as headings) that will be the same on every run of this report. You write Xs and 9s to represent the variable data (such as the items, their prices, and their quantities) that will change from run to run.

**FIGURE 3-13:** PRINT CHART WITH GENERIC DATA

|   | 1 2 3 4 5 6 7 8 9 0 1 2 3 4 5 6 7 8 9 0 1 2 3 4 5 6 7 8 9 0 1 2 3 4 5 6 7 8 9 0 1 2 3 4 5 6 7 8 9 0 1 2 3 4 5 6 7 |
|---|---|
| 1 | |
| 2 | INVENTORY REPORT |
| 3 | |
| 4 | ITEM NAME          PRICE        QUANTITY IN STOCK |
| 5 | |
| 6 | XXXXXXXXXXXXXXX 999.99       9999 |
| 7 | XXXXXXXXXXXXXXX 999.99       9999 |
| 8 | |
| 9 | |
| 10 | |
| 11 | |
| 12 | |
| 13 | |
| 14 | |

In the inventory report layout shown in Figure 3-13, the headings truly are constant, but you should not assume that all headings are completely constant. Let's say that your user decides to include the date in the inventory report heading. The report might now have a layout like that of Figure 3-14. Notice that now there is variable data, the date, in the report heading.

**FIGURE 3-14:** PRINT CHART CONTAINING VARIABLE DATA IN REPORT HEADING

|   | 1 2 3 4 5 6 7 8 9 0 1 2 3 4 5 6 7 8 9 0 1 2 3 4 5 6 7 8 9 0 1 2 3 4 5 6 7 8 9 0 1 2 3 4 5 6 7 8 9 0 1 2 3 4 5 6 7 |
|---|---|
| 1 | |
| 2 | INVENTORY REPORT FOR WEEK OF 99/99/9999 |
| 3 | |
| 4 | ITEM NAME          PRICE        QUANTITY IN STOCK |
| 5 | |
| 6 | |
| 7 | |
| 8 | |
| 9 | |
| 10 | |
| 11 | |
| 12 | |
| 13 | |
| 14 | |

For a long report that requires multiple pages, perhaps the user will also decide that the headings should appear at the top of every printed page, and that page numbers should also be added. Figure 3-15 shows how you might indicate page numbers.

**FIGURE 3-15:** PRINT CHART CONTAINING HEADING WITH PAGE NUMBERS

```
              1111111111222222222233333333334444444444555555 5
    12345678901234567890123456789012345678901234567890123456 7
 1
 2           INVENTORY REPORT FOR WEEK OF 99/99/9999 PAGE 99
 3
 4    ITEM NAME          PRICE      QUANTITY IN STOCK
 5
 6
 7
 8
 9
10
11
12
13
14
```

Just as variable data might appear in a heading, constants might appear in the detail lines. For example, a company might choose to display a dollar sign to the left of every price listed on a report. In this case, the dollar sign would appear literally on each line, as shown in Figure 3-16.

**FIGURE 3-16:** PRINT CHART WITH DOLLAR SIGN IN EACH DETAIL LINE

```
              1111111111222222222233333333334444444444555555 5
    12345678901234567890123456789012345678901234567890123456 7
 1
 2           INVENTORY REPORT
 3
 4    ITEM NAME          PRICE      QUANTITY IN STOCK
 5
 6    XXXXXXXXXXXXXXX    $999.99         9999
 7    XXXXXXXXXXXXXXX    $999.99         9999
 8
 9
10
11
12
13
14
```

Besides header lines and detail lines, reports often include special lines at the end of a report. These may contain variable information only, as in Figure 3-17, or constant information only, as in Figure 3-18. Most often, however, reports will have both, as in Figure 3-19. Even though lines at the end of a report don't always contain numeric totals, they are usually referred to generically as **total lines** or **summary lines**.

**FIGURE 3-17:** REPORT WITH VARIABLE DATA AT END

A print chart with columns numbered 1 through 57. The content is as follows:

| Line | Content (column positions) |
|------|----------------------------|
| 2 | INVENTORY REPORT (beginning at column 15) |
| 4 | ITEM NAME (col 4), PRICE (col 23), QUANTITY IN STOCK (col 37) |
| 6 | XXXXXXXXXXXXXXX (col 4), 999.99 (col 23), 9999 (col 44) |
| 7 | XXXXXXXXXXXXXXX (col 4), 999.99 (col 23), 9999 (col 44) |
| 9 | 99999 (col 44) |

**FIGURE 3-18:** REPORT WITH CONSTANT DATA AT END

A print chart with columns numbered 1 through 57. The content is as follows:

| Line | Content (column positions) |
|------|----------------------------|
| 2 | INVENTORY REPORT (beginning at column 15) |
| 4 | ITEM NAME (col 4), PRICE (col 23), QUANTITY IN STOCK (col 37) |
| 6 | XXXXXXXXXXXXXXX (col 4), 999.99 (col 23), 9999 (col 44) |
| 7 | XXXXXXXXXXXXXXX (col 4), 999.99 (col 23), 9999 (col 44) |
| 9 | THANK YOU FOR USING THIS PROGRAM (col 4) |

**FIGURE 3-19:** REPORT WITH COMBINED CONSTANT AND VARIABLE DATA AT END

```
            1111111111222222222233333333334444444444555555555
  1234567890123456789012345678901234567890123456789012345 67
 1
 2               INVENTORY REPORT
 3
 4  ITEM NAME        PRICE       QUANTITY IN STOCK
 5
 6  XXXXXXXXXXXXXX   999.99               9999
 7  XXXXXXXXXXXXXX   999.99               9999
 8
 9                   GRAND TOTAL:    999999
10
11
12
13
14
```

Printed reports do not necessarily contain detail lines. A report might contain only headers and summary lines. For example, a payroll report might contain only a heading and a total gross payroll figure for each department in the company, or a college might print a report showing how many students have declared each available major. These reports contain no detail—no information about individual employees or students—but they do contain summaries. Figure 3-20 shows an example of a print chart for a summary report.

**FIGURE 3-20:** PRINT CHART FOR PAYROLL SUMMARY REPORT

```
            1111111111222222222233333333334444444444555555555
  1234567890123456789012345678901234567890123456789012345 67
 1                 PAYROLL SUMMARY REPORT
 2
 3              DEPT   TOTAL GROSS PAYROLL
 4
 5              101    999,999,999.99
 6              102    999,999,999.99
 7              103    999,999,999.99
 8              104    999,999,999.99
 9              105    999,999,999.99
10              106    999,999,999.99
11              107    999,999,999.99
12
13
14
```

Not all program output takes the form of printed reports. If your program's output will appear on a monitor screen, particularly if you are working in a **GUI**, or graphical user interface environment like Windows, your design issues will differ. In a GUI program, the user sees a screen, and can typically make selections using a mouse or other pointing device. Instead of a print chart, your output design might resemble a sketch of a screen. Figure 3-21 shows how inventory records might be displayed in a graphical environment. On a monitor, you might choose to allow the user to see only one or a few records at a time, so one concern is providing a means for users to scroll through displayed records. In Figure 3-21, records are accessed using a single button that the user can click to read the next record; in a more sophisticated design, the user might be able to "jump" to the first or last record, or look up a specific record.

**FIGURE 3-21:** INVENTORY RECORDS DISPLAYED IN A GUI ENVIRONMENT

**TIP** ☐ ☐ ☐ ☐   A printed report is also called a **hard copy**, whereas screen output is referred to as a **soft copy**.

**TIP** ☐ ☐ ☐ ☐   Achieving good screen design is an art that requires much study and thought to master. Besides being visually pleasing, good screen design also requires ease of use and accessibility.

**TIP** ☐ ☐ ☐ ☐   GUI programs often include several different screen formats that a user will see while running a program. In such cases, you would design several screens.

## INPUT DOCUMENTATION

Once you have planned the design of the output, you need to know what input is available to produce this output. If you are producing a report from stored data, you frequently will be provided with a **file description** that describes the data contained in a file. You usually find a file's description as part of an organization's information systems documentation; physically, the description might be on paper in a binder in the Information Systems department, or it might be stored on a disk. If the file you will use comes from an outside source, the person requesting the report will have to provide you with a description of the data stored on the file. For example, Figure 3-22 shows an inventory file description for a file that could be used to produce the report described in Figure 3-13.

**TIP** ☐ ☐ ☐ ☐   Not all programs use previously stored input files. Some use interactive input data supplied by a user during the execution of a program. Some programs produce an output file that is stored directly on a storage device, such as a disk. If your program produces file output instead of printed report output, you will create a file description for your output. Other programs then may use your output file description as an input description.

**FIGURE 3-22:** INVENTORY FILE DESCRIPTION

```
INVENTORY FILE DESCRIPTION
File name: INVTRY
FIELD DESCRIPTION      POSITIONS    DATA TYPE    DECIMALS
Name of item           1—15         Character
Price of item          16—20        Numeric      2
Quantity in stock      21—24        Numeric      0
```

The inventory file description in Figure 3-22 shows that each item's name occupies the first 15 bytes of each record in the file. A **byte** is a unit of computer storage that can contain any of 256 combinations of 0s and 1s that often represent a character. The code of 0s and 1s depends on the type of computer system you are using. Popular coding schemes include ASCII (American Standard Code for Information Interchange), EBCDIC (Extended Binary Coded Decimal Interchange Code), and Unicode. Each of these codes uses a different combination of 1s and 0s to represent characters—you can see a listing of each code's values in Appendix B. For example, in ASCII, an uppercase "A" is represented by 01000001. Programmers seldom care about the code used; for example, if an "A" is stored as part of a person's name, the programmer's only concern is that the "A" in the name appears correctly on output—not the combination of 0s and 1s that represents it. This book assumes that one stored character occupies one byte in an input file.

Some item names may require all 15 positions allowed for the name in the input file, for example "12 by 16 carpet", which contains exactly 15 characters, including spaces. Other item names require fewer than the allotted 15 positions, for example "door mat". In such cases, the remaining allotted positions remain blank. When only 15 storage positions are allowed for a name, some names might have to be truncated or abbreviated. For example, "hand woven carpet" might be stored as "hand woven carp". Whether the item name requires all 15 positions or not, you can see from the input file description in Figure 3-22 that the price for each item begins in position 16 of each input record.

The price of any item in the inventory file is allowed five positions, 16 through 20. It is natural to assume, therefore, that a price contains five digits. However, very often numeric values are stored on disk in a format that allows many more digits to be stored in a five-byte area. For convenience, this book assumes that a five-byte numeric storage location holds five digits, but keep in mind that, in reality, it would hold a much larger number in most systems.

**TIP** ▫ ▫ ▫ ▫ | Some systems store numbers in a format called "unpacked," in which a number like 456 is stored in three bytes as +4, +5, and +6, and a number like –23789 is stored in five bytes as –2, –3, –7, –8, and –9. In each case, the sign (+ or –) occupies half a byte, and the digit occupies the other half of the byte. However, if a number is positive, the entire number is positive, and if a number is negative, the entire number is negative, so storing the sign with each digit is redundant. Therefore, some systems store numbers in a format called "packed." In these systems, the sign is stored only once with each multidigit number, and each digit occupies half a byte—so +456 occupies only two bytes (one for the + and the 4, and the other for the 5 and the 6), and –23789 requires only three bytes (containing – and 2, 3 and 7, and 8 and 9).

The input file description in Figure 3-22 shows that two of the positions in the price are reserved for decimal places. Typically, decimal points themselves are not stored in data files; they are **implied**, or **assumed**. Also typically, numeric data are stored with leading zeros so that all allotted positions are occupied. Thus, an item valued at $345.67 is stored as 34567, and an item valued at $1.23 is stored as 00123.

**TIP** ☐ ☐ ☐ ☐ Decimal points are implied in data files, but occupy positions on printed reports. Within data files, it is most efficient to save space. On printed reports, it is most important to represent information in a way that is easy for the reader to interpret. Leading zeros fill numeric fields within files, but are not used on printed reports. Within data files, numeric fields must be totally numeric, so spaces are not allowed within numeric fields. On printed reports, information must be easy for the reader to interpret; readers usually do not expect to see leading zeros in numeric data.

**TIP** ☐ ☐ ☐ ☐ Just as repetitious decimal points are not stored in numeric fields, data files often do not store other repeated characters whose position is assumed—for example, dashes in Social Security numbers or telephone numbers, or a period after a middle initial.

Typically, programmers create one program variable for each field that is part of the input file. In addition to the field descriptions contained in the input documentation, the programmer might be given specific variable names to use for each field, particularly if such variable names must agree with the ones that other programmers working on the project are using. In many cases, however, programmers are allowed to choose their own variable names. Therefore, you can choose `itemName`, `nameOfItem`, `itemDescription`, or any other reasonable one-word variable name when you refer to the item name within your program. The variable names you use within your program need not match constants printed on the report. Thus, the variable `itemName` might hold the characters that will print under the column heading NAME OF ITEM.

For example, examine the input file description in Figure 3-22. When this file is used for a project in which the programmer can choose variable names, he or she might choose the following variable declaration list:

```
char itemName
num itemPrice
num itemQuantity
```

Each data field in the list is declared using the data type that corresponds to the data type indicated in the file description, and has an appropriate, easy-to-read, single-word variable name.

**TIP** ☐ ☐ ☐ ☐ When a programmer uses an identifier like `itemName`, that variable identifier exists in computer memory only for the duration of the program in which the variable is declared. Another program can use the same input file and refer to the same field as `nameOfItem`. Variable names exist in memory during the run of a program—they are not stored in the data file. Variable names simply represent memory addresses at which pieces of data are stored while a program executes.

Recall the data hierarchy relationship introduced in Chapter 1:

- Database
- File
- Record
- Field
- Character

Whether the inventory file is part of a database or not, it will contain many records; each record will contain an item name, price, and quantity, which are fields. In turn, the field that holds the name of an item might contain up to 15 characters, for example "12 by 16 carpet", "blue miniblinds", or "diskette holder".

Organizations may use different forms to relay the information about records and fields, but the very least the programmer needs to know is:

- What is the name of the file?
- What data does it contain?
- How much room do the file and each of its fields take up?
- What type of data can be stored in each field—character or numeric?

Notice that a data field's position on the input file never has to correspond with the same item's position in an output file or in a print chart. For example, you can use the data file described in Figure 3-22 to produce the report shown in Figure 3-13. In the input data file, the item name appears in positions 1 through 15. However, on the printed report, the same information appears in columns 4 through 18. In an input file, data are "squeezed" together—no human being will read this file, and there is no need for it to be attractively spaced. However, on printed output, you typically include spaces between data items so they are legible as well as attractive. Figure 3-23 illustrates how input fields are read by the program and converted to output fields.

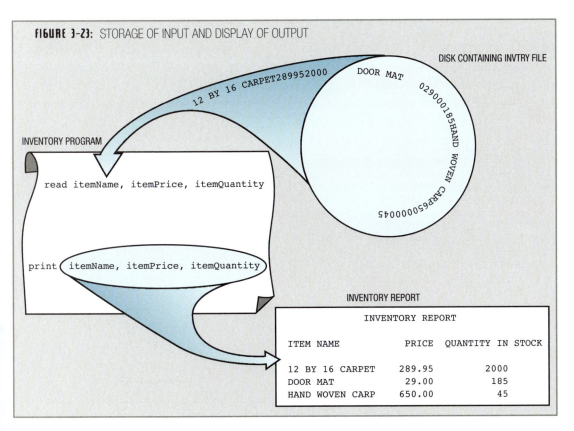

**FIGURE 3-23:** STORAGE OF INPUT AND DISPLAY OF OUTPUT

DISK CONTAINING INVTRY FILE

12 BY 16 CARPET289952000    DOOR MAT    02900018 5HAND WOVEN CARP65000045

INVENTORY PROGRAM

```
read itemName, itemPrice, itemQuantity

print ( itemName, itemPrice, itemQuantity )
```

INVENTORY REPORT

INVENTORY REPORT

| ITEM NAME | PRICE | QUANTITY IN STOCK |
|---|---|---|
| 12 BY 16 CARPET | 289.95 | 2000 |
| DOOR MAT | 29.00 | 185 |
| HAND WOVEN CARP | 650.00 | 45 |

TIP ☐ ☐ ☐ ☐   You are never required to output all the available characters in a field that exist on input. For example, even though the item name in the input file description in Figure 3-22 shows that each item contains 15 stored characters, you might decide to display only 10 of them on output, especially if your output report contained many columns and you were "crunched" for space.

The inventory file description in Figure 3-22 contains all the information the programmer needs to create the output requested in Figure 3-13—the output lists each item's name, price, and quantity, and the input records clearly contain that data. Often, however, a file description more closely resembles the description in Figure 3-24.

---

**FIGURE 3-24:** EXPANDED INVENTORY FILE DESCRIPTION

```
INVENTORY FILE DESCRIPTION
File name: INVTRY
```

| FIELD DESCRIPTION | POSITIONS | DATA TYPE | DECIMALS |
|---|---|---|---|
| Item number | 1–4 | Numeric | 0 |
| Name of item | 5–19 | Character | |
| Size | 20 | Numeric | 0 |
| Manufacturing cost of item | 21–25 | Numeric | 2 |
| Retail price of item | 26–30 | Numeric | 2 |
| Quantity in stock | 31–34 | Numeric | 0 |
| Reorder point | 35–38 | Numeric | 0 |
| Sales rep | 39–48 | Character | |
| Amt sold last year | 49–54 | Numeric | 0 |

---

The file description in Figure 3-24 contains nine fields. With this file description, it's harder to pinpoint the information needed for the report, but the necessary data fields are available, and you still can write the program. The input file contains more information than you need for the report you want to print, so you will ignore some of the input fields, such as Item number and Sales rep. These fields certainly may be used in other reports within the company. Typically, data input files contain more data than any one program requires. For example, your credit card company stores historical data about your past purchases, but these are not included on every bill. Similarly, your school records contain more data than are printed on each report card or tuition bill.

However, if the input file description resembles Figure 3-25, then there are not enough data to produce the requested report.

---

**FIGURE 3-25:** INSUFFICIENT INVENTORY FILE DESCRIPTION

```
INVENTORY FILE DESCRIPTION
File name: INVTRY
```

| FIELD DESCRIPTION | POSITIONS | DATA TYPE | DECIMALS |
|---|---|---|---|
| Item number | 1–4 | Numeric | 0 |
| Name of item | 5–19 | Character | |
| Size | 20 | Numeric | 0 |
| Manufacturing cost of item | 21–25 | Numeric | 2 |
| Retail price of item | 26–30 | Numeric | 2 |
| Reorder point | 35–38 | Numeric | 0 |
| Sales rep | 39–48 | Character | |
| Amt sold last year | 49–54 | Numeric | 0 |

In Figure 3-25, there is no indication that the input file contains a figure for quantity in stock. If the user really needs (or wants) the report as requested, it's out of the programmer's hands until the data can be collected from some source and stored in a file the programmer can use.

Each field printed on a report does not need to exist on the input file. Assume that a user requests a report in the format shown in Figure 3-26, which includes a column labeled "PROFIT", and that the input file description is the one in Figure 3-25. In this case, it's difficult to determine whether you can create the requested report, because the input file does not contain a `profit` field. However, because the input data include the company's cost and selling price for each item, you can calculate the `profit` within your program by subtracting the cost from the price, and then produce the desired output.

**FIGURE 3-26:** REQUESTED PROFIT REPORT

|  | ITEM NUMBER | PROFIT REPORT | PRICE | COST | PROFIT |
|---|---|---|---|---|---|
| 2 |  | PROFIT REPORT |  |  |  |
| 4 | ITEM NUMBER |  | PRICE | COST | PROFIT |
| 6 | 9999 |  | 999.99 | 999.99 | 999.99 |
| 7 | 9999 |  | 999.99 | 999.99 | 999.99 |

## COMPLETING THE DOCUMENTATION

When you have designed the output and confirmed that it is possible to produce it from the input, then you can plan the logic of the program, code the program, and test the program. The original output design, input description, flowchart or pseudocode, and program code all become part of the program documentation. These pieces of documentation are typically stored together in a binder within the programming department of an organization, where they can be studied later, when program changes become necessary.

In addition to this program documentation, you typically must create user documentation. **User documentation** includes all the manuals or other instructional materials that nontechnical people use, as well as the operating instructions that computer operators and data-entry personnel need. It needs to be written clearly, in plain language, with reasonable expectations of the users' expertise. Within a small organization, the programmer may prepare the user documentation. In a large organization, user documentation is usually prepared by technical writers or systems analysts, who oversee programmers' work and coordinate programmers' efforts. These professionals consult with the programmer to ensure that the user documentation is complete and accurate.

The areas addressed in user documentation may include:

- How to prepare input for the program
- To whom the output should be distributed
- How to interpret the normal output
- How to interpret and react to any error message generated by the program
- How frequently the program needs to run

 Complete documentation also might include operations support documentation. This type of documentation provides backup and recovery information, run-time instructions, and security considerations for computer center personnel who run large applications within data centers.

All these issues must be addressed before a program can be fully functional in an organization. When users throughout an organization can supply input data to computer programs and obtain the information they need in order to do their jobs well, then a skilled programmer has provided a complete piece of work.

## CHAPTER SUMMARY

☐ Programmers break programming problems down into smaller, reasonable units called modules, subroutines, procedures, functions, or methods. Modularization provides abstraction, allows multiple programmers to work on a problem, makes it easy to reuse your work, and allows you to identify structures more easily.

☐ When you create a module or subroutine, you give the module a name that a calling program uses when the module is about to execute. The flowchart symbol used to call a subroutine is a rectangle with a bar across the top; the name of the module that you are calling is inside the rectangle. You draw a flowchart for each module separately, with its own sentinel symbols.

☐ A module can call other modules.

☐ Declaring a variable involves providing a name for the memory location where the computer will store the variable value, and notifying the computer of what type of data to expect.

☐ You can use a hierarchy chart to illustrate modules' relationships.

☐ Documentation refers to all of the supporting material that goes with a program.

☐ Output documentation is usually written first. You can design a printed report on a printer spacing chart to represent both constant and variable data.

☐ A file description lists the data contained in a file, including a description, size, and data type. Typically, numeric data are stored with leading zeros and without decimal points.

☐ In addition to program documentation, you typically must create user documentation, which includes the manuals or other instructional materials that nontechnical people use, as well as the operating instructions that computer operators and data-entry personnel may need.

## KEY TERMS

**Modules** are small program units that you can use together to make a program. Programmers also refer to modules as **subroutines**, **procedures**, **functions**, or **methods**.

The process of breaking a program into modules is called **modularization**.

**Abstraction** is the process of paying attention to important properties while ignoring nonessential details.

**Low-level** details are small, nonabstract steps.

**High-level** programming languages allow you to use English-like vocabulary in which one broad statement corresponds to dozens of machine instructions.

**Reusability** is the feature of modular programs that allows individual modules to be used in a variety of applications.

**Reliability** is the feature of modular programs that assures you that a module has been tested and proven to function correctly.

A **calling program** is one that calls a module.

A **main program** runs from start to stop and calls other modules.

A **prompt** is a message that is displayed on a monitor, asking the user for a response.

The **functional cohesion** of a module is a measure of the degree to which all the module statements contribute to the same task.

**Declaring a variable** involves providing a name for the memory location where the computer will store the variable value, and notifying the computer of what type of data to expect.

**Local variables** are declared within each module that uses them.

**Global variables** are given a type and name once, and then are used in all modules of the program.

An **annotation symbol** or **annotation box** is a flowchart symbol that represents an attached box containing notes.

A **data dictionary** is a list of every variable name used in a program, along with its type, size, and description.

A **hierarchy chart** is a diagram that illustrates modules' relationships to each other.

**Documentation** refers to all of the supporting material that goes with a program.

**End users**, or **users**, are people who use computer programs.

**Program documentation** is the set of instructions that programmers use when they begin to plan the logic of a program.

**Internal program documentation** is documentation within a program.

**Program comments** are nonexecuting statements that programmers place within their code to explain program statements in English.

**External program documentation** includes all the supporting paperwork that programmers develop before they write a program.

A **printer spacing chart**, which is also referred to as a **print chart** or a **print layout**, is a tool for planning program output.

**Constant** output does not change based on any conditions.

A **detail line** on a report is a line that contains data details. Most reports contain many detail lines.

**Heading lines** on a report, which contain the title and any column headings, usually appear only once per page.

**Total lines** or **summary lines** contain end-of-report information.

A **GUI**, or graphical user interface environment, uses screens to display program output. Users interact with GUI programs with a device such as a mouse.

A **hard copy** is a printed copy.

A **soft copy** is a screen copy.

A **file description** is a document that describes the data contained in a file.

A **byte** is a unit of computer storage that can contain any of 256 combinations of 0s and 1s that often represent a character.

When pieces of data are **implied** or **assumed**, they do not exist explicitly.

**User documentation** includes all the manuals or other instructional materials that nontechnical people use, as well as the operating instructions that computer operators and data-entry personnel need.

## REVIEW QUESTIONS

1.  **Which of the following is *not* a term used for modules in any programming language?**

    a. structure

    b. procedure

    c. method

    d. function

2.  **Which of the following is *not* a reason to use modularization?**

    a. Modularization provides abstraction.

    b. Modularization allows multiple programmers to work on a problem.

    c. Modularization allows you to reuse your work.

    d. Modularization eliminates the need for structure.

3.  **What is the name for the process of paying attention to important properties while ignoring nonessential details?**

    a. structure

    b. iteration

    c. abstraction

    d. modularization

4.  **All modern programming languages that use English-like vocabulary to create statements that correspond to dozens of machine instructions are referred to as _____.**

    a. high-level

    b. object-oriented

    c. modular

    d. obtuse

5.  **Modularizing a program makes it _____ to identify structures.**

    a. unnecessary

    b. easier

    c. more difficult

    d. impossible

6.  **Programmers say that one module can _____ another, meaning that the first module causes the second module to execute.**

    a. declare

    b. define

    c. enact

    d. call

7. **A message that appears on a monitor, asking the user for a response is a _____ .**

     a. call

     b. prompt

     c. command

     d. declaration

8. **The more that a module's statements contribute to the same job, the greater the _____ of the module.**

     a. structure

     b. modularity

     c. functional cohesion

     d. size

9. **When you declare a variable, you must provide _____ .**

     a. a name

     b. a name and a type

     c. a name, a type, and a value

     d. a name, a type, a value, and a purpose

10. **A _____ is a list of every variable name used in a program, along with its type, size, and description.**

     a. flowchart

     b. hierarchy chart

     c. data dictionary

     d. variable map

11. **A hierarchy chart tells you _____ .**

     a. what tasks are to be performed within each program module

     b. when a module executes

     c. which routines call which other routines

     d. all of the above

12. **Two broad categories of documentation are the documentation intended for _____ .**

     a. management and workers

     b. end users and programmers

     c. people and the computer

     d. defining variables and defining actions

13. **Nonexecuting statements that programmers place within their code to explain program statements in English are called _____ .**

     a. comments

     b. pseudocode

     c. trivia

     d. user documentation

14. **The first type of documentation usually created when writing a program pertains to _____ .**

    a. end users
    b. input
    c. output
    d. data

15. **Lines of output that never change, no matter what data values are input, are referred to as _____ .**

    a. detail lines
    b. headers
    c. rigid
    d. constant

16. **Report lines that contain the information stored in individual data records are known as _____ .**

    a. headers
    b. footers
    c. detail lines
    d. X-lines

17. **Summary lines appear _____ .**

    a. at the end of every printed report
    b. at the end of some printed reports
    c. in printed reports, but never in screen output
    d. only when detail lines also appear

18. **If an input file description allows 15 characters for a first name, and the stored name for the first record is "John", then typically _____ .**

    a. the actual field for the first record will be shortened to four characters
    b. the fields for first name in all subsequent records will be shortened to four characters
    c. the first name field in the first record will end with 11 zeros
    d. the first name field in the first record will end with 11 blanks

19. **In most computer systems, when numbers that contain a decimal point are stored, _____ .**

    a. the decimal point is not stored; its position is assumed
    b. the decimal point occupies one byte of storage
    c. the decimal point occupies two bytes of storage
    d. Most systems cannot store numbers containing a decimal point.

20. **A field holding a student's last name is stored in bytes 10 through 29 of each student record. Therefore, when you design a print chart for a report that contains each student's last name, _____ .**

    a. the name must print in positions 10 through 29 of the print chart
    b. the name must occupy exactly 20 positions on the print chart
    c. Both of these are true.
    d. Neither of these is true.

## EXERCISES

1.   Redraw the following flowchart so that the decisions and compensation calculations are in a module.

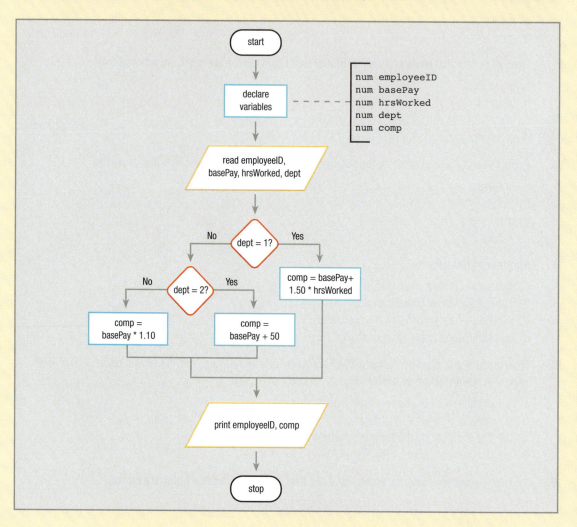

2. Rewrite the following pseudocode so the discount decisions and calculations are in a module.

```
start
      read customerRecord
      if quantityOrdered > 100 then
            discount = .20
      else
            if quantityOrdered > 12 then
                  discount = .10
            endif
        endif
        total = priceEach * quantityOrdered
        total = total - discount * total
        print total
   stop
```

3. What are the final values of variables a, b, and c after the following program runs?

```
start
      a = 2
      b = 4
      c = 10
      while c > 6
            perform changeBAndC()
      endwhile
      if a = 2 then
            perform changeA()
      endif
      if c = 10 then
            perform changeA()
      else
            perform changeBAndC()
      endif
      print a,b,c
   stop

changeBAndC()
      b = b + 1
      c = c - 1
   return

changeA()
      a = a + 1
      b = b - 1
   return
```

4. **What are the final values of variables d, e, and f after the following program runs?**

```
start
     d = 1
     e = 3
     f = 100
     while e > d
           perform module1()
     endwhile
     if f > 0 then
           perform module2()
     else
           d = d + 5
     endif
     print d, e, f
stop

module1()
     f = f - 50
     e = e + 1
     d = d + 3
return

module2()
     f = f + 13
     d = d * 10
return
```

5. **Draw a typical hierarchy chart for a paycheck-producing program. Try to think of at least 10 separate modules that might be included. For example, one module might calculate an employee's dental insurance premium.**

6. **Design a print chart for a payroll roster that is intended to list the following items for every employee: employee's first name, last name, and salary.**

7. **Design a print chart for a payroll roster that is intended to list the following items for every employee: employee's first name, last name, hours worked, rate per hour, gross pay, federal withholding tax, state withholding tax, union dues, and net pay.**

8.  **Given the following input file description, determine if there is enough information provided to produce each of the requested reports:**

    ```
    INSURANCE PREMIUM LIST
    File name: INSPREM
    FIELD DESCRIPTION            POSITIONS      DATA TYPE      DECIMALS
    Name of insured driver       1-40           Character
    Birth date                   41-46          Numeric        0
    Gender                       47             Character
    Make of car                  48-57          Character
    Year of car                  58-61          Numeric        0
    Miles driven per year        62-67          Numeric        0
    Number of traffic tickets    68-69          Numeric        0
    Balance owed                 70-75          Numeric        2
    ```

    a.  a list of the names of all insured drivers
    b.  a list of very high-risk insured drivers, defined as male, under 25 years old, with more than two tickets
    c.  a list of low-risk insured drivers, defined as those with no tickets in the last three years, and over 30 years old
    d.  a list of insured drivers to contact about a special premium offer for those with a passenger car who drive under 10,000 miles per year
    e.  a list of the names of female drivers whose balance owed is more than $99.99

9.  **Given the INSPREM file description in Exercise 8, design a print chart to satisfy each of the following requests:**

    a.  a list of every driver's name and make of car
    b.  a list of the names of all insured drivers who drive more than 20,000 miles per year
    c.  a list of the name, gender, make of car, and year of car for all drivers who have more than two tickets
    d.  a report that summarizes the number of tickets held by drivers who were born in 1940 or before, from 1941–1960, from 1961–1980, and from 1981 on
    e.  a report that summarizes the number of tickets held by drivers in the four birth-date categories listed in part d, grouped by gender

10. A program calculates the gown size that a student needs for a graduation ceremony. The program accepts as input a student's height in feet and inches and weight in pounds. It converts the student's height to centimeters and weight to grams. Then, it calculates the graduation gown size needed by adding ⅓ of the weight in grams to the height in centimeters. Finally, the program prints the results. There are 2.54 centimeters in an inch and 453.59 grams in a pound. Write the pseudocode that matches the following flowchart.

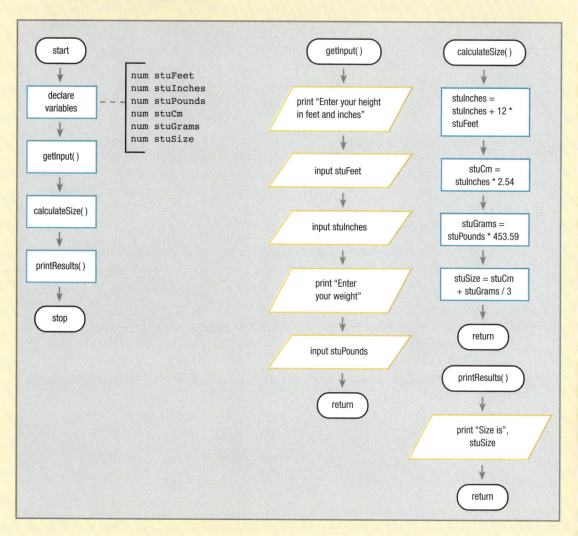

11. A program calculates the service charge a customer owes for writing a bad check. The program accepts a customer's name, the date the check was written (month, day, and year), the current date (month, day, and year), and the amount of the check in dollars and cents. The service charge is $20.00 plus 2% of the amount of the check, plus $5 for every month that has passed since the check was written. Draw the flowchart that matches the pseudocode.

(This pseudocode assumes that all checks entered are already written—that is, their dates are prior to today's date. Additionally, a check is one month late as soon as a new month starts—so a bad check written on September 30 is one month overdue on October 1.)

```
start
    declare variables
        char custName
        num checkMonth
        num checkDay
        num checkYear
        num todayMonth
        num todayDay
        num todayYear
        num checkAmount
        num serviceCharge
        num baseCharge
        num extraCharge
        num yearsLate
        num monthsLate
        num checkWorkField
        num todayWorkField
    perform getInput()
    perform calculateServiceCharge()
    perform printResults()
stop

getInput()
    print "Enter customer name"
    input custName
    perform getDates()
    print "Enter check amount"
    input checkAmount
return
```

```
getDates()
    print "Enter the date of the check"
    input checkMonth
    input checkDay
    input checkYear
    print "Enter today's date"
    input todayMonth
    input todayDay
    input todayYear
return

calculateServiceCharge()
    baseCharge = 20.00
    extraCharge = .02 * checkAmount
    serviceCharge = baseCharge + extraCharge +
        monthsLate * 5
return

printResults()
    print custName, serviceCharge
return
```

12. Draw the hierarchy chart that corresponds to the pseudocode presented in Exercise 11.

# 4

# WRITING AND DESIGNING A COMPLETE PROGRAM

## After studying Chapter 4, you should be able to:

- ☐ Plan the mainline logic for a complete program
- ☐ Describe typical housekeeping tasks
- ☐ Describe tasks typically performed in the main loop of a program
- ☐ Describe tasks performed in the end-of-job module
- ☐ Understand the need for good program design
- ☐ Appreciate the advantages of storing program components in separate files
- ☐ Select superior variable and module names
- ☐ Design clear module statements
- ☐ Understand the need for maintaining good programming habits

## UNDERSTANDING THE MAINLINE LOGICAL FLOW THROUGH A PROGRAM

You're ready to plan the logic for your first complete computer program. The output is an inventory report, as shown in Figure 4-1. The report lists inventory items along with the price, cost, and profit of each item.

**FIGURE 4-1:** PRINT CHART FOR INVENTORY REPORT

|   |   | | | | | | | | | |1|1|1|1|1|1|1|1|1|1|2|2|2|2|2|2|2|2|2|2|3|3|3|3|3|3|3|3|3|3|4|4|4|4|4|4|4|4|4|4|5|5|5|5|5|5|5|5|5|5|6|6|
|---|---|
|   |1|2|3|4|5|6|7|8|9|0|1|2|3|4|5|6|7|8|9|0|1|2|3|4|5|6|7|8|9|0|1|2|3|4|5|6|7|8|9|0|1|2|3|4|5|6|7|8|9|0|1|2|3|4|5|6|7|8|9|0|1|

Row 1
Row 2: INVENTORY REPORT
Row 3
Row 4: ITEM — RETAIL PRICE — MANUFACTURING — PROFIT PER
Row 5: DESCRIPTION — EACH — COST EACH — ITEM
Row 6
Row 7: XXXXXXXXXXXXXXX — 999.99 — 999.99 — 999.99
Row 8: XXXXXXXXXXXXXXX — 999.99 — 999.99 — 999.99
Rows 9–14

Figure 4-2 shows the input INVENTORY file description, Figure 4-3 shows some typical data that might exist in the input file, and Figure 4-4 shows how the output would actually look if the input file in Figure 4-3 were used.

**FIGURE 4-2:** INVENTORY FILE DESCRIPTION

```
INVENTORY FILE DESCRIPTION
File name: INVENTORY
```

| FIELD DESCRIPTION | POSITIONS | DATA TYPE | DECIMALS |
|---|---|---|---|
| Item name | 1–15 | Character | |
| Price | 16–20 | Numeric | 2 |
| Cost | 21–25 | Numeric | 2 |
| Quantity in stock | 26–29 | Numeric | 0 |

**FIGURE 4-3:** TYPICAL DATA THAT MIGHT BE STORED IN INVENTORY FILE

| | | | |
|---|---|---|---|
| cotton shirt | 01995 | 01457 | 2500 |
| wool scarf | 01450 | 01125 | 0060 |
| silk blouse | 16500 | 04850 | 0525 |
| cotton shorts | 01750 | 01420 | 1500 |

**TIP** In some older operating systems, file names are limited to eight characters, in which case INVENTORY might be an unacceptable file name.

**FIGURE 4-4:** TYPICAL OUTPUT FOR INVENTORY REPORT PROGRAM

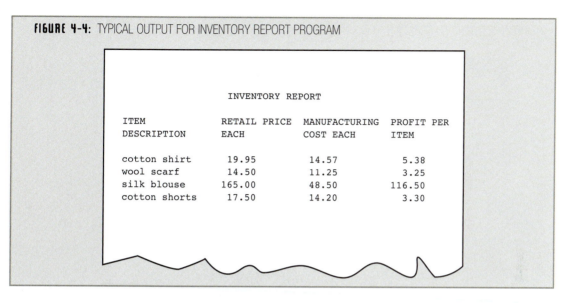

```
                        INVENTORY REPORT

     ITEM              RETAIL PRICE   MANUFACTURING   PROFIT PER
     DESCRIPTION       EACH           COST EACH       ITEM

     cotton shirt       19.95          14.57            5.38
     wool scarf         14.50          11.25            3.25
     silk blouse       165.00          48.50          116.50
     cotton shorts      17.50          14.20            3.30
```

Examine the print chart and the input file description. Your first task is to make sure you understand what the report requires; your next job is to determine whether you have all the data you need to produce the report. (Figure 4-5 shows this process.) The output requires the item name, price, and cost, and you can see that all three are data items on the input file. The output also requires a profit figure for each item; you need to understand how profit is calculated—which could be done differently in various companies. If there is any doubt as to what a term used in the output means or as to how a value is calculated, you must ask the **user**, or your **client**—the person who has requested this program and who will read and use this report to make management decisions. In this case, suppose you are told you can determine the profit by subtracting an item's cost from its selling price. The input record contains an additional field, "Quantity in stock." Input records often contain more data than an application needs, so you will ignore this field in your program. You have all the necessary data, so you can begin to plan the program.

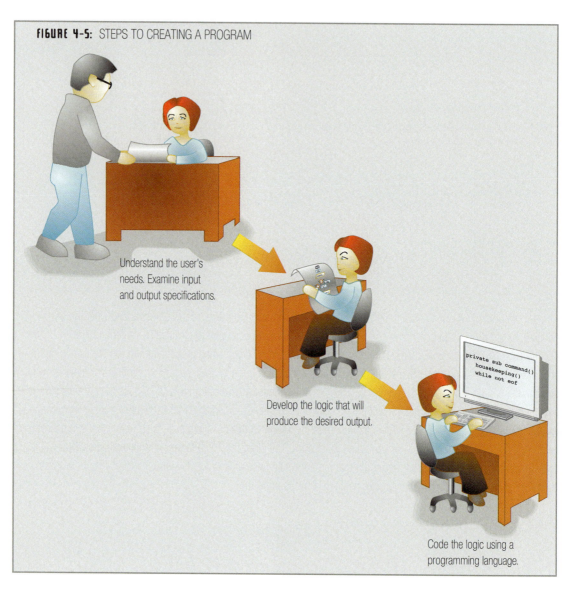

**FIGURE 4-5:** STEPS TO CREATING A PROGRAM

Understand the user's needs. Examine input and output specifications.

Develop the logic that will produce the desired output.

```
private sub command()
    housekeeping()
    while not eof
```

Code the logic using a programming language.

**TIP** ☐ ☐ ☐ ☐   It is very common for input records to contain more data than an application uses. For example, although your doctor stores your blood pressure in your patient record, that field does not appear on your bill, and although your school stores your grades from your first semester, they do not appear on your report card for your second semester.

Where should you begin? It's wise to try to understand the big picture first. You can write a program that reads records from an input file and produces a printed report as a **procedural program**—that is, a program in which one procedure follows another from the beginning until the end. You write the entire set of instructions for a procedural program, and when the program executes, instructions take place one at a time, following your program's logic. The overall logic, or **mainline logic**, of almost every procedural computer program can follow a general structure that consists of three distinct parts:

1. Performing housekeeping, or initialization tasks. **Housekeeping** includes steps you must perform at the beginning of a program to get ready for the rest of the program.
2. Performing the main loop repeatedly within the program. The **main loop** contains the instructions that are executed for every record until you reach the end of the input of records, or `eof`.
3. Performing the end-of-job routine. The **end-of-job routine** holds the steps you take at the end of the program to finish the application.

**TIP** ▫ ▫ ▫ ▫ | Not all programs are procedural; some are object-oriented. A distinguishing feature of many (but not all) object-oriented programs is that they are event-driven; often the user determines the timing of events in the main loop of the program by using an input device such as a mouse. As you advance in your knowledge of programming, you will learn more about object-oriented techniques.

You can write any procedural program as one long series of programming language statements, but most programmers prefer to break their programs into at least three parts. The main program can call the three major modules, as shown in the flowchart and pseudocode in Figure 4-6. The module or subroutine names, of course, are entirely up to the programmer.

**TIP** ▫ ▫ ▫ ▫ | Reducing a large program into more manageable modules is sometimes called **functional decomposition**.

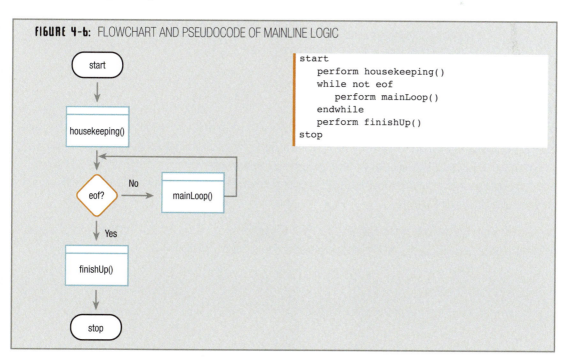

**FIGURE 4-6:** FLOWCHART AND PSEUDOCODE OF MAINLINE LOGIC

```
start
    perform housekeeping()
    while not eof
        perform mainLoop()
    endwhile
    perform finishUp()
stop
```

Figure 4-7 shows the hierarchy chart for this program.

**FIGURE 4-7:** HIERARCHY CHART FOR INVENTORY REPORT PROGRAM

In summary, breaking down a big program into three basic procedures, or modularizing the program, helps keep the job manageable, allowing you to tackle a large job one step at a time. Dividing the work into routines also might allow you to assign the three major procedures to three different programmers, if you choose. It also helps you keep the program structured.

## HOUSEKEEPING TASKS

Housekeeping tasks include all the steps that must take place at the beginning of a program. Very often, this includes four major tasks:

- You declare variables.
- You open files.
- You perform any one-time-only tasks that should occur at the beginning of the program, such as printing headings at the beginning of a report.
- You read the first input record.

### DECLARING VARIABLES

Your first task in writing any program is to declare variables. When you declare variables, you assign reasonable names to memory locations, so you can store and retrieve data there. Declaring a variable involves selecting a name and a type. When you declare a variable in program code, the operating system reserves space in memory to hold the contents of the variable. It uses the type (`num` or `char`) to determine how to store the information; it stores numeric and character values in different formats.

For example, within the inventory report program, you need to supply variable names for the data fields that appear in each input record. You might decide on the variable names and types shown in Figure 4-8.

**FIGURE 4-8:** VARIABLE DECLARATIONS FOR THE INVENTORY FILE

```
char    invItemName
num     invPrice
num     invCost
num     invQuantity
```

TIP □ □ □ □ | Some languages require that you provide storage size, in addition to a type and name, for each variable. Other languages provide a predetermined amount of storage based on the variable type: for example, four bytes for an integer or one byte for a character. Also, many languages require you to provide a length for strings of characters. For simplicity, this book just declares variables as either character or numeric.

You can provide any names you choose for your variables. When you write another program that uses the same input file, you are free to choose completely new variable names. Similarly, other programmers can write programs that use the same file and choose their own variable names. The variable names just represent memory positions, and are internal to your program. The files do not contain any variable names; files contain only data. When you read the characters "cotton shirt" from an input file, it doesn't matter whether you store those characters at a memory location named `invItemName`, `nameOfItem`, `productDescription`, or any other one-word variable name. The variable name is simply an easy-to-remember name for a specific memory address where those characters are stored.

TIP □ □ □ □ | Programmers always must decide between descriptive, but long, variable names and cryptic, but short, variable names. In general, more descriptive names are better, but certain abbreviations are almost always acceptable in the business world. For example, SSN is commonly used as an abbreviation for Social Security number, and if you use it as a variable name, it will be interpreted correctly by most of your associates who read your program.

Each of the four variable declarations in Figure 4-8 contains a type (character or numeric) and a name. You can choose any one-word names for the variables, but a typical practice involves beginning similar variables with a common **prefix**, for example, `inv`. In a large program in which you eventually declare dozens of variables, the `inv` prefix will help you immediately identify a variable as part of the inventory file.

TIP □ □ □ □ | Organizations sometimes enforce different rules for programmers to follow when naming variables. Some use a variable-naming convention called **Hungarian notation**, in which a variable's data type or other information is stored as part of the name.

Creating the inventory report as planned in Figure 4-1 involves using the `invItemName`, `invPrice`, and `invCost` fields, but you do not need to use the `invQuantity` field in this program. However, the information regarding quantity does take room in the input file. If you imagine the surface of a disk as pictured in Figure 4-9, you can envision how the data fields follow one another in the file.

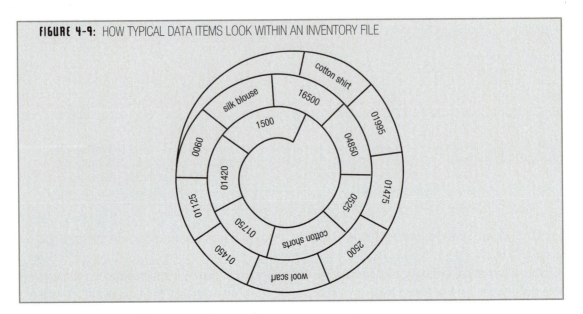

**FIGURE 4-9:** HOW TYPICAL DATA ITEMS LOOK WITHIN AN INVENTORY FILE

When you ask the program to read in an inventory record, four "chunks" of data will be transferred from the input device to the computer's main memory: name, price, cost, and quantity. When you declare the variables that represent the input data, you must provide a memory position for each of the four pieces of data, whether or not they all are used within this program.

**TIP** □ □ □ □  Some languages do not require you to use a unique name for each data field in an input record. For example, in COBOL, you can use the generic name FILLER for all unused data positions. This frees you from the task of creating variable names for items you do not intend to use. The examples in this book always provide a unique identifier for each variable in a file.

**TIP** □ □ □ □  Considering that dozens of programs within the organization might access the INVENTORY file, some organizations create the data file descriptions for you. This system is efficient because the description of variable names and types is stored in one location, and each programmer who uses the file simply imports the data file description into his or her own program. Of course, the organization must provide the programmer with documentation specifying and describing the chosen names.

In most programming languages, you can give a group of associated variables a **group name**. This allows you to handle several associated variables using a single instruction. Just as it is easier to refer to "The Andersons" than it is to list "Nancy, Bud, Jim, Tom, Julie, Jane, Kate, and John," the benefit of using a group name is the ability to reference several variables with one all-encompassing name. For example, writing `read invRecord` is simpler than writing `read invItemName`, `invPrice`, `invCost`, and `invQuantity`. The way you assign a group name to several variables differs in each programming language. This book follows the convention of underlining any group name and indenting the group members beneath, as shown in Figure 4-10.

---

**FIGURE 4-10:** VARIABLE DECLARATIONS FOR THE INVENTORY FILE INCLUDING A GROUP NAME

```
invRecord
        char    invItemName
        num     invPrice
        num     invCost
        num     invQuantity
```

---

**TIP** ▫ ▫ ▫ ▫  A group of variables is often called a *data structure*, or more simply, a *structure*. Some object-oriented languages refer to a group as a *class*, although a class often contains method definitions as well as variables.

**TIP** ▫ ▫ ▫ ▫  The ability to group variable names does not automatically provide you with the ability to perform every sort of operation with a group. For example, you cannot multiply or divide one invRecord by another (unless, with some languages, you write special code to do so). In this book, assume that you can use one input or output statement on a set of fields that constitute a record.

In addition to declaring variables, sometimes you want to provide a variable with an initial value. Providing a variable with a value when you create it is known as **initializing**, or **defining**, **the variable**. For example, for the inventory report print chart shown in Figure 4-1, you might want to create a variable named `mainHeading` and store the value "INVENTORY REPORT" in that variable. The declaration is `char mainHeading = "INVENTORY REPORT"`. This indicates that `mainHeading` is a character variable, and that the character contents are the words "INVENTORY REPORT".

**TIP** ▫ ▫ ▫ ▫  *Declaring* a variable provides it with a name and type. *Defining*, or initializing, a variable also provides it with a value.
In some programming languages, you can declare a variable such as `mainHeading` to be constant, or never changing. Even though `invItemName`, `invPrice`, and the other fields in the input file will hold a variety of values when a program executes, the `mainHeading` value will never change.

In many programming languages, if you do not provide an initial value when declaring a variable, then the value is unknown or **garbage**. Some programming languages do provide you with an automatic starting value; for example in Java, BASIC, or RPG, all numeric variables automatically begin with the value zero. However, in C++, C#, Pascal, and COBOL, variables do not receive any initial value unless you provide one. No matter which programming language you use, it is always clearest to provide a value for those variables that require them.

**TIP** ▫ ▫ ▫ ▫  Be especially careful to make sure all variables you use in calculations have initial values. If you perform arithmetic with garbage values, the result will also contain garbage.

When you declare the variables `invItemName`, `invPrice`, `invCost`, and `invQuantity`, you do not provide them with any initial value. The values for these variables will be assigned when the first file record is read into memory. It would be *legal* to assign a value to input file record variables—for example, `invItemName = "cotton shirt"`—but it would be a waste of time and might mislead others who read your program. The first `invItemName` will come from an input device, and may or may not be "cotton shirt."

The report illustrated in Figure 4-1 contains three individual heading lines. The most common practice is to declare one variable or constant for each of these lines. The three declarations are as follows:

```
char mainHeading = "INVENTORY REPORT"
char columnHead1 = "ITEM            RETAIL PRICE
      MANUFACTURING        PROFIT PER"
char columnHead2 = "DESCRIPTION   EACH
      COST EACH          ITEM"
```

Within the program, when it is time to write the heading lines to an output device, you will code:

```
print mainHeading
print columnHead1
print columnHead2
```

You are not required to create variables for your headings. Your program can contain the following statements, in which you use literal strings of characters instead of variable names. The printed results are the same either way.

```
print "INVENTORY REPORT"
print "ITEM            RETAIL PRICE   MANUFACTURING   PROFIT PER"
print "DESCRIPTION   EACH            COST EACH       ITEM"
```

Using variable names, as in `print mainHeading`, is usually more convenient than spelling out the heading's contents within the statement that prints, especially if you will use the headings in multiple locations within your program. Additionally, if the contents of all of a program's heading lines can be found in one location at the start of the program, it is easier to locate them all if changes need to be made in the future.

**TIP** □ □ □ □  When you write a program, you type spaces between the words within column headings so the spacing matches the print chart you created for the program. For convenience, some languages provide you with a tab character. The goal is to provide well-spaced output in readable columns.

Dividing the headings into three lines is not required either, but it is a common practice. In most programming languages, you could write all the headings in one statement, using a code that indicates a new line at every appropriate position. Alternately, most programming languages let you produce a character for output without advancing to a new line. You could write out the headings using separate print statements to display one character at a time, advancing to a new line only after all the line's characters had been individually printed, although this approach seems painstakingly detailed. Storing and writing one complete line at a time is a reasonable compromise.

Every programming language provides you with a means to physically advance printer paper to the top of a page when you print the first heading. Similarly, every language provides you with a means for producing double- and triple-spaced lines of text by sending specific codes to the printer or monitor. Because the methods and codes differ from language to language, examples in this book assume that if a print chart shows a heading that prints at the top of the page and then skips a line, any corresponding variable you create, such as `mainHeading`, will also print in this manner. You can add the appropriate language-specific codes to implement the `mainHeading` spacing when you write the actual computer program. Similarly, if you create a print chart that shows detail lines as double-spaced, assume your detail lines will double-space when you execute the step to write them.

Often, you must create dozens of variables when you write a computer program. If you are using a flowchart to diagram the logic, it is physically impossible to fit the variables in one flowchart box. Therefore, you might want to use an annotation symbol. The beginning of a flowchart for the `housekeeping()` module of the inventory report program is shown in Figure 4-11.

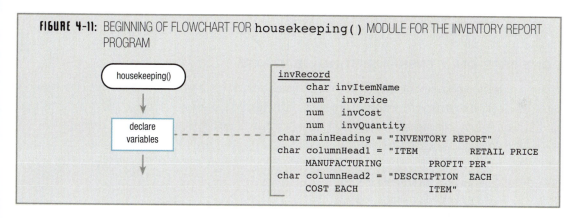

**FIGURE 4-11:** BEGINNING OF FLOWCHART FOR `housekeeping()` MODULE FOR THE INVENTORY REPORT PROGRAM

```
invRecord
       char invItemName
       num    invPrice
       num    invCost
       num    invQuantity
char mainHeading = "INVENTORY REPORT"
char columnHead1 = "ITEM          RETAIL PRICE
       MANUFACTURING        PROFIT PER"
char columnHead2 = "DESCRIPTION   EACH
       COST EACH            ITEM"
```

**TIP** □ □ □ □ | You learned about the annotation symbol in Chapter 3.

Notice that the three heading variables defined in Figure 4-11 are not indented under `invRecord` as the `invRecord` fields are. This shows that although `invItemName`, `invPrice`, `invCost`, and `invQuantity` are part of the `invRecord` group, `mainHeading`, `columnHead1`, and `columnHead2` are not.

In Figure 4-11, notice that columnHead1 contains only the words that appear in the first line of column headings, in row 4 of the print chart in Figure 4-1: "ITEM     RETAIL PRICE     MANUFACTURING     PROFIT PER". Similarly, columnHead2 contains only the words that appear in the second row of column headings.

## OPENING FILES

If a program will use input files, you must tell the computer where the input is coming from—for example, a specific disk drive, CD, or tape drive. This process is known as **opening a file**. Because a disk can have many files stored on it, the program also needs to know the name of the file being opened. In many languages, if no input file is opened, input is accepted from a default or **standard input device**, most often the keyboard.

If a program will have output, you must also open a file for output. Perhaps the output file will be sent to a disk or tape. Although you might not think of a printed report as a file, computers treat a printer as just another output device, and if output will go to a printer, then you must open the printer output device as well. Again, if no file is opened, a default or **standard output device**, usually the monitor, is used.

When you create a flowchart, you usually write the command to open the files within a parallelogram. You use the parallelogram because it is the input/output symbol, and you are opening the input and output devices. You can use an annotation box to list the files that you open, as shown in Figure 4-12.

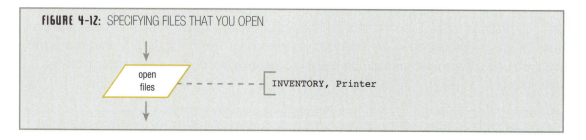

**FIGURE 4-12:** SPECIFYING FILES THAT YOU OPEN

## A ONE-TIME-ONLY TASK—PRINTING HEADINGS

Within a program's housekeeping module, besides declaring variables and opening files, you perform any other tasks that occur only at the beginning of the program. A common housekeeping task involves printing headings at the top of a report. In the inventory report example, three lines of headings appear at the beginning of the report. In this example, printing the heading lines is straightforward:

```
print mainHeading
print columnHead1
print columnHead2
```

## READING THE FIRST INPUT RECORD

The last task you execute in the `housekeeping()` module of most computer programs is to read the first data record into memory. When you read the four data fields for the inventory file data, you can write `read invItemName, invPrice, invCost, invQuantity`, but if you have declared a group name such as `invRecord`, it is simpler to write `read invRecord`. Using the group name is a shortcut for writing each field name.

The last task within the `housekeeping()` module is to read the first `invRecord`; the first task following `housekeeping()` is to check for `eof` on the file that contains the inventory records. An input device recognizes that it has reached the end of a file when it attempts to read a record and finds no records available. Recall the mainline logic of the inventory report program from Figure 4-6—`eof` is tested immediately after `housekeeping()` ends.

If the input file has no records, when you read the first record the computer recognizes the end-of-file condition and proceeds to the `finishUp()` module, never executing `mainLoop()`. More commonly, an input file does have records, and after the first `read` the computer determines that the `eof` condition is false, and the logic proceeds to the `mainLoop()`.

Immediately after reading from a file, the next step always should determine whether `eof` was encountered. Notice in Figure 4-6 that the `eof` question always follows both the `housekeeping()` module and the `mainLoop()` module. When the last instruction in each of these modules reads a record, then the `eof` question correctly follows each `read` instruction immediately.

Not reading the first record within the `housekeeping()` module is a mistake. If `housekeeping()` does not include a step to read a record from the input file, you must read a record as the first step in the `mainLoop()`, as shown on the left side of Figure 4-13. In this program, a record is read, a profit is calculated, and a line is printed. Then, if it is not `eof`, another record is read, a profit calculated, and a line printed. The program works well, reading records, calculating profits, and printing information until reaching a `read` command in which the computer encounters the `eof` condition. When this last read occurs, the next steps involve computing a profit and writing a line—but there isn't any data to process. Depending on the programming language you use, either garbage data will calculate and print, or a repeat of the data from the last record before `eof` will print.

TIP ▫ ▫ ▫ ▫ | Reading an input record in the `housekeeping()` section is an example of a priming read. You learned about the priming read in Chapter 2.
In some modern programming languages, such as Visual Basic, file `read` commands can look ahead to determine if the *next* record is empty. With these languages, the priming read is no longer necessary. Because most languages do not currently have this type of read statement, and because the priming read is always necessary when input is based on user response rather than reading from a file, this book uses the conventional priming read.

The flowchart in the lower part of Figure 4-13 shows correct record-reading logic. The appropriate place for the priming record `read` is at the end of the preliminary housekeeping steps, and the appropriate place for all subsequent reads is at the end of the main processing loop.

**FIGURE 4-13:** COMPARING FAULTY AND CORRECT RECORD-READING LOGIC

FAULTY RECORD-READING LOGIC

```
start
    │
    ▼
┌──────────────┐
│ housekeeping()│
│  (without    │
│   read)      │
└──────────────┘
    │
    ▼
  ◇ eof? ◇ ──No──▶ ╱ read      ╱
    │              ╱ InvRecord ╱
   Yes             │
    │              ▼
    ▼           ┌──────────┐
              │ profit = │
              │ invPrice │
              │    −     │
              │ invCost  │
              └──────────┘
                   │
                   ▼
              ╱ print        ╱
              ╱ invItemName, ╱
              ╱ invPrice,    ╱
              ╱ invCost,profit╱
```

```
FAULTY RECORD-READING LOGIC
start
     perform housekeeping() (without read)
     while not eof
          read invRecord
          profit = invPrice - invCost
          print invItemName, invPrice, invCost, profit
     endwhile
```

CORRECT RECORD-READING LOGIC

```
start
    │
    ▼
┌──────────────┐
│ housekeeping()│
│  (with read) │
└──────────────┘
    │
    ▼
  ◇ eof? ◇ ──No──▶ ┌──────────┐
    │              │ profit = │
   Yes             │ invPrice │
    │              │    −     │
    ▼              │ invCost  │
                   └──────────┘
                        │
                        ▼
                   ╱ print        ╱
                   ╱ invItemName, ╱
                   ╱ InvPrice,    ╱
                   ╱ invCost,profit╱
                        │
                        ▼
                   ╱ read      ╱
                   ╱ InvRecord ╱
```

```
CORRECT RECORD-READING LOGIC
start
     perform housekeeping() (with read)
     while not eof
          profit = invPrice - invCost
          print invItemName, invPrice, invCost, profit
          read invRecord
     endwhile
```

Figure 4-14 shows a completed `housekeeping()` routine for the inventory program in both flowchart and pseudocode versions.

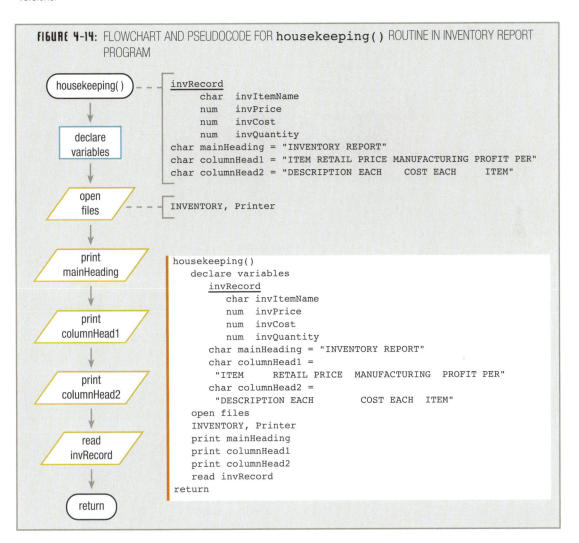

**FIGURE 4-14:** FLOWCHART AND PSEUDOCODE FOR `housekeeping()` ROUTINE IN INVENTORY REPORT PROGRAM

As an alternative to including `print mainHeading`, `print columnHead1`, and `print columnHead2` within the `housekeeping()` module, you can place the three heading line statements in their own subroutine. In this case, the flowchart and pseudocode for `housekeeping()` will look like Figure 4-15, with the steps in the newly created `headings()` module appearing in Figure 4-16. Either approach is fine; the logic of the program is the same whether or not the heading line statements are segregated into their own routine. The programmer can decide on the program organization that makes the most sense.

**FIGURE 4-15:** FLOWCHART AND PSEUDOCODE FOR ALTERNATIVE `housekeeping()` MODULE THAT CALLS `headings()` MODULE

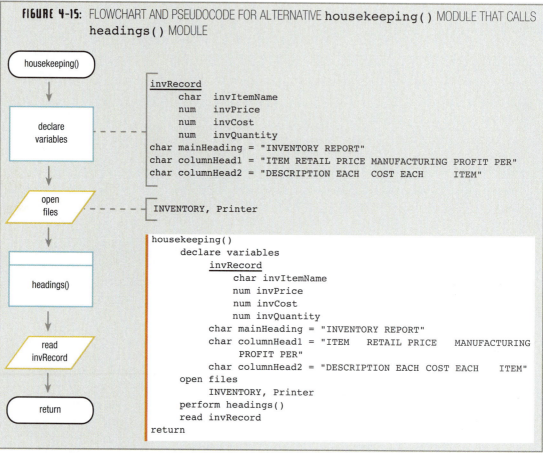

```
housekeeping()
    declare variables
        invRecord
            char invItemName
            num invPrice
            num invCost
            num invQuantity
        char mainHeading = "INVENTORY REPORT"
        char columnHead1 = "ITEM    RETAIL PRICE    MANUFACTURING
            PROFIT PER"
        char columnHead2 = "DESCRIPTION EACH COST EACH    ITEM"
    open files
        INVENTORY, Printer
    perform headings()
    read invRecord
return
```

**FIGURE 4-16:** FLOWCHART AND PSEUDOCODE FOR `headings()` MODULE CALLED BY MAINLINE IN FIGURE 4-15

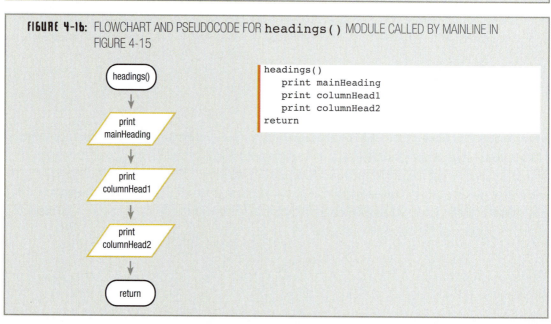

```
headings()
    print mainHeading
    print columnHead1
    print columnHead2
return
```

## WRITING THE MAIN LOOP

After you declare the variables for a program and perform the housekeeping tasks, the "real work" of the program begins. The inventory report described at the beginning of this chapter and depicted in Figure 4-1 needs just one set of variables and one set of headings, yet there might be hundreds or thousands of inventory items to process. The main loop of a program, controlled by the `eof` decision, is the program's "workhorse." Each data record will pass once through the main loop, where calculations are performed with the data and the results printed.

**TIP** □ □ □ □   If the inventory report contains more records than will fit on a page of output, you probably will want to print a new set of headings at the top of each page. You will learn how to do this in Chapter 7.

For the inventory report program to work, the `mainLoop()` module must include three steps:

1. Calculate the profit for an item.
2. Print the item information on the report.
3. Read the next inventory record.

At the end of `housekeeping()`, you read one data record into the computer's memory. As the first step in the `mainLoop()`, you can calculate an item's profit by subtracting its manufacturing cost from its retail price: `profit = invPrice - invCost`. The name `profit` is the programmer-created variable name for a new spot in computer memory where the value of the profit is stored. Although it is legal to use any variable name to represent profit, naming it `invProfit` would be misleading. Using the `inv` prefix would lead those who read your program to believe that profit was part of the input record, like the other variable names that start with `inv`. The profit is not part of the input record however; it represents a memory location used to store the arithmetic difference between two other variables.

**TIP** □ □ □ □   Recall that the standard way to express mathematical statements is to assign values from the right side of an equal sign to the left. That is, `profit = invPrice - invCost` assigns a value to `profit`. The statement `invPrice - invCost = profit` is an illegal statement.

Because you have a new variable, you must add `profit` to the list of declared variables at the beginning of the program. Programmers often work back and forth between the variable list and the logical steps during the creation of a program, listing some of the variables they will need as soon as they start to plan, and adding others later as they think of them. Because `profit` will hold the result of a mathematical calculation, you should declare it as a numeric variable when you add it to the variable list, as shown in Figure 4-17. Notice that, like the headings, `profit` is not indented under `invRecord`. You want to show that `profit` is not part of the `invRecord` group; instead, it is a separate variable that you are declaring to store a calculated value.

**TIP** □ □ □ □   You can declare `mainHeading`, `columnHead1`, `columnHead2`, and `profit` in any order. The important point is that none of these four variables is part of the `invRecord` group.

**FIGURE 4-17:** VARIABLE LIST FOR INVENTORY REPORT PROGRAM, INCLUDING PROFIT

```
invRecord
   char   invItemName
   num    invPrice
   num    invCost
   num    invQuantity
char mainHeading = "INVENTORY         REPORT"
char columnHead1 = "ITEM              RETAIL PRICE   MANUFACTURING   PROFIT PER"
char columnHead2 = "DESCRIPTION       EACH           COST EACH       ITEM"
num profit
```

After you determine an item's profit, you can write a detail line of information on the inventory report: `print invItemName, invPrice, invCost, profit`. Notice that in the flowchart and pseudocode for the `mainLoop()` routine in Figure 4-15, the output statement is not `print invRecord`. For one thing, the entire `invRecord` is not printed—the quantity is not part of the report. Also, the calculated profit is included in the detail line—it does not appear on the input record. Even if the report detail lines listed each of the `invRecord` fields in the exact same order as on the input file, the print statement still would most often be written listing the individual fields to be printed. Usually, you would include a formatting statement with each printed field to control the spacing within the detail line. Because the way you space fields on detail lines differs greatly in programming languages, discussion of the syntax to space fields is not included in this book. However, the fields that are printed are listed separately, as you would usually do when coding in a specific programming language.

The last step in the `mainLoop()` module of the inventory report program involves reading in the next `invRecord`. Figure 4-18 shows the flowchart and pseudocode for `mainLoop()`.

Just as headings are printed one full line at a time, detail lines are also printed one line at a time. You can print each field separately, as in the following code, but it is clearer and most efficient to write one full line at a time, as shown in Figure 4-18.

```
print invItemName
print invPrice
print invCost
print profit
```

In most programming languages, you also have the option of calculating the profit and printing it in one statement, as in the following:

```
print invItemName, invPrice, invCost, invPrice - invCost
```

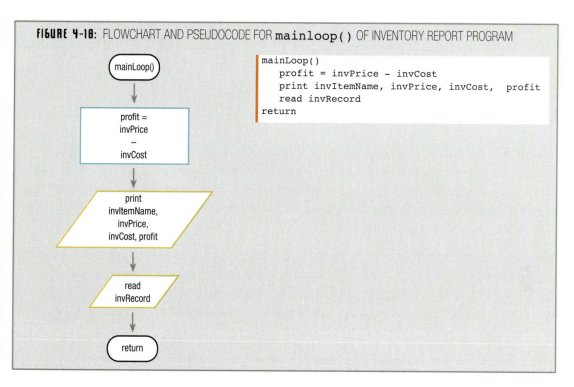

**FIGURE 4-18:** FLOWCHART AND PSEUDOCODE FOR `mainloop()` OF INVENTORY REPORT PROGRAM

```
mainLoop()
    profit = invPrice - invCost
    print invItemName, invPrice, invCost,  profit
    read invRecord
return
```

If the language you use allows this type of statement, in which a calculation takes place within the output statement, it is up to you to decide which format to use. Performing the arithmetic as part of the `print` statement allows you to avoid declaring a `profit` variable. However, if you need the `profit` figure for further calculations, then it makes sense to compute the profit and store it in a `profit` field. Using a separate **work variable** or **work field** such as `profit` to temporarily hold a calculation is never wrong, and often it's the clearest course of action.

**TIP** ▫ ▫ ▫ ▫  As with performing arithmetic within a print statement, different languages often provide multiple ways to combine several steps into one. For example, many languages allow you to print multiple lines of output or read a record and check for end of file using one statement. This book uses only the most common combinations, such as performing arithmetic within a print statement.

**TIP** ▫ ▫ ▫ ▫  Although a language may allow you to combine actions in a single statement, you are never required to do so. If the program is clearer using separate statements, then that is what you should do.

After the detail line containing the item name, price, cost, and profit has been written, the last step you take before leaving the `mainLoop()` module is to read the next record from the input file into memory. When you exit the `mainLoop()`, the logic flows back to the `eof` question in the mainline logic. If it is not `eof`—that is, if an additional data record exists—then you enter the `mainLoop()` again, compute profit on the second record, print the detail line, and read the third record.

Eventually, during an execution of the `mainLoop()`, the program will read a new record and encounter the end of the file. Then, when you ask the `eof` question in the main line of the program, the answer will be *yes*, and the program will not enter the `mainLoop()` again. Instead, the program logic will enter the `finishUp()` routine.

## PERFORMING END-OF-JOB TASKS

Within any program, the end-of-job routine holds the steps you must take at the end of the program, after all input records are processed. Some end-of-job modules print summaries or grand totals at the end of a report. Others might print a message such as "End of Report," so readers can be confident that they have received all the information that should be included. Such end-of-job message lines often are called **footer lines**, or **footers** for short. Very often, end-of-job modules must close any open files.

The end-of-job module for the inventory report program is very simple. The print chart does not indicate that any special messages, such as "Thank you for reading this report", print after the detail lines end. Likewise, there are no required summary or total lines; nothing special happens. Only one task needs to be performed in the end-of-job routine that this program calls `finishUp()`. In `housekeeping()`, you opened files; in `finishUp()`, you close them. The complete `finishUp()` module is flowcharted and written in pseudocode in Figure 4-19.

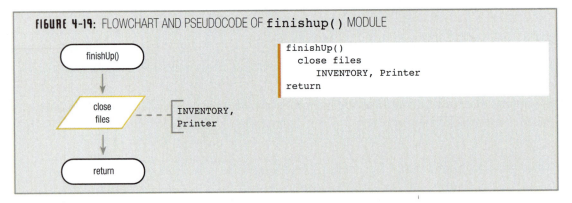

**FIGURE 4-19**: FLOWCHART AND PSEUDOCODE OF `finishup()` MODULE

Many programmers wouldn't bother with a subroutine for just one statement, but as you create more complicated programs, your end-of-job routines will get bigger, and it will make more sense to see the necessary job-finishing tasks together in a module.

For your convenience, Figure 4-20 shows the flowchart and pseudocode for the entire inventory report program. Make sure you understand the importance of each flowchart symbol and each pseudocode line. There is nothing superfluous—each is included to accomplish a specific part of the program that creates the completed inventory report.

**FIGURE 4-20:** FLOWCHART AND PSEUDOCODE FOR INVENTORY REPORT PROGRAM

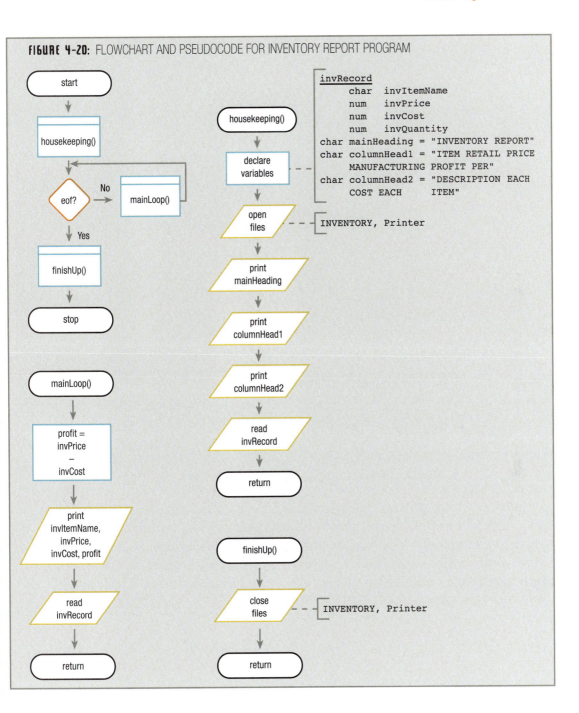

**FIGURE 4-20:** FLOWCHART AND PSEUDOCODE FOR INVENTORY REPORT PROGRAM (CONTINUED)

```
start                              housekeeping()
   perform housekeeping()            declare variables
   while not eof                        invRecord
        perform mainLoop()                  char    invItemName
   endwhile                                 num     invPrice
   perform finishUp()                       num     invCost
stop                                        num     invQuantity
                                     char mainHeading = "INVENTORY REPORT"
                                     char columnHead1 =
                                      "ITEM          RETAIL PRICE  MANUFACTURING  PROFIT PER"
                                     char columnHead2 =
                                      "DESCRIPTION EACH          COST EACH      ITEM"
                                     open files
                                        INVENTORY, Printer
                                     print mainHeading
                                     print columnHead1
                                     print columnHead2
                                     read invRecord
                                  return


mainLoop()                                           finishUp()
   profit = invPrice - invCost                          close files
   print invItemName, invPrice, invCost,  profit           INVENTORY, Printer
   read invRecord                                     return
return
```

## UNDERSTANDING THE NEED FOR GOOD PROGRAM DESIGN

As your programs become larger and more complicated, the need for good planning and design increases. Think of an application you use, such as a word processor or a spreadsheet. The number and variety of user options are staggering. Not only would it be impossible for a single programmer to write such an application, but without thorough planning and design, the components would never work together properly. Ideally, each program module you design needs to work well as a stand-alone module and as an element of larger systems. Just as a house with poor plumbing or a car with bad brakes is fatally flawed, a computer-based application can be great only if each component is designed well.

## STORING PROGRAM COMPONENTS IN SEPARATE FILES

When you start to work on professional programs, you will see that many of them are quite lengthy, with some containing hundreds of variables and thousands of lines of code. Earlier in this chapter, you learned you can manage lengthy procedural programs by breaking them into modules. Although modularization helps you to organize your programs, sometimes it is still difficult to manage all of a program's components.

Most modern programming languages allow you to store program components in separate files. If you write a module and store it in the same file as the program that uses it, your program files become large and hard to work with, whether you are trying to read them on a screen or on multiple printed pages. In addition, when you define a useful module, you might want to use it in many programs. Of course, you can copy module definitions from one file to another, but this method is time-consuming as well as prone to error. A better solution (if you are using a language that allows it) is to store your modules in individual files and use an instruction to include them in any program that uses them. The statement needed to access modules from separate files varies from language to language, but it usually involves using a verb such as *include*, *import*, or *copy*, followed by the name of the file that contains the module.

For example, suppose your company has a standard employee record definition, part of which is shown in Figure 4-21. Files with the same format are used in many applications within the organization—personnel reports, production reports, payroll, and so on. It would be a tremendous waste of resources if every programmer rewrote this file definition in multiple applications. Instead, once a programmer writes the statements that constitute the file definition, those statements should be imported in their entirety into any program that uses a record with the same structure. For example, Figure 4-22 shows how the data fields in Figure 4-21 would be defined in the C++ programming language. If the statements in Figure 4-22 are saved in a file named Employees, then any C++ program can contain the statement `#include Employees` and all the data fields are automatically defined.

**TIP** ▢ ▢ ▢ ▢  The pound sign (#) is used with the include statement in C++ to notify the compiler that it is part of a special type of statement called a *pre-processor directive*.

**FIGURE 4-21:** PARTIAL EMPLOYEES FILE DESCRIPTION

*EMPLOYEE FILE DESCRIPTION*

*FILE NAME: EMPLOYEES*

| Field description | Data type | Decimals |
|---|---|---|
| Employee ID | numeric | 0 |
| Last name | character | |
| First name | character | |
| Hire date | numeric | 0 |
| Hourly wage | numeric | 2 |
| Birth date | numeric | 0 |
| Termination date | numeric | 0 |

**FIGURE 4-22:** DATA FIELDS IN FIGURE 4-21 DEFINED IN THE C++ LANGUAGE

```
class Employee
{
     int employeeID;
     string lastName;
     string firstName;
     long hireDate;
     double hourlyWage;
     long birthDate;
     long terminationDate;
};
```

**TIP** ▫ ▫ ▫ ▫  Don't be concerned with the syntax used in the file description in Figure 4-22. The words *class*, *int*, *string*, *long*, and *double* are all part of the C++ programming language and are not important to you now. Simply concentrate on how the variable names reflect the field descriptions in Figure 4-21.

Suppose you write a useful module that checks dates to guarantee their validity. For example, the two digits that represent a month can be neither less than 01 nor greater than 12, and the two digits that represent the day can contain different possible values, depending on the month. Any program that uses the employee file description shown in Figure 4-21 might want to call the date-validating module several times in order to validate any employee's hire date, birth date, and termination date. Not only do you want to call this module from several locations within any one program, you want to call it from many programs. For example, programs used for company ordering and billing would each contain several dates. If the date-validating module is useful and well-written, you might even want to market it to other companies. By storing the module in its own file, you enable its use to be flexible. When you write a program of any length, you should consider storing each of its components in its own file.

Storing components in separate files can provide an advantage beyond ease of reuse. When you let others use your programs or modules, you often provide them with only the compiled (that is, machine-language) version of your code, not the **source code**, which is composed of readable statements. Storing your program statements in a separate, non-readable, compiled file is an example of **implementation hiding**, or hiding the details of how the program or module works. Other programmers can use your code, but cannot see the statements you used to create it. A programmer who cannot see your well-designed modules is more likely to use them simply as they were intended; the programmer also will not be able to attempt to make adjustments in your code, thereby introducing error. Of course, in order to work with your modules or data definitions, a programmer must know the names and types of data you are using. Typically, you provide programmers who use your definitions with written documentation of the data names and purposes.

**TIP** ▫ ▫ ▫ ▫  Recall from Chapter 1 that when you write a program in a programming language, you must compile or interpret it into machine language before the computer can actually carry out your instructions.

## SELECTING VARIABLE AND MODULE NAMES

An often-overlooked element in program design is the selection of good data and module names (sometimes generically called **identifiers**). In Chapter 1, you learned that every programming language has specific rules for the construction of names—some languages limit the number of characters, some allow dashes, and so on—but there are other general guidelines:

- Use meaningful names. Creating a data field named `someData` or a module named `firstModule()` makes a program cryptic. Not only will others find it hard to read your programs, but you will forget the purpose of these identifiers even within your own programs. All programmers occasionally use short, nondescriptive names such as `x` or `temp` in a quick program written to test a procedure; however, in most cases, data and module names should be meaningful. Programmers refer to programs that contain meaningful names as **self-documenting**. This means that even without further documentation, the program code explains itself to readers.

- Usually, you should use pronounceable names. A variable name like `pzf` is neither pronounceable nor meaningful. A name that looks meaningful when you write it might not be as meaningful when someone else reads it; for instance, `preparead()` might mean "Prepare ad" to you, but is "Prep a read" to others. Look at your names critically to make sure they are pronounceable. Very standard abbreviations do not have to be pronounceable. For example, most business people would interpret `ssn` as a Social Security number.

**TIP** ▫ ▫ ▫ ▫ | Don't forget that not all programmers share your culture. An abbreviation whose meaning seems obvious to you might be cryptic to someone in a different part of the world.

- Be judicious in your use of abbreviations. You can save a few keystrokes when creating a module called `getStat()`, but is its purpose to find the state in which a city is located, output some statistics, or determine the status of some variables? Similarly, is a variable named `fn` meant to hold a first name, file number, or something else?

**TIP** ▫ ▫ ▫ ▫ | To save typing time when you develop a program, you can use a short name like `efn`. After the program operates correctly, you can use an editor's Search and Replace feature to replace your coded name with a more meaningful name such as `employeeFirstName`. Some newer compilers support an automatic statement completion feature that saves typing time. After the first time you use a name like `employeeFirstName`, you need to type only the first few letters before the compiler editor offers a list of available names from which to choose. The list is constructed from all names you have used in the file that begin with the same characters.

- Usually, avoid digits in a name. Zeroes get confused with the letter "O", and lowercase "l"s are misread as the numeral 1. Of course, use your judgment: `budgetFor2005` is probably not going to be misinterpreted.

- Use the system your language allows to separate words in long, multiword variable names. For example, if the programming language you use allows dashes or underscores, then use a method name like `initialize-data()` or `initialize_data()`, which is easier to read than `initializedata()`. If you use a language that allows camel casing, then use `initializeData()`. If you use a language that is case sensitive, it is legal but confusing to use variable names that differ only in case, for example `empName`, `EmpName`, and `Empname`.

■ Consider including a form of the verb *to be*, such as *is* or *are*, in names for variables that are intended to hold a status. For example, use `isFinished` as a flag variable that holds a "Y" or "N" to indicate whether a file is exhausted. The shorter name `finished` is likely to be confused with a module that executes when a program is done.

When you begin to write programs, the process of determining what data variables and modules you will need and what to name them all might seem overwhelming. The design process is crucial, however. When you acquire your first professional programming assignment, the design process might very well be completed already. Most likely, your first assignment will be to write or make modifications to one small member module of a much larger application. The more the original programmers stuck to these guidelines, the better the original design was, and the easier your job of modification will be.

## DESIGNING CLEAR MODULE STATEMENTS

In addition to selecting good identifiers, you can use the following tactics to contribute to the clarity of the statements within your program modules.

■ Avoid confusing line breaks.

■ Use temporary variables to clarify long statements.

■ Use constants where appropriate.

### AVOIDING CONFUSING LINE BREAKS

Some older programming languages require that program statements be placed in specific columns. Most modern programming languages are free-form; you can arrange your lines of code any way you see fit. As in real life, with freedom comes responsibility; when you have flexibility in arranging your lines of code, you must take care to make sure your meaning is clear. With free-form code, programmers often do not provide enough line breaks, or they provide inappropriate ones.

Figure 4-23 shows an example of code (part of the housekeeping module from Figure 4-14) that does not provide enough line breaks for clarity. If you have been following the examples used throughout this book, the code in Figure 4-24 looks clearer to you; it will also look clearer to most other programmers.

**FIGURE 4-23:** PART OF A `housekeeping()` MODULE WITH INSUFFICIENT LINE BREAKS

```
open files   print mainHeading   print columnHead1
  print columnHead2   read invRecord
```

---

**FIGURE 4-24:** PART OF A `housekeeping()` MODULE WITH APPROPRIATE LINE BREAKS

```
open files
print mainHeading
print columnHead1
print columnHead2
read invRecord
```

---

Figure 4-24 shows that more, but shorter, lines usually improve your ability to understand a program's logic; appropriately breaking lines will become even more important as you introduce decisions and loops into your programs in the next chapters.

## USING TEMPORARY VARIABLES TO CLARIFY LONG STATEMENTS

When you need several mathematical operations to determine a result, consider using a series of temporary variables to hold intermediate results. For example, Figure 4-25 shows two ways to calculate a value for a real estate `salespersonCommission` variable. Each method achieves the same result—the salesperson's commission is based on the square feet multiplied by the price per square foot plus any premium for a lot with special features, such as a wooded or waterfront lot. However, the second example uses two temporary variables, `sqFootPrice` and `totalPrice`. When the computation is broken down into less complicated, individual steps, it is easier to see how the total price is calculated. In calculations with even more computation steps, performing the arithmetic in stages would become increasingly helpful.

**TIP** ☐ ☐ ☐ ☐  Programmers might say using temporary variables, like the example in Figure 4-25, is *cheap*. When executing a lengthy arithmetic statement, even if you don't explicitly name temporary variables, the programming language compiler creates them behind the scenes, so declaring them yourself does not cost much in terms of program execution time.

---

**FIGURE 4-25:** TWO WAYS OF ACHIEVING THE SAME `salespersonCommission` RESULT

```
salespersonCommission = (sqFeet * pricePerSquareFoot + lotPremium) *
    commissionRate
sqFootPrice = sqFeet * pricePerSquareFoot
totalPrice = sqFootPrice + lotPremium
salespersonCommission = totalPrice * commissionRate
```

---

## USING CONSTANTS WHERE APPROPRIATE

Whenever possible, use named values in your programs. If your program contains a statement like `salesTax = price * taxRate` instead of `salesTax = price * .06`, you gain two benefits:

- It is easier for readers to know that the price is being multiplied by a tax rate instead of a discount, commission, or some other rate represented by .06.

- When the tax rate changes, you make one change to the value where `taxRate` is defined, rather than searching through a program for every instance of .06.

For example, the program segment in Figure 4-26 uses the constants `tuitionPerCreditHour` and `athleticFee`. If the values of these variables change in the future, then the changes to the constants can be made in the declaration list, and the actual program code does not have to be disturbed.

**FIGURE 4-26:** PROGRAM SEGMENT THAT CALCULATES STUDENT BALANCE DUE USING DEFINED CONSTANTS

```
declare variables
    studentRecord
          num studentId
          num creditsEnrolled
    num tuitionDue
    num totalDue
    num tuitionPerCreditHour = 74.50
    num athleticFee = 25.00
read studentRecord
tuitionDue = creditsEnrolled * tuitionPerCreditHour
totalDue = tuitionDue + athleticFee
```

**TIP** ▫ ▫ ▫ ▫ | Some programmers refer to numeric constants that are hard coded into a program as "magic numbers." They feel that using magic numbers should always be avoided, and that you should provide a descriptive name for every numeric constant you use.

## MAINTAINING GOOD PROGRAMMING HABITS

When you learn a programming language and begin to write lines of program code, it is easy to forget the principles you have learned in this text. Having some programming knowledge and a keyboard at your fingertips can lure you into typing lines of code before you think things through. But every program you write will be better if you plan before you code. If you maintain the habits of first drawing flowcharts or writing pseudocode, as you have learned here, your future programming projects will go more smoothly. If you walk through your program logic on paper (called **desk-checking**) before starting to type statements in C++, COBOL, Visual Basic, or Java, your programs will run correctly sooner. If you think carefully about the variable and module names you use, and design your program statements so they are easy for others to read, you will be rewarded with programs that are easier to get up and running, and are easier to maintain as well.

## CHAPTER SUMMARY

- ☐ When you write a complete program, you first determine whether you have all the necessary data to produce the report. Then, you plan the mainline logic, which usually includes modules to perform housekeeping, a main loop that contains the steps that repeat for every record, and an end-of-job routine.

- ☐ Housekeeping tasks include all steps that must take place at the beginning of a program. These tasks include declaring variables, opening files, performing any one-time-only tasks—such as printing headings at the beginning of a report—and reading the first input record.

- ☐ The main loop of a program is controlled by the `eof` decision. Each data record passes once through the main loop, where calculations are performed with the data and results are printed.

- ☐ Within any program, the end-of-job module holds the steps you must take at the end of the program, after all the input records have been processed. Typical tasks include printing summaries, grand totals, or final messages at the end of a report, and closing all open files.

- ☐ As your programs become larger and more complicated, the need for good planning and design increases.

- ☐ Most modern programming languages allow you to store program components in separate files and use instructions to include them in any program that uses them. Storing components in separate files can provide the advantages of easy reuse and implementation hiding.

- ☐ When selecting data and module names, use meaningful, pronounceable names. Be judicious in your use of abbreviations, avoid digits in a name, and visually separate words in multiword names. Consider including a form of the verb *to be*, such as *is* or *are*, in names for variables and those that are intended to hold a status.

- ☐ When writing program statements, you should avoid confusing line breaks, use temporary variables to clarify long statements, and use constants where appropriate.

## KEY TERMS

A **user**, or **client**, is a person who requests a program, and who will actually use the output of the program.

A **procedural program** is a program in which one procedure follows another from the beginning until the end.

The **mainline logic** of a program is the overall logic of the main program from beginning to end.

A **housekeeping** module includes steps you must perform at the beginning of a program, to get ready for the rest of the program.

The **main loop** of a program contains the steps that are repeated for every record.

The **end-of-job routine** holds the steps you take at the end of the program, to finish the application.

**Functional decomposition** is the act of reducing a large program into more manageable modules.

A **prefix** is a set of characters used at the beginning of related variable names.

**Hungarian notation** is a variable-naming convention in which a variable's data type or other information is stored as part of its name.

A **group name** is a name for a group of associated variables.

**Initializing**, or **defining**, **a variable** is the process of providing a variable with a value, as well as a name and a type, when you create it.

**Garbage** is the unknown value of an undefined variable.

**Opening a file** is the process of telling the computer where the input is coming from—for example, a specific disk drive, CD, or tape drive.

The **standard input device** is the default device from which input comes, most often the keyboard.

The **standard output device** is the default device to which output is sent, usually the monitor.

A **work variable**, or **work field**, is a variable you use to temporarily hold a calculation.

**Footer lines**, or **footers**, are end-of-job message lines.

**Source code** is the readable statements of a program, written in a programming language.

**Implementation hiding** is hiding the details of the way a program or module works.

**Identifiers** are the names of variables and modules.

**Self-documenting** programs are those that contain meaningful data and module names that describe the programs' purpose.

**Desk-checking** is the process of walking through a program's logic on paper.

## REVIEW QUESTIONS

1. **Input records usually contain _____.**
   a. less data than an application needs
   b. more data than an application needs
   c. exactly the amount of data an application needs
   d. none of the data an application needs

2. **A program in which one operation follows another from the beginning until the end is a _____ program.**
   a. modular
   b. functional
   c. procedural
   d. object-oriented

3. **The mainline logic of many computer programs contains _____.**
   a. calls to housekeeping, record processing, and finishing routines
   b. steps to declare variables, open files, and read the first record
   c. arithmetic instructions that are performed for each record on the input file
   d. steps to print totals and close files

4.  **Modularizing a program _____.**

    a.  keeps large jobs manageable
    b.  allows work to be divided easily
    c.  helps keep a program structured
    d.  all of the above

5.  **Which of the following is not a typical housekeeping module task?**

    a.  declaring variables
    b.  printing summaries
    c.  opening files
    d.  performing a priming read

6.  **When a programmer uses a data file and names the first field stored in each record `idNumber`, then other programmers who use the same file _____ in their programs.**

    a.  must also name the field `idNumber`
    b.  might name the field `idNumber`
    c.  cannot name the field `idNumber`
    d.  cannot name the field

7.  **If you use a data file containing student records, and the first field is the student's last name, then you can name the field _____.**

    a.  `stuLastName`
    b.  `studentLastName`
    c.  `lastName`
    d.  any of the above

8.  **If a field in a data file used for program input contains "Johnson", then the best choice from among the following names for a programmer to use when declaring a memory location for the data is _____.**

    a.  Johnson
    b.  n
    c.  `lastName`
    d.  A programmer cannot declare a variable name for this field; it is already called Johnson.

9.  **The purpose of using a group name is _____.**

    a.  to be able to handle several variables with a single instruction
    b.  to eliminate the need for machine-level instructions
    c.  to be able to use both character and numeric values within the same program
    d.  to be able to use multiple input files concurrently

10. **Defining a variable means the same as _____ it.**

    a.  declaring
    b.  initializing
    c.  deleting
    d.  assigning

11. **In most programming languages, the initial value of unassigned variables is _____.**

    a. 0

    b. spaces

    c. 0 or spaces, depending on whether the variable is numeric or character

    d. unknown

12. **The types of variables you usually do not initialize are _____.**

    a. those that will never change value during a program

    b. those representing fields on an input file

    c. those that will be used in mathematical statements

    d. those that will not be used in mathematical statements

13. **The name programmers use for unknown variable values is _____.**

    a. default

    b. trash

    c. naive

    d. garbage

14. **Preparing an input device to deliver data records to a program is called _____ a file.**

    a. prompting

    b. opening

    c. refreshing

    d. initializing

15. **A computer system's standard input device is most often _____.**

    a. a mouse

    b. a floppy disk

    c. a keyboard

    d. a compact disc

16. **The last task performed in a housekeeping module is most often to _____.**

    a. open files

    b. close files

    c. check for eof

    d. read an input record

17. **Most business programs contain a _____ that executes once for each record on an input file.**

    a. housekeeping module

    b. main loop

    c. finish routine

    d. terminal symbol

18. Which of the following pseudocode statements is equivalent to this pseudocode:

```
salePrice = salePrice - discount
finalPrice = salePrice + tax
print finalPrice
```

a. `print salePrice + tax`
b. `print salePrice - discount`
c. `print salePrice - discount + tax`
d. `print discount + tax - salePrice`

19. Common end-of-job module tasks in programs include all of the following except _____ .

a. opening files
b. printing totals
c. printing end-of-job messages
d. closing files

20. Which of the following is never performed in an end-of-job module?

a. closing files
b. checking for eof
c. printing the message "End of report"
d. adding two values

## EXERCISES

1. A pet store owner needs a weekly sales report. The output consists of a printed report titled PET SALES, with column headings TYPE OF ANIMAL and PRICE. Fields printed on output are: type of animal and price. After all records print, a footer line END OF REPORT prints. The input file description is shown below.

```
File name: PETS
```

| FIELD DESCRIPTION | POSITIONS | DATA TYPE | DECIMALS |
|---|---|---|---|
| Type of Animal | 1-20 | Character | |
| Price of Animal | 21-26 | Numeric | 2 |

a. Design the print chart for this program.
b. Draw the hierarchy chart for this program.
c. Draw the flowchart for this program.
d. Write the pseudocode for this program.

2. **An employer wants to produce a personnel report. The output consists of a printed report titled ACTIVE PERSONNEL. Fields printed on output are: last name of employee, first name of employee, and current weekly salary. Include appropriate column headings and a footer. The input file description is shown below.**

```
File name: PERSONNEL
FIELD DESCRIPTION        POSITIONS        DATA TYPE        DECIMALS
Last Name                1-15             Character
First Name               16-30            Character
Soc. Sec. Number         31-39            Numeric          0
Department               40-41            Numeric          0
Current Salary           42-47            Numeric          2
```

a. Design the print chart for this program.
b. Draw the hierarchy chart for this program.
c. Draw the flowchart for this program.
d. Write the pseudocode for this program.

3. **An employer wants to produce a personnel report that shows the end result if she gives everyone a 10 percent raise in salary. The output consists of a printed report entitled PROJECTED RAISES. Fields printed on output are: last name of employee, first name of employee, current weekly salary, and projected weekly salary. The input file description is shown below.**

```
File name: PERSONNEL
FIELD DESCRIPTION        POSITIONS        DATA TYPE        DECIMALS
Last Name                1-15             Character
First Name               16-30            Character
Soc. Sec. Number         31-39            Numeric          0
Department               40-41            Numeric          0
Current Salary           42-47            Numeric          2
```

a. Design the print chart for this program.
b. Draw the hierarchy chart for this program.
c. Draw the flowchart for this program.
d. Write the pseudocode for this program.

4. **A furniture store maintains an inventory file that includes data about every item it sells. The manager wants a report that lists each stock number, description, and profit, which is the retail price minus the wholesale price. The fields include a stock number, description, wholesale price, and retail price. The input file description is shown below.**

```
File name: FURNITURE
FIELD DESCRIPTION        POSITIONS        DATA TYPE        DECIMALS
Stock Number             1-4              Numeric          0
Description              5-29             Character
Wholesale Price          30-35            Numeric          2
Retail Price             36-41            Numeric          2
```

a. Design the print chart for this program.
b. Draw the hierarchy chart for this program.

c. Draw the flowchart for this program.

d. Write the pseudocode for this program.

5.   A summer camp keeps a record for every camper, including first name, last name, birth date, and skill scores that range from 1 to 10 in four areas: swimming, tennis, horsemanship, and crafts. (The birth date is stored in the format MMDDYYYY without any punctuation.) The camp wants a printed report listing each camper's data, plus a total score that is the sum of the camper's four skill scores. The input file description is shown below.

File name: CAMPERS

| FIELD DESCRIPTION | POSITIONS | DATA TYPE | DECIMALS |
|---|---|---|---|
| First Name | 1-15 | Character | |
| Last Name | 16-30 | Character | |
| Birth Date | 31-38 | Numeric | 0 |
| Swimming Skill | 39-40 | Numeric | 0 |
| Tennis Skill | 41-42 | Numeric | 0 |
| Horsemanship Skill | 43-44 | Numeric | 0 |
| Crafts Skill | 45-46 | Numeric | 0 |

a. Design the print chart for this program.

b. Draw the hierarchy chart for this program.

c. Draw the flowchart for this program.

d. Write the pseudocode for this program.

6.   An employer needs to determine how much tax to withhold for each employee. This withholding amount computes as 20 percent of each employee's weekly pay. The output consists of a printed report titled WITHHOLDING FOR EACH EMPLOYEE. Fields printed on output are: last name of employee, first name of employee, hourly pay, weekly pay based on a 40-hour work week, and withholding amount per week. The input file description is shown below.

File name: EMPLOYEES

| FIELD DESCRIPTION | POSITIONS | DATA TYPE | DECIMALS |
|---|---|---|---|
| Company ID | 1-5 | Numeric | 0 |
| First Name | 6-17 | Character | |
| Last Name | 18-29 | Character | |
| Hourly Rate | 30-34 | Numeric | 2 |

a. Design the print chart for this program.

b. Draw the hierarchy chart for this program.

c. Draw the flowchart for this program.

d. Write the pseudocode for this program.

7. A baseball team manager wants a report showing her players' batting statistics. A batting average is computed as hits divided by at-bats, and it is usually expressed to three decimal positions, for example: .235. The output consists of a printed report titled TEAM STATISTICS. Fields printed on output are: player number, first name, last name, and batting average. The input file description is shown below.

```
File name: BASEBALL
FIELD DESCRIPTION        POSITIONS       DATA TYPE       DECIMALS
Player Number            1-2             Numeric         0
First Name               3-18            Character
Last Name                19-35           Character
At-bats                  36-38           Numeric         0
Hits                     39-41           Numeric         0
```

a. Design the print chart for this program.
b. Draw the hierarchy chart for this program.
c. Draw the flowchart for this program.
d. Write the pseudocode for this program.

# 5

# MAKING DECISIONS

## After studying Chapter 5, you should be able to:

- ☐ Evaluate Boolean expressions to make comparisons
- ☐ Use the logical comparison operators
- ☐ Understand AND logic
- ☐ Understand OR logic
- ☐ Use selections within ranges
- ☐ Understand precedence when combining AND and OR selections
- ☐ Understand the case structure
- ☐ Use decision tables

## EVALUATING BOOLEAN EXPRESSIONS TO MAKE COMPARISONS

The reason people think computers are smart lies in the computer program's ability to make decisions. A medical diagnosis program that can decide if your symptoms fit various disease profiles seems quite intelligent, as does a program that can offer you different potential vacation routes based on your destination.

The selection structure (sometimes called a decision structure) involved in such programs is not new to you—it's one of the basic structures of structured programming. See Figures 5-1 and 5-2.

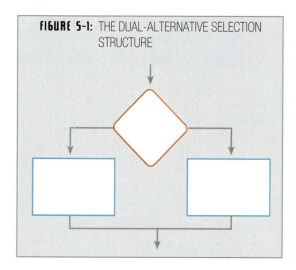

FIGURE 5-1: THE DUAL-ALTERNATIVE SELECTION STRUCTURE

FIGURE 5-2: THE SINGLE-ALTERNATIVE SELECTION STRUCTURE

You can refer to the structure in Figure 5-1 as a **dual-alternative**, or **binary**, selection because there is an action associated with each of two possible outcomes. Depending on the answer to the question represented by the diamond, the logical flow proceeds either to the left branch of the structure or to the right. The choices are mutually exclusive; that is, the logic can flow only to one of the two alternatives, never to both. This selection structure is also called an **if-then-else** structure because it fits the statement:

```
if the answer to the question is yes, then
    do something
else
    do somethingElse
endif
```

The flowchart segment in Figure 5-2 represents a **single-alternative**, or **unary**, selection where action is required for only one outcome of the question. You call this form of the if-then-else structure an **if-then**, because no alternative or "else" action is necessary.

TIP ▫ ▫ ▫ ▫  You can call a single-alternative decision (or selection) a *single-sided decision*. Similarly, a dual-alternative decision is a *double-sided decision* (or selection).

For example, Figure 5-3 shows the flowchart and pseudocode for a typical if-then-else decision in a business program. Many organizations pay employees time and a half (one and one-half times their usual hourly rate) for hours in excess of 40 per week. The logic segments in the figure show this decision.

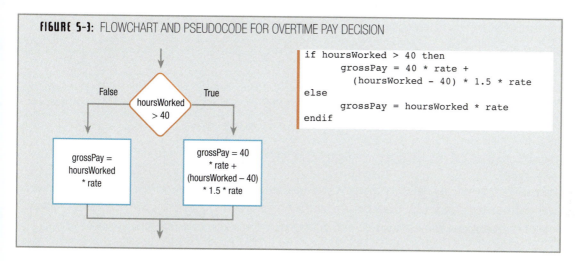

**FIGURE 5-3:** FLOWCHART AND PSEUDOCODE FOR OVERTIME PAY DECISION

```
if hoursWorked > 40 then
      grossPay = 40 * rate +
         (hoursWorked - 40) * 1.5 * rate
else
      grossPay = hoursWorked * rate
endif
```

In the example in Figure 5-3, the longer calculation that adds a time-and-a-half factor to an employee's gross pay executes only when the expression `hoursWorked > 40` is true. The long calculation exists in the **if clause** of the decision—the part of the decision that holds the action or actions that execute when the tested condition in the decision is true. The shorter calculation, which produces `grossPay` by multiplying `hoursWorked` by `rate`, constitutes the **else clause** of the decision—the part that executes only when the tested condition in the decision is false.

The typical if-then decision in Figure 5-4 shows the employee's paycheck being reduced if the employee participates in the dental plan. No action is taken if the employee is not a dental plan participant.

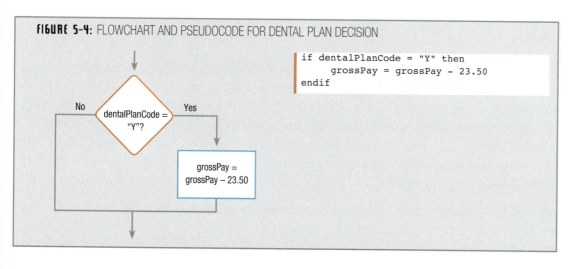

**FIGURE 5-4:** FLOWCHART AND PSEUDOCODE FOR DENTAL PLAN DECISION

```
if dentalPlanCode = "Y" then
      grossPay = grossPay - 23.50
endif
```

The expressions `hoursWorked > 40` and `dentalPlanCode = "Y"` that appear in Figures 5-3 and 5-4 are Boolean expressions. A **Boolean expression** is one that represents only one of two states, usually expressed as true or false. Every decision you make in a computer program involves evaluating a Boolean expression. True/false evaluation is "natural" from a computer's standpoint, because computer circuitry consists of two-state, on-off switches, often represented by 1 or 0. Every computer decision yields a true-or-false, yes-or-no, 1-or-0 result.

 George Boole was a mathematician who lived from 1815 to 1864. He approached logic more simply than his predecessors did, by expressing logical selections with common algebraic symbols. He is considered the founder of symbolic logic, and Boolean (true/false) expressions are named for him.

## USING THE LOGICAL COMPARISON OPERATORS

Usually, you can compare only values that are of the same type; that is, you can compare numeric values to other numeric values, and character values to other characters. You can ask every programming question by using one of only three types of comparison operators in a Boolean expression. For any two values that are the same type, you can decide whether:

- The two values are equal.
- The first value is greater than the second value.
- The first value is less than the second value.

 Usually, character variables are not considered to be equal unless they are identical, including the spacing and whether they appear in upper or lowercase. For example, "black pen" is *not* equal to "blackpen", "BLACK PEN", or "Black Pen".

 Some programming languages allow you to compare a character to a number. If this is the case, then a single character's numeric code value is used in the comparison. For example, most microcomputers use the ASCII coding system, in which an uppercase "A" is represented numerically as a 65, an uppercase "B" is a 66, and so on.

In any Boolean expression, the two values used can be either variables or constants. For example, the expression `currentTotal = 100?` compares a variable, `currentTotal`, to a numeric constant, 100. Depending on the `currentTotal` value, the expression is true or false. In the expression `currentTotal = previousTotal?`, both values are variables, and the result is also true or false depending on the values stored in each of the two variables. Although it's legal to do so, you would never use expressions in which you compare two constants, for example `20 = 20?` or `30 = 40?`. Such expressions are considered **trivial** because each will always evaluate to the same result: true for the first expression and false for the second.

Each programming language supports its own set of **logical comparison operators**, or comparison symbols, that express these Boolean tests. For example, many languages such as Visual Basic and Pascal use the equal sign (=) to express testing for equivalency, so `balanceDue = 0?` compares `balanceDue` to zero. COBOL programmers can use the equal sign, but they also can spell out the expression, as in `balanceDue equal to 0?`. RPG programmers use the two-letter operator `EQ` in place of a symbol. C#, C++, and Java programmers use two equal signs to test for equivalency, so they write `balanceDue == 0?` to compare the two values. Although each programming language supports its own syntax for comparing values' equivalency, all languages provide for the same logical concept of equivalency.

> The reason some languages use two equal signs for comparisons is to avoid confusion with assignment statements such as `balanceDue = 0`. In C++ or Java, this statement only assigns the value 0 to `balanceDue`; it does not compare `balanceDue` to zero.

> Whenever you use a comparison operator, you must provide a value on each side of the operator. Comparison operators are sometimes called *binary operators* because of this requirement.

Most languages allow you to use the algebraic signs for greater than (>) and less than (<) to make the corresponding comparisons. Additionally, COBOL, which is very similar to English, allows you to spell out the comparisons in expressions like `daysPastDue is greater than 30?` or `packageWeight is less than maximumWeightAllowed?`. RPG uses the two-letter abbreviations `GT` and `LT` to represent greater than or less than. When you create a flowchart or pseudocode, you can use any form of notation you want to express "greater than" and "less than." It's simplest to use the symbols > and < if you are comfortable with their meaning. As with equivalency, the syntax changes when you change languages, but the concepts of greater than and less than exist in all programming languages.

In addition to the three basic comparisons you can make, most programming languages provide three others. For any two values that are the same type, you can decide whether:

- The first is greater than or equal to the second.
- The first is less than or equal to the second.
- The two are not equal.

Most programming languages allow you to express "greater than or equal to" by typing a greater-than sign immediately followed by an equal sign (>=). When you are drawing a flowchart or writing pseudocode, you might prefer a greater-than sign with a line under it (≥) because mathematicians use that symbol to mean "greater than or equal to." However, when you write a program, you type >= as two separate characters, because no single key on the keyboard expresses this concept. Similarly, "less than or equal to" is written with two symbols, < immediately followed by =.

> The operators >= and <= are always treated as a single unit; no spaces separate the two parts of the operator. Also, the equal sign always appears second. No programming language allows => or =< as a comparison operator.

Any logical situation can be expressed using just three types of comparisons: equal, greater than, and less than. You never need the three additional comparisons (greater than or equal to, less than or equal to, or not equal to), but using them often makes decisions more convenient. For example, assume you need to issue a 10 percent discount to any customer whose age is 65 or greater, and charge full price to other customers. You can use the greater-than-or-equal-to symbol to write the logic as follows:

```
if customerAge >= 65 then
        discount = 0.10
else
        discount = 0
endif
```

As an alternative, if you want to use only the three basic comparisons (=, >, and <) you can express the same logic by writing:

```
if customerAge < 65 then
        discount = 0
else
        discount = 0.10
endif
```

In any decision for which a >= b is true, then a < b is false. Conversely, if a >= b is false, then a < b is true. By rephrasing the question and swapping the actions taken based on the outcome, you can make the same decision in multiple ways. The clearest route is often to ask a question so the positive or true outcome results in the unusual action. When your company policy is to "provide a discount for those who are 65 and older," the phrase "greater than or equal to" comes to mind, so it is the most natural to use. Conversely, if your policy is to "provide no discount for those under 65," then it is more natural to use the "less than" syntax. Either way, the same people receive a discount.

Comparing two amounts to decide if they are *not* equal to each other is the most confusing of all the comparisons. Using "not equal to" in decisions involves thinking in double negatives, which makes you prone to include logical errors in your programs. For example, consider the flowchart segment in Figure 5-5.

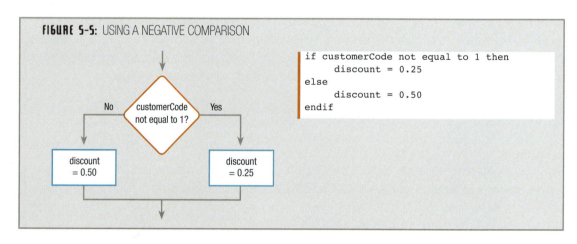

**FIGURE 5-5:** USING A NEGATIVE COMPARISON

```
if customerCode not equal to 1 then
        discount = 0.25
else
        discount = 0.50
endif
```

In Figure 5-5, if the value of `customerCode` *is* equal to 1, the logical flow follows the false branch of the selection. If `customerCode not equal to 1` is true, the `discount` is 0.25; if `customerCode not equal to 1` is not true, it means the `customerCode` *is* 1, and the `discount` is 0.50. Even using the phrase "`customerCode not equal to 1 is not true`" is awkward.

Figure 5-6 shows the same decision, this time asked in the positive. Making the decision `if customerCode is 1 then discount = 0.50` is clearer than trying to determine what `customerCode` is *not*.

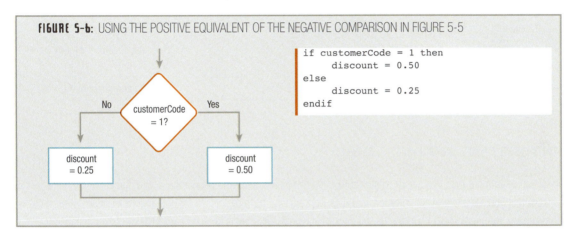

**FIGURE 5-6:** USING THE POSITIVE EQUIVALENT OF THE NEGATIVE COMPARISON IN FIGURE 5-5

```
if customerCode = 1 then
     discount = 0.50
else
     discount = 0.25
endif
```

Besides being awkward to use, the "not equal to" comparison operator is the one most likely to be different in the various programming languages you may use. COBOL allows you to write "not equal to"; Pascal uses a less-than sign followed immediately by a greater-than sign (<>); C#, C++, C, and Java use an exclamation point followed by an equal sign (!=). In a flowchart or in pseudocode, you can use the symbol that mathematicians use to mean "not equal," an equal sign with a slash through it ($\neq$). When you program, you will not be able to use this symbol, because no single key on the keyboard produces it.

**TIP** □ □ □ □ | Although NOT comparisons can be awkward to use, there are times when your meaning is clearest if you use one. Frequently, this occurs when you take action only when some condition is false. An example would be: if customerZipCode is not equal to localZipCode, then add deliveryCharge to total. The mainline logic of many programs, including those you have worked with in this book, includes a negative comparison that controls a loop. The pseudocode you have seen for almost every program includes a statement similar to: while not eof, perform mainLoop().

Figure 5-7 summarizes the six comparison operators and contrasts trivial (both true and false) examples with typical examples of their use.

**FIGURE 5-7:** LOGICAL COMPARISONS

| Comparison | Trivial true example | Trivial false example | Typical example |
|---|---|---|---|
| Equal to | 7 = 7? | 7 = 4? | amtOrdered = 12? |
| Greater than | 12 > 3? | 4 > 9? | hoursWorked > 40? |
| Less than | 1 < 8? | 13 < 10? | hourlyWage < 5.65? |
| Greater than or equal to | 5 >= 5? | 3 >= 9? | customerAge >= 65? |
| Less than or equal to | 4 <= 4? | 8 <= 2? | daysOverdue <= 60? |
| Not equal to | 16 <> 3? | 18 <> 18? | customerBalance <> 0? |

## UNDERSTANDING AND LOGIC

Often, you need more than one selection structure to determine whether an action should take place. For example, suppose that your employer wants a report that lists workers who have registered for both insurance plans offered by the company: the medical plan and the dental plan. This type of situation is known as an **AND decision** because the employee's record must pass two tests—participation in the medical plan *and* participation in the dental plan—before you write that employee's information on the report. A compound, or AND, decision requires a **nested decision**, or a **nested if**—that is, a decision "inside of" another decision. The logic looks like Figure 5-8.

 You first learned about nesting structures in Chapter 2.

 A series of nested if statements can also be called a **cascading if statement**.

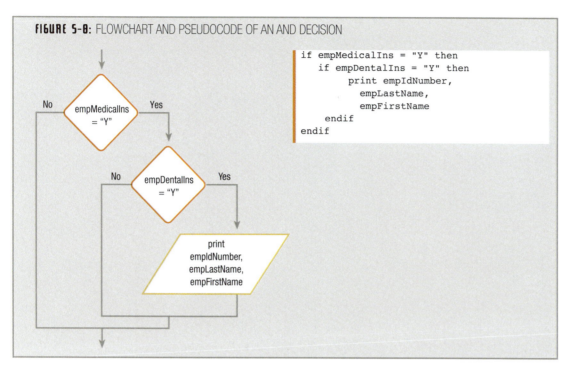

**FIGURE 5-8**: FLOWCHART AND PSEUDOCODE OF AN AND DECISION

```
if empMedicalIns = "Y" then
    if empDentalIns = "Y" then
        print empIdNumber,
            empLastName,
            empFirstName
    endif
endif
```

The AND decision shown in Figure 5-8 is part of a much larger program. To help you develop this program, suppose your employer provides you with the employee data file description shown in Figure 5-9, and you learn that the medical and dental insurance fields contain a single character, "Y" or "N", indicating each employee's participation status. With your employer's approval, you develop the print chart shown in Figure 5-10.

**FIGURE 5-9**: EMPLOYEE FILE DESCRIPTION

```
EMPLOYEE FILE DESCRIPTION
File Name: EMPFILE
```

| FIELD DESCRIPTION | POSITIONS | DATA | DECIMALS | EXAMPLE |
|---|---|---|---|---|
| ID Number | 1—4 | Numeric | 0 | 1234 |
| Last Name | 5—20 | Character | | Kroening |
| First Name | 21—35 | Character | | Ginny |
| Department | 36 | Numeric | 0 | 3 |
| Hourly Rate | 37—40 | Numeric | 2 | 17.50 |
| Medical Plan | 41 | Character | | Y |
| Dental Plan | 42 | Character | | N |
| Number of Dependents | 43—44 | Numeric | 0 | 2 |

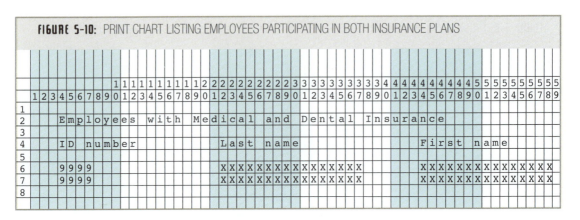

**FIGURE 5-10:** PRINT CHART LISTING EMPLOYEES PARTICIPATING IN BOTH INSURANCE PLANS

| | 1 2 3 4 5 6 7 8 9 | 1 0 | 1 1 | 1 2 | 1 3 | 1 4 | 1 5 | 1 6 | 1 7 | 1 8 | 1 9 | 2 0 | 2 1 | 2 2 | 2 3 | 2 4 | 2 5 | 2 6 | 2 7 | 2 8 | 2 9 | 3 0 | 3 1 | 3 2 | 3 3 | 3 4 | 3 5 | 3 6 | 3 7 | 3 8 | 3 9 | 4 0 | 4 1 | 4 2 | 4 3 | 4 4 | 4 5 | 4 6 | 4 7 | 4 8 | 4 9 | 5 0 | 5 1 | 5 2 | 5 3 | 5 4 | 5 5 | 5 6 | 5 7 | 5 8 | 5 9 |

The print chart shows:
- Row 2: `Employees with Medical and Dental Insurance`
- Row 4: `ID number        Last name              First name`
- Row 6: `9999            XXXXXXXXXXXXXXXXX      XXXXXXXXXXXXXXX`
- Row 7: `9999            XXXXXXXXXXXXXXXXX      XXXXXXXXXXXXXXX`

The mainline logic and `housekeeping()` routines for this program are diagrammed in Figures 5-11 and 5-12.

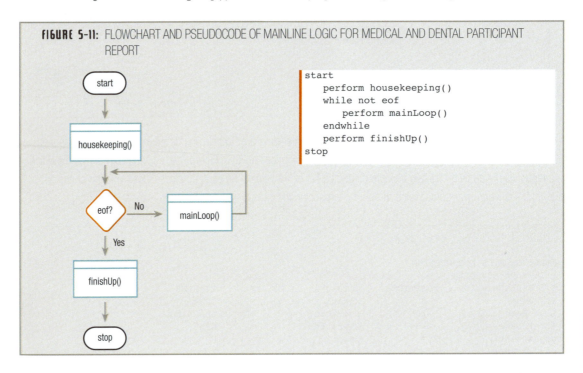

**FIGURE 5-11:** FLOWCHART AND PSEUDOCODE OF MAINLINE LOGIC FOR MEDICAL AND DENTAL PARTICIPANT REPORT

```
start
    perform housekeeping()
    while not eof
        perform mainLoop()
    endwhile
    perform finishUp()
stop
```

**FIGURE 5-12:** FLOWCHART AND PSEUDOCODE OF `housekeeping()` MODULE FOR MEDICAL AND DENTAL PARTICIPANT REPORT

```
empRecord
        num empIdNumber
        char empLastName
        char empFirstName
        num empDept
        num empRate
        char empMedicalIns
        char empDentalIns
        num empDependents
char heading1 = "Employees with Medical
   and Dental Insurance"
char heading2 = "ID number   Last name   First name"
```

```
housekeeping()
    declare variables
    open files
    print heading1
    print heading2
    read empRecord
return
```

At the end of the `housekeeping()` module, the first employee record is read into computer memory. Assuming that the `eof` condition is not yet met, the logical flow proceeds to the `mainLoop()`. If the program required data for all employees to be printed, you would simply print the information from the current record and get the next record. However, in this case, the output should contain only the names of those employees who participate in both the medical and dental insurance plans. Therefore, within the `mainLoop()` module of this program, you ask the questions that determine whether the current employee's record will print; if the employee's data meet the medical and dental insurance requirements, then you print the record. Whether or not you take the path that prints the record, the last thing you do in the `mainLoop()` is to read the next input record. Figure 5-13 shows the `mainLoop()` module.

**FIGURE 5-13:** `mainLoop()` OF PROGRAM THAT LISTS EMPLOYEES WHO ARE BOTH MEDICAL AND DENTAL INSURANCE PROGRAM PARTICIPANTS

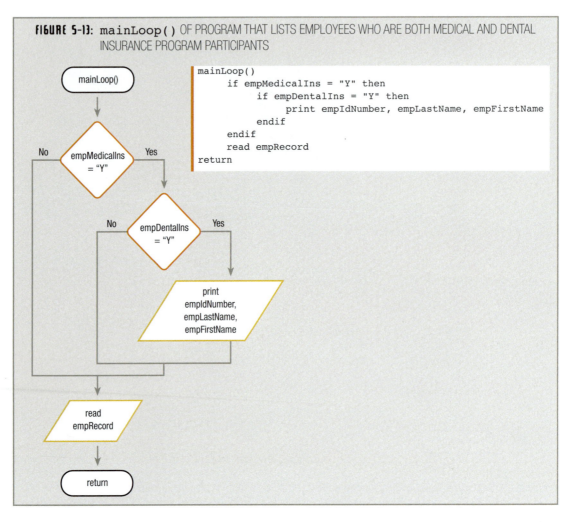

```
mainLoop()
    if empMedicalIns = "Y" then
        if empDentalIns = "Y" then
            print empIdNumber, empLastName, empFirstName
        endif
    endif
    read empRecord
return
```

The `mainLoop()` module works like this: If the employee has medical insurance, *then* and *only then*, test to see if the employee has dental insurance. If so, *then* and *only then*, print the employee's data. The dental insurance question is nested entirely within half of the medical insurance question structure. If an employee does not carry medical insurance, there is no need to ask about the dental insurance; the employee is already disqualified from the report. Pseudocode for the entire program is shown in Figure 5-14. Notice how the second (dental insurance) decision within the `mainLoop()` is indented within the first (medical insurance) decision. This technique shows that the second question is asked only when the result of the first comparison is true.

**FIGURE 5-14:** PSEUDOCODE OF PROGRAM THAT PRINTS RECORDS OF EMPLOYEES WHO PARTICIPATE IN BOTH THE MEDICAL AND DENTAL INSURANCE PLANS

```
start
    perform houskeeping()
    while not eof
        perform mainLoop()
    endwhile
    perform finishUp()              empRecord
stop                                    num empIdNumber
                                        char empLastName
housekeeping()                          char empFirstName
    declare variables- - - - -          num empDept
    open files                          num empRate
    print heading1                      char empMedicalIns
    print heading2                      char empDentalIns
    read empRecord                      num empDependents
return                              char heading1 = "Employees with Medical
                                              and Dental Insurance"
mainLoop()                          char heading2 = "ID number    Last name
    if empMedicalIns = "Y" then                First name"
        if empDentalIns = "Y" then
            print empIdNumber, empLastName, empFirstName
        endif
    endif
    read empRecord
return

finishUp()
     close files
return
```

## WRITING NESTED AND DECISIONS FOR EFFICIENCY

When you nest decisions because the resulting action requires that two conditions be true, you must decide which of the two decisions to make first. Logically, either selection in an AND decision can come first. However, when there are two selections, you often can improve your program's performance by making an appropriate choice as to which selection to make first.

For example, Figure 5-15 shows the nested decision structure in the `mainLoop()` logic of the program that produces a report of employees who participate in both the medical and dental insurance plans.

**FIGURE 5-15:** FINDING MEDICAL AND DENTAL PLAN PARTICIPANTS

```
if empMedicalIns = "Y" then
    if empDentalIns = "Y" then
         print empIdNumber, empLastName, empFirstName
    endif
endif
```

Alternately, you can write the decision as in Figure 5-16.

**FIGURE 5-16:** FINDING DENTAL AND MEDICAL PLAN PARTICIPANTS

```
if empDentalIns = "Y" then
    if empMedicalIns = "Y" then
        print empIdNumber, empLastName, empFirstName
    endif
endif
```

Examine the decision statements in the preceding figures. If you want to print employees who participate in the medical AND dental plans, you can ask about the medical plan first, eliminate those employees who do not participate, and ask about the dental plan only for those employees who "pass" the medical insurance test. Or, you could ask about the dental plan first, eliminate those who do not participate, and ask about the medical plan only for those employees who "pass" the dental insurance test. Either way, the final list contains only those employees who have both kinds of insurance.

Does it make a difference which question is asked first? As far as the output goes, no. Either way, the same employee names appear on the report—those with both types of insurance. As far as program efficiency goes, however, it *might* make a difference which question is asked first.

Assume you know that out of 1,000 employees in your company, about 90 percent, or 900, participate in the medical insurance plan. Assume you also know that out of 1,000 employees, only about half, or 500, participate in the dental plan.

The medical and dental insurance program will ask the first question in the `mainLoop()` 1,000 times during its execution—once for each employee record contained on the input file. If the program uses the logic in Figure 5-15, it asks the first question `empMedicalIns = "Y"`? 1,000 times. For approximately 90 percent of the employees, or 900 of the records, the answer is `true`, meaning the `empMedicalIns` field contains the character "Y". So 100 employees are eliminated, and 900 proceed to the next question about dental insurance. Only about half of the employees participate in the dental plan, so 450 out of the 900 will appear on the printed report.

Using the alternate logic in Figure 5-16, the program asks the first question `empDentalIns = "Y"`? 1,000 times. Because only about half of the company's employees participate, only 500 will "pass" this test and proceed to the medical insurance question. Then about 90 percent of the 500, or 450 employees, will appear on the printed report. Whether you use the logic in Figure 5-15 or 5-16, the same 450 employees who have both types of insurance appear on the report.

The difference lies in the fact that when you use the logic in Figure 5-15, the program must ask 1,900 questions to produce the report—the medical insurance question tests all 1,000 employee records, and 900 continue to the dental insurance question. If you use the logic in Figure 5-16 to produce the report, the program asks only 1,500 questions— all 1,000 records are tested for dental insurance, but only 500 proceed to the medical insurance question. By asking about the dental insurance first, you "save" 400 decisions.

The 400-question difference between the first set of decisions and the second set really doesn't take much time on most computers. But it will take *some* time, and if there are hundreds of thousands of employees instead of only 1,000, or if many such decisions have to be made within a program, performance time can be significantly improved by asking questions in the proper order.

In many AND decisions, you have no idea which of two events is more likely to occur; in that case, you can legitimately ask either question first. In addition, even though you know the probability of each of two conditions, the two events might not be mutually exclusive; that is, one might depend on the other. For example, if employees with dental insurance are significantly more likely to carry medical insurance than those who don't carry dental insurance, the order in which to ask the questions might matter less or not matter at all. However, if you do know the probabilities of the conditions, or can make a reasonable guess, the general rule is: *In an AND decision, first ask the question that is less likely to be true*. This eliminates as many records as possible from having to go through the second decision, which speeds up processing time.

## COMBINING DECISIONS IN AN AND SELECTION

Most programming languages allow you to ask two or more questions in a single comparison by using a **logical AND operator**. For example, if you want to select employees who carry both medical and dental insurance, you can use nested `if`s, or you can include both decisions in a single statement by writing `empDentalIns = "Y" AND empMedicalIns = "Y"?`. When you use one or more AND operators to combine two or more Boolean expressions, each Boolean expression must be true in order for the entire expression to be evaluated as true. For example, if you ask, "Are you at least 18, and are you a registered voter, and did you vote in the last election?", the answer to all three parts of the question must be "yes" before the response can be a single, summarizing "yes". If any part of the question is false, then the entire question is false.

If the programming language you use allows an AND operator, you still must realize that the question you place first is the question that will be asked first, and cases that are eliminated based on the first question will not proceed to the second question. The computer can ask only one question at a time; even when your logic follows the flowchart segment in Figure 5-17, the computer will execute the logic in the flowchart in Figure 5-18.

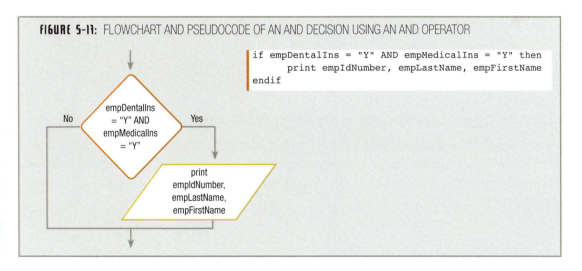

FIGURE 5-17: FLOWCHART AND PSEUDOCODE OF AN AND DECISION USING AN AND OPERATOR

```
if empDentalIns = "Y" AND empMedicalIns = "Y" then
        print empIdNumber, empLastName, empFirstName
endif
```

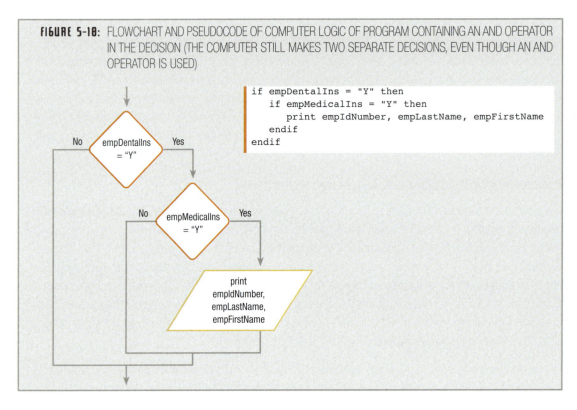

**FIGURE 5-18:** FLOWCHART AND PSEUDOCODE OF COMPUTER LOGIC OF PROGRAM CONTAINING AN AND OPERATOR IN THE DECISION (THE COMPUTER STILL MAKES TWO SEPARATE DECISIONS, EVEN THOUGH AN AND OPERATOR IS USED)

```
if empDentalIns = "Y" then
    if empMedicalIns = "Y" then
        print empIdNumber, empLastName, empFirstName
    endif
endif
```

**TIP** ▢▢▢▢ The AND operator in Java, C++, and C# consists of two ampersands, with no spaces between them (&&).

**TIP** ▢▢▢▢ Using an AND operator in a decision that involves multiple conditions does not eliminate your responsibility for determining which of the conditions to test first. Even when you use an AND operator, the computer makes decisions one at a time, and makes them in the order you ask them. If the first question in an AND expression evaluates to false, then the entire expression is false, and the second question will not even be tested.

## AVOIDING COMMON ERRORS IN AN AND SELECTION

When you must satisfy two or more criteria to initiate an event in a program, you must make sure that the second decision is made entirely within the first decision. For example, if a program's objective is to print a report of those employees who carry both medical and dental insurance, then the program segment shown in Figure 5-19 contains three different types of logic errors.

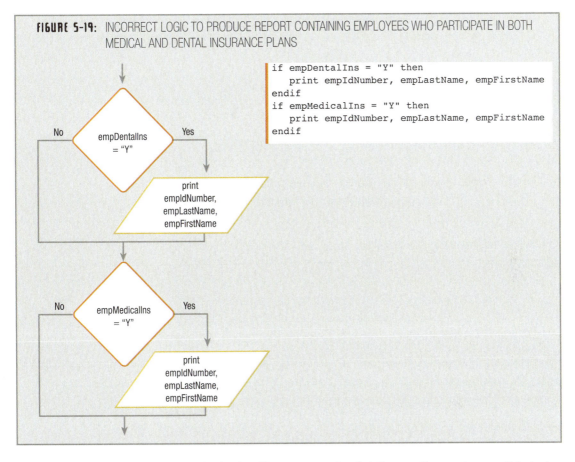

**FIGURE 5-19:** INCORRECT LOGIC TO PRODUCE REPORT CONTAINING EMPLOYEES WHO PARTICIPATE IN BOTH MEDICAL AND DENTAL INSURANCE PLANS

```
if empDentalIns = "Y" then
    print empIdNumber, empLastName, empFirstName
endif
if empMedicalIns = "Y" then
    print empIdNumber, empLastName, empFirstName
endif
```

The diagram shows that the program asks the dental insurance question first. However, if an employee participates in the dental program, the employee's record prints immediately. The employee record should not print, because the employee might not have the medical insurance. In addition, the program should eliminate an employee without dental insurance from the next selection, but every employee's record proceeds to the medical insurance question, where it might print, whether the employee has dental insurance or not. Additionally, any employee who has both medical and dental insurance, having passed each test successfully, will appear twice on this report. For many reasons, the logic shown in Figure 5-19 is *not* correct for this problem.

Beginning programmers often make another type of error when they must make two comparisons on the same field while using a logical AND operator. For example, suppose you want to list employees who make between $10.00 and $11.99 per hour, inclusive. When you make this type of decision, you are basing it on a **range** of values—every value between low and high limits. For example, you want to select employees whose `empRate` is greater than or equal to 10.00 AND whose `empRate` is less than 12.00; therefore, you need to make two comparisons on the same field. Without the logical AND operator, the comparison is:

```
if empRate >= 10.00 then
    if empRate < 12.00 then
```

```
                        print empIdNumber, empLastName, empFirstName
                endif
        endif
```

**TIP** ▫ ▫ ▫ ▫   To check for `empRate` values that are 10.00 and greater, you can use either `empRate >` `9.99?` or `empRate >= 10.00?`. To check for `empRate` values under 12.00, you can write `empRate <= 11.99?` or `empRate < 12.00?`.

The correct way to make this comparison with the AND operator is as follows:

```
        if empRate >= 10.00 AND empRate < 12.00 then
                print empIdNumber, empLastName, empFirstName
        endif
```

You substitute the AND operator for the phrase `then if`. However, some programmers might try to make the comparison as follows:

```
        if empRate >= 10.00 AND < 12.00 then
                print empIdNumber, empLastName, empFirstName
        endif
```

In most languages, the phrase `empRate >= 10.00 AND < 12.00` is incorrect. The logical AND is usually a binary operator that requires a complete Boolean expression on each side. The expression to the right of the AND, `< 12.00`, is not a complete Boolean expression; you must indicate *what* is being compared to 12.00.

**TIP** ▫ ▫ ▫ ▫   In some programming languages, such as COBOL and RPG, you can write the equivalent of `empRate >= 10.00 AND < 12.00?` and the `empRate` variable is implied for both comparisons. Still, it is clearer, and therefore preferable, to use the two full expressions, `empRate >= 10.00 AND empRate < 12.00?`.

## UNDERSTANDING OR LOGIC

Sometimes, you want to take action when one *or* the other of two conditions is true. This is called an **OR decision** because either one condition must be met *or* some other condition must be met, in order for an event to take place. If someone asks you, "Are you free Friday or Saturday?"only one of the two conditions has to be true in order for the answer to the whole question to be "yes"; only if the answers to both halves of the question are false is the value of the entire expression false.

For example, suppose your employer wants a list of all employees who participate in either the medical or dental plan. Assuming you are using the same input file described in Figure 5-9, the mainline logic and `housekeeping()` module for this program are identical to those used in Figures 5-11 and 5-12. You only need to change the heading on the print chart (Figure 5-10) and change the `heading1` variable in Figure 5-12 from `heading1 = "Employees with Medical` *and* `Dental Insurance"` to `heading1 = "Employees with Medical` *or* `Dental Insurance"`. The only substantial changes to the program occur in the `mainLoop()` module.

Figure 5-20 shows the possible logic for `mainLoop()` in this OR selection. As each record enters the `mainLoop()`, you ask the question `empMedicalIns = "Y"?`, and if the result is true, you print the employee data. Because the employee needs to participate in only one of the two insurance plans to be selected for printing, there is no need for further questioning after you have determined that an employee has medical insurance. If the employee does not participate in the medical insurance plan, only then do you need to ask if `empDentalIns = "Y"?`. If the employee does not have medical insurance, but does have dental, you want this employee information to print on the report.

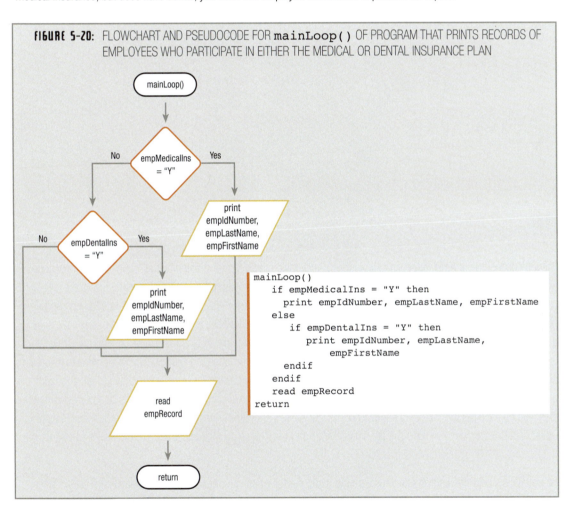

**FIGURE 5-20:** FLOWCHART AND PSEUDOCODE FOR `mainLoop()` OF PROGRAM THAT PRINTS RECORDS OF EMPLOYEES WHO PARTICIPATE IN EITHER THE MEDICAL OR DENTAL INSURANCE PLAN

```
mainLoop()
    if empMedicalIns = "Y" then
        print empIdNumber, empLastName, empFirstName
    else
        if empDentalIns = "Y" then
            print empIdNumber, empLastName,
                empFirstName
        endif
    endif
    read empRecord
return
```

## AVOIDING COMMON ERRORS IN AN OR SELECTION

You might have noticed that the statement `print empIdNumber, empLastName, empFirstName` appears twice in the flowchart and in the pseudocode shown in Figure 5-20. The temptation is to redraw the flowchart in Figure 5-20 to look like Figure 5-21. Logically, you can argue that the flowchart in Figure 5-21 is correct because the correct employee records print. However, this flowchart is not allowed because it is not structured.

**FIGURE 5-21:** INCORRECT FLOWCHART FOR `mainLoop()` MODULE

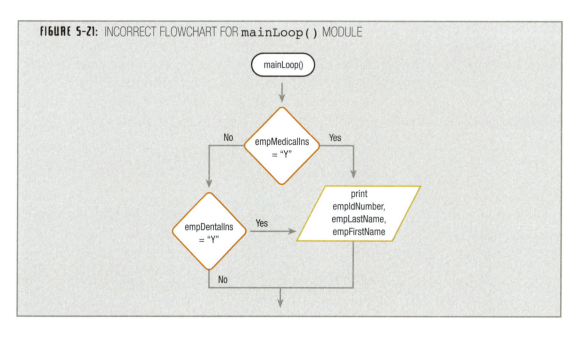

**TIP** ▫ ▫ ▫ ▫ | If you do not see that Figure 5-21 is not structured, go back and review Chapter 2. In particular, review the example that begins at Figure 2-21.

An additional source of error that is specific to the OR selection stems from a problem with language and the way people use it too casually. When your boss needs a report of all employees who carry medical or dental insurance, she is likely to say, "I need a report of all the people who have medical insurance and all those who have dental insurance." The request contains the word "and," and the report contains people who have one type of insurance "and" people who have another. However, the records you want to print are those from employees who have medical insurance OR dental insurance OR both. The logical situation requires an OR decision. Instead of saying "people who have medical insurance and people who have dental insurance," it would be clearer if your boss asked for "people who have medical or dental insurance." In other words, it would be more correct to put the question-joining "or" conjunction between the insurance types held by each person than between the people, but bosses and other human beings often do not speak like computers. As a programmer, you have the job of clarifying what really is being requested, and determining that often a request for A *and* B means a request for A *or* B.

The way we casually use English can cause another type of error when you require a decision based on a value falling within a range of values. For example, a movie theater manager might say, "Provide a discount to patrons who are under 13 years old and those who are over 64 years old; otherwise charge the full price." Because the manager has used the word "and" in the request, you might be tempted to create the decision shown in Figure 5-22; however, this logic will not provide a discounted price for any movie patron. You must remember that every time the decision in Figure 5-22 is made, it is made using a single data record. If the age field in that record contains an age lower than 13, then it cannot possibly contain an age over 64. Similarly, if it contains an age over 64, then there is no way it can contain an age under that. Therefore, there is no value that could be stored in the age field of a movie patron record for which both parts of the AND question could be true—and the price will never be set to the `discountPrice` for any record. Figure 5-23 shows the correct logic.

**FIGURE 5-22:** INCORRECT LOGIC THAT ATTEMPTS TO PROVIDE A DISCOUNT FOR MOVIE PATRONS UNDER 13 AND FOR MOVIE PATRONS OVER 64

```
if patronAge < 13 AND patronAge > 64 then
    price = discountPrice
else
    price = fullPrice
endif
```

**FIGURE 5-23:** CORRECT LOGIC THAT PROVIDES A DISCOUNT FOR MOVIE PATRONS UNDER 13 AND FOR MOVIE PATRONS OVER 64

```
if patronAge < 13 OR patronAge > 64 then
    price = discountPrice
else
    price = fullPrice
endif
```

A similar error can occur in your logic if the theater manager says something like, "Don't give a discount—that is, charge full price—if a patron is over 12 or under 65." Because the word "or" appears in the request, you might plan your logic like that shown in Figure 5-24.

As in Figure 5-22, in Figure 5-24, no patron ever receives a discount, because every patron is either over 12 or under 65. Remember, in an OR decision, only one of the conditions needs to be true in order for the entire expression to be evaluated as true. So, for example, because a patron who is 10 is under 65, the full price is charged, and because a patron who is 70 is over 12, the full price also is charged. Figure 5-25 shows the correct logic for this decision.

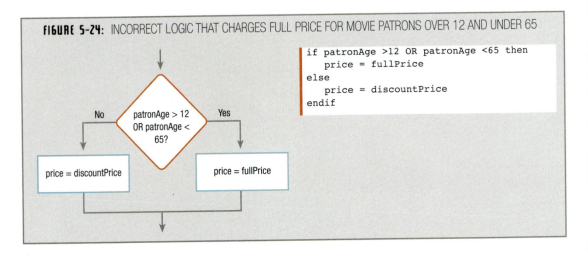

**FIGURE 5-24:** INCORRECT LOGIC THAT CHARGES FULL PRICE FOR MOVIE PATRONS OVER 12 AND UNDER 65

```
if patronAge >12 OR patronAge <65 then
    price = fullPrice
else
    price = discountPrice
endif
```

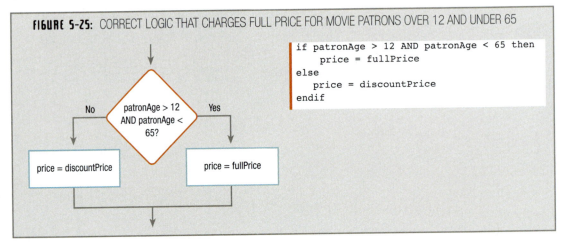

**FIGURE 5-25:** CORRECT LOGIC THAT CHARGES FULL PRICE FOR MOVIE PATRONS OVER 12 AND UNDER 65

```
if patronAge > 12 AND patronAge < 65 then
    price = fullPrice
else
    price = discountPrice
endif
```

**TIP** □ □ □ □ Using an OR operator in a decision that involves multiple conditions does not eliminate your responsibility for determining which of the conditions to test first. Even when you use an OR operator, the computer makes decisions one at a time, and makes them in the order you ask them. If the first question in an OR expression evaluates to true, then the entire expression is true, and the second question will not even be tested.

## WRITING OR DECISIONS FOR EFFICIENCY

You can write a program that creates a report containing all employees who have either the medical or dental insurance by using the `mainLoop()` in either Figure 5-26 or Figure 5-27.

**FIGURE 5-2b:** `mainLoop()` TO SELECT EMPLOYEES WITH MEDICAL OR DENTAL INSURANCE, USING MEDICAL DECISION FIRST

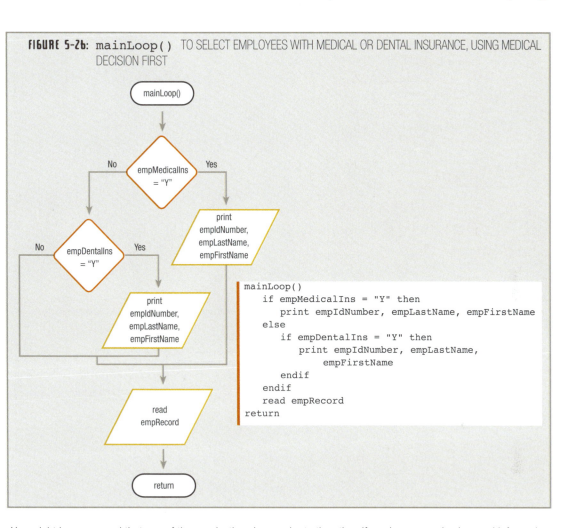

```
mainLoop()
    if empMedicalIns = "Y" then
        print empIdNumber, empLastName, empFirstName
    else
        if empDentalIns = "Y" then
            print empIdNumber, empLastName,
                empFirstName
        endif
    endif
    read empRecord
return
```

You might have guessed that one of these selections is superior to the other, if you have some background information about the relative likelihood of each condition you are testing. For example, once again assume you know that out of 1,000 employees in your company, about 90 percent, or 900, participate in the medical insurance plan, and about half, or 500, participate in the dental plan.

When you use the logic shown in Figure 5-26 to select employees who participate in either insurance plan, you first ask about medical insurance. For 900 employees, the answer is true; you print these employee records. Only about 100 records continue to the next question regarding dental insurance, where about half, or 50, fulfill the requirements to print. In the end, you print about 950 employees.

If you use Figure 5-27, you ask `empDentalIns = "Y"`? first. The result is true for 50 percent, or 500 employees, whose names then print. Five hundred employee records then progress to the medical insurance question, after which 90 percent, or 450, of them print.

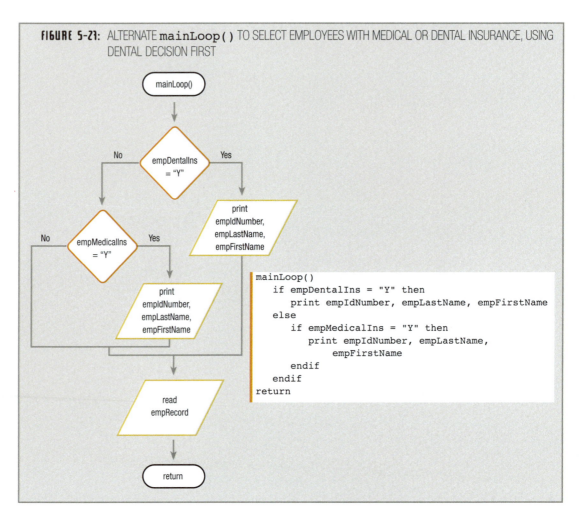

**FIGURE 5-27:** ALTERNATE `mainLoop()` TO SELECT EMPLOYEES WITH MEDICAL OR DENTAL INSURANCE, USING DENTAL DECISION FIRST

```
mainLoop()
    if empDentalIns = "Y" then
        print empIdNumber, empLastName, empFirstName
    else
        if empMedicalIns = "Y" then
            print empIdNumber, empLastName,
                empFirstName
        endif
    endif
return
```

Using either scenario, 950 employee records appear on the list, but the logic used in Figure 5-26 requires 1,100 decisions, whereas the logic used in Figure 5-27 requires 1,500 decisions. The general rule is: *In an OR decision, first ask the question that is more likely to be true.* Because a record qualifies for printing as soon as it passes one test, asking the more likely question first eliminates as many records as possible from having to go through the second decision. The time it takes to execute the program is decreased.

## COMBINING DECISIONS IN AN OR SELECTION

When you need to take action when either one or the other of two conditions is met, you can use two separate, nested selection structures, as in the previous examples. However, most programming languages allow you to ask two or more questions in a single comparison by using a **logical OR operator**—for example, `empDentalIns = "Y" OR empMedicalIns = "Y"`. When you use the logical OR operator, only one of the listed conditions must be met for the resulting action to take place. If the programming language you use allows this construct, you still must realize that the question you place first is the question that will be asked first, and cases eliminated by the first question will not proceed to the second question. The computer can ask only one question at a time; even when you draw the flowchart in Figure 5-28, the computer will execute the logic in the flowchart in Figure 5-29.

**TIP** ▫ ▫ ▫ ▫ | C#, C++, C, and Java use the symbol ‖ to represent the logical OR.

**FIGURE 5-28:** FLOWCHART AND PSEUDOCODE OF AN OR DECISION USING AN OR OPERATOR

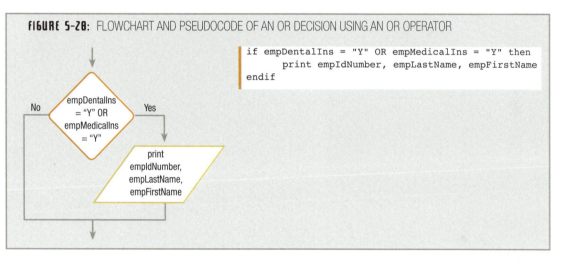

```
if empDentalIns = "Y" OR empMedicalIns = "Y" then
        print empIdNumber, empLastName, empFirstName
endif
```

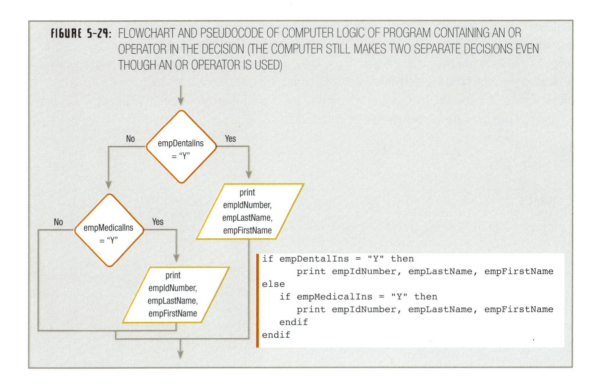

**FIGURE 5-29:** FLOWCHART AND PSEUDOCODE OF COMPUTER LOGIC OF PROGRAM CONTAINING AN OR OPERATOR IN THE DECISION (THE COMPUTER STILL MAKES TWO SEPARATE DECISIONS EVEN THOUGH AN OR OPERATOR IS USED)

```
if empDentalIns = "Y" then
      print empIdNumber, empLastName, empFirstName
else
   if empMedicalIns = "Y" then
      print empIdNumber, empLastName, empFirstName
   endif
endif
```

## USING SELECTIONS WITHIN RANGES

Business programs often need to make selections based on a variable falling within a range of values. For example, suppose you want to print a list of all employees and the names of their supervisors. An employee's supervisor is assigned according to the employee's department number, as shown in Figure 5-30.

**FIGURE 5-30:** SUPERVISORS BY DEPARTMENT

| DEPARTMENT NUMBER | SUPERVISOR |
|---|---|
| 1–3 | Dillon |
| 4–7 | Escher |
| 8–9 | Fontana |

When you write the program that reads each employee's record, you could make nine decisions before printing the supervisor's name, such as `empDept = 1?`, `empDept = 2?`, and so on. However, it is more convenient to find the supervisor by using a range check.

When you use a **range check**, you compare a variable to a series of values between limits. To perform a range check, make comparisons using either the lowest or highest value in each range of values you are using. For example, to find each employee's supervisor as listed in Figure 5-30, either use the values 1, 4, and 8, which represent the low ends of each supervisor's department range, or use the values 3, 7, and 9, which represent the high ends.

Figure 5-31 shows the flowchart and pseudocode that represent the logic for choosing a supervisor name by using the high-end range values. You test the `empDept` value for less than or equal to the high end of the lowest range group. If the comparison evaluates as true, you know the `supervisorName`. If not, you continue checking.

**FIGURE 5-31:** USING HIGH-END VALUES FOR A RANGE CHECK

```
if empDept >= 8 then
    supervisorName = "Fontana"
else
    if empDept >= 4 then
        supervisorName = "Escher"
    else
        supervisorName = "Dillon"
    endif
endif
```

**TIP** ☐ ☐ ☐ ☐   In Figure 5-31, notice how each `else` aligns vertically with its corresponding `if`.

For example, consider records containing three different values for `empDept`, and compare how they would be handled by the set of decisions in Figure 5-31.

- First, assume that the value of `empDept` for a record is 2. Using the logic in Figure 5-31, the value of the Boolean expression `empDept <= 3` is true, the `supervisorName` is set to "Dillon", and the `if` structure ends. In this case, the second decision, `empDept <= 7`, is never made, because the `else` half of the `empDept <= 3` never executes.

- Next, assume that for another record, the value of `empDept` is 7. Then, `empDept <= 3` evaluates as false, so the `else` clause of the decision executes. There, `empDept <= 7` is evaluated, and found to be true, so `supervisorName` becomes "Escher".

- Finally, assume that the value of `empDept` is 9. In this case, the first decision, `empDept <= 3`, is false, so the `else` clause executes. Then, the second decision, `empDept <=7`, also evaluates as false, so the `else` clause of the second decision executes, and the `supervisorName` is set to "Fontana". In this example, "Fontana" can be called a **default value**, because if neither of the two decision expressions is true, the `supervisorName` becomes "Fontana" by default. A default value is the value assigned after a series of selections are all false.

**TIP** ▫ ▫ ▫ ▫ Using the logic in Figure 5-31, the `supervisorName` becomes "Fontana" even if the `empDept` is a high, invalid value such as 10, 12, or even 300. The example is intended to be simple, using only two decisions. However, in a business application, you might consider amending the logic so an additional, third decision is made that compares `empDept` less than or equal to 9. Then, you could assign "Fontana" as the supervisor name if the `empDept` is less than or equal to 9, and issue an error message if the `empDept` is not. You might also want to insert a similar decision at the beginning of the program segment to make sure the `empDept` is not less than 1.

The flowchart and pseudocode for choosing a supervisor name using the reverse of this method, by comparing the employee department to the low end of the range values that represent each supervisor's area, appear in Figure 5-32. Using the technique shown in Figure 5-32, you compare `empDept` to the low end (8) of the highest range (8 to 9) first; if the `empDept` falls in the range, the `supervisorName` is known; otherwise, you check the next lower group. In this example, "Dillon" becomes the default value. That is, if the department number is not greater than or equal to 8, and it is also not greater than or equal to 4, then by default, the supervisor name is set to "Dillon".

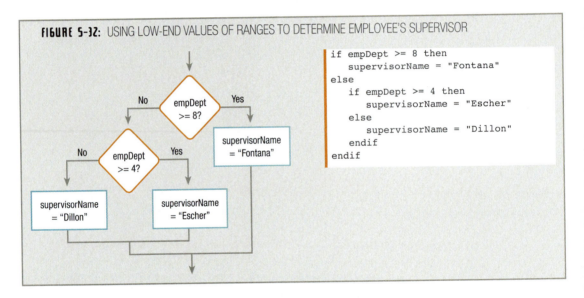

**FIGURE 5-32:** USING LOW-END VALUES OF RANGES TO DETERMINE EMPLOYEE'S SUPERVISOR

```
if empDept >= 8 then
    supervisorName = "Fontana"
else
    if empDept >= 4 then
        supervisorName = "Escher"
    else
        supervisorName = "Dillon"
    endif
endif
```

## COMMON ERRORS USING RANGE CHECKS

Two common errors that occur when programmers perform range checks both entail doing more work than is necessary. Figure 5-33 shows a range check in which the programmer has asked one question too many. If you know that all `empDept` values are positive numbers, then if the `empDept` is not greater than or equal to 8, and it is also not greater than or equal to 4, then by default it must be greater than or equal to 1. Asking whether `empDept` is greater than or equal to 1 is a waste of time; no employee record can ever travel the logical path on the far left. You might say that the path that can never be traveled is a **dead** or **unreachable path**, and that the statements written there constitute dead or unreachable code. Providing such a path is always a logical error.

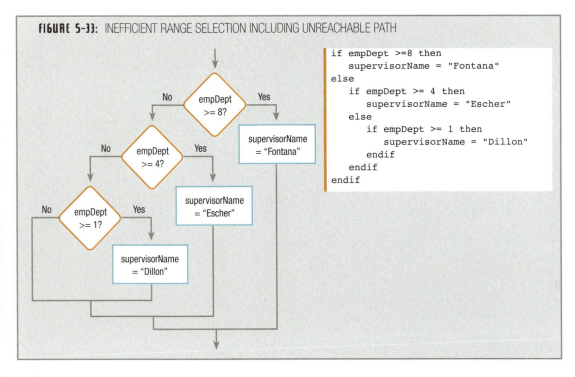

**FIGURE 5-33:** INEFFICIENT RANGE SELECTION INCLUDING UNREACHABLE PATH

```
if empDept >=8 then
    supervisorName = "Fontana"
else
    if empDept >= 4 then
        supervisorName = "Escher"
    else
        if empDept >= 1 then
            supervisorName = "Dillon"
        endif
    endif
endif
```

**TIP** ▫ ▫ ▫ ▫   When you ask questions of human beings, you sometimes ask a question to which you already know the answer. For example, in court, a good trial lawyer seldom asks a question if the answer will be a surprise. With computer logic, however, such questions are an inefficient waste of time.

Another error that programmers make when writing the logic to perform a range check also involves asking unnecessary questions. You should never ask a question if there is only one possible answer or outcome. Figure 5-34 shows an inefficient range selection that asks two unneeded questions. In the figure, if `empDept` is greater than or equal to 8, "Fontana" is the supervisor. If the `empDept` is not greater than or equal to 8, then it must be less than 8, so the next question does not have to check for less than 8. The computer logic will never execute the second decision unless the `empDept` is already less than 8—that is, unless it follows the false branch of the first selection. If you use the logic in Figure 5-34, you are wasting computer time asking a question that has previously been answered. Similarly, if the `empDept` is not greater than or equal to 8 and it is also not greater than or equal to 4, then it must be less than 4. Therefore, there is no reason to compare `empDept` to 4 to determine whether "Dillon" is the supervisor. If the logic makes it past the first two `if` statements in Figure 5-34, then the supervisor must be "Dillon".

**TIP** ▫ ▫ ▫ ▫   Beginning programmers sometimes justify their use of unnecessary questions as "just making really sure." Such caution is unnecessary when writing computer logic.

**FIGURE 5-34:** INEFFICIENT RANGE SELECTION INCLUDING UNNECESSARY QUESTION

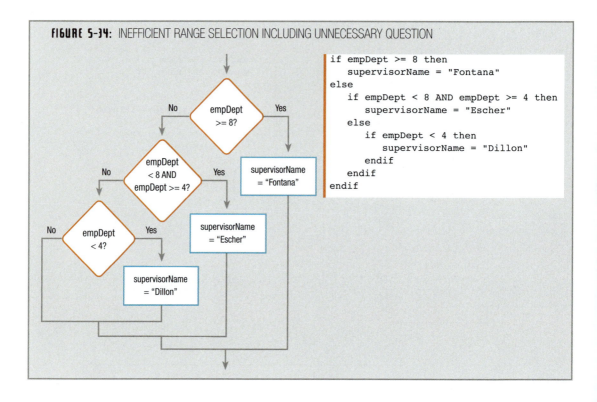

```
if empDept >= 8 then
    supervisorName = "Fontana"
else
    if empDept < 8 AND empDept >= 4 then
        supervisorName = "Escher"
    else
        if empDept < 4 then
            supervisorName = "Dillon"
        endif
    endif
endif
```

## UNDERSTANDING PRECEDENCE WHEN COMBINING AND AND OR SELECTIONS

Most programming languages allow you to combine as many AND and OR operators in an expression as you need. For example, assume you need to achieve a score of at least 75 on each of three tests in order to pass a course. When multiple conditions must be true before performing an action, you can use an expression like the following:

```
if score1 >= 75 AND score2 >= 75 AND score3 >= 75 then
    classGrade = "Pass"
else
    classGrade = "Fail"
endif
```

On the other hand, if you need to pass only one test in order to pass the course, then the logic is as follows:

```
if score1 >= 75 OR score2 >= 75 OR score3 >= 75 then
    classGrade = "Pass"
else
    classGrade = "Fail"
endif
```

The logic becomes more complicated when you combine AND and OR operators within the same statement. When you combine AND and OR operators, the AND operators take **precedence**, meaning their Boolean values are evaluated first.

For example, consider a program that determines whether a movie theater patron can purchase a discounted ticket. Assume discounts are allowed for children (age 12 and under) and senior citizens (age 65 and older) who attend "G"-rated movies. The following code looks reasonable, but produces incorrect results, because the AND operator evaluates before the OR.

```
if age <= 12 OR age >= 65 AND rating = "G" then
    print "Discount applies"
```

For example, assume a movie patron is 10 years old and the movie rating is "R". The patron should not receive a discount— or be allowed to see the movie! However, within the previous `if` statement, the part of the expression containing the AND, `age >= 65 AND rating = "G"`, evaluates first. For a 10 year old and an "R" rated movie, the question is false (on both counts), so the entire `if` statement becomes the equivalent of the following:

```
if age <= 12 OR aFalseExpression
```

Because the patron is 10, `age <= 12` is true, so the original `if` statement becomes the equivalent of:

```
if aTrueExpression OR aFalseExpression
```

which evaluates as true. Therefore, the statement "Discount applies" prints when it should not.

Many programming languages allow you to use parentheses to correct the logic and force the expression `age <= 12 OR age >= 65` to evaluate first, as shown in the following pseudocode.

```
if (age <= 12 OR age >= 65) AND rating = "G" then
    print "Discount applies"
```

With the added parentheses, if the patron's age is 12 or under OR 65 or over, the expression is evaluated as:

```
if aTrueExpression AND rating = "G"
```

When the age value qualifies a patron for a discount, then the rating value must also be acceptable before the discount applies. This was the original intention of the statement.

You always can avoid the confusion of mixing AND and OR decisions by nesting `if` statements instead of using ANDs and ORs. With the flowchart and pseudocode shown in Figure 5-35, it is clear which movie patrons receive the discount. In the flowchart in the figure, you can see that the OR is nested entirely within the Yes branch of the `rating = "G"?` selection. Similarly, by examining the pseudocode in Figure 5-35, you can see by the alignment that if the rating is not "G", the logic proceeds directly to the last `endif` statement, bypassing any checking of the age at all.

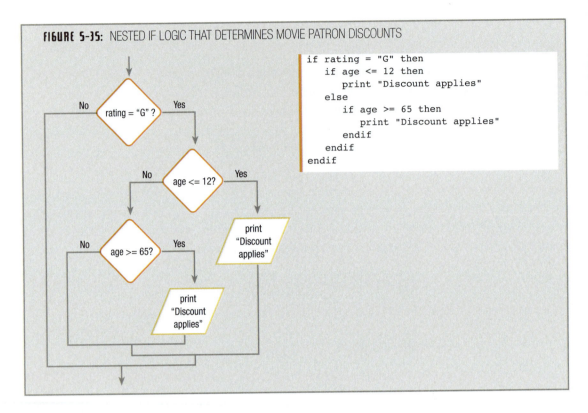

**FIGURE 5-35:** NESTED IF LOGIC THAT DETERMINES MOVIE PATRON DISCOUNTS

```
if rating = "G" then
    if age <= 12 then
        print "Discount applies"
    else
        if age >= 65 then
            print "Discount applies"
        endif
    endif
endif
```

**TIP** □ □ □ □ In every programming language, multiplication has precedence over addition in an arithmetic statement. That is, the value of 2 + 3 * 4 is 14 because the multiplication occurs before the addition. Similarly, in every programming language, AND has precedence over OR. That's because computer circuitry treats the AND operator as multiplication and the OR operator as addition. In every programming language, 1 represents true and 0 represents false. So, for example, aTrueExpression AND aTrueExpression results in true, because 1 * 1 is 1, and aTrueExpression AND aFalseExpression is false, because 1 * 0 is 0. Similarly, aFalseExpression OR aFalseExpression AND aTrueExpression evaluates to aFalseExpression because 0 + 0 * 1 is 0, whereas aFalseExpression AND aFalseExpression OR aTrueExpression evaluates to aTrueExpression result because 0 * 0 + 1 evaluates to 1.

## UNDERSTANDING THE CASE STRUCTURE

When you have a series of decisions based on the value stored in a single variable, most languages allow you to use a case structure. You first learned about the case structure in Chapter 2. There, you learned that you can solve any programming problem using only the three basic structures—sequence, selection, and loop. You are never required to use a case structure—you can always substitute a series of selections. The **case structure** simply provides a convenient alternative to using a series of decisions when you must make choices based on the value stored in a single variable.

For example, suppose you work for a real estate developer who is selling houses that have one of three different floor plans. The logic segment of a program that determines the base price of the house might look like the logic shown in Figure 5-36.

**FIGURE 5-36:**  FLOWCHART AND PSEUDOCODE OF HOUSING MODEL USING IFS

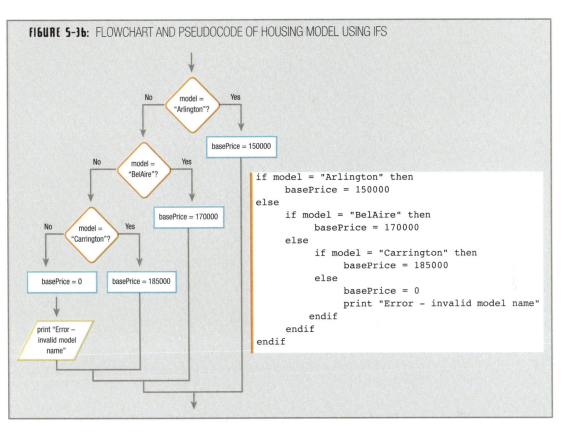

```
if model = "Arlington" then
      basePrice = 150000
else
      if model = "BelAire" then
            basePrice = 170000
      else
            if model = "Carrington" then
                  basePrice = 185000
            else
                  basePrice = 0
                  print "Error - invalid model name"
            endif
      endif
endif
```

The logic shown in Figure 5-36 is completely structured. However, rewriting the logic using a case structure, as shown in Figure 5-37, might make it easier to understand. When using the case structure, you test a variable against a series of values, taking appropriate action based on the variable's value.

In Figure 5-37, the `model` variable is compared in turn with "Arlington", "BelAire", and "Carrington", and an appropriate `basePrice` value is set. The default case is the case that executes in the event no other cases execute. The logic shown in Figure 5-36 is identical to that shown in Figure 5-37; your choice of method to set the housing model prices is entirely a matter of preference.

**TIP** ▫ ▫ ▫ ▫    When you look at a nested `if-else` structure containing an outer and inner selection, if the inner nested `if` is within the `if` portion of the outer `if`, the program segment is a candidate for AND logic. On the other hand, if the inner `if` is within the `else` portion of the outer `if`, the program segment might be a candidate for the case structure.

**TIP** ▫ ▫ ▫ ▫    Some languages require a break statement at the end of each case selection segment. In those languages, once a case is true, all the following cases execute until a break statement is encountered. When you study a specific programming language, you will learn how to use break statements if they are required in that language.

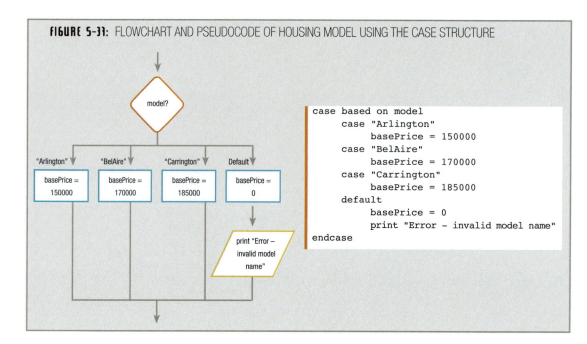

**FIGURE 5-37:** FLOWCHART AND PSEUDOCODE OF HOUSING MODEL USING THE CASE STRUCTURE

```
case based on model
    case "Arlington"
        basePrice = 150000
    case "BelAire"
        basePrice = 170000
    case "Carrington"
        basePrice = 185000
    default
        basePrice = 0
        print "Error - invalid model name"
endcase
```

## USING DECISION TABLES

Some programs require multiple decisions to produce the correct output. Managing all possible outcomes of multiple decisions can be a difficult task, so programmers sometimes use a tool called a decision table to help organize the possible decision outcome combinations.

A **decision table** is a problem-analysis tool that consists of four parts:

- Conditions
- Possible combinations of Boolean values for the conditions
- Possible actions based on the conditions
- The specific action that corresponds to each Boolean value of each condition

For example, suppose a college collects input data like that shown in Figure 5-38. Each student's data record includes the student's age and a variable that indicates whether the student has requested a residence hall that enforces quiet study hours.

**FIGURE 5-38:** STUDENT FILE DESCRIPTION

```
STUDENT FILE DESCRIPTION
File Name: STURESFILE
FIELD DESCRIPTION      POSITION      DATA TYPE      DECIMALS      EXAMPLE
ID Number              1—4           Numeric        0             5377
Last Name              5—20          Character                    Bowers
First Name             21—35         Character                    Laurel
Age                    36—37         Numeric        0             19
Request for Hall       38            Character                    Y
  with Quiet Hours
```

Assume the residence hall director makes residence hall assignments based on the following rules:

- Students who are under 21 years old and who request a residence hall with quiet study hours are assigned to Addams Hall.

- Students who are under 21 years old and who do not request a residence hall with quiet study hours are assigned to Grant Hall.

- Students who are 21 years old and over and who request a residence hall with quiet study hours are assigned to Lincoln Hall.

- Students who are 21 years old and over and who do not request a residence hall with quiet study hours are also assigned to Lincoln Hall.

You can create a program that assigns each student to the appropriate residence hall and prints a list of students along with each student's hall assignment. The print chart for the report is shown in Figure 5-39. The mainline logic for this program appears in Figure 5-40. Most programs you write will contain the same basic mainline logic: Each performs start-up or housekeeping tasks, a main loop that acts repeatedly—once for each input record, and a finishing module that performs any necessary program-ending tasks, including closing the open files.

**FIGURE 5-39:** PRINT CHART FOR STUDENT RESIDENCE HALL ASSIGNMENTS REPORT

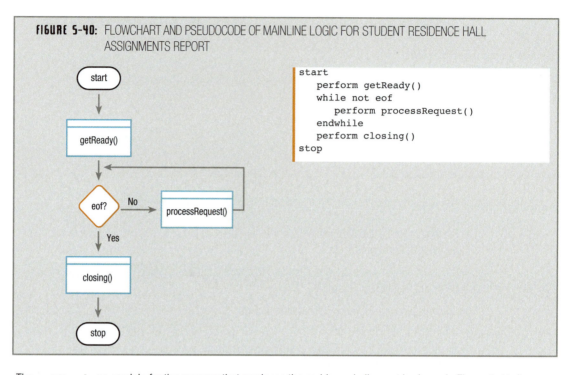

**FIGURE 5-40:** FLOWCHART AND PSEUDOCODE OF MAINLINE LOGIC FOR STUDENT RESIDENCE HALL ASSIGNMENTS REPORT

```
start
    perform getReady()
    while not eof
        perform processRequest()
    endwhile
    perform closing()
stop
```

The `getReady()` module for the program that produces the residence hall report is shown in Figure 5-41. It declares variables, opens the files, prints the report headings, and reads the first data record into memory.

Before you draw a flowchart or write the pseudocode for the `processRequest()` module, you can create a decision table to help you manage all the decisions. You can begin to create a decision table by listing all possible conditions. They are:

- stuAge < 21, or not
- stuQuietRequest = "Y", or not

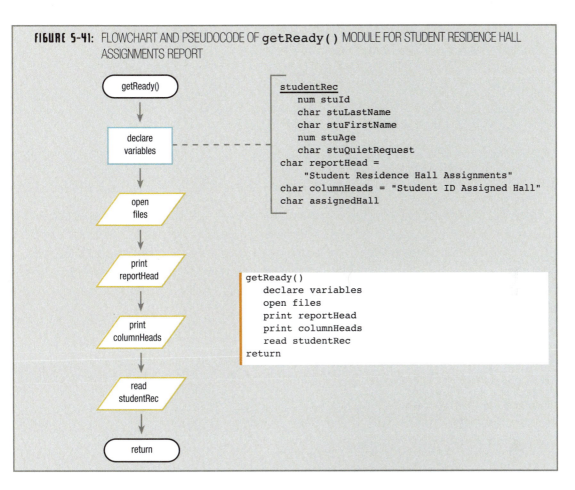

**FIGURE 5-41:** FLOWCHART AND PSEUDOCODE OF `getReady()` MODULE FOR STUDENT RESIDENCE HALL ASSIGNMENTS REPORT

```
getReady()
    declare variables
    open files
    print reportHead
    print columnHeads
    read studentRec
return
```

Next determine how many possible Boolean value combinations exist for the conditions. In this case, there are four possible combinations, shown in Figure 5-42. A student can be under 21, request a residence hall with quiet hours, both, or neither. Because each condition has two outcomes and there are two conditions, there are 2 * 2, or four, possibilities. Three conditions would produce eight possibilities (2 * 2 * 2); four conditions would produce 16 possible outcome combinations (2 * 2 * 2 * 2), and so on.

**FIGURE 5-42:** POSSIBLE OUTCOMES OF RESIDENCE HALL REQUEST CONDITIONS

| Condition | Outcome | | | |
|---|---|---|---|---|
| stuAge < 21 | T | T | F | F |
| stuQuietRequest = "Y" | T | F | T | F |

Next, add rows to the decision table to list the possible outcome actions. A student might be assigned to Addams, Grant, or Lincoln Hall. Figure 5-43 shows an expanded decision table that includes these three possible outcomes.

**FIGURE 5-43:** DECISION TABLE INCLUDING POSSIBLE OUTCOMES OF RESIDENCE HALL DECISIONS

| Condition | Outcome | | | |
|---|---|---|---|---|
| stuAge < 21 | T | T | F | F |
| stuQuietRequest = "Y" | T | F | T | F |
| assignedHall = "Addams" | | | | |
| assignedHall = "Grant" | | | | |
| assignedHall = "Lincoln" | | | | |

You choose one required outcome for each possible combination of conditions. As shown in Figure 5-44, you place an X in the Addams Hall row when `stuAge` is less than 21 and the student requests a residence hall with quiet study hours. You place an X in the Grant Hall row under the condition when a student is under 21 but does not request a residence hall with quiet hours. Finally, you place Xs in the Lincoln Hall row for both `stuQuietRequest` values when a student is not under 21 years old—only one residence hall is available for students 21 and over, whether they have requested a hall with quiet hours or not.

**FIGURE 5-44:** COMPLETED DECISION TABLE FOR RESIDENCE HALL SELECTION

| Condition | Outcome | | | |
|---|---|---|---|---|
| stuAge < 21 | T | T | F | F |
| stuQuietRequest = "Y" | T | F | T | F |
| assignedHall = "Addams" | X | | | |
| assignedHall = "Grant" | | X | | |
| assignedHall = "Lincoln" | | | X | X |

The decision table is complete (count the Xs—there are four possible outcomes). Take a moment and confirm that each residence hall selection is the appropriate value based on the original specifications. Now that the decision table is complete, you can start to plan the logic.

If you choose to use a flowchart to express the logic, you start by drawing a path to the outcome shown in the first column. This result (which occurs when `stuAge < 21` and `stuQuietRequest = "Y"`) sets the residence hall to "Addams". Next, add the resulting action shown in the second column of the decision table, which occurs when `stuAge < 21` is true and `stuQuietRequest = "Y"` is false. In those cases, the residence hall becomes "Grant". See Figure 5-45.

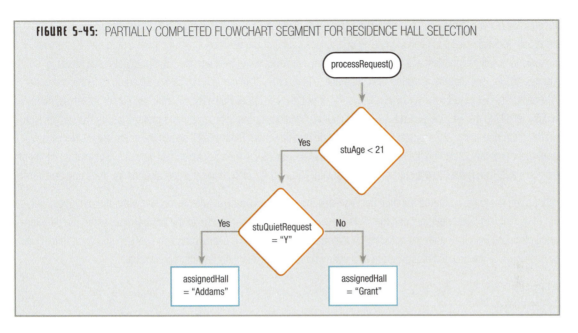

**FIGURE 5-45:** PARTIALLY COMPLETED FLOWCHART SEGMENT FOR RESIDENCE HALL SELECTION

Next, on the false outcome side of the `stuAge < 21` question, you add the resulting action shown in the third column of the decision table—set the residence hall to "Lincoln". This action occurs when `stuAge < 21` is false and `stuQuietRequest = "Y"` is true. Finally, add the resulting action shown in the fourth column of the decision table, which occurs when both conditions are false. When a student is not under 21 and does not request a hall with quiet study hours, then the assigned hall is "Lincoln". See Figure 5-46.

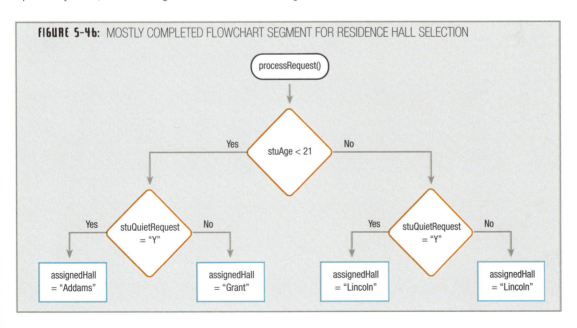

**FIGURE 5-46:** MOSTLY COMPLETED FLOWCHART SEGMENT FOR RESIDENCE HALL SELECTION

The decision making in the flowchart segment is now complete and accurately assigns each student to the correct residence hall. To finish it, all you need to do is tie up the loose ends of the decision structure, print a student's ID number and residence hall assignment, and read the next record. However, if you examine the two rightmost result boxes in Figure 5-46, you see that the assigned residence hall is identical—"Lincoln" in both cases. When a student is not under 21, whether the `stuQuietRequest` equals "Y" or not, the residence hall assignment is the same; therefore, there is no point in asking the `stuQuietRequest` question. Additionally, many programmers prefer that the True or Yes side of a flowchart decision always appears on the right side of a flowchart. Figure 5-47 shows the complete residence hall assignment program, including the redrawn `processRequest()` module, which has only one "Lincoln" assignment statement and True results to the right of each selection. Figure 5-47 also shows the pseudocode for the same problem.

Perhaps you could have created the final decision-making `processRequest()` module without creating the decision table first. If so, you need not use the table. Decision tables are more useful to the programmer when the decision-making process becomes more complicated. Additionally, they serve as a useful graphic tool when you want to explain the decision-making process of a program to a user who is not familiar with flowcharting symbols.

**TIP** ▫ ▫ ▫ ▫ In Appendix C, you can walk through the process used to create a larger decision table.

**FIGURE 5-47:** COMPLETE FLOWCHART AND PSEUDOCODE FOR RESIDENCE HALL SELECTION PROBLEM

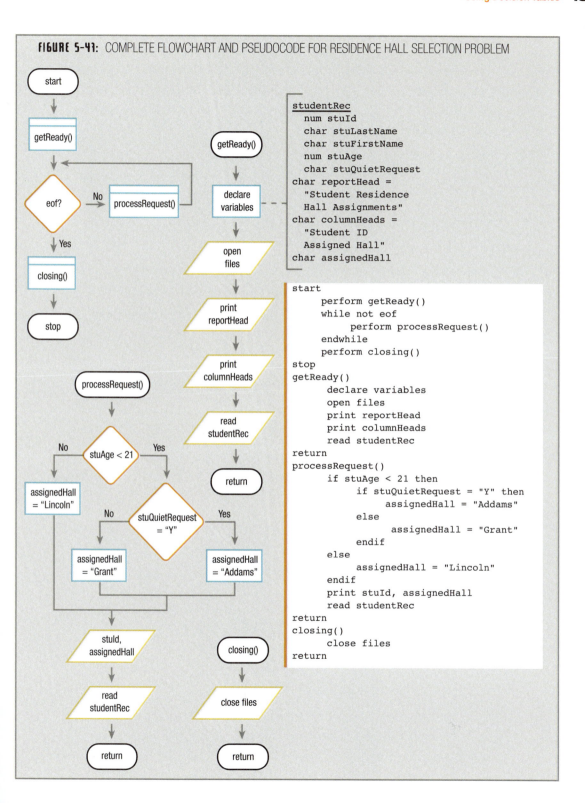

```
studentRec
  num stuId
  char stuLastName
  char stuFirstName
  num stuAge
  char stuQuietRequest
char reportHead =
  "Student Residence
  Hall Assignments"
char columnHeads =
  "Student ID
  Assigned Hall"
char assignedHall
```

```
start
    perform getReady()
    while not eof
        perform processRequest()
    endwhile
    perform closing()
stop
getReady()
    declare variables
    open files
    print reportHead
    print columnHeads
    read studentRec
return
processRequest()
    if stuAge < 21 then
        if stuQuietRequest = "Y" then
            assignedHall = "Addams"
        else
            assignedHall = "Grant"
        endif
    else
        assignedHall = "Lincoln"
    endif
    print stuId, assignedHall
    read studentRec
return
closing()
    close files
return
```

## CHAPTER SUMMARY

☐ Every decision you make in a computer program involves evaluating a Boolean expression. You can use dual-alternative, or binary, selections or if-then-else structures to choose between two possible outcomes. You also can use single-alternative, or unary, selections or if-then structures when there is only one outcome for the question where action is required.

☐ For any two values that are the same type, you can use logical comparison operators to decide whether the two values are equal, the first value is greater than the second value, or the first value is less than the second value. The two values used in a Boolean expression can be either variables or constants.

☐ An AND decision occurs when two conditions must be true in order for a resulting action to take place. An AND decision requires a nested decision or a nested if.

☐ In an AND decision, first ask the question that is less likely to be true. This eliminates as many records as possible from the number that have to go through the second decision, which speeds up processing time.

☐ Most programming languages allow you to ask two or more questions in a single comparison by using a logical AND operator.

☐ When you must satisfy two or more criteria to initiate an event in a program, you must make sure that the second decision is made entirely within the first decision, and that you use a complete Boolean expression on both sides of the AND.

☐ An OR decision occurs when you want to take action when one or the other of two conditions is true.

☐ Errors occur in OR decisions when programmers do not maintain structure. An additional source of errors that are particular to the OR selection stems from people using the word AND to express OR requirements.

☐ In an OR decision, first ask the question that is more likely to be true.

☐ Most programming languages allow you to ask two or more questions in a single comparison by using a logical OR operator.

☐ To perform a range check, make comparisons with either the lowest or highest value in each range of values you are using.

☐ Common errors that occur when programmers perform range checks include asking unnecessary and previously answered questions.

☐ The case structure provides a convenient alternative to using a series of decisions when you must make choices based on the value stored in a single variable.

☐ A decision table is a problem-analysis tool that consists of conditions, possible combinations of Boolean values for the conditions, possible actions based on the conditions, and the action that corresponds to each Boolean value of each condition.

## KEY TERMS

A **dual-alternative**, or **binary**, selection offers two actions, each associated with one of two possible outcomes. It is also called an **if-then-else** structure.

In a **single-alternative**, or **unary**, selection, action is required for only one outcome of the question. You call this form of the selection structure an **if-then**, because no "else" action is necessary.

An **if clause** of a decision holds the action that results when a Boolean expression in a decision is true.

The **else clause** of a decision holds the action or actions that execute only when the Boolean expression in the decision is false.

A **Boolean expression** is one that represents only one of two states, usually expressed as true or false.

A **trivial** Boolean expression is one that always evaluates to the same result.

**Logical comparison operators** are the symbols that express Boolean comparisons. Examples include =, >, <, >=, <=, and <>.

With an **AND decision**, two conditions must both be true for an action to take place. An AND decision requires a **nested decision**, or a **nested if**—that is, a decision "inside of" another decision. A series of nested if statements can also be called a **cascading if statement**.

A **logical AND operator** is a symbol that you use to combine decisions so that two (or more) conditions must be true for an action to occur.

A **range** of values encompasses every value between a high and low limit.

An **OR decision** contains two (or more) decisions; if at least one condition is met, the resulting action takes place.

A **logical OR operator** is a symbol that you use to combine decisions when any one condition can be true for an action to occur.

When you use a **range check**, you compare a variable to a series of values between limits.

A **default value** is one that is assigned after all test conditions are found to be false.

A **dead** or **unreachable path** is a logical path that can never be traveled.

When an operator has **precedence**, it is evaluated before others.

The **case structure** provides a convenient alternative to using a series of decisions when you must make choices based on the value stored in a single variable.

A **decision table** is a problem-analysis tool that consists of four parts: conditions, possible combinations of Boolean values for the conditions, possible actions based on the conditions, and the specific action that corresponds to each Boolean value of each condition.

## REVIEW QUESTIONS

1. The selection statement `if quantity > 100 then discountRate = 0.20` is an example of a _____.

   a. single-alternative selection
   b. dual-alternative selection
   c. binary selection
   d. all of the above

2. The selection statement `if dayOfWeek = "S" then price = 5.00 else price = 6.00` is an example of a _____.

   a. unary selection
   b. single-alternative selection
   c. binary selection
   d. all of the above

3. All selection statements must have _____.

   a. an `if` clause
   b. an `else` clause
   c. both of these
   d. neither of these

4. An expression like `amount < 10` is a _____ expression.

   a. Gregorian
   b. Boolean
   c. unary
   d. binary

5. Usually, you compare only variables that have the same _____.

   a. value
   b. size
   c. name
   d. type

6. Symbols like > and < are known as _____ operators.

   a. arithmetic
   b. logical comparison
   c. sequential
   d. scripting accuracy

7. If you could use only three logical comparison operators, you could get by with _____.

   a. greater than, less than, and greater than or equal to
   b. less than, less than or equal to, and not equal to
   c. equal to, less than, and greater than
   d. equal to, not equal to, and less than

8. **If a > b is false, then which of the following is always true?**

   a. a < b

   b. a <= b

   c. a = b

   d. a >= b

9. **Usually, the most difficult comparison operator to work with is _____.**

   a. equal to

   b. greater than

   c. less than

   d. not equal to

10. **Which of the lettered choices is equivalent to the following decision?**

```
if x > 10 then
    if y > 10 then
        print "X"
    endif
endif
```

   a. if x > 10 AND y > 10 then print "X"

   b. if x > 10 OR y > 10 then print "X"

   c. if x > 10 AND x > y then print "X"

   d. if y > x then print "X"

11. **The Midwest Sales region of Acme Computer Company consists of five states—Illinois, Indiana, Iowa, Missouri, and Wisconsin. Suppose you have input records containing Acme customer data, including state of residence. To most efficiently select and display all customers who live in the Midwest Sales region, you would use _____.**

   a. five completely separate unnested if statements

   b. nested if statements using AND logic

   c. nested if statements using OR logic

   d. Not enough information is given.

12. **The Midwest Sales region of Acme Computer Company consists of five states—Illinois, Indiana, Iowa, Missouri, and Wisconsin. About 50 percent of the regional customers reside in Illinois, 20 percent in Indiana, and 10 percent in each of the other three states. Suppose you have input records containing Acme customer data, including state of residence. To most efficiently select and display all customers who live in the Midwest Sales region, you would ask first about residency in _____.**

   a. Illinois

   b. Indiana

   c. Wisconsin

   d. either Iowa, Missouri, or Wisconsin—it does not matter which one is first

13. The Boffo Balloon Company makes helium balloons. Large balloons cost $13.00 a dozen, medium-sized balloons cost $11.00 a dozen, and small balloons cost $8.60 a dozen. About 60 percent of the company's sales are the smallest balloons, 30 percent are the medium, and large balloons constitute only 10 percent of sales. Customer order records include customer information, quantity ordered, and size. When you write a program to determine price based on size, for the most efficient decision, you should ask first whether the size is _____.

   a. large
   b. medium
   c. small
   d. It does not matter.

14. The Boffo Balloon Company makes helium balloons in 3 sizes, 12 colors, and with a choice of 40 imprinted sayings. As a promotion, the company is offering a 25-percent discount on orders of large, red "Happy Valentine's Day" balloons. To most efficiently select the orders to which a discount applies, you would use _____.

   a. three completely separate unnested `if` statements
   b. nested `if` statements using AND logic
   c. nested `if` statements using OR logic
   d. Not enough information is given.

15. Radio station FM-99 keeps a record of every song played on the air in a week. Each record contains the day, hour, and minute the song started, and the title and artist of the song. The station manager wants a list of every title played during the important 8 a.m. commute hour on the two busiest traffic days, Monday and Friday. Which logic would select the correct titles?

```
a. if day = "Monday" OR day = "Friday" OR hour = 8 then
        print title
   endif
b. if day = "Monday" then
        if hour = 8 then
            print title
        else
            if day = "Friday" then
                print title
            endif
        endif
   endif
c. if hour = 8 AND day = "Monday" OR day = "Friday" then
        print title
   endif
d. if hour = 8 then
        if day = "Monday" OR day = "Friday" then
            print title
        endif
   endif
```

16. **In the following pseudocode, what percentage raise will an employee in Department 5 receive?**

```
if department < 3 then
    raise = 25
else
    if department < 5 then
        raise = 50
    else
        raise = 75
    endif
endif
```

    a. 25

    b. 50

    c. 75

    d. impossible to tell

17. **In the following pseudocode, what percentage raise will an employee in Department 8 receive?**

```
if department < 5 then
    raise = 100
else
    if department < 14 then
        raise = 250
    else
        if department < 9 then
            raise = 375
        endif
    endif
endif
```

    a. 100

    b. 250

    c. 375

    d. impossible to tell

18. **In the following pseudocode, what percentage raise will an employee in Department 10 receive?**

```
if department < 2 then
    raise = 1000
else
    if department < 6 then
        raise = 2500
    else
        if department < 10 then
            raise = 3000
        endif
    endif
endif
```

    a. 1000

    b. 2500

    c. 3000

    d. impossible to tell

19. **When you use a range check, you compare a variable to the _____ value in the range.**

    a. lowest

    b. middle

    c. highest

    d. lowest or highest

20. **Which of the following is not a part of a decision table?**

    a. conditions

    b. declarations

    c. possible actions

    d. specific actions that will take place under given conditions

## EXERCISES

1. **Assume the following variables contain the values shown:**

    **numberRed = 100**        **numberBlue = 200**        **numberGreen = 300**

    **wordRed = "Wagon"**       **wordBlue = "Sky"**        **wordGreen = "Grass"**

    **For each of the following Boolean expressions, decide whether the statement is true, false, or illegal.**

    a. numberRed = numberBlue?

    b. numberBlue > numberGreen?

    c. numberGreen < numberRed?

    d. numberBlue = wordBlue?

    e. numberGreen = "Green"?

    f. wordRed = "Red"?

    g. wordBlue = "Blue"?

    h. numberRed <= numberGreen?

    i. numberBlue >= 200?

    j. numberGreen >= numberRed + numberBlue?

2. **A candy company wants a list of its best-selling items, including item number and name of candy. Best-selling items are those that sell over 2,000 pounds per month. Input records contain fields for the item number (three digits), the name of the candy (20 characters), the price per pound (four digits, two assumed decimal places), and the quantity in pounds sold last month (four digits, no decimals).**

    a. Design the print chart for this program.

    b. Draw the hierarchy chart for this program.

    c. Draw the flowchart for this program.

    d. Write the pseudocode for this program.

3.  The same candy company described in Exercise 2 wants a list of its high-priced, best-selling items. Best-selling items are those that sell over 2,000 pounds per month. High-priced items are those that sell for $10 per pound or more.

    a.  Design the print chart for this program.
    b.  Draw the hierarchy chart for this program.
    c.  Draw the flowchart for this program.
    d.  Write the pseudocode for this program.

4.  The Literary Honor Society needs a list of English majors who have a grade point average of 3.5 or higher. The student record file includes students' last names and first names (15 characters each), major (10 characters, for example "History" or "English"), and grade point average (two digits, one assumed decimal place, for example 3.9 or 2.0).

    a.  Design the print chart for this program.
    b.  Draw the hierarchy chart for this program.
    c.  Draw the flowchart for this program.
    d.  Write the pseudocode for this program.

5.  A telephone company charges 10 cents per minute for all calls outside the customer's area code that last over 20 minutes. All other calls are 13 cents per minute. The phone company has a file with one record for every call made in one day. (In other words, a single customer might have many such records on file.) Fields for each call include customer area code (three digits), customer phone number (seven digits), called area code (three digits), called number (seven digits), and call time in minutes (four digits). The company wants a report listing one detail line for each call, including the customer area code and number, the called area code and number, the minutes, and the total charge.

    a.  Design the print chart for this program.
    b.  Draw the hierarchy chart for this program.
    c.  Create a decision table to use while planning the logic for this program.
    d.  Draw the flowchart for this program.
    e.  Write the pseudocode for this program.

6.  A nursery maintains a file of all plants in stock. Each record contains the name of a plant, its price, and fields that indicate the plant's light and soil requirements. The light field contains either "sunny", "partial sun", or "shady". The soil field contains either "clay" or "sandy". Only 20 percent of the nursery stock does well in shade, and 50 percent does well in sandy soil. Customers have requested a report that lists the name and price of each plant that would be appropriate in a shady, sandy yard.

    a.  Design the print chart for this program.
    b.  Draw the hierarchy chart for this program.
    c.  Create a decision table to use while planning the logic for this program.
    d.  Draw the flowchart for this program.
    e.  Write the pseudocode for this program.

7.  You have declared variables for an insurance company program as follows:

```
FIELD                     POSITIONS       EXAMPLE
num custPolicyNumber      1-6             223356
char custLastName         7-20            Falkenburg
```

```
num custAge              21-23        25
num custDueMonth         24-25        06
num custDueDay           26-27        24
num custDueYear          28-31        2005
num custAccidents        32-34        2
```

**Draw the flowchart or write the pseudocode for the selection structures that print the
`custPolicyNumber` and `custLastName` for customers whose data satisfy the following
requests for lists of policyholders:**

a. over 35 years old
b. at least 21 years old
c. no more than 30 years old
d. due no later than March 15 any year
e. due up to and including January 1, 2005
f. due by April 27, 2008
g. due as early as December 1, 2004
h. fewer than 11 accidents
i. no more than 5 accidents
j. no accidents

8. **Student files contain an ID number (four digits), last and first names (15 characters each), and major
field of study (10 characters). Plan a program that lists ID numbers and names for all French or
Spanish majors.**

a. Design the print chart for this program.
b. Draw the hierarchy chart for this program.
c. Create a decision table to use while planning the logic for this program.
d. Draw the flowchart for this program.
e. Write the pseudocode for this program.

9. **A florist wants to send coupons to her best customers, so she needs a list of names and addresses
for customers who placed orders more than three times last year or spent more than $200 last year.
The input file description follows:**

```
File name: FLORISTCUSTS
FIELD DESCRIPTION        POSITIONS      TYPE          DECIMALS
Customer ID              1-3            Numeric       0
First Name               4-16           Character
Last Name                17-30          Character
Street Address           31-51          Character
Orders Last Year         52-55          Numeric       0
Amount Spent             56-62          Numeric       2
  Last Year
```

**(Note: To save room, don't include city or state. Assume all the florist's best customers are in town.)**

a. Design the print chart for this program.
b. Draw the hierarchy chart for this program.

c. Create a decision table to use while planning the logic for this program.

d. Draw the flowchart for this program.

e. Write the pseudocode for this program.

10. A carpenter needs a program that computes the price of any desk a customer orders, based on the following input fields: order number, desk length and width in inches (three digits each, no decimals), type of wood (20 characters), and number of drawers (two digits). The price is computed as follows:

☐ The charge for all desks is a minimum $200.

☐ If the surface (length * width) is over 750 square inches, add $50.

☐ If the wood is "mahogany", add $150; for "oak", add $125. No charge is added for "pine".

☐ For every drawer in the desk, there is an additional $30 charge.

a. Design the print chart for this program.

b. Draw the hierarchy chart for this program.

c. Create a decision table to use while planning the logic for this program.

d. Draw the flowchart for this program.

e. Write the pseudocode for this program.

11. A company is attempting to organize carpools to save energy. Each input record contains an employee's name and town of residence. Ten percent of the company's employees live in Wonder Lake. Thirty percent of the employees live in Woodstock. Because these towns are both north of the company, the company wants a list of employees who live in either town, so it can recommend that these employees drive to work together.

a. Design the print chart for this program.

b. Draw the hierarchy chart for this program.

c. Create a decision table to use while planning the logic for this program.

d. Draw the flowchart for this program.

e. Write the pseudocode for this program.

12. A supervisor in a manufacturing company wants to produce a report showing which employees have increased their production this year over last year, so that she can issue them a certificate of commendation. She wants to have a report with three columns: last name, first name, and either the word "UP" or blanks printed under the column heading PRODUCTION. "UP" is printed when this year's production is a greater number than last year's production. Input exists as follows:

```
PRODUCTION FILE DESCRIPTION
File name: PRODUCTION
```

| FIELD DESCRIPTION | POSITIONS | DATA TYPE | DECIMALS |
|---|---|---|---|
| Last Name | 1-20 | Character | |
| First Name | 21-30 | Character | |
| Last Year's Production | 31-34 | Numeric | 0 |
| This Year's Production | 35-38 | Numeric | 0 |

    a. Design the print chart for this program.

    b. Draw the hierarchy chart for this program.

    c. Create a decision table to use while planning the logic for this program.

    d. Draw the flowchart for this program.

    e. Write the pseudocode for this program.

13. **A supervisor in the same manufacturing company as described in Exercise 12 wants to produce a report from the PRODUCTION input file showing bonuses she is planning to give based on this year's production. She wants to have a report with three columns: last name, first name, and bonus. The bonuses will be distributed as follows.**

**If this year's production is:**

    ☐ 1,000 units or fewer, the bonus is $25

    ☐ 1,001 to 3,000 units, the bonus is $50

    ☐ 3,001 to 6,000 units, the bonus is $100

    ☐ 6,001 units and up, the bonus is $200

    a. Design the print chart for this program.

    b. Draw the hierarchy chart for this program.

    c. Create a decision table to use while planning the logic for this program.

    d. Draw the flowchart for this program.

    e. Write the pseudocode for this program.

14. **Modify Exercise 13 to reflect the following new facts, and have the program execute as efficiently as possible:**

    ☐ Only employees whose production this year is higher than it was last year will receive bonuses. This is true for approximately 30 percent of the employees.

    ☐ Sixty percent of employees produce over 6,000 units per year; 20 percent produce 3,001 to 6,000; 15 percent produce 1,001 to 3,000 units; and only 5 percent produce fewer than 1,001.

    a. Design the print chart for this program.

    b. Draw the hierarchy chart for this program.

    c. Create a decision table to use while planning the logic for this program.

    d. Draw the flowchart for this program.

    e. Write the pseudocode for this program.

15. **The Richmond Riding Club wants to assign the title of Master or Novice to each of its members. A member earns the title of Master by accomplishing two or more of the following:**

☐ Participating in at least eight horse shows

☐ Winning a first or second place ribbon in at least two horse shows, no matter how many shows the member has participated in

☐ Winning a first, second, third, or fourth place ribbon in at least four horse shows, no matter how many shows the member has participated in

**Create a report that prints each club member's name along with the designation "Master" or "Novice". Input exists as follows:**

```
PRODUCTION FILE DESCRIPTION
File name: RIDING
FIELD DESCRIPTION          POSITIONS      DATA TYPE      DECIMALS
Last Name                  1-15           Character
First Name                 16-25          Character
Number of shows            26-28          Numeric        0
First Place Ribbons        29-31          Numeric        0
Second Place Ribbons       32-34          Numeric        0
Third Place Ribbons        35-37          Numeric        0
Fourth Place Ribbons       38-40          Numeric        0
```

a. Design the print chart for this program.

b. Draw the hierarchy chart for this program.

c. Create a decision table to use while planning the logic for this program.

d. Draw the flowchart for this program.

e. Write the pseudocode for this program.

# 6

# LOOPING

## After studying Chapter 6, you should be able to:

- ☐ Understand the advantages of looping
- ☐ Control a `while` loop using a loop control variable
- ☐ Increment a counter to control a loop
- ☐ Loop with a variable sentinel value
- ☐ Control a loop by decrementing a loop control variable
- ☐ Avoid common loop mistakes
- ☐ Use a `for` loop
- ☐ Use a `do until` loop
- ☐ Recognize the characteristics shared by all loops
- ☐ Nest loops
- ☐ Use a loop to accumulate totals

## UNDERSTANDING THE ADVANTAGES OF LOOPING

If making decisions is what makes computers seem intelligent, it's looping that makes computer programming worthwhile. When you use a loop within a computer program, you can write one set of instructions that operates on multiple, separate sets of data. Consider the following set of tasks required for each employee in a typical payroll program:

- Determine regular pay.
- Determine overtime pay, if any.
- Determine federal withholding tax based on gross wages and number of dependents.
- Determine state withholding tax based on gross wages, number of dependents, and state of residence.
- Determine insurance deduction based on insurance code.
- Determine Social Security deduction based on gross pay.
- Subtract federal tax, state tax, Social Security, and insurance from gross pay.

In reality, this list is too short—companies deduct stock option plans, charitable contributions, union dues, and other items from checks in addition to the items mentioned in this list. Also, they might pay bonuses and commissions and provide sick days and vacation days that must be taken into account and handled appropriately. As you can see, payroll programs are complicated.

The advantage of having a computer perform payroll calculations is that all of the deduction instructions need to be written *only once* and can be repeated over and over again for each paycheck, using a **loop**, the structure that repeats actions while some condition continues.

## USING A WHILE LOOP WITH A LOOP CONTROL VARIABLE

Recall the loop, or do-while structure, that you learned about in Chapter 2. (See Figure 6-1.) In Chapter 4, you learned that almost every program has a **main loop**, or a basic set of instructions that is repeated for every record. The main loop is a typical loop—within it, you write one set of instructions that executes repeatedly while records continue to be read from an input file. Several housekeeping tasks execute at the start of most programs, and a few clean-up tasks execute at the end. However, most of a program's tasks are located in a main loop; these tasks repeat over and over for many records (sometimes hundreds, thousands, or millions).

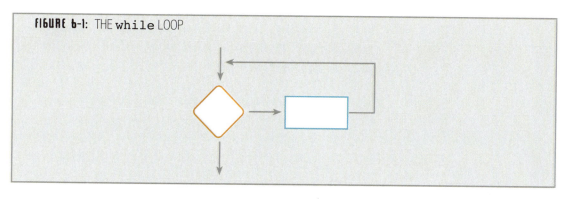

FIGURE 6-1: THE while LOOP

In addition to this main loop, loops also appear within subroutines. They are used any time you need to perform a task several times and don't want to write identical or similar instructions over and over. Suppose, for example, as part of a much larger program, you want to print a warning message on the computer screen when the user has made a potentially dangerous menu selection (for example, "Delete all files"). To get the user's attention, you want to print the message four times. You can write this program segment as shown in Figure 6-2, but using a loop, as shown in Figure 6-3, is much more efficient.

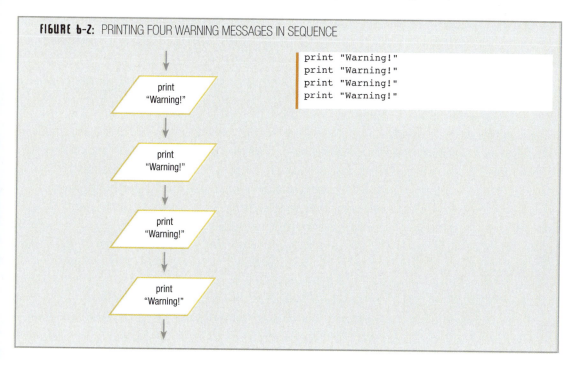

FIGURE 6-2: PRINTING FOUR WARNING MESSAGES IN SEQUENCE

```
print "Warning!"
print "Warning!"
print "Warning!"
print "Warning!"
```

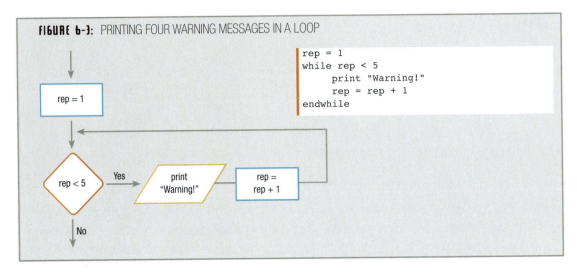

**FIGURE 6-3:** PRINTING FOUR WARNING MESSAGES IN A LOOP

```
rep = 1
while rep < 5
    print "Warning!"
    rep = rep + 1
endwhile
```

The flowchart and pseudocode segments in Figure 6-3 show three steps that must occur in every loop:

1. You must initialize a variable that will control the loop. The variable in this case is named `rep`.
2. You must compare the variable to some value that controls whether the loop continues or stops. In this case, you compare `rep` to the value 5.
3. Within the loop, you must alter the variable that controls the loop. In this case, you alter `rep` by adding 1 to it.

On each pass through the loop, the value in the `rep` variable determines whether the loop will continue. Therefore, variables like `rep` are known as **loop control variables**. Any variable that determines whether a loop will continue is a loop control variable. To stop a loop, you compare the loop control value to a **sentinel value** (also known as a limit, or ending value), in this case the value 5. The decision that controls every loop is always based on a Boolean comparison. You can use any of the six comparison operators that you learned about in Chapter 5 to control a loop—equal to, greater than, less than, greater than or equal to, less than or equal to, and not equal to.

**TIP** □ □ □ □ | Just as with a selection, the Boolean comparison that controls a `while` loop must compare same-type values: numeric values are compared to other numeric values, and character values to other character values.

The statements that execute within a loop are known as the **loop body**. The body of a loop might contain any number of statements, including subroutine calls, decisions, and other loops. Once your program enters the body of a structured loop, the entire loop body must execute. Your program can leave a structured loop only at the comparison that tests the loop control variable.

## USING A COUNTER TO CONTROL LOOPING

Suppose you own a factory and have decided to place a label on every product you manufacture. The label contains the words "Made for you personally by" followed by the first name of one of your employees. For one week's production, you need 100 personalized labels for each employee.

Assume you already have a personnel file that can be used for input. This file has more information than you'll need for this program: an employee last name, first name, Social Security number, address, date hired, and salary. The important feature of the file is that it does contain each employee's name stored in a separate record. The input file description appears in Figure 6-4.

**FIGURE 6-4:** EMPLOYEE DATA FILE DESCRIPTION

```
File Name: EMPLOYEES
FIELD DESCRIPTION          POSITIONS      DATA TYPE      DECIMALS
Employee Last Name         1–20           Character
Employee First Name        21–35          Character
Social Security Number     36–44          Numeric        0
Address                    45–60          Character
Date Hired                 61–68          Numeric        0
Hourly Salary              69–72          Numeric        2
```

In the main line of this program, you call three modules: a housekeeping module (**housekeep()**), a main loop (**mainLoop()**), and a finish routine (**finishUp()**). See Figure 6-5.

**FIGURE 6-5:** MAINLINE LOGIC FOR LABEL-MAKING PROGRAM

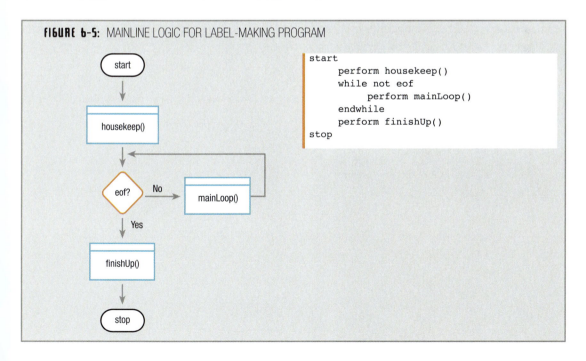

```
start
      perform housekeep()
      while not eof
            perform mainLoop()
      endwhile
      perform finishUp()
stop
```

The first task for the label program involves naming the fields on the input record so you can refer to them within the program. As a programmer, you can choose any variable names you like, for example: `inLastName`, `inFirstName`, `inSSN`, `inAddress`, `inDate`, and `inSalary`.

TIP ☐ ☐ ☐ ☐ In Chapter 4 you learned that starting all field names in the input record with the same prefix, such as `in`, is a common programming technique to help identify these fields in a large program and differentiate them from work areas and output areas that will have other names. Another benefit to using a prefix like `in` is that some language compilers also produce a dictionary of variable names when you compile your program. These dictionaries show at which lines in the program each data name is referenced. If all your input field names start with the same prefix, they will be together alphabetically in the dictionary, and perhaps be easier to find and work with.

You also can set up a variable to hold the characters "Made for you personally by" and name it `labelLine`. You eventually will print this `labelLine` variable followed by the employee's first name (`inFirstName`).

You will need one more variable: a location called a counter. A **counter** is any numeric variable you use to count the number of times an event has occurred; in this example, you need a counter to keep track of how many labels have been printed at any point. Each time you read an employee record, the counter variable is set to 0. Then every time a label is printed, you add 1 to the counter. Adding 1 to a variable is called **incrementing** the variable. Before the next employee label is printed, the program checks the variable to see if it has reached 100 yet. When it has, that means 100 labels have been printed, and the job is done for that employee. While the counter remains below 100, you continue to print labels. As with all variables, the programmer can choose any name for a counter; this program uses `labelCounter`. In this example, `labelCounter` is the loop control variable.

The `housekeep()` routine for the label program, shown in Figure 6-6, includes a step to open the files: the employee file and the printer. Unlike a program that produces a report, this program has no headings, so the next and last task performed in `housekeep()` is to read the first input record.

TIP ☐ ☐ ☐ ☐ Remember, you can give any name you like to subroutines within your programs. This program uses `housekeep()` for its first routine, but `housekeeping()`, `startUp()`, `prep()`, or any other name with the same general meaning could be used.

TIP ☐ ☐ ☐ ☐ If you don't know why the first record is read in the `housekeep()` module, go back and review the concept of the priming read, presented in Chapter 2.

## FIGURE 6-6:   THE `housekeep()` MODULE FOR THE LABEL PROGRAM

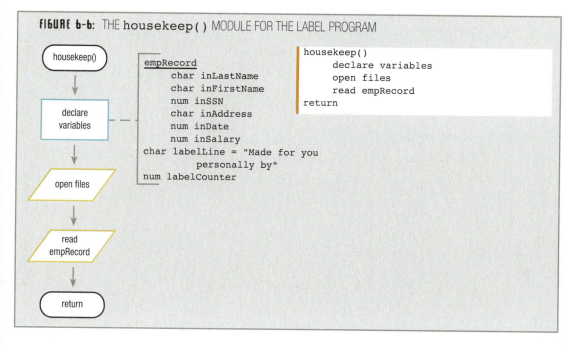

TIP ☐ ☐ ☐ ☐ In previous chapters, the list of declared variables was shown with both the flowchart and the pseudocode. To save space in the rest of the chapters in this book, the variable list will be shown only with the flowchart.

When the `housekeep()` module is done, the logical flow returns to the `eof` question in the main line. If you attempt to read the first record at the end of `housekeep()` and for some reason there is no record, the answer to `eof?` is Yes, so then the `mainLoop()` is never entered; instead, the logic of the program flows directly to the `finishUp()` module.

Usually, however, employee records will exist and the program will enter the `mainLoop()` module, which is shown in Figure 6-7. When this happens, the first employee record is sitting in memory waiting to be processed. During one execution of the `mainLoop()` module, 100 labels will be printed for one employee. As the last event within the `mainLoop()` module, the program reads the next employee record. Control of the program then returns to the `eof` question. If the new read process has not resulted in the `eof` condition, control reenters the `mainLoop()` module, where 100 more labels print for the new employee.

**FIGURE 6-7:** THE `mainLoop()` MODULE FOR THE LABEL PROGRAM

```
mainLoop()
      labelCounter = 0
      while labelCounter < 100
            print labelLine, inFirstName
            labelCounter = labelCounter + 1
      endwhile
      read empRecord
return
```

The `mainLoop()` of this label program contains three parts:

- Set the `labelCounter` to 0.
- Compare the `labelCounter` to 100.
- While the `labelCounter` is less than 100, print the `labelLine` and the `inFirstName`, and add 1 to the `labelCounter`.

When the first employee record enters the `mainLoop()` module, the `labelCounter` is set to 0. Comparing the `labelCounter` to 100 results in a true condition, so the record enters the label-making loop. One label prints for the first employee, the `labelCounter` increases by one, and the logical flow returns to the question `labelCounter < 100?`. After the first label is printed, the `labelCounter` holds a value of only 1. It is nowhere near 100 yet, so the value of the Boolean expression is true, and the loop is entered for a second time, thus printing a second label.

After the second printing, `labelCounter` holds a value of 2. After the third printing, it holds a value of 3. Finally, after the 100th label prints, `labelCounter` has a value of 100. When the question `labelCounter < 100?` is asked, the answer will finally be No, and the loop will exit.

Before leaving `mainLoop()`, and after the program prints 100 labels for an employee, there is one final step: the next input record is read from the EMPLOYEES file. When `mainLoop()` is over, control returns to the `eof` question in the main line of the logic. If it is not `eof` (if another employee record is present), the program enters `mainLoop()` again, resets `labelCounter` to 0, and prints 100 new labels with the next employee's name.

**TIP** ☐ ☐ ☐ ☐ Setting the `labelCounter` to 0 when the `mainLoop()` is entered is important. With each new record, the `labelCounter` must begin at 0 if 100 labels are to print. When the first employee's set of labels is complete, `labelCounter` holds the value 100. If it is not reset to 0 for the second employee, then no labels will ever print for that employee.

At some point while attempting to read a new record, the program encounters the end of the file, the `mainLoop()` is not entered again, and control passes to the `finishUp()` module. In this program the `finishUp()` module simply closes the files. See Figure 6-8.

**FIGURE 6-8:** THE `finishUp()` MODULE FOR THE LABEL PROGRAM

```
finishUp()
    close files
return
```

## LOOPING WITH A VARIABLE SENTINEL VALUE

Sometimes you don't want to be forced to repeat every pass through a loop the same number of times. For example, instead of printing 100 labels for each employee, you might want to vary the number of labels based on how many items a worker actually produces. That way, high-achieving workers won't run out of labels, and less productive workers won't have too many. Instead of printing the same number of labels for every employee, a more sophisticated program prints a different number of labels for each employee, depending on that employee's previous week's production. For example, you might decide to print enough labels to cover 110% of each employee's production rate from the previous week; this ensures that the employee will have enough labels for the week, even if his or her production level improves.

For example, assume that employee production data exists in an input file called EMPPRODUCTION in the format shown in Figure 6-9.

**FIGURE 6-9:** EMPLOYEE PRODUCTION FILE DESCRIPTION

```
File Name: EMPPRODUCTION
```

| FIELD DESCRIPTION | POSITIONS | DATA TYPE | DECIMALS |
|---|---|---|---|
| Last Name | 1–20 | Character | |
| First Name | 21–35 | Character | |
| Production Last Week | 36–38 | Numeric | 0 |

A real-life production file would undoubtedly have more fields in each record, but these fields supply more than enough information to produce the labels. You need the first name to print on the label, and you need the field that holds production for the last week in order to calculate the number of labels to print for each employee. This field can contain any number from 0 through 999.

To write a program that produces an appropriate number of labels for each employee, you can make some minor modifications to the original label-making program. For example, the input file variables have changed; you must declare a variable for an `inLastProduction` field. Additionally, you might want to create a numeric field named `labelsToPrint` that can hold a value equal to 110% of a worker's `inLastProduction`.

The major modification to the original label-making program is in the question that controls the label-producing loop. Instead of asking if `labelCounter < 100`, you now can ask if `labelCounter < labelsToPrint`. The sentinel or limit value can be a variable like `labelsToPrint` just as easily as it can be a constant like 100. See Figure 6-10 for the flowchart as well as the pseudocode.

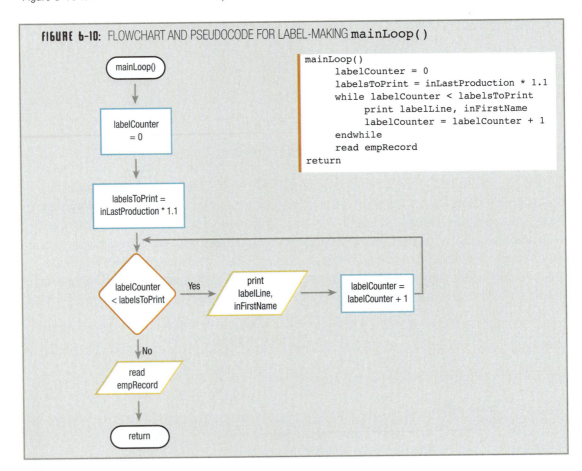

**FIGURE 6-10:** FLOWCHART AND PSEUDOCODE FOR LABEL-MAKING `mainLoop()`

```
mainLoop()
     labelCounter = 0
     labelsToPrint = inLastProduction * 1.1
     while labelCounter < labelsToPrint
          print labelLine, inFirstName
          labelCounter = labelCounter + 1
     endwhile
     read empRecord
return
```

**TIP** ☐ ☐ ☐ ☐ The statement `labelsToPrint = inLastProduction * 1.1` calculates `labelsToPrint` as 110% of `inLastProduction`. Alternately, you can perform the calculation as `labelsToPrint = inLastProduction + 0.10 * inLastProduction`. The mathematical result is the same.

## LOOPING BY DECREMENTING

Rather than increasing a loop control variable until it passes some sentinel value, sometimes it is more convenient to reduce a loop control variable on every cycle through a loop. For example, again assume you want to print enough labels for every worker to cover 110% production. As an alternative to setting a `labelCounter` variable to 0 and increasing it after each label prints, you initially can set `labelCounter` equal to the number of labels to print (`inLastProduction * 1.1`), and subsequently reduce the `labelCounter` value every time a label prints. You continue printing labels and reducing the `labelCounter` until you have counted down to zero. Decreasing a variable by one is called **decrementing** the variable.

For example, when you write the following, you produce enough labels to equal 110% of `inLastProduction`:

```
labelCounter = inLastProduction * 1.1
while labelCounter > 0
     print labelLine, inFirstName
     labelCounter = labelCounter - 1
endwhile
```

When you decrement, you can avoid declaring a special variable for the `labelsToPrint`. The `labelCounter` variable starts with a value that represents the labels to print, and works its way down to zero.

Yet another alternative allows you to eliminate the `labelCounter` variable. You could use the `inLastProduction` variable itself to keep track of the labels. For example, the following pseudocode segment also produces a number of labels equal to 110% of each worker's `inLastProduction` value:

```
inLastProduction = inLastProduction * 1.1
while inLastProduction > 0
     print labelLine, inFirstName
     inLastProduction = inLastProduction - 1
endwhile
```

In this example, `inLastProduction` is first increased by 10%. Then, while it remains above 0, there are more labels to print; when it is eventually reduced to hold the value 0, all the needed labels will have been printed. With this method, you do not need to create any new counter variables such as `labelCounter`, because `inLastProduction` itself acts as a counter. However, you can't use this method if you need to use the value of `inLastProduction` for this record later in the program. By decrementing the variable, you are changing its value on every cycle through the loop; when you have finished, the original value in `inLastProduction` has been lost.

TIP □ □ □ □ Do not think the value of `inLastProduction` is gone forever when you alter it. The original value still exists within the data file. It is the main memory location called `inLastProduction` that is being reduced.

## AVOIDING COMMON LOOP MISTAKES

The mistakes programmers make most often with loops are:

- Neglecting to initialize the loop control variable
- Neglecting to alter the loop control variable
- Using the wrong comparison with the loop control variable
- Including statements inside the loop that belong outside the loop
- Initializing a variable that does not require initialization

### NEGLECTING TO INITIALIZE THE LOOP CONTROL VARIABLE

It is always a mistake to fail to initialize a loop's control variable. For example, assume you remove the statement `labelCounter = 0` from the program illustrated in Figure 6-10. When `labelCounter` is compared to `labelsToPrint` at the start of the `while` loop, it is impossible to predict whether any labels will print. Because uninitialized values contain unknown, unpredictable garbage, comparing such a variable to another value is meaningless. Even if you initialize `labelCounter` to 0 in the `housekeep()` module of the program, you must reset `labelCounter` to 0 for each new record that is processed within the `while` loop. If you fail to reset the `labelCounter`, it never surpasses 100 because after it reaches 100, the answer to the question `labelCounter < 100` is always No, and the logic never enters the loop where a label can be printed.

### NEGLECTING TO ALTER THE LOOP CONTROL VARIABLE

A different sort of error occurs if you remove the statement that adds 1 to the `labelCounter` from the program in Figure 6-10. This error results in the following code:

```
while labelCounter < labelsToPrint
    print labelLine, inFirstName
endwhile
```

Following this logic, if `labelCounter` is 0 and `labelsToPrint` is, for example, 110, then `labelCounter` will be less than `labelsToPrint` forever. Nothing in the loop changes either variable, so when `labelCounter` is less than `labelsToPrint` once, then `labelCounter` is less than `labelsToPrint` forever, and labels will continue to print. A loop that never stops executing is called an **infinite loop**. It is always incorrect to create a loop that cannot terminate.

## USING THE WRONG COMPARISON WITH THE LOOP CONTROL VARIABLE

Programmers must be careful to use the correct comparison in the statement that controls a loop. Although there is only a one-keystroke difference between the following two code segments, one performs the loop 10 times and the other performs the loop 11 times.

```
counter = 0
while counter < 10
    perform someModule()
    counter = counter + 1
endwhile
```

and

```
counter = 0
while counter <= 10
    perform someModule()
    counter = counter + 1
endwhile
```

The seriousness of the error of using <= or >= when only < or > is needed depends on the actions performed within the loop. For example, if such an error occurred in a loan company program, each customer might be charged a month's additional interest; if the error occurred in an airline's program; it might overbook a flight; and if it occurred in a pharmacy's drug-dispensing program, each patient might receive one extra (and possibly harmful) unit of medication.

## INCLUDING STATEMENTS INSIDE THE LOOP THAT BELONG OUTSIDE THE LOOP

When you run a computer program that uses the loop in Figure 6-10, hundreds or thousands of employee records might pass through the `mainLoop()`. If there are 100 employee records, then `labelCounter` is set to 0 exactly 100 times; it must be reset to 0 once for each employee, in order to count each employee's labels correctly. Similarly, `labelsToPrint` is reset (to 1.1 times the current `inLastProduction` value) once for each employee.

If the average employee produces 100 items during a week, then the loop within the `mainLoop()`, the one controlled by the statement `while labelCounter < labelsToPrint`, executes 11,000 times—110 times each for 100 employees. This number of repetitions is necessary in order to print the correct number of labels.

A repetition that is *not* necessary would be to execute 11,000 separate multiplication statements to recalculate the value to compare to `labelCounter`. See Figure 6-11.

**FIGURE 6-11:** INEFFICIENT PSEUDOCODE FOR LABEL-MAKING `mainLoop()`

```
mainLoop()
    labelCounter = 0
    while labelCounter < inLastProduction * 1.1
        print labelLine, inFirstName
        labelCounter = labelCounter + 1
    endwhile
    read empRecord
return
```

Although the logic shown in Figure 6-11 will produce the correct number of labels for every employee, the statement `while labelCounter < inLastProduction * 1.1` executes an average of 110 times for each employee. That means the arithmetic operation that is part of the question—multiplying `inLastProduction` by 1.1—occurs 110 separate times for each employee. Performing the same calculation that results in the same mathematical answer 110 times in a row is inefficient. Instead, it is superior to perform the multiplication just once for each employee and use the result 110 times, as shown in the original version of the program in Figure 6-10. In the pseudocode in Figure 6-10, you still must recalculate `labelsToPrint` once for each record, but not once for each label, so you have improved the program's efficiency.

The modules illustrated in Figures 6-10 and 6-11 do the same thing: print enough labels for every employee to cover 110% of production. As you become more proficient at programming, you will recognize many opportunities to perform the same tasks in alternative, more elegant, and more efficient ways.

## INITIALIZING A VARIABLE THAT DOES NOT REQUIRE INITIALIZATION

Another common error made by beginning programmers involves initializing a variable that does not require initialization. When declaring variables for the label-making program, you might be tempted to declare `num labelsToPrint = inLastProduction * 1.1`. It seems as though this declaration statement indicates that the value of the `labelsToPrint` will always be 110% of the `inLastProduction` figure. However, this approach is incorrect for two reasons. First, at the time `labelsToPrint` is declared, the first employee record has not yet been read into memory, so the value of `inLastProduction` is garbage; therefore, the result in `labelsToPrint` after multiplication will also be garbage. Second, even if you read the first `empRecord` into memory before declaring the `labelsToPrint` variable, the mathematical calculation of the `labelsToPrint` within the `housekeep()` module would be valid for the first record only. The value of `labelsToPrint` must be recalculated for each employee record in the input file. Therefore, calculation of the `labelsToPrint` correctly belongs within the `mainLoop()`, as shown in Figure 6-10.

## USING THE FOR LOOP

The label-making programs discussed in this chapter each contain two loops. For example, Figures 6-12 and 6-13 show the loop within the mainline program as well as the loop within the `mainLoop()` module for a program that produces exactly 100 labels for each employee.

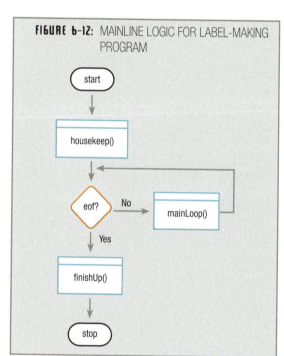

**FIGURE 6-12:** MAINLINE LOGIC FOR LABEL-MAKING PROGRAM

**FIGURE 6-13:** THE `mainLoop()` LOGIC FOR LABEL-MAKING PROGRAM

Entry to the `mainLoop()` in the mainline logic is controlled by the `eof` decision. Within the `mainLoop()`, label production is controlled by the `labelCounter` decision. When you execute the mainline logic, you cannot predict how many times the `mainLoop()` module will execute. Depending on the size of the input file, any number of records might be processed; while the program runs, you don't know what the total number of records finally will be. Until you attempt to read a record and encounter the end of the file, you don't know if more records are going to become available. Of course, not being able to predict the number of input records is valuable—it allows the program to function correctly no matter how many employees exist from week to week or year to year. Because you can't determine ahead of time how many records there might be and, therefore, how many times the loop might execute, the mainline loop in the label-making program is called an **indeterminate**, or **indefinite**, **loop**.

With some loops, you know exactly how many times they will execute. If every employee needs 100 printed labels, then the loop within the `mainLoop()` module executes exactly 100 times for each employee. This kind of loop, in which you definitely know the repetition factor, is a **definite loop**.

Every high-level computer programming language contains a **while statement** that you can use to code any loop, including indefinite loops (like the mainline loop) and definite loops (like the label-printing loop). You can write statements like the following:

```
while not eof
      perform mainLoop()
endwhile
```

and

```
while labelCounter < 100
      print labelLine, inFirstName
      labelCounter = labelCounter + 1
endwhile
```

In addition to the `while` statement, most computer languages also support a `for` statement. You can use the **for statement**, or **for loop**, with definite loops—those for which you know how many times the loop will repeat. The `for` statement provides you with three actions in one compact statement. The `for` statement uses a loop control variable that it automatically:

- initializes
- evaluates
- increments

The `for` statement usually takes the form:

```
for initialValue to finalValue
      do something
endfor
```

For example, to print 100 labels you can write:

```
for labelCounter = 0 to 99
      print labelLine, inFirstName
endfor
```

This `for` statement accomplishes several tasks at once in a compact form:

- The `for` statement initializes the `labelCounter` to 0.
- The `for` statement checks the `labelCounter` against the limit value 99 and makes sure that the `labelCounter` is less than or equal to that value.
- If the evaluation is true, the `for` statement body that prints the label executes.
- After the `for` statement body executes, the `labelCounter` increases by 1 and the comparison to the limit value is made again.

**TIP** ☐ ☐ ☐ ☐ | As an alternative to using the loop `for labelCounter = 0 to 99`, you can use `for labelCounter = 1 to 100`. You can use any combination of values, as long as there are 100 whole number values between (and including) the two limits.

You are never required to use a `for` statement; the label loop executes correctly using a `while` statement with `labelCounter` as a loop control variable. However, when a loop is based on a loop control variable progressing from a known starting value to a known ending value in equal increments, the `for` loop presents you with a convenient shorthand.

**TIP** ☐ ☐ ☐ ☐ | The programmer needs to know neither the starting nor the ending value for the loop control variable; only the program must know those values. For example, you don't know the value of a worker's `inLastProduction`, but when you tell the program to read a record, the program knows. To use this value as a limit value, you can write a `for` loop that begins `for labelCounter = 1 to inLastProduction`.

**TIP** ☐ ☐ ☐ ☐ | In most programming languages, you can provide a `for` loop with a step value. A step value is a number you use to increase a loop control variable on each pass through a loop. In most programming languages, the default loop step value is 1. You specify a step value when you want each pass through the loop to change the loop control variable by a value other than 1.

## USING THE DO UNTIL LOOP

When you use either a `while` or a `for` loop, the body of the loop may never execute. For example, in the mainline logic in Figure 6-5, the last action in the `housekeep()` module is to read an input record. If the input file contains no records, the result of the `eof` decision is true, and the program executes the `finishUp()` module without ever entering the `mainLoop()` module.

Similarly, when you produce labels within the `mainLoop()` module shown in Figure 6-10, labels are produced `while labelCounter < labelsToPrint`. Suppose an employee record contains a 0 in the `inLastProduction` field—for example, in the case of a new employee or an employee who was on vacation during the previous week. In such a case, the value of `labelsToPrint` would be 0, and the label-producing body of the loop would never execute. With a `while` loop, you evaluate the loop control variable prior to executing the loop body, and the evaluation might indicate that you can't enter the loop.

When you want to ensure that a loop's body executes at least one time, you can use a **do until** loop. In a **do until** loop, the loop control variable is evaluated after the loop body executes instead of before. Therefore, the body always executes at least one time.

You first learned about the **do until** loop in Chapter 2. Review Chapter 2 to reinforce your understanding of the differences between a **while** loop and a **do until** loop.

Because the question that controls a **while** loop is asked before you enter the loop body, programmers say a **while** loop has a pretest. Because the question that controls a **do until** loop occurs after the loop body executes, programmers say the **do until** loop contains a posttest.

For example, suppose you want to produce one label for each employee to wear as identification, before you produce enough labels to cover 110% of last week's production. You can write the **do until** loop that appears in Figure 6-14.

In Figure 6-14, the `labelCounter` variable is set to 0 and `labelsToPrint` is calculated. Suppose `labelsToPrint` is computed to be 0. The **do** loop will be entered, a label will print, 1 will be added to the `labelCounter`, and then and only then will `labelCounter` be compared to `labelsToPrint`. Because `labelCounter` is now 1 and `labelsToPrint` is only 0, the loop is exited, having printed a single identification label and no product labels.

As a different example using the logic in Figure 6-14, suppose that for a worker `labelsToPrint` is calculated to be 1. In this case, the loop is entered, a label prints, and 1 is added to `labelCounter`. Now, the value of `labelCounter` is not yet greater than the value of `labelsToPrint`, so the loop repeats, a second label prints, and `labelCounter` is incremented again. This time `labelCounter` (with a value of 2) does exceed `labelsToPrint` (with a value of 1), so the loop ends. This employee gets an identification label as well as one product label.

**FIGURE 6-14:** USING A **do until** LOOP TO PRINT ONE IDENTIFICATION LABEL, THEN PRINT ENOUGH TO COVER PRODUCTION REQUIREMENTS

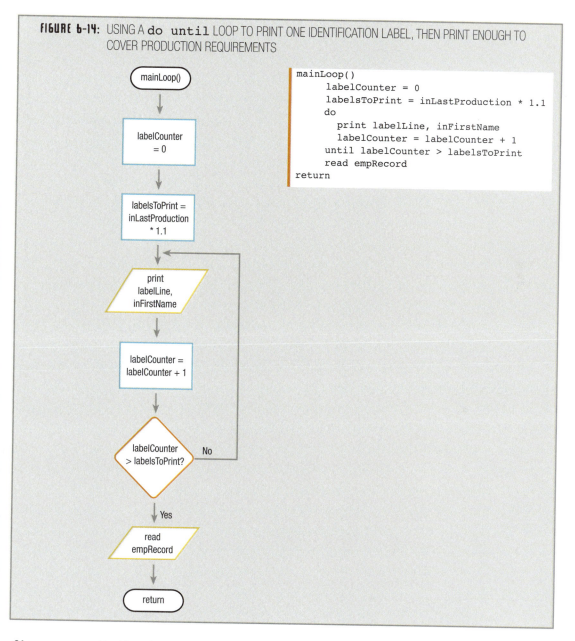

```
mainLoop()
    labelCounter = 0
    labelsToPrint = inLastProduction * 1.1
    do
        print labelLine, inFirstName
        labelCounter = labelCounter + 1
    until labelCounter > labelsToPrint
    read empRecord
return
```

Of course, you could achieve the same results by printing one label, then entering a **while** loop, as in Figure 6-15. In this example, one label prints before **labelCounter** is compared to **labelsToPrint**. No matter what the value of **labelsToPrint** is, one identification label is produced.

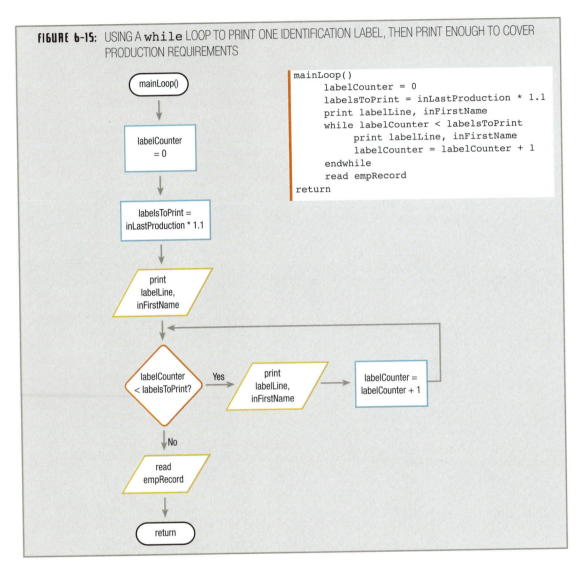

**FIGURE 6-15:** USING A `while` LOOP TO PRINT ONE IDENTIFICATION LABEL, THEN PRINT ENOUGH TO COVER PRODUCTION REQUIREMENTS

```
mainLoop()
    labelCounter = 0
    labelsToPrint = inLastProduction * 1.1
    print labelLine, inFirstName
    while labelCounter < labelsToPrint
        print labelLine, inFirstName
        labelCounter = labelCounter + 1
    endwhile
    read empRecord
return
```

**TIP** □ □ □ □     The logic in Figure 6-15, in which you print one label, then test a value to determine whether you will print more, takes the same form as the mainline logic in most of the programs you have worked with so far. When you read records from a file, you read one record (the priming read) and then test for `eof` before continuing. In effect, the first label printed in Figure 6-15 is a "priming label."

The results of the programs shown in Figures 6-14 and 6-15 are the same. Using either, every employee will receive an identification label and enough labels to cover production. Each module works correctly, and neither is logically superior to the other. There is almost always more than one way to solve the same programming problem. As you learned in Chapter 3, a `do until` loop can always be replaced by pairing a sequence and a `do while` loop. Which method you choose depends on your (or your instructor's or supervisor's) preferences.

**TIP** □ □ □ □ There are several additional ways to approach the logic shown in the programs in Figures 6-14 and 6-15. For example, after calculating `labelsToPrint`, you could immediately add 1 to the value. Then, you could use the logic in Figure 6-14, as long as you change the loop-ending question to `labelCounter >= labelsToPrint` (instead of only >). Alternatively, using the logic in Figure 6-15, after adding 1 to `labelsToPrint`, you could remove the lone first label-printing instruction; that way, one identification label would always be printed, even if the last production figure was 0.

## RECOGNIZING THE CHARACTERISTICS SHARED BY ALL LOOPS

You can see from Figure 6-15 that you are never required to use a `do until` loop. The same results always can be achieved by performing the loop body steps once before entering a `while` loop. If you follow the logic of either of the loops shown in Figures 6-14 and 6-15, you will discover that when an employee has an `inLastProduction` value of 3, then exactly four labels print. Likewise, when an employee has an `inLastProduction` value of 0, then in both cases exactly one label prints. You can accomplish the same results with either type of loop; the `do until` loop is simply a convenience when you need a loop to execute at least one time.

**TIP** □ □ □ □ In some languages, the `do until` loop is called a `repeat until` loop.

**TIP** □ □ □ □ If you can express the logic you want to perform by saying "while a is true, keep doing b," you probably want to use a `while` loop. If what you want to accomplish seems to fit the statement "do a until b is true," you can probably use a `do until` loop.

As you examine Figures 6-14 and 6-15, notice that with the `do until` loop, the loop-controlling question is placed at the *end* of the sequence of the steps that repeat. With the `while` loop, the loop-controlling question is placed at the *beginning* of the steps that repeat. All structured loops share these characteristics:

- The loop-controlling question provides either entry to or exit from the repeating structure.
- The loop-controlling question provides the *only* entry to or exit from the repeating structure.

You should also notice the difference between *unstructured* loops and the structured `do until` and `while` loops. Figure 6-16 diagrams the outline of two unstructured loops. In each case, the decision labeled X breaks out of the loop prematurely. In each case, the loop control variable (labeled `LC`) does not provide the only entry to or exit from the loop.

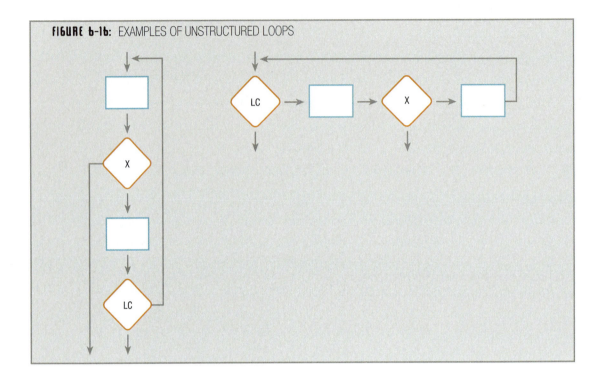

**FIGURE 6-16:** EXAMPLES OF UNSTRUCTURED LOOPS

## NESTING LOOPS

Program logic gets more complicated when you must use loops within loops, or **nesting loops**. When one loop appears inside another, the loop that contains the other loop is called the **outer loop**, and the loop that is contained is called the **inner loop**. For example, suppose you work for a company that pays workers twice per month. The company has decided on an incentive plan to provide each employee with a one-fourth of one percent raise for each pay period during the coming year, and it wants a report like that shown in Figure 6-17. A list will be printed for each employee showing the exact paycheck amounts for each of the next 24 pay periods—two per month for 12 months. As an example of how the report looks for one employee, see Figure 6-18. A description of each employee input record is shown in Figure 6-19.

**FIGURE 6-17:** PRINT CHART FOR PROJECTED PAYROLL REPORT

```
          1 1 1 1 1 1 1 1 1 1 2 2 2 2 2 2 2 2 2 2 3 3 3 3 3 3 3 3 3 3 4 4 4 4 4 4 4 4 4 4 5 5 5 5 5 5 5 5 5 5
  1 2 3 4 5 6 7 8 9 0 1 2 3 4 5 6 7 8 9 0 1 2 3 4 5 6 7 8 9 0 1 2 3 4 5 6 7 8 9 0 1 2 3 4 5 6 7 8 9 0 1 2 3 4 5 6 7 8 9
1     P r o j e c t e d   P a y r o l l   f o r
      x x x x x x x x   x x x x x x x x x x x x
2
3     M o n t h   C h e c k   A m o u n t
4
5       9 9         9         9 9 9 9 . 9 9
6       9 9         9         9 9 9 9 . 9 9
7       9 9         9         9 9 9 9 . 9 9
8       9 9         9         9 9 9 9 . 9 9
9
```

**FIGURE 6-18:** SAMPLE PROJECTED PAYROLL REPORT FOR ONE EMPLOYEE

Projected Payroll for
Roberto Martinez

| Month | Check | Amount |
|-------|-------|--------|
| 1 | 1 | 501.25 |
| 1 | 2 | 502.50 |
| 2 | 1 | 503.76 |
| 2 | 2 | 505.02 |
| 3 | 1 | 506.28 |

**FIGURE 6-19:** EMPLOYEE PAYROLL RECORD DATA FILE DESCRIPTION

File Name: EMPPAY

| FIELD DESCRIPTION | POSITIONS | DATA TYPE | DECIMALS |
|-------------------|-----------|-----------|----------|
| Employee Last Name | 1-12 | Character | |
| Employee First Name | 13-20 | Character | |
| Weekly salary at start of year | 21-26 | Numeric | 2 |

To produce the Projected Payroll report, you need to maintain two separate counters to control two separate loops. One counter will keep track of the month (1 through 12), and another will keep track of the pay period within the month (1 through 2). When nesting loops, you must maintain individual loop control variables—one for each loop—and alter each at the appropriate time.

Figure 6-20 shows the mainline, `housekeeping()`, and `finish()` logic for the program. These modules are standard. Besides the input file variables and the headers that print for each employee, the list of declared variables includes two counters. One, named `monthCounter`, keeps track of the month that is currently printing. The other, named `checkCounter`, keeps track of which check within the month is currently printing. Three additional declarations hold the number of months in a year (12), the number of checks in a month (2), and the rate of increase (0.0025). Declaring these variables is not required; the program could just use the numeric constants 12, 2, and 0.0025, but providing those values with names serves two purposes. First, the program becomes more **self-documenting**—that is, it describes itself to the reader. When other programmers read a program and encounter a number like 2, they might wonder about the meaning. Instead, if the value is named `numberOfChecksInMonth`, the meaning of the value is much clearer. Second, after the program is in production, the company might choose to change one of the values, for example, by going to an 11-month year, producing more or fewer paychecks in a month, or changing the raise rate. In those cases, the person who modifies the program would not have to search for appropriate spots to make those changes, but would simply redefine the values assigned to the appropriate variables.

**FIGURE 6-20:** MAINLINE LOGIC, `housekeeping()`, AND `finish()` MODULES FOR PROJECTED PAYROLL REPORT PROGRAM

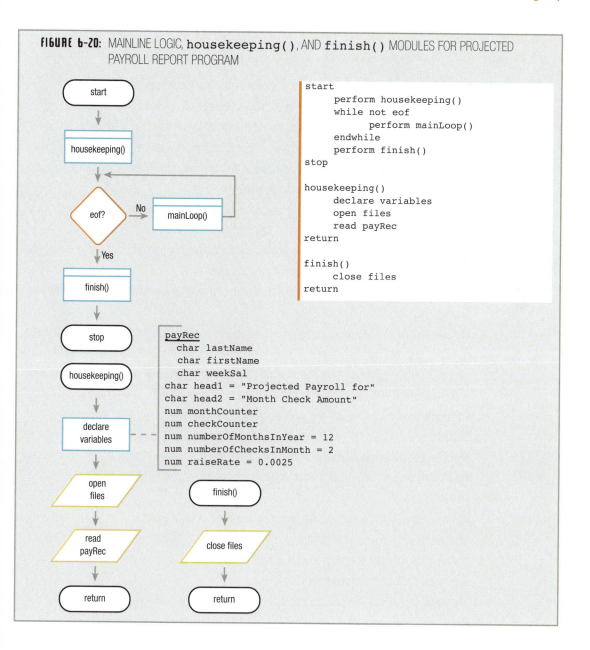

```
start
     perform housekeeping()
     while not eof
              perform mainLoop()
     endwhile
     perform finish()
stop

housekeeping()
     declare variables
     open files
     read payRec
return

finish()
     close files
return
```

```
payRec
  char lastName
  char firstName
  char weekSal
char head1 = "Projected Payroll for"
char head2 = "Month Check Amount"
num monthCounter
num checkCounter
num numberOfMonthsInYear = 12
num numberOfChecksInMonth = 2
num raiseRate = 0.0025
```

At the end of the `housekeeping()` module in Figure 6-20, the first employee record is read into main memory. Figure 6-21 shows how the record is processed in the `mainLoop()` module. The program proceeds as follows:

1. The first heading prints, followed by the employee name and the column headings.
2. The `monthCounter` variable is set to 1; the `monthCounter` variable is the loop control variable for the outer loop, and this step provides it with its initial value.
3. The `monthCounter` is compared to the number of months in a year, and because the comparison evaluates as true, the outer loop is entered. Within this loop, the `checkCounter` variable is used as a loop control variable for an inner loop.
4. The `checkCounter` is initialized to 1, and then compared to the number of checks in a month. Because this comparison evaluates as true, the inner loop is entered.
5. Within this inner loop, the employee's weekly salary is increased by one-quarter of one percent (the old salary plus 0.0025 of the old salary).
6. The month number (currently 1), check number (also currently 1), and newly calculated salary are printed.
7. The check number is increased (to 2), and the inner loop reaches its end; this causes the logical control to return to the top of the inner loop, where the `while` condition is tested again. Because the check number (2) is still less than or equal to the number of checks in a month, the inner loop is entered again.
8. The pay amount increases, and the month (still 1), the check number (2), and the new salary are printed.
9. Then, the check number becomes 3. Now, when the loop condition is tested for the third time, the check number is no longer less than or equal to the number of checks in a month, so the inner loop ends.
10. As the last step in the outer loop, the `monthCounter` becomes 2.
11. After the `monthCounter` increases to 2, control returns to the entry point of the outer loop.
12. The `while` condition is tested, and because 2 is not greater than the number of months in a year, the outer loop is entered for a second time.
13. The `checkCounter` is reset to 1 so that it will correctly count two checks for this month.
14. Because the newly reset `checkCounter` is not more than the number of checks in a month, the salary is increased, and the amount prints for month 2, check 1.
15. The `checkCounter` increases to 2 and another value is printed for month 2, check 2 before the inner loop ends and the `monthCounter` is increased to 3.
16. Then, month 3, check 1 prints, followed by month 3, check 2.

**FIGURE 6-21:** THE `mainLoop()` MODULE FOR THE PROJECTED PAYROLL REPORT PROGRAM

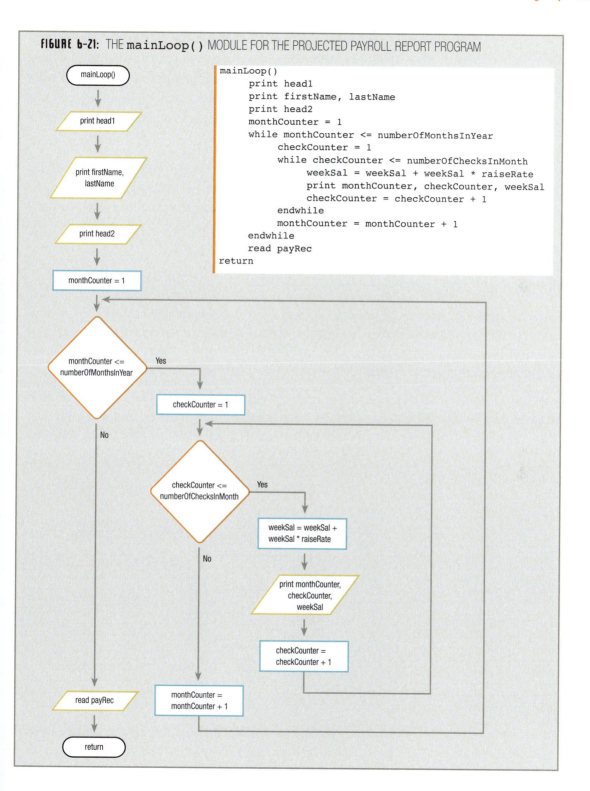

```
mainLoop()
     print head1
     print firstName, lastName
     print head2
     monthCounter = 1
     while monthCounter <= numberOfMonthsInYear
          checkCounter = 1
          while checkCounter <= numberOfChecksInMonth
               weekSal = weekSal + weekSal * raiseRate
               print monthCounter, checkCounter, weekSal
               checkCounter = checkCounter + 1
          endwhile
          monthCounter = monthCounter + 1
     endwhile
     read payRec
return
```

17. The `mainLoop()` continues printing two check amounts for each of 12 months before the outer loop is finished, when the `monthCounter` eventually exceeds 12. Only then is the next employee record read into memory, and control leaves the `mainLoop()` module and returns to the mainline logic where the end of file is tested. If a new record exists, control returns to the `mainLoop()` for the new employee, for whom headings are printed, and the `monthCounter` is set to 1 to start the set of 24 calculations for this employee.

There is no limit to the number of loop-nesting levels a program can contain. For instance, suppose that in the projected payroll example, the company wanted to provide a slight raise each hour or each day of each pay period in each month for each of several years. No matter how many levels deep the nesting goes, each loop must still contain a loop control variable that is initialized, tested, and altered.

## USING A LOOP TO ACCUMULATE TOTALS

Business reports often include totals. The supervisor requesting a list of employees who participate in the company dental plan is often as much interested in *how many* such employees there are as in *who* they are. When you receive your telephone bill at the end of the month, you are usually more interested in the total than in the charges for the individual calls. Some business reports list no individual detail records, just totals. Such reports are called **summary reports**.

For example, a real estate broker might maintain a file of company real estate listings. Each record in the file contains the street address and the asking price of a property for sale. The broker wants a listing of all the properties for sale; she also wants a total value for all the company's listings. The print chart appears in Figure 6-22.

**FIGURE 6-22:** PRINT CHART FOR REAL ESTATE REPORT

| | 1 | PROPERTIES FOR SALE |
|---|---|---|
| 2 | | PROPERTIES FOR SALE |
| 4 | STREET ADDRESS | ASKING PRICE |
| 7 | XXXXXXXXXXXXXXX | 9,999,999 |
| 8 | XXXXXXXXXXXXXXX | 9,999,999 |
| 10 | TOTAL VALUE | 99,999,999 |

When you read a real estate listing record, besides printing it you must add its value to an accumulator. An **accumulator** is a variable that you use to gather or accumulate values. An accumulator is very similar to a counter. The difference lies in the value that you add to the variable; usually, you add just one to a counter, whereas you add some other value to an accumulator. If the real estate broker wants to know how many listings the company holds, you count them. When she wants to know total real estate value, you accumulate it.

In order to accumulate total real estate prices, you declare a numeric variable at the beginning of the program, as shown in the `housekeep()` module in Figure 6-23. You must initialize the accumulator, `accumValue`, to zero. In Chapter 4, you learned that when using most programming languages, declared variables do not automatically assume any particular value; the unknown value is called garbage. When you read the first real estate record, you will add its value to the accumulator. If the accumulator contains garbage, the addition will not work. Some programming languages issue an error message if you don't initialize a variable you use for accumulating; others let you accumulate, but the results are worthless because you start with garbage.

**FIGURE 6-23:** THE REAL ESTATE PROGRAM

If you name the input record fields `realAddress` and `realPrice`, then the `mainLoop()` module of the real estate listing program can be written as shown in Figure 6-23. For each real estate record, you print it and add its value to the accumulator `accumValue`. Then you can read the next record.

After the program reaches the end of the file, the accumulator will hold the grand total of all the real estate values. When you reach the end of the file, the `finishUp()` module executes, and it is within the `finishUp()` module that you print the accumulated value, `accumValue`. After printing the total, you can close both the input and the output files and return to the main line where the program ends.

New programmers often want to reset the `accumValue` to zero after printing it. Although you *can* take this step without harming the execution of the program, it does not serve any useful purpose. You cannot set `accumValue` to zero in anticipation of having it ready for the next program, or even for the next time you execute this program. Program variables exist only for the life of the program, and even if a future program happens to contain a variable named `accumValue`, the variable will not necessarily occupy the same memory location as this one. Even if you run the program a second time, the variables might occupy physical memory locations different from those they occupied during the first run. At the beginning of the program, it is the programmer's responsibility to initialize all variables that must start with a specific value. There is no benefit to changing a variable's value when it will never be used again during the current execution of the program.

It is especially important to avoid changing the value of a variable unnecessarily when the change occurs within a loop. One extra, unnecessary statement in a loop that executes hundreds of thousands of times can significantly slow a program's performance speed.

## CHAPTER SUMMARY

☐ When you use a loop within a computer program, you can write one set of instructions that operates on multiple, separate sets of data.

☐ Three steps must occur in every loop: You must initialize a loop control variable, compare the variable to some value that controls whether the loop continues or stops, and alter the variable that controls the loop.

☐ A counter is a numeric variable you use to count the number of times an event has occurred. You can count occurrences by incrementing a variable.

☐ You can use a variable sentinel value to control a loop.

☐ Sometimes, it is convenient to reduce or decrement a loop control variable on every cycle through a loop.

☐ The two mistakes programmers make most often with loops are neglecting to initialize the loop control variable, and neglecting to alter the loop control variable. Additionally, when a calculation can be performed once before entering a loop, it is inefficient to place the calculation within the loop. It is incorrect to attempt to initialize a variable by using data values that have not been read into memory yet.

☐ Most computer languages support a `for` statement or `for` loop that you can use with definite loops when you know how many times a loop will repeat. The `for` statement uses a loop control variable that it automatically initializes, evaluates, and increments.

☐ When you want to ensure that a loop's body executes at least one time, you can use a `do until` loop, in which the loop control variable is evaluated after the loop body executes.

☐ All structured loops share these characteristics: The loop-controlling question provides either entry to or exit from the repeating structure, and the loop-controlling question provides the *only* entry to or exit from the repeating structure.

☐ When you must use loops within loops, you use nesting loops. When nesting loops, you must maintain two individual loop control variables and alter each at the appropriate time.

☐ Business reports often include totals. Summary reports list no detail records—only totals. An accumulator is a variable that you use to gather or accumulate values.

## KEY TERMS

A loop is a structure that repeats actions while some condition continues.

A main loop is a basic set of instructions that is repeated for every record.

A loop control variable is a variable that determines whether a loop will continue.

A sentinel value is a limit, or ending, value.

A loop body is the set of statements that executes within a loop.

A counter is any numeric variable you use to count the number of times an event has occurred.

Adding 1 to a variable is called incrementing the variable.

Decreasing a variable by one is called decrementing the variable.

A loop that never stops executing is called an infinite loop.

An indeterminate, or indefinite, loop is one for which you cannot predetermine the number of executions.

A loop for which you definitely know the repetition factor is a definite loop.

A while statement can be used to code any loop.

A for statement, or for loop, can be used to code definite loops. It contains a loop control variable that it automatically initializes, evaluates, and increments.

Nesting loops are loops within loops.

When one loop appears inside another, the loop that contains the other loop is called the outer loop, and the loop that is contained is called the inner loop.

A self-documenting program is one that describes itself to the reader.

A summary report lists only totals, without individual detail records.

An accumulator is a variable that you use to gather or accumulate values.

## REVIEW QUESTIONS

1. The structure that allows you to write one set of instructions that operates on multiple, separate sets of data is the _____.
   a. sequence
   b. selection
   c. loop
   d. case

2. Which of the following is not a step that must occur in every loop?
   a. Initialize a loop control variable.
   b. Compare the loop control value to a sentinel.
   c. Set the loop control value equal to a sentinel.
   d. Alter the loop control variable.

3. The statements executed within a loop are known collectively as the _____.
   a. sentinels
   b. loop controls
   c. sequences
   d. loop body

4. **A counter keeps track of** _____.

    a.  the number of times an event has occurred

    b.  the number of machine cycles required by a segment of a program

    c.  the number of loop structures within a program

    d.  a total that prints at the end of a summary report

5. **Adding 1 to a variable is also called** _____.

    a.  digesting

    b.  incrementing

    c.  decrementing

    d.  resetting

6. **In the following pseudocode, what is printed?**

```
a = 1
b = 2
c = 5
while a < c
     a = a + 1
     b = b + c
endwhile
print a, b, c
```

    a.  1 2 5

    b.  5 22 5

    c.  5 6 5

    d.  6 22 9

7. **In the following pseudocode, what is printed?**

```
d = 4
e = 6
f = 7
while d > f
     d = d + 1
     e = e - 1
endwhile
print d, e, f
```

    a.  7 3 7

    b.  8 2 8

    c.  4 6 7

    d.  5 5 7

8. **When you decrement a variable, you** _____.

   a. set it to 0

   b. reduce it by one-tenth

   c. subtract 1 from it

   d. remove it from a program

9. **In the following pseudocode, what is printed?**

   ```
   g = 4
   h = 6
   while g < h
        g = g + 1
   endwhile
   print g, h
   ```

   a. nothing

   b. 4 6

   c. 5 6

   d. 6 6

10. **Most programmers use a `for` loop** _____.

    a. for every loop they write

    b. when they know the exact number of times a loop will repeat

    c. when they do not know the exact number of times a loop will repeat

    d. when a loop will not repeat

11. **Unlike a `do while` loop, you use a `do until` loop when** _____.

    a. you can predict the exact number of loop repetitions

    b. the loop body might never execute

    c. the loop body must execute exactly one time

    d. the loop body must execute at least one time

12. **Which of the following is a characteristic shared by `while` loops and `do until` loops?**

    a. Both have one entry and one exit.

    b. Both have a body that executes at least once.

    c. Both compare a loop control variable at the top of the loop.

    d. All of these are true.

13. **A comparison with a loop control variable provides** _____.

    a. the only entry to a `while` loop

    b. the only exit from a `do until` loop

    c. both of the above

    d. none of the above

14. **When two loops are nested, the loop that is contained by the other is the _____ loop.**
    a. inner
    b. outer
    c. unstructured
    d. captive

15. **In the following pseudocode, how many times is "Hello" printed?**

```
j = 2
k = 5
m = 6
n = 9
while j < k
      while m < n
            print "Hello"
            m = m + 1
      endwhile
      j = j + 1
endwhile
```

    a. zero
    b. three
    c. six
    d. nine

16. **In the following pseudocode, how many times is "Hello" printed?**

```
j = 2
k = 5
n = 9
while j < k
      m = 6
      while m < n
            print "Hello"
            m = m + 1
      endwhile
      j = j + 1
endwhile
```

    a. zero
    b. three
    c. six
    d. nine

17. **In the following pseudocode, how many times is "Hello" printed?**

```
p = 2
q = 4
while p < q
        print "Hello"
        r = 1
        while r < q
                print "Hello"
                r = r + 1
        endwhile
        p = p + 1
endwhile
```

   a. zero
   b. four
   c. six
   d. eight

18. **A report that lists no details about individual records, but totals only, is a(n) _____ report.**

   a. accumulator
   b. final
   c. summary
   d. detailless

19. **Typically, the value added to a counter variable is _____.**

   a. 0
   b. 1
   c. 10
   d. 100

20. **Typically, the value added to an accumulator variable is _____.**

   a. zero
   b. one
   c. smaller than a value added to a counter variable
   d. larger than a value added to a counter variable

## EXERCISES

1.  **Design the logic for a module that would print every number from 1 through 10.**

    a.  Draw the flowchart.
    b.  Design the pseudocode.

2.  **Design the logic for a module that would print every number from 1 through 10 along with its square and cube.**

    a.  Draw the flowchart.
    b.  Design the pseudocode.

3.  **Design a program that reads credit card account records and prints payoff schedules for customers. Input records contain an account number, customer name, and balance due. For each customer, print the account number and name; then print the customer's projected balance each month for the next 10 months. Assume that there is no finance charge on this account, that the customer makes no new purchases, and that the customer pays off the balance with equal monthly payments, which are 10% of the original bill.**

    a.  Design the print chart for this program.
    b.  Design the hierarchy chart for this program.
    c.  Design the flowchart for this program.
    d.  Write pseudocode for this program.

4.  **Design a program that reads credit card account records and prints payoff schedules for customers. Input records contain an account number, customer name, and balance due. For each customer, print the account number and name; then print the customer's payment amount and new balance each month until the card is paid off. Assume that when the balance reaches $10 or less, the customer can pay off the account. At the beginning of every month, 1.5% interest is added to the balance, and then the customer makes a payment equal to 5% of the current balance. Assume the customer makes no new purchases.**

    a.  Design the print chart for this program.
    b.  Design the hierarchy chart for this program.
    c.  Design the flowchart for this program.
    d.  Write pseudocode for this program.

5.  **Assume you have a bank account that compounds interest on a yearly basis. In other words, if you deposit $100 for two years at 4% interest, at the end of 1 year you will have $104. At the end of 2 years, you will have the $104 plus 4% of that, or $108.16. Create the logic for a program that would (1) read in records containing a deposit amount, a term in years, and an interest rate, and (2) for each record, print the running total balance for each year of the term.**

    a.  Design the print chart for this program.
    b.  Design the hierarchy chart for this program.
    c.  Design the flowchart for this program.
    d.  Write pseudocode for this program.

6. **A school maintains class records in the following format:**

```
CLASS FILE DESCRIPTION
File name: CLASS
```

| FIELD DESCRIPTION | POSITIONS | DATA TYPE | DECIMALS | EXAMPLE |
|---|---|---|---|---|
| Class Code | 1-6 | Character | | CIS111 |
| Section No. | 7-9 | Numeric | 0 | 101 |
| Teacher | 10-29 | Character | | Gable |
| Enrollment | 30-31 | Numeric | 0 | 24 |
| Room | 32-35 | Character | | A213 |

**There is one record for each class section offered in the college. Design the program that would print as many stickers as a class needs to provide one for each enrolled student, plus one for the teacher. Each sticker would leave a blank for the student's (or teacher's) name like this:**

Hello!

My name is _____

Class: XXXXXX Section: 999

**This border is preprinted, but you must design the program to print all the text you see on the sticker. (You do not need to design a print chart—the image of the sticker serves as a print chart.)**

a. Design the hierarchy chart for this program.
b. Design the flowchart for this program.
c. Write pseudocode for this program.

7. **A mail-order company often sends multiple packages per order. For each customer order, print enough mailing labels to use on each of the separate boxes that will be mailed. The mailing labels contain the customer's complete name and address, along with a box number in the form "Box 9 of 9". For example, an order that requires three boxes produces three labels: Box 1 of 3, Box 2 of 3, and Box 3 of 3. The file description is as follows:**

```
SHIPPING FILE DESCRIPTION
File name: ORDERS
```

| FIELD DESCRIPTION | POSITIONS | DATA TYPE | DECIMALS | EXAMPLE |
|---|---|---|---|---|
| Title | 1-3 | Character | | Ms |
| First Name | 4-14 | Character | | Kathy |
| Last Name | 15-25 | Character | | Lewis |
| Street | 26-40 | Character | | 847 Pine |
| City | 41-51 | Character | | Aurora |
| State | 52-53 | Character | | IL |

| | | | | |
|---|---|---|---|---|
| Boxes | 54-55 | Numeric | 0 | 3 |
| Balance Due | 56-61 | Numeric | 2 | 129.95 |

   a. Design the print chart for this program.
   b. Design the hierarchy chart for this program.
   c. Design the flowchart for this program.
   d. Write pseudocode for this program.

8.   A secondhand store is having a seven-day sale during which the price of any unsold item drops 10% each day. The inventory file includes an item number, description, and original price on day one. For example, an item that costs $10.00 on the first day costs 10% less, or $9.00, on the second day. On the third day, the same item is 10% less than $9.00, or $8.10. Produce a report that shows the price of the item on each day, one through seven.

   a. Design the print chart for this program.
   b. Design the hierarchy chart for this program.
   c. Design the flowchart for this program.
   d. Write pseudocode for this program.

9.   The state of Florida maintains a census file in which each record contains the name of a county, the current population, and a number representing the rate at which population is increasing per year. The governor wants a report listing each county and the number of years it will take for the population of the county to double, assuming the present rate of growth remains constant.

CENSUS FILE DESCRIPTION
File name: CENSUS

| FIELD DESCRIPTION | POSITIONS | DATA TYPE | DECIMALS | EXAMPLE |
|---|---|---|---|---|
| County Name | 1-20 | Character | | Dade |
| Current | | | | |
|   Population | 21-28 | Numeric | 0 | 525000 |
| Rate of Growth | 29-30 | Numeric | 2 | .07 |

   a. Design the print chart for this program.
   b. Design the hierarchy chart for this program.
   c. Design the flowchart for this program.
   d. Write pseudocode for this program.

10.   A Human Resources Department wants a report that shows its employees the benefits of saving for retirement. Produce a report that shows 12 predicted retirement account values for each employee—the values if the employee saves 5, 10, or 15% of his or her annual salary for 10, 20, 30, or 40 years. The department maintains a file in which each record contains the name of an employee and the employee's current annual salary. Assume that savings grow at a rate of 8% per year.

   a. Design the print chart for this program.
   b. Design the hierarchy chart for this program.
   c. Design the flowchart for this program.
   d. Write pseudocode for this program.

11. Randy's Recreational Vehicles pays its salespeople once every three months. Salespeople receive one-quarter of their annual base salary plus 7% of all sales made in the last three-month period. Randy creates an input file with four records for each salesperson. The first of the four records contains the salesperson's name and annual salary, while each of the three records that follow contains the name of a month and the monthly sales figure. For example, the first eight records in the file might contain the following data:

| Kimball | 20000 |
|---------|-------|
| April | 30000 |
| May | 40000 |
| June | 60000 |
| Johnson | 15000 |
| April | 65000 |
| May | 78000 |
| June | 135500 |

Because the two types of records contain data in the same format, a character field followed by a numeric field, you can define one input record format containing two variables that you use with either type of record. Design the logic for the program that reads a salesperson's record, and if not at `eof`, reads the next three records in a loop, accumulating sales and computing commissions. For each salesperson, print the quarterly base salary, the three commission amounts, and the total salary, which is the quarterly base plus the three commission amounts.

   a. Design the print chart for this program.
   b. Design the hierarchy chart for this program.
   c. Design the flowchart for this program.
   d. Write pseudocode for this program.

12. Mr. Furly owns 20 apartment buildings. Each building contains 15 units that he rents for $800 per month each. Design the logic for the program that would print 12 payment coupons for each of the 15 apartments in each of the 20 buildings. Each coupon should contain the building number (1 through 20), the apartment number (1 through 15), the month (1 through 12), and the amount of rent due.

   a. Design the print chart for this program.
   b. Design the hierarchy chart for this program.
   c. Design the flowchart for this program.
   d. Write pseudocode for this program.

13.   Mr. Furly owns 20 apartment buildings. Each building contains 15 units that he rents. The usual monthly rent for apartments numbered 1 through 9 in each building is $700; the monthly rent is $850 for apartments numbered 10 through 15. The usual rent is due every month except July and December; in those months Mr. Furly gives his renters a 50% credit, so they owe only half the usual amount. Design the logic for the program that would print 12 payment coupons for each of the 15 apartments in each of the 20 buildings. Each coupon should contain the building number (1 through 20), the apartment number (1 through 15), the month (1 through 12), and the amount of rent due.

   a.  Design the print chart for this program.
   b.  Design the hierarchy chart for this program.
   c.  Design the flowchart for this program.
   d.  Write pseudocode for this program.

# CONTROL BREAKS

## After studying Chapter 7, you should be able to:

- [ ] Understand control break logic
- [ ] Perform single-level control breaks
- [ ] Use control data within a heading in a control break module
- [ ] Use control data within a footer in a control break module
- [ ] Perform control breaks with totals
- [ ] Perform multiple-level control breaks
- [ ] Perform page breaks

## UNDERSTANDING CONTROL BREAK LOGIC

A **control break** is a temporary detour in the logic of a program. In particular, programmers refer to a program as a **control break program** when a change in the value of a variable initiates special actions or causes special or unusual processing to occur. You usually write control break programs to organize output for programs that handle data records that are organized logically in groups based on the value in a field. As you read in records, you examine the same field in each record, and when you encounter a record that contains a different value from the ones that preceded it, you perform a special action. If you have ever read a report that lists items in groups, with each group followed by a subtotal, then you have read a type of **control break report**. Some other examples of control break reports produced by control break programs include:

- All employees listed in order by department number, with a new page started for each department
- All company clients listed in order by state of residence, with a count of clients after each state's client list
- All books for sale in a bookstore in order by category (such as reference or self-help), with a dollar total following each category of book for the value of all books
- All items sold in order by date of sale, with a different ink color for each new month

Each of these reports shares two traits:

- The records used in each report are listed in order by a specific variable: department, state, category, or date.
- When that variable changes, the program takes special action: starts a new page, prints a count or total, or switches ink color.

To generate a control break report, your input records must be organized in sequential order based on the field that will cause the breaks. In other words, if you are going to write a program that prints employee records on separate pages based on their departments, then the records must be arranged in department-number order before you begin processing. As you grow more proficient in programming logic, you will learn techniques for writing programs that sort records before you proceed with control break logic. Programs that **sort** records take records that are not in order and rearrange them so that they are in order. For now, assume that a sorting program has already been used to presort your records before you begin the part of a program that requires control breaks.

**TIP** □ □ □ □ | You will learn techniques for processing unsorted records in Chapter 8.

## PERFORMING A SINGLE-LEVEL CONTROL BREAK TO START A NEW PAGE

Suppose you want to print a list of employees, advancing to a new page for each department. Figure 7-1 shows the input file description, from which you can see that the employee department is a two-digit numeric field, and that the file has been presorted so that the records will arrive in a program in employee-department-number order. Figure 7-2 shows the desired output—a simple list of employee names.

## FIGURE 7-1: EMPLOYEE FILE DESCRIPTION

```
File name: EMPSBYDEPT
Sorted by: Department
FIELD DESCRIPTION        POSITIONS      DATA TYPE       DECIMALS
Department               1-2            Numeric         0
Last Name                3-14           Character
First Name               15-26          Character
```

## FIGURE 7-2: PRINT CHART FOR EMPLOYEES LISTED BY DEPARTMENT

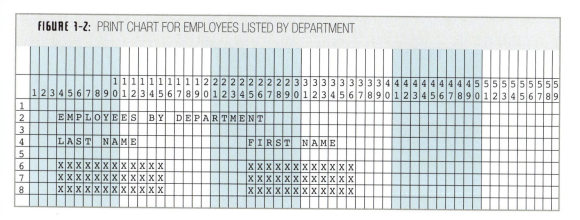

The basic logic of the program works like this: Each time you read an employee record from the input file, you will determine whether the employee belongs to the same department as the previous employee. If so, you simply print the employee record and read another record, without any special processing. If there are 20 employees in a department, these steps are repeated 20 times in a row—read an employee record in and print the employee record out. However, eventually you will read in an employee who does not belong to the same department. At that point, before you print the employee who is in the new department, you must print headings on the top of a new page. Then, you can proceed to read and print employees who belong to the new department, and you continue to do so until the next time you encounter an employee in a different department. This type of program contains a **single-level control break**, a break in the logic of the program (pausing or detouring to print new headings) that is based on the value of a single variable (the department number).

However, there is a slight problem you must solve before you can determine whether a newly input record contains the same department number as the previously input record. When you read a record from an input file, the data items that represent department, last name, and first name occupy specific physical locations in computer memory. For each new record, new data must occupy the same positions, and the previous set of data is lost. For example, if you read a record containing data for Alan Andrews in Department 1, when you read the next record for Barbara Bailey in Department 2, "Barbara" replaces "Alan", "Bailey" replaces "Andrews", and 2 replaces 1. After you read in a new record, there is no way to look back at the previous record to determine whether that record had a different department number. The previous record's data has been replaced by the new record's data.

The technique you must use to "remember" the old department number is to create a special variable, called a **control break field**, to hold the previous department number. With a control break field, every time you read in a record and print it, you also can save the crucial part of the record that will signal the change or control the program break. In this case, you want to store the department number in this specially created variable. Comparing the new and old department-number values will determine when it is time to print headings at the top of a new page.

The mainline logic for the Employees by Department report is the same as the mainline logic for all the other programs you've analyzed so far. It performs a `housekeeping()` module, after which an `eof` question controls execution of a `mainLoop()`. At `eof`, a `finish()` module executes. See Figure 7-3.

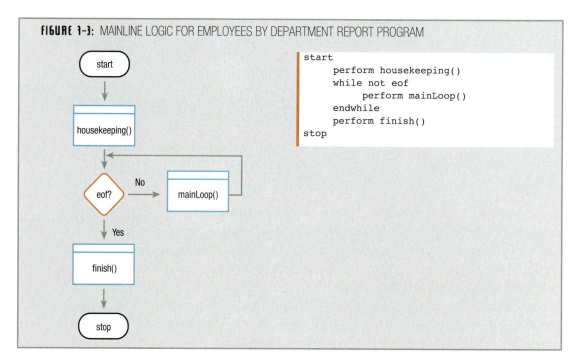

**FIGURE 7-3:** MAINLINE LOGIC FOR EMPLOYEES BY DEPARTMENT REPORT PROGRAM

```
start
        perform housekeeping()
        while not eof
                perform mainLoop()
        endwhile
        perform finish()
stop
```

The `housekeeping()` module begins similarly to others you have seen. You declare variables as shown in Figure 7-4, including those you will use for the input data: `empDept`, `empLast`, and `empFirst`. You can also declare variables to hold the headings, and an additional variable that is named `oldDept` in this example. The purpose of `oldDept` is to serve as the control break field. Every time you read a record, you can save its department number in `oldDept` before you read the next record.

Note that it would be incorrect to initialize `oldDept` to the value of `empDept` when you declare `oldDept` in the `housekeeping()` module. When you declare variables at the beginning of the `housekeeping()` module, you have not yet read in the first record; therefore, `empDept` does not yet have any usable value. You use the value of the first `empDept` at the end of the module, only after you read the first input record.

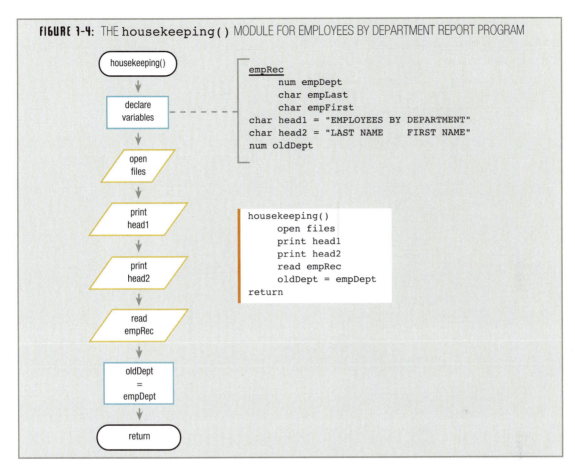

**FIGURE 7-4:** THE `housekeeping()` MODULE FOR EMPLOYEES BY DEPARTMENT REPORT PROGRAM

```
empRec
     num empDept
     char empLast
     char empFirst
char head1 = "EMPLOYEES BY DEPARTMENT"
char head2 = "LAST NAME    FIRST NAME"
num oldDept
```

```
housekeeping()
     open files
     print head1
     print head2
     read empRec
     oldDept = empDept
return
```

In the `housekeeping()` module, after declaring variables, you also open files, print headings, and read the first input record. Before you leave the `housekeeping()` module, you can set the `oldDept` variable to equal the `empDept` value in the first input record. You will write the `mainLoop()` of the program to check for any change in department number; that's the signal to print headings at the top of a new page. Because you just printed headings and read in the first record, you do not want to print headings again for this first record, so you want to ensure that the `empDept` and `oldDept` are equal when you enter the `mainLoop()`.

**TIP** □ □ □ □  As an alternative to the `housekeeping()` logic shown here, you can remove printing headings from the `housekeeping()` module and set the `oldDept` to any impossible value, for example, −1. Then, in the `mainLoop()`, the first record will force the control break, and the headings will print in the `newPage()` control break routine.

The first task within the `mainLoop()` module is to check whether the `empDept` holds the same value as `oldDept`. For the first record, on the first pass through the `mainLoop()`, the values are equal; you set them to be equal in the `housekeeping()` module. Therefore, you proceed without performing the `newPage()` module, printing the first employee's record and reading a second record. At the end of the `mainLoop()` shown in Figure 7-5, the logical flow returns to the mainline logic shown in Figure 7-3. If it is not `eof`, the flow travels back into the `mainLoop()` module.

There, you compare the second record's `empDept` to `oldDept`. If the second record holds an employee from the same department as the first employee, then you simply print that second employee's record, and read a third record into memory. As long as each new record holds the same `empDept` value, you continue reading and printing, never pausing to perform the `newPage()` module.

FIGURE 7-5: THE `mainLoop()` MODULE FOR EMPLOYEES BY DEPARTMENT REPORT PROGRAM

```
mainLoop()
        if empDept not = oldDept then
                perform newPage()
        endif
        print empLast, empFirst
        read empRec
return
```

**TIP** ☐ ☐ ☐ ☐ In the flowchart in Figure 7-5, you could change the question to `empDept <> oldDept` or `empDept not = oldDept`. Then, the Yes branch of the decision structure would perform the `newPage()` module, and the No branch would be null. This format would more closely resemble the pseudocode in Figure 7-5, but the logic would be identical to the version shown here, in which the question is asked in the positive rather than the negative.

Eventually, you will read in an employee whose `empDept` is not the same as `oldDept`. That's when the control break routine, `newPage()`, executes. The `newPage()` module must perform two tasks:

- It must print headings at the top of a new page.
- It must update the control break field.

Figure 7-6 shows the `newPage()` module.

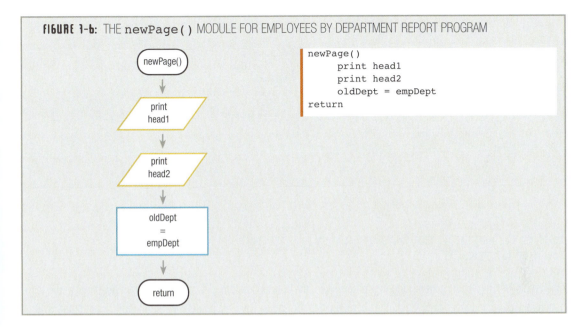

FIGURE 7-6: THE `newPage()` MODULE FOR EMPLOYEES BY DEPARTMENT REPORT PROGRAM

```
newPage()
     print head1
     print head2
     oldDept = empDept
return
```

TIP □ □ □ □ In Chapter 4, you learned that specific programming languages each provide you with a means to physically advance printer paper to the top of a page. Usually, you insert a language-specific code just before the first character in the first heading that will appear on a page. For this book, if a print chart shows a heading printing at the top of the page, then you can assume that printing the heading causes the paper in the printer to advance to the top of a new page. The appropriate language-specific codes can be added when you code the program.

When you read an employee whose `empDept` is not the same as `oldDept`, you cause a break in the normal flow of the program. The new employee record must "wait" while headings print and the control break field `oldDept` acquires a new value. After the `oldDept` field has been updated, and before the `mainLoop()` module ends, the waiting employee record prints on the new page. When you read the *next* employee record (and it is not `eof`), the `mainLoop()` module is reentered and the next employee's `empDept` is compared to the updated `oldDept`. If the new employee works in the same department as the one just preceding, then normal processing continues with the print-and-read statements.

The `newPage()` module in the employee report program performs two tasks required in all control break modules:

- It performs any necessary processing for the new group—in this case, it prints headings.
- It updates the control break field—in this case, the `oldDept` field.

TIP □ □ □ □ As an alternative to updating the control break field within the control break routine, you could set the `oldDept` equal to `empDept` just before you read each record. However, if there are 200 employees in Department 55, then you set the `oldDept` to the same value 200 times. It's more efficient to set `oldDept` to a different value only when there is a change in the value of the department.

The `finish()` module for the Employees by Department report program requires only that you close the files. See Figure 7-7.

**FIGURE 7-7:** THE `finish()` MODULE FOR EMPLOYEES BY DEPARTMENT REPORT PROGRAM

## USING CONTROL DATA WITHIN A HEADING IN A CONTROL BREAK MODULE

In the Employees by Department report program example, the control break module printed constant headings at the top of each new page; in other words, each page heading was the same. However, sometimes you need to use control data within the heading. For example, consider the report layout shown in Figure 7-8.

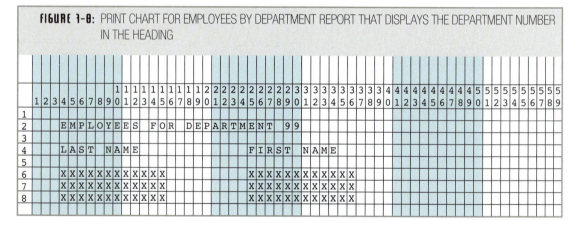

**FIGURE 7-8:** PRINT CHART FOR EMPLOYEES BY DEPARTMENT REPORT THAT DISPLAYS THE DEPARTMENT NUMBER IN THE HEADING

The difference between Figure 7-2 and Figure 7-8 lies in the heading. Figure 7-8 shows variable data in the heading—a different department number prints at the top of each page of employees. To create this kind of program, you must make two changes in the existing program. First, you modify the `newPage()` module, as shown within the `newPage()` module in Figure 7-9. Instead of printing a fixed heading on each new page, you print a heading that contains two parts: a constant beginning ("EMPLOYEES FOR DEPARTMENT") and a variable ending (the department number for the employees who appear on the page). Notice that you use the `empDept` number that belongs to the employee record that is waiting to be printed while this control break module executes. Additionally, you must modify the `housekeeping()` module to ensure that the first heading on the report prints correctly. As Figure 7-9 shows, you must modify the `housekeeping()` module from Figure 7-4 so that you read the first `empRec` prior to printing the headings. The reason is that you must know the first employee's department number before you can print the heading for the top of the first page.

**FIGURE 7-9:** MODIFIED `newPage()` AND `housekeeping()` MODULES FOR EMPLOYEES BY DEPARTMENT REPORT THAT DISPLAYS THE DEPARTMENT NUMBER IN THE HEADING

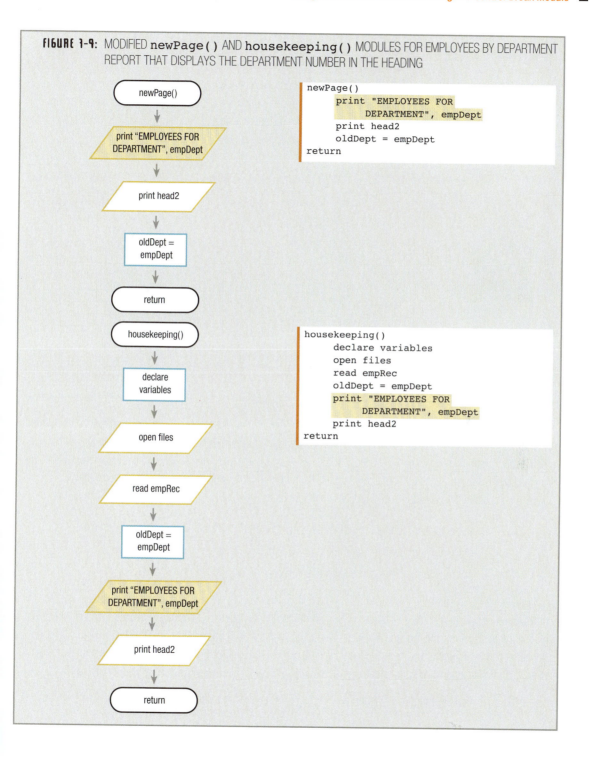

```
newPage()
    print "EMPLOYEES FOR
        DEPARTMENT", empDept
    print head2
    oldDept = empDept
return
```

```
housekeeping()
    declare variables
    open files
    read empRec
    oldDept = empDept
    print "EMPLOYEES FOR
        DEPARTMENT", empDept
    print head2
return
```

## USING CONTROL DATA WITHIN A FOOTER IN A CONTROL BREAK MODULE

In the previous section, you learned how to use control break data in a heading. Figure 7-10 shows a different print chart. For this report, the department number prints *following* the employee list for the department. A message that prints at the end of a page or other section of a report is called a **footer**. Headings usually require information about the *next* record; footers usually require information about the *previous* record.

**FIGURE 7-10:** PRINT CHART FOR EMPLOYEES BY DEPARTMENT REPORT IN WHICH DEPARTMENT NUMBERS APPEAR IN A FOOTER

```
 2  EMPLOYEES  BY  DEPARTMENT
 4  LAST NAME                FIRST NAME
 6  XXXXXXXXXXXX             XXXXXXXXXXXX
 7  XXXXXXXXXXXX             XXXXXXXXXXXX
 8  XXXXXXXXXXXX             XXXXXXXXXXXX
10  END OF DEPARTMENT  99
```

Figure 7-11 shows a program that prints a list of employees by department, including a footer that displays the department number at the end of each department's list. When you write a program that produces the report shown in Figure 7-10, you continuously read records with `empLast`, `empFirst`, and `empDept` fields. Each time an `empDept` does not equal the `oldDept`, it means that you have reached a department break and that you should perform the `newPage()` module. The `newPage()` module has three tasks:

- It must print the footer for the previous department at the bottom of the employee list.
- It must print headings at the top of a new page.
- It must update the control break field.

When the `newPage()` module prints the footer at the bottom of the old page, you must use the `oldDept` number. For example, assume you have printed several employees from Department 12. When you read a record with an employee from Department 13 (or any other department), the first thing you must do is print "END OF DEPARTMENT 12". You print the correct department number by accessing the value of the `oldDept`, not `empDept`. Then, you can print the other headings at the top of a new page and update `oldDept` to the current `empDept`, which in this example is 13.

The `newPage()` module in Figure 7-11 performs three tasks required in all control break routines:

- It performs any necessary processing for the previous group—in this case, it prints the footer.
- It performs any necessary processing for the new group—in this case, it prints headings.
- It updates the control break field.

**FIGURE 7-11:** PROGRAM THAT LISTS EMPLOYEES BY DEPARTMENT, INCLUDING DEPARTMENT NUMBER IN THE FOOTER

```
start
      perform housekeeping()
      while not eof
            perform mainLoop()
      endwhile
      perform finish()
stop



housekeeping()
      declare variables
      open files
      print head1
      print head2
      read empRec
      oldDept = empDept
return
```

```
finish()
      print foot, oldDept
      close files
return
```

```
empRec
      num empDept
      char empLast
      char empFirst
char head1 =  "EMPLOYEES BY DEPARTMENT"
char head2 =  " LAST NAME    FIRSTNAME"
char foot = "END OF DEPARTMENT"
num oldDept
```

```
mainloop()
      if empDept not = oldDept then
            perform newPage()
      endif
      print empLast, empFirst
      read empRec
return

newPage()
      print foot, oldDept
      print head1
      print head2
      oldDept = empDept
return
```

When you printed the department number in the header in the example in the previous section, you needed a special step in the `housekeeping()` module. When you print the department number in the footer, the `finish()` module requires an extra step. Imagine that the last five records on the input file include two employees from Department 78, Amy and Bill, and three employees from Department 85, Carol, Don, and Ellen. The logical flow proceeds as follows:

1. After the first Department 78 employee (Amy) prints, you read in the second Department 78 employee (Bill).
2. At the top of the `mainLoop()` module, Bill's department is compared to `oldDept`. The departments are the same, so the second Department 78 employee (Bill) is printed. Then, you read in the first Department 85 employee (Carol).
3. At the top of the `mainLoop()`, Carol's `empDept` and the `oldDept` are different, so you perform the `newPage()` module, while Carol's record waits in memory.
4. In the `newPage()` module, you print "END OF DEPARTMENT 78". Then, you print headings at the top of the next page. Finally, you set `oldDept` to 85, and then return to the `mainLoop()`.
5. Back in the `mainLoop()`, you print a line of data for the first Department 85 employee (Carol), whose record waited while `newPage()` executed. Then, you read in the record for the second Department 85 employee (Don).
6. At the top of `mainLoop()`, you compare Don's department number to `oldDept`. The numbers are the same, so you print Don's employee data and read in the last Department 85 employee (Ellen).
7. At the top of `mainLoop()`, you determine that Ellen has the same department number, so you print Ellen's data and attempt to read from the input file, where you encounter `eof`.
8. The `eof` decision in the mainline logic sends you to the `finish()` module.

You have printed the last Department 85 employee (Ellen), but the department footer for Department 85 has not printed. That's because every time you attempt to read an input record, you don't know whether there will be more records. The mainline logic checks for the `eof` condition, but if it determines that it is `eof`, the logic does not flow back into the `mainLoop()` where the `newPage()` module can execute.

To print the footer for the last department, you must print a footer one last time within the `finish()` routine. The `finish()` module that is part of the complete program in Figure 7-11 illustrates this. Taking this action is similar to printing the first heading in the `housekeeping()` module. The very first heading prints separately from all the others at the beginning; the very last footer must print separately from all the others at the end.

## PERFORMING CONTROL BREAKS WITH TOTALS

Suppose you run a bookstore, and one of the files you maintain is called BOOKFILE, which has one record for every book title that you carry. Each record has fields such as `bookTitle`, `bookAuthor`, `bookCategory` (fiction, reference, self-help, and so on), `bookPublisher`, and `bookPrice`, as shown in the file description in Figure 7-12.

---

**FIGURE 7-12:** BOOKFILE FILE DESCRIPTION

```
File name: BOOKFILE
Sorted by: Category
FIELD DESCRIPTION      POSITIONS      DATA TYPE      DECIMALS
Title                  1-30           Character
Author                 31-46          Character
Category               47-56          Character
Publisher              57-72          Character
Price                  73-77          Numeric            2
```

---

Suppose you want to print out a list of all the books that your store carries, with a total number of books at the bottom of the list, as shown in Figure 7-13. You can use the logic shown in Figure 7-14. In the main loop module, named `bookListLoop()`, you print a book title, add 1 to the `grandTotal`, and read the next record. At the end of the program, in the `closeDown()` module, you print the `grandTotal` before you close the files.

**FIGURE 7-13:** PRINT CHART FOR BOOK LIST

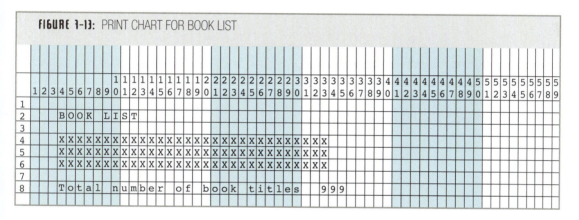

As you can see from the pseudocode in Figure 7-14, the `bookListLoop()` module performs three major tasks:

- Prints a book title
- Adds 1 to the `grandTotal`
- Reads in the next book record

The `closeDown()` module prints the `grandTotal`. You can't print `grandTotal` any earlier in the program because the `grandTotal` value isn't complete until the last record has been read.

The logic of the preceding program is pretty straightforward. Suppose, however, that you decide you want a count for each category of book rather than just one grand total. For example, if all the book records contain a category that is either fiction, reference, or self-help, then the book records might be sorted to be in alphabetical order by category, and the output would consist of a list of all fiction books first, followed by a count; then all reference books, followed by a count; and finally all self-help books, followed by a count. The report is a control break report, and the control break field is the `bookCategory`.

**FIGURE 7-14:** FLOWCHART AND PSEUDOCODE FOR BOOKSTORE PROGRAM

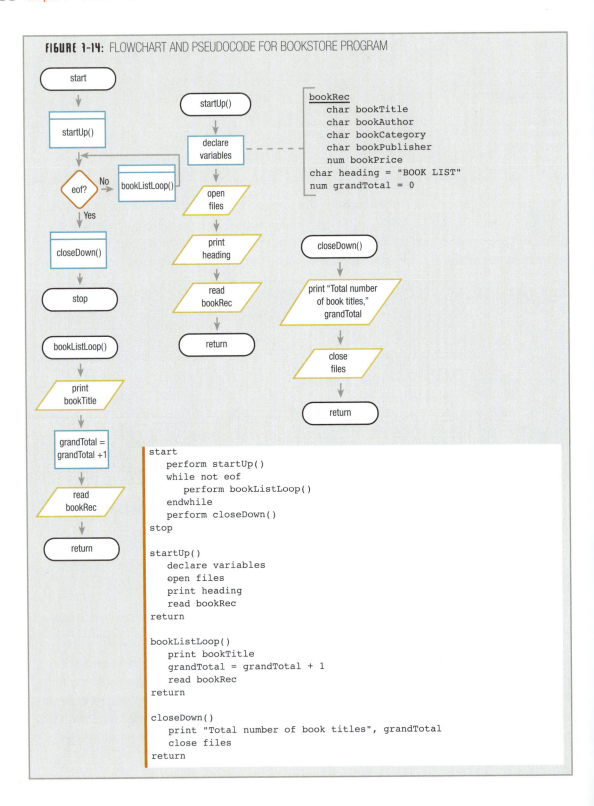

```
start
   perform startUp()
   while not eof
      perform bookListLoop()
   endwhile
   perform closeDown()
stop

startUp()
   declare variables
   open files
   print heading
   read bookRec
return

bookListLoop()
   print bookTitle
   grandTotal = grandTotal + 1
   read bookRec
return

closeDown()
   print "Total number of book titles", grandTotal
   close files
return
```

To produce the report with subtotals by category, you must declare two new variables: `previousCategory` and `categoryTotal`. Every time you read in a book record, you compare `bookCategory` to `previousCategory`; when there is a category change, you print the count of books for the previous category. The `categoryTotal` variable holds that count. See Figure 7-15.

 **TIP** When you draw a flowchart, it usually is clearer to ask questions positively, as in "`bookCategory = previousCategory?`", and draw appropriate actions on the Yes or No side of the decision. In pseudocode, when action occurs only on the No side of a decision, it is usually clearer to ask negatively, as in "`bookCategory not equal to previousCategory?`". Figure 7-15 uses these tactics.

When you read the first record from the input file in the `startUp()` module of the program in Figure 7-15, you save the value of `bookCategory` in the `previousCategory` variable. Every time a record enters the `bookListLoop()` module, the program checks to see if the current record represents a new category of work, by comparing `bookCategory` to the variable called `previousCategory`. When you process the first record, the categories match, so the book title prints, the `categoryTotal` increases by one, and you read the next record. If this next record's `bookCategory` value matches the `previousCategory` value, processing continues as usual with printing a line and adding 1 to the `categoryTotal`.

At some point, the `bookCategory` for an input record does not match the `previousCategory`. At that point, you perform the `categoryChange()` module. Within the `categoryChange()` module, you print the count of the previous category of books. Then, you add the `categoryTotal` to the `grandTotal`. Adding a total to a higher-level total is called **rolling up the totals**.

You could write the `bookListLoop()` so that as you process each book, you add one to the `categoryTotal` and add one to the `grandTotal`. Then, there would be no need to roll totals up in the `categoryChange()` module. If there are 120 fiction books, you add 1 to `categoryTotal` 120 times; you also would add 1 to `grandTotal` 120 times. This technique would yield correct results, but you can eliminate executing 119 addition instructions by waiting until you have accumulated all 120 category counts before adding the total figure to `grandTotal`.

This control break report containing totals performs the five tasks required in all control break routines that include totals:

- ▪ It performs any necessary processing for the previous group—in this case, it prints the `categoryTotal`.
- ▪ It rolls up the current-level totals to the next higher level—in this case, it adds `categoryTotal` to `grandTotal`.
- ▪ It resets the current level's totals to zero—in this case, the `categoryTotal` is set to zero.
- ▪ It performs any necessary processing for the new group—in this case, there is none.
- ▪ It updates the control break field—in this case, `previousCategory`.

**FIGURE 7-15:** FLOWCHART AND PSEUDOCODE FOR BOOKSTORE PROGRAM CONTAINING A COUNT AFTER EACH BOOK CATEGORY GROUP

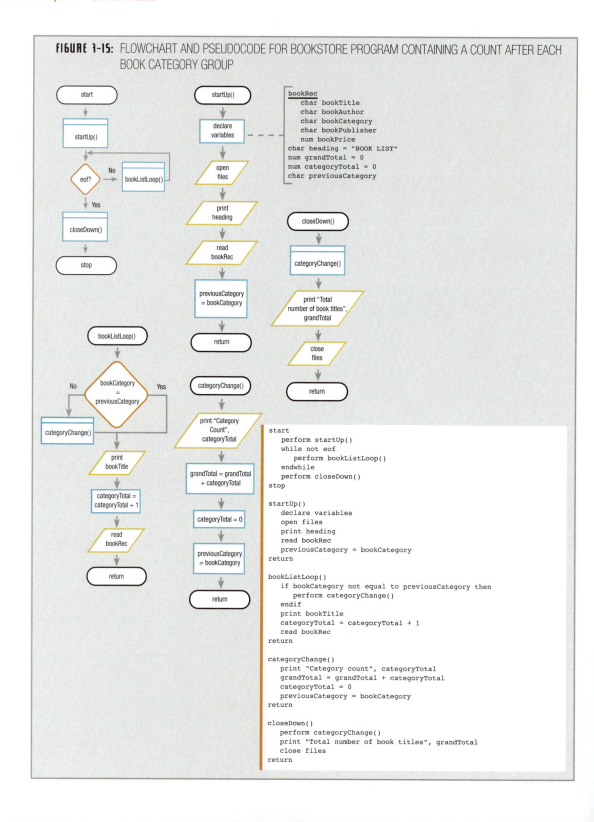

```
start
   perform startUp()
   while not eof
      perform bookListLoop()
   endwhile
   perform closeDown()
stop

startUp()
   declare variables
   open files
   print heading
   read bookRec
   previousCategory = bookCategory
return

bookListLoop()
   if bookCategory not equal to previousCategory then
      perform categoryChange()
   endif
   print bookTitle
   categoryTotal = categoryTotal + 1
   read bookRec
return

categoryChange()
   print "Category count", categoryTotal
   grandTotal = grandTotal + categoryTotal
   categoryTotal = 0
   previousCategory = bookCategory
return

closeDown()
   perform categoryChange()
   print "Total number of book titles", grandTotal
   close files
return
```

The `closeDown()` routine for this type of program is more complicated than it might first appear. It seems as though you should print the `grandTotal`, close the files, and return to the mainline logic. However, when you read the last record, the mainline `eof` decision sends the logical flow to the `closeDown()` routine. You have not printed the last `categoryTotal`, nor have you added the count for the last category into the `grandTotal`. You must take care of both these tasks before printing the `grandTotal`. You can perform these two tasks as separate steps in `closeDown()`, but it is often simplest just to remember to perform the control break routine `categoryChange()` one last time. The `categoryChange()` module already executes after every previous category completes—that is, every time you encounter a new category during the execution of the program. You also can execute this module after the final category completes, at end of file. Encountering the end of the file is really just another form of break; it signals that the last category has finally completed. The `categoryChange()` module prints the category total and rolls the totals up to the `grandTotal` level.

TIP ▫ ▫ ▫ ▫ | When you call the `categoryChange()` module from within `closeDown()`, it performs a few tasks you don't need, such as setting the value of `previousCategory`. You have to weigh the convenience of calling the already-written `categoryChange()` module, and executing a few unneeded statements, against taking the time to write a new module that would execute only the statements that are absolutely necessary.

It is very important to note that this control break program works whether there are three categories of books or 300. Note further that it does not matter what the categories of books are. For example, the program never asks `bookCategory = "fiction"?`. Instead, the control of the program breaks when the category field *changes*, and it is in no way dependent on *what* that change is.

## PERFORMING MULTIPLE-LEVEL CONTROL BREAKS

Let's say your bookstore from the last example is so successful that you have a chain of them across the country. Every time a sale is made, you create a record with the fields `bookTitle`, `bookPrice`, `bookCity`, and `bookState`. You want a report that prints a summary of books sold in each city and each state, similar to the one shown in Figure 7-16. A report such as this one, which does not include any information about individual records, but instead includes only group totals, is a **summary report**.

This program contains a **multiple-level control break**—that is, the normal flow of control (reading records and counting book sales) breaks away to print totals in response to more than just one change in condition. In this report, a control break occurs in response to either (or both) of two conditions: when the contents of the `bookCity` variable changes as well as when the contents of the `bookState` variable changes.

Just as the file you use to create a single-level control break report must be presorted, so must the input file you use to create a multiple-level control break report. The input file that you use for the book sales report must be sorted by `bookCity` *within* `bookState`. That is, all of one state's records, for example all records from IA, come first; then all the records from another state, such as IL, follow. Within any one state, all of one city's records come first, then all of the next city's records follow. For example, the input file that produces the report shown in Figure 7-16 contains 200 records for book sales in Ames, IA, followed by 814 records for book sales in Des Moines, IA. The basic processing entails reading a book sale record, adding one to a counter, and reading the next book sale record. At the end of any city's records, you print a total for that city; at the end of a state's records, you print a total for that state.

**FIGURE 7-16:** SAMPLE RUN OF BOOK SALES BY CITY AND STATE REPORT

| BOOK SALES BY CITY AND STATE | |
|---|---|
| Ames | 200 |
| Des Moines | 814 |
| Iowa City | 291 |
| Total for IA | 1305 |
| Chicago | 1093 |
| Crystal Lake | 564 |
| McHenry | 213 |
| Springfield | 365 |
| Total for IL | 2235 |
| Springfield | 289 |
| Worcester | 100 |
| Total for MA | 389 |
| Grand Total | 3929 |

The `housekeeping()` module of the Book Sales by City and State report program looks similar to the `housekeeping()` module in the previous control break program, in which there was a single control break for change in category of book. In each program, you declare variables, open files, and read the first record. This time, however, there are multiple fields to save and compare to the old fields. Here, you declare two special variables, `prevCity` and `prevState`, as shown in Figure 7-17. In addition, the Book Sales report shows three kinds of totals, so you declare three new variables that will serve as holding places for the total in the Book Sales report: `cityCounter`, `stateCounter`, and `grandTotal`, which are all initialized to zero.

This program prints both `bookState` and `bookCity` totals, so you need two control break modules, `cityBreak()` and `stateBreak()`. Every time there is a change in the `bookCity` field, the `cityBreak()` routine performs these standard control break tasks:

- It performs any necessary processing for the previous group—in this case, it prints totals for the previous city.
- It rolls up the current-level totals to the next higher level—in this case, it adds the city count to the state count.
- It resets the current level's totals to zero—in this case, it sets the city count to zero.
- It performs any necessary processing for the new group—in this case, there is none.
- It updates the control break field—in this case, it sets `prevCity` to `bookCity`.

**FIGURE 7-17:** FLOWCHART AND PSEUDOCODE FOR `housekeeping()` MODULE IN BOOK SALES BY CITY AND STATE REPORT PROGRAM

Within the `stateBreak()` module, you must perform one new type of task, as well as the control break tasks you are familiar with. The new task is the first task: Within the `stateBreak()` module, you must first perform a `cityBreak()` automatically (because if there is a change in the state, there must also be a change in the city). The `stateBreak()` module does the following:

- It processes the lower-level break—in this case, `cityBreak()`.
- It performs any necessary processing for the previous group—in this case, it prints totals for the previous state.
- It rolls up the current-level totals to the next higher level—in this case, it adds the state count to the grand total.
- It resets the current level's totals to zero—in this case, it sets the state count to zero.
- It performs any necessary processing for the new group—in this case, there is none.
- It updates the control break field—in this case, it sets `prevState` to `bookState`.

The `mainLoop()` of this multiple-level control break program checks for any change in two different variables: `bookCity` and `bookState`. When the `bookCity` changes, a city total is printed, and when the `bookState` changes, a state total is printed. As you can see from the sample report in Figure 7-16, all city totals for each state print before the state total for the same state, so it might seem logical to check for a change in `bookCity` before checking for a change in `bookState`. However, the opposite is true. For the totals to be correct, you must check for any `bookState` change first. You do so because when a `bookCity` changes, the `bookState` also *might* be changing, but when the `bookState` changes, it means the `bookCity` *must* be changing.

Consider the sample input records shown in Figure 7-18, which are sorted by `bookCity` within `bookState`:

**FIGURE 7-18:** SAMPLE DATA FOR BOOK SALES BY CITY AND STATE REPORT

| TITLE | PRICE | CITY | STATE |
|---|---|---|---|
| *A Brief History of Time* | 20.00 | Iowa City | IA |
| *The Scarlet Letter* | 15.99 | Chicago | IL |
| *Math Magic* | 4.95 | Chicago | IL |
| *She's Come Undone* | 12.00 | Springfield | IL |
| *The Joy of Cooking* | 2.50 | Springfield | IL |
| *Walden* | 9.95 | Springfield | MA |
| *A Bridge Too Far* | 3.50 | Springfield | MA |

When you get to the point in the program where you read the first Illinois record (*The Scarlet Letter*), "Iowa City" is the value stored in the field `prevCity`, and "IA" is the value stored in `prevState`. Because the values in the `bookCity` and `bookState` variables on the new record are both different from the `prevCity` and `prevState` fields, both a city and state total will print. However, consider the problem when you read the first record for Springfield, MA (*Walden*). At this point in the program, `prevState` is IL, but `prevCity` is the same as the current `bookCity`; both contain Springfield. If you check for a change in `bookCity`, you won't find one at all, and no city total will print, even though Springfield, MA, is definitely a different city from Springfield, IL.

Cities in different states can have the same name; when cities with the same name but in different states follow each other, if you have written your control break program to check for a change in city name first, the program will not recognize that you are working with a new city. Instead, you should always check for the major-level break first. If the records are sorted by `bookCity` within `bookState`, then a change in `bookState` causes a **major-level break**, and a change in `bookCity` causes a **minor-level break**. When the `bookState` value "MA" is not equal to the `prevState` value "IL", you force a `cityBreak()`, printing a city total for Springfield, IL, before a state total for IL and before continuing with the Springfield, MA, record. You check for a change in `bookState` first, and if there is one, you perform a `cityBreak()`. In other words, if there is a change in `bookState`, there is an implied change in `bookCity`, even if the cities happen to have the same name.

**TIP** ▫ ▫ ▫ ▫ If you needed totals to print by `bookCity` within a field defined as `bookCounty` within `bookState`, you could say you have minor-, intermediate-, and major-level breaks.

Figure 7-19 shows the `mainLoop()` for the Book Sales by City and State Report program. You check for a change in the `bookState` value. If there is no change, you check for a change in the `bookCity` value. If there is no change there either, you add 1 to the counter for the city and read the next record. When there is a change in the `bookCity` value, you print the city total and add the city total to the state total. When there is a change in the `bookState` value, you perform the break routine for the last city in the state, then you print the state total and add it to the grand total.

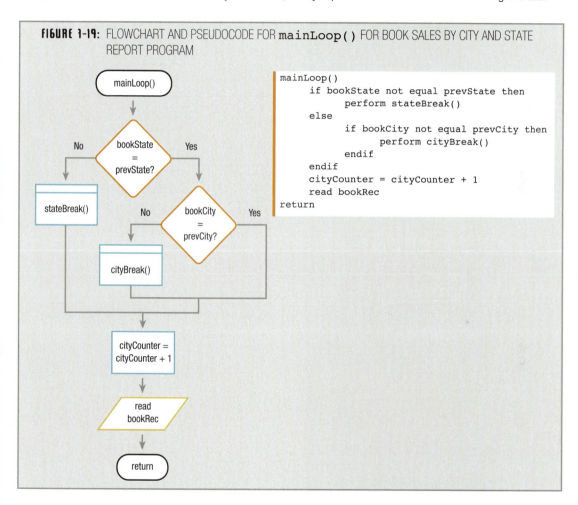

**FIGURE 7-19:** FLOWCHART AND PSEUDOCODE FOR `mainLoop()` FOR BOOK SALES BY CITY AND STATE REPORT PROGRAM

```
mainLoop()
        if bookState not equal prevState then
                perform stateBreak()
        else
                if bookCity not equal prevCity then
                        perform cityBreak()
                endif
        endif
        cityCounter = cityCounter + 1
        read bookRec
return
```

Figures 7-20 and 7-21 show the `stateBreak()` and `cityBreak()` modules. The two modules are very similar; the `stateBreak()` routine contains just one extra type of task. When there is a change in `bookState`, you perform the `cityBreak()` automatically before you perform any of the other necessary steps to change states.

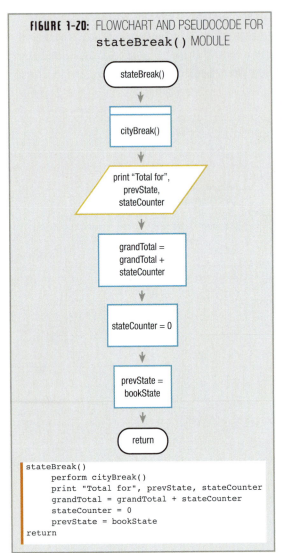

**FIGURE 7-20:** FLOWCHART AND PSEUDOCODE FOR `stateBreak()` MODULE

```
stateBreak()
    perform cityBreak()
    print "Total for", prevState, stateCounter
    grandTotal = grandTotal + stateCounter
    stateCounter = 0
    prevState = bookState
return
```

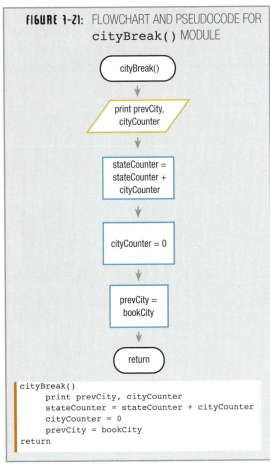

**FIGURE 7-21:** FLOWCHART AND PSEUDOCODE FOR `cityBreak()` MODULE

```
cityBreak()
    print prevCity, cityCounter
    stateCounter = stateCounter + cityCounter
    cityCounter = 0
    prevCity = bookCity
return
```

The sample report containing book sales by city and state shows that you print the grand total for all book sales, so within the `closeDown()` module, you must print the `grandTotal` variable. Before you can do so, however, you must perform both the `cityBreak()` and the `stateBreak()` modules one last time. You can accomplish this by performing `stateBreak()`, because the first step within `stateBreak()` is to perform `cityBreak()`.

Consider the sample data shown in Figure 7-18. While you continue to read records for books sold in Springfield, MA, you continue to add to the `cityCounter` for that city. At the moment you attempt to read one more record past the end of the file, you do not know whether there will be more records; therefore, you have not yet printed either the `cityCounter` for Springfield or the `stateCounter` for MA. In the `closeDown()` module, you perform `stateBreak()`, which immediately performs `cityBreak()`. Within `cityBreak()`, the count for Springfield prints and rolls up to the `stateCounter`. Then, after the logic transfers back to the `stateBreak()` module, the total for MA prints and rolls up to the `grandTotal`. Finally, you can print the `grandTotal`, as shown in Figure 7-22.

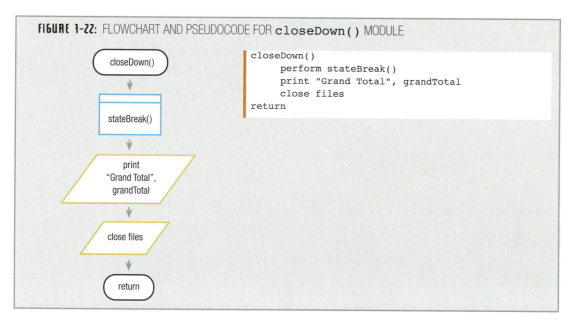

**FIGURE 7-22:** FLOWCHART AND PSEUDOCODE FOR `closeDown()` MODULE

```
closeDown()
    perform stateBreak()
    print "Grand Total", grandTotal
    close files
return
```

Every time you write a program where you need control break routines, you should check whether you need to complete each of the following tasks within the modules:

- Performing the lower-level break, if any
- Performing any control break processing for the previous group
- Rolling up the current-level totals to the next higher level
- Resetting the current level's totals to zero
- Performing any control break processing for the new group
- Updating the control break field

## PERFORMING PAGE BREAKS

Many business programs use a form of control break logic to start a new page when a printed page fills up with output. In other words, you might want the change to a new page to be based on the number of lines already printed, rather than on the contents of an input field, such as department number. The logic in these programs involves counting the lines printed, pausing to print headings when the counter reaches some predetermined value, and then going on. This common business task is just another example of providing a break in the usual flow of control.

TIP ☐ ☐ ☐ ☐  Some programmers may prefer to reserve the term *control break* for situations in which the break is based on the contents of one of the fields in an input record, rather than on the contents of a work field such as a line counter.

Let's say you have a file called CUSTOMERFILE containing 1,000 customers, with two character fields that you have decided to call `custLast` and `custFirst`. You want to print a list of these customers, 60 detail lines to a page, in the format shown in Figure 7-23. The mainline logic of the program is familiar. The only new feature is a variable called a line counter. You will use a **line-counter** variable to keep track of the number of printed lines, so that you can break to a new page after printing 60 lines. See Figure 7-24.

TIP ☐ ☐ ☐ ☐  You first learned about detail lines in Chapter 3. Detail lines contain individual record data, as opposed to summary lines, which typically contain counts, totals, or other group information culled from multiple records.

**FIGURE 7-23:** PRINT CHART FOR CUSTOMER REPORT

|   |   |   |   |   |   |   |   |   |   |   |   |   |   |   |   |   |   |   |   |   |   |   |   |   |   |   |   |   |   |   |   |   |   |   |   |   |   |   |   |   |   |   |   |   |   |   |   |   |   |   |   |   |   |   |   |   |   |   |
|---|---|---|---|---|---|---|---|---|---|---|---|---|---|---|---|---|---|---|---|---|---|---|---|---|---|---|---|---|---|---|---|---|---|---|---|---|---|---|---|---|---|---|---|---|---|---|---|---|---|---|---|---|---|---|---|---|---|---|
| 1 | | | | | | C | u | s | t | o | m | e | r | | L | i | s | t | | | | | | | | | | | | | | | | | | | | | | | | | | | | | | | | | | | | | | |
| 2 | | | | | | | | | | | | | | | | | | | | | | | | | | | | | | | | | | | | | | | | | | | | | | | | | | | | | | | | |
| 3 | | L | A | S | T | | N | A | M | E | | | | | | | | | | | F | I | R | S | T | | N | A | M | E | | | | | | | | | | | | | | | | | | | | | | | | |
| 4 | | | | | | | | | | | | | | | | | | | | | | | | | | | | | | | | | | | | | | | | | | | | | | | | | | | | | | |
| 6 | | X | X | X | X | X | X | X | X | X | X | X | X | | | | | | | X | X | X | X | X | X | X | X | X | X | X | X | | | | | | | | | | | | | | | | |
| 7 | | X | X | X | X | X | X | X | X | X | X | X | X | | | | | | | X | X | X | X | X | X | X | X | X | X | X | X | | | | | | | | | | | | | | | | |
| 8 | | X | X | X | X | X | X | X | X | X | X | X | X | | | | | | | X | X | X | X | X | X | X | X | X | X | X | X | | | | | | | | | | | | | | | | |

TIP ☐ ☐ ☐ ☐  When creating a printed report, you need to clarify whether the user wants a specific number of *total* lines per page, including headings, or a specific number of *detail* lines per page following the headings.

Within the `getReady()` module (Figure 7-25), you declare the variables, open the files, print the headings, and read the first record. Within the `produceReport()` module (Figure 7-26), you compare the `lineCounter` to 60. When you process the first record, the `lineCounter` is zero, so you print the record, add one to the `lineCounter`, and read the next record.

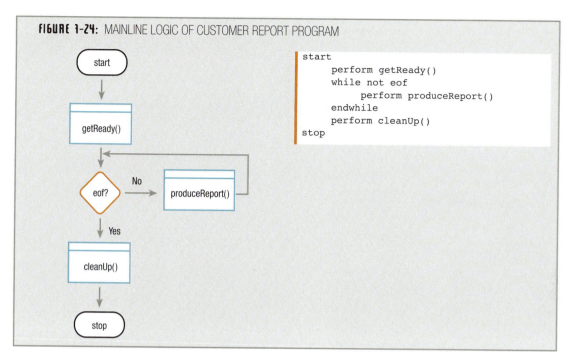

**FIGURE 7-24:** MAINLINE LOGIC OF CUSTOMER REPORT PROGRAM

```
start
    perform getReady()
    while not eof
        perform produceReport()
    endwhile
    perform cleanUp()
stop
```

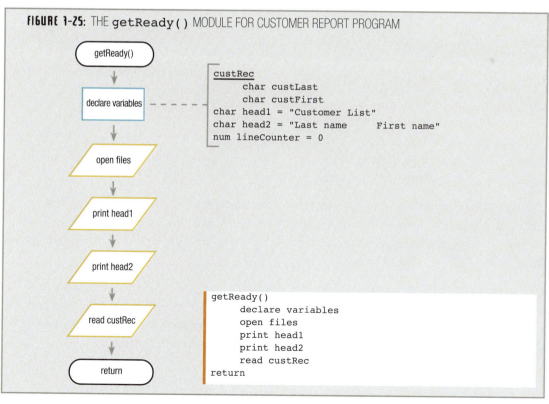

**FIGURE 7-25:** THE `getReady()` MODULE FOR CUSTOMER REPORT PROGRAM

```
custRec
    char custLast
    char custFirst
char head1 = "Customer List"
char head2 = "Last name      First name"
num lineCounter = 0
```

```
getReady()
    declare variables
    open files
    print head1
    print head2
    read custRec
return
```

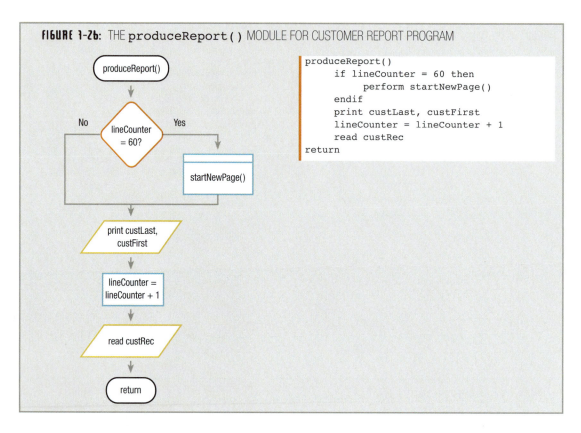

**FIGURE 7-26:** THE `produceReport()` MODULE FOR CUSTOMER REPORT PROGRAM

```
produceReport()
     if lineCounter = 60 then
          perform startNewPage()
     endif
     print custLast, custFirst
     lineCounter = lineCounter + 1
     read custRec
return
```

**TIP** ☐ ☐ ☐ ☐ In Figure 7-25, instead of printing head1 and head2, you could perform a module that starts a new page. Figure 7-27 shows a startNewPage() module that the getReady() module could call.

On every cycle through the `produceReport()` module, you check the line counter to see if it is 60 yet. When the first record is written, `lineCounter` is 1. You read the second record, and if there is a second record (that is, if it is not `eof`), you return to the top of the `produceReport()` module. In that module, you compare `lineCounter` to 60, print another line, and add 1 to `lineCounter`, making it equal to 2.

After 60 records read and write, `lineCounter` holds a value of 60. When you read the sixty-first record (and if it is not `eof`), you enter the `produceReport()` module for the 61st time. The answer to the question `lineCounter = 60?` is yes, and you break to perform the `startNewPage()` module. The `startNewPage()` module is a control break routine.

The `startNewPage()` module, shown in Figure 7-27, must print the headings that appear at the top of a new page, and it must also set the `lineCounter` back to zero. If you neglect to reset the `lineCounter`, its value will increase with each successive record and never be equal to 60 again. When resetting the `lineCounter` for a new page, you force execution of the `startNewPage()` module after 60 more records (120 total) print.

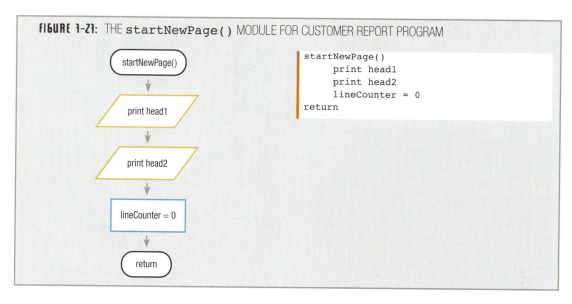

FIGURE 7-27:  THE `startNewPage()` MODULE FOR CUSTOMER REPORT PROGRAM

```
startNewPage()
    print head1
    print head2
    lineCounter = 0
return
```

The `startNewPage()` module is simpler than many control break modules because no record counters or accumulators are being maintained. In fact, the `startNewPage()` module must perform only two of the tasks you have seen required by control break routines.

- It does not perform the lower-level break, because there is none.
- It does not perform any control break processing for the previous group, because there is none.
- It does not roll up the current-level totals to the next higher level, because there are no totals.
- It does not reset the current level's totals to zero, because there are no totals (other than the `lineCounter`, which is the control break field).
- It does perform control break processing for the new group by printing headings at the top of the new page.
- It does update the control break field—the line counter.

You might want to employ one little trick that you can use to remove the statements that print the headings from the `getReady()` module. If you initialize `lineCounter` to 60 when defining the variables at the beginning of the program, on the first pass through `mainLoop()`, you can "fool" the computer into printing the first set of headings automatically. When you initialize the `lineCounter` to 60, you can remove the statements `print head1` and `print head2` from the `getReady()` module. With this change, when you enter the `produceReport()` module for the first time, `lineCounter` is already set to 60, and the `startNewPage()` module prints the headings and resets the `lineCounter` to zero before processing the first record from the input file. Figure 7-28 shows the entire program.

As with control break report programs that break based on the contents of one of a record's fields, in any program that starts new pages based on a line count, you always must update the line-counting variable that causes the unusual action. Using page breaks or control breaks (or both) within reports adds a new degree of organization to your printed output and makes it easier for the user to interpret and use.

**FIGURE 7-28:** THE COMPLETE CUSTOMER REPORT PROGRAM

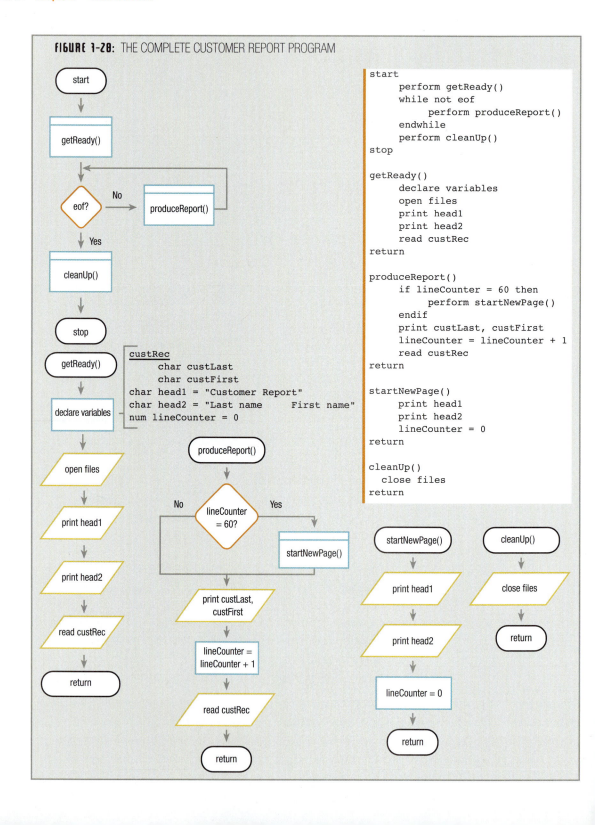

```
start
    perform getReady()
    while not eof
        perform produceReport()
    endwhile
    perform cleanUp()
stop

getReady()
    declare variables
    open files
    print head1
    print head2
    read custRec
return

produceReport()
    if lineCounter = 60 then
        perform startNewPage()
    endif
    print custLast, custFirst
    lineCounter = lineCounter + 1
    read custRec
return

startNewPage()
    print head1
    print head2
    lineCounter = 0
return

cleanUp()
  close files
return
```

```
custRec
    char custLast
    char custFirst
char head1 = "Customer Report"
char head2 = "Last name     First name"
num lineCounter = 0
```

# CHAPTER SUMMARY

☐ A control break is a temporary detour in the logic of a program; programmers refer to a program as a control break program when a change in the value of a variable initiates special actions or causes special or unusual processing to occur. To generate a control break report, your input records must be organized in sorted order based on the field that will cause the breaks.

☐ You use a control break field to hold data from a previous record. You decide when to perform a control break routine by comparing the value in the control break field to the corresponding value in the current record. At minimum, the simplest control break routines perform necessary processing for the new group and update the control break field.

☐ Sometimes, you need to use control data within a control break module, such as in a heading that requires information about the next record, or in a footer that requires information about the previous record. The very first heading prints separately from all the others at the beginning; the very last footer must print separately from all the others at the end.

☐ A control break report contains and prints totals for the previous group, rolls up the current-level totals to the next higher level, resets the current level's totals to zero, performs any other needed control break processing, and updates the control break field.

☐ In a program containing a multiple-level control break, the normal flow of control breaks away for special processing in response to a change in more than one field. You should always test for a major-level break before a minor-level break, and include a call to the minor break routine within the major break module.

☐ Every time you write a program in which you need control break routines, you should check whether you need to perform each of the following tasks within the routines: any lower-level break, any control break processing for the previous group, rolling up the current-level totals to the next higher level, resetting the current level's totals to zero, any control break processing for the new group, and updating the control break field.

☐ To perform page breaks, you count the lines printed and pause to print headings when the counter reaches some predetermined value.

### KEY TERMS

A control break is a temporary detour in the logic of a program.

A control break program is one in which a change in the value of a variable initiates special actions or causes special or unusual processing to occur.

A control break report lists items in groups. Frequently, each group is followed by a subtotal.

Programs that sort records take records that are not in order and rearrange them so that they are in an order based on some field.

A single-level control break is a break in the logic of a program based on the value of a single variable.

A control break field is a variable that holds the value that signals a break in a program.

A footer is a message that prints at the end of a page or other section of a report.

Rolling up the totals is the process of adding a total to a higher-level total.

A summary report is one that does not include any information about individual records, but instead includes only group totals.

A multiple-level control break is one in which the normal flow of control breaks away for special processing in response to a change in more than one field.

A major-level break is a break in the flow of logic that is caused by a change in the value of a higher-level field.

A minor-level break is a break in the flow of logic that is caused by a change in the value of a lower-level field.

A line counter is a variable that keeps track of the number of printed lines on a page.

# REVIEW QUESTIONS

1. **A control break occurs when a program** _____.
   a. takes one of two alternate courses of action for every record
   b. pauses to perform special processing based on the value of a field
   c. ends prematurely, before all records have been processed
   d. passes logical control to a module contained within another program

2. **Which of the following is an example of a control break report?**
   a. a list of all employees in a company, with a message "Retain" or "Dismiss" following each employee record
   b. a list of all students in a school, arranged in alphabetical order, with a total count at the end of the report
   c. a list of all customers of a business in ZIP code order, with a count of the number of customers who reside in each ZIP code
   d. a list of some of the patients of a medical clinic—those who have not seen a doctor for at least two years

3. **Placing records in sequential order based on the value in one of the fields is called** _____.
   a. sorting
   b. collating
   c. merging
   d. categorizing

4. **In a program with a single-level control break,** _____.
   a. the input file must contain a variable that contains a single digit
   b. the hierarchy chart must contain a single level below the main level
   c. special processing occurs based on the value in a single field
   d. the control break module must not contain any submodules

5. **A control break field** _____.
   a. always prints prior to any group of records on a control break report
   b. always prints after any group of records on a control break report
   c. never prints on a report
   d. causes special processing to occur

6. **The value stored in a control break field** _____.
   a. can be printed at the end of each group of records
   b. can be printed with each record
   c. both of these
   d. neither of these

7. Within any control break module, you must _____.

    a. declare a control break field

    b. set the control break field to zero

    c. print the control break field

    d. update the value in the control break field

8. An insurance agency employs 10 agents and wants to print a report of claims based on the insurance agent who sold each policy. The agent's name should appear in a heading prior to the list of each agent's claims. In the housekeeping module for this program, you should _____.

    a. read the first record before printing the first heading

    b. print the first heading before reading the first record

    c. read all the records that represent clients of the first agent before printing the heading

    d. print the first heading, but do not read the first record until the main loop

9. In contrast to using control break data in a heading, when you use control break data in a footer, you usually need data from the _____ record in the input data file.

    a. previous

    b. next

    c. first

    d. priming

10. An automobile dealer wants a list of cars sold, grouped by model, with a total dollar amount sold at the end of each group. The program contains four modules, appropriately named `housekeeping()`, `mainLoop()`, `modelBreak()`, and `finish()`. The total for the last car model group should be printed in the _____.

    a. `mainLoop()` module, after the last time the control break module is called

    b. `mainLoop()` module, as the last step in the module

    c. `modelBreak()` module when it is called from within the `mainLoop()` module

    d. `modelBreak()` module when it is called from within the `finish()` module

11. The Hampton City Zoo has a file that contains information about each of the animals it houses. Each animal record contains such information as the animal's ID number, date acquired by the zoo, and species. The zoo wants to print a list of animals, grouped by species, with a count after each group. As an example, a typical summary line might be "Species: Giraffe   Count: 7". Which of the following happens within the control break module that prints the count?

    a. The previous species count prints, and then the previous species field is updated.
    b. The previous species field is updated, and then the previous species count prints.
    c. Either of these will produce the desired results.
    d. Neither of these will produce the desired results.

12. Adding a total to a higher-level total is called _____ the totals.

    a. sliding
    b. advancing
    c. rolling up
    d. replacing

13. The Academic Dean of Creighton College wants a count of the number of students who have declared each of the college's 45 major courses of study, as well as a grand total count of students enrolled in the college. Individual student records contain each student's name, ID number, major, and other data, and are sorted in alphabetical order by major. A control break module executes when the program encounters a change in student major. Within this model, what must occur?

    a. The total count for the previous major prints.
    b. The total count for the previous major prints, and the total count is added to the grand total.
    c. The total count for the previous major prints, the total count for the major is added to the grand total, and the total count for the major is reset to zero.
    d. The total count for the previous major prints, the total count for the major is added to the grand total, the total count for the major is reset to zero, and the grand total is reset to zero.

14. In a control break program containing printed group totals and a grand total, the final module that executes must _____.

    a. print the group total for the last group
    b. roll up the total for the last group
    c. both of these
    d. neither of these

15. A summary report _____.

    a. contains detail lines
    b. contains total lines
    c. both of these
    d. neither of these

16. The Cityscape Real Estate Agency wants a list of all housing units sold last year that includes a subtotal of sales that occurred each month. Within each month group, there are also subtotals of each type of property—single-family homes, condominiums, commercial properties, and so on. This report is a _____ control break report.

    a. single-level
    b. multiple-level
    c. semilevel
    d. trilevel

17. The Packerville Parks Commission has a file that contains picnic permit information for the coming season. They need a report that lists each day's picnic permit information, including permit number and name of permit holder, starting on a separate page each day of the picnic season. (Figure 7-29 shows a sample page of output for the Packerville Parks report.) Within each day's permits, they want subtotals that count permits in each of the city's 30 parks. The permit records have been sorted by park name within date. In the main loop of the report program, the first decision should check for a change in _____.

**FIGURE 7-29:**

```
        Packerville Parks Commission - Daily Count of Permits by Park
Day: June 24

        Permit Number          Permit Holder
        200501932              Paul Martin
        200502003              Brownie Troop 176
        200502015              Dorothy Wintergreen
                                        Alcott Park Count - 3
        200500080              YMCA Day Camp
        200501200              Packerville Rotary Club
        200501453              Harold Martinez
        200502003              Wendy Sudo
                                        Browning Park Count - 4
```

    a. park name
    b. date
    c. permit number
    d. any of these

18. Which of the following is *not* a task you need to complete in any control break module that has multiple levels and totals at each level?

    a. Perform lower-level breaks.
    b. Roll up the totals.
    c. Update the control break field.
    d. Reset the current-level totals to the previous-level totals.

19. The election commission for the state of Illinois maintains a file that contains the name of each registered voter, the voter's county, and precinct within the county. The commission wants to produce a report that counts the voters in each precinct and county. The file should be sorted in _____.

    a. county order within precinct
    b. last name order within precinct
    c. last name order within county
    d. precinct order within county

20. A variable that determines when a new page should start based on the number of detail lines printed on a page is a(n) _____.

    a. detail counter
    b. line counter
    c. page counter
    d. break counter

## EXERCISES

1. What fields might you want to use as the control break fields to produce a report that lists all inventory items in a grocery store? (For example, you might choose to group items by grocery store department.) Design the print chart for the report.

2. What fields might you want to use as the control break fields to produce a report that lists all the people you know? (For example, you might choose to group friends by city of residence.) Design the print chart for the report.

3. Cool's Department Store keeps a record of every sale in the following format:

```
DEPARTMENT STORE SALES FILE DESCRIPTION
File name: DEPTSALES
Sorted by: Department
```

| FIELD DESCRIPTION | POSITIONS | DATA TYPE | DECIMALS | EXAMPLE |
|---|---|---|---|---|
| Transaction Number | 1-7 | Numeric | 0 | 2615441 |
| Amount | 8-13 | Numeric | 2 | 012599 |
| Department | 14-16 | Numeric | 0 | 501 |

Create the logic for a program that would print each transaction's details, with a total at the end of each department.

   a. Create the print chart.
   b. Create the hierarchy chart.
   c. Create the flowchart.
   d. Create the pseudocode.

4. A used-car dealer keeps track of sales in the following format:

```
AUTO SALES FILE DESCRIPTION
File name: AUTO
Sorted by: Salesperson
```

| FIELD DESCRIPTION | POSITIONS | DATA TYPE | DECIMALS | EXAMPLE |
|---|---|---|---|---|
| Salesperson | 1-20 | Character | | Miller |
| Make of Car | 21-30 | Character | | Ford |
| Vehicle Type | 31-40 | Character | | Sedan |
| Sale Price | 41-45 | Numeric | 0 | 12500 |

By the end of the week, a salesperson may have sold no cars, one car, or many cars. Create the logic of a program that would print one line for each salesperson, with that salesperson's total sales for the week and commission earned, which is 4% of the total sales.

   a. Create the print chart.
   b. Create the hierarchy chart.
   c. Create the flowchart.
   d. Create the pseudocode.

5.  A community college maintains student records in the following format:

```
STUDENT FILE DESCRIPTION
File name: STUDENTS
Sorted by: Hour of First Class
FIELD DESCRIPTION        POSITIONS    DATA TYPE    DECIMALS    EXAMPLE
Student Name             1-20         Character                Amy Lee
City                     21-30        Character                Woodstock
Hour of First Class      31-32        Numeric      0           08
Phone Number             33-42        Numeric      0           8154379823
```

The records have been sorted by hour of the day. The Hour of First Class is a two-digit number based on a 24-hour clock (that is, a 1 p.m. first class is recorded as 13).

Create a report that students can use to organize carpools. The report lists the names and phone numbers of students from the city of Huntley. Note that some students come from cities other than Huntley; these students should not be listed on the report.

Start a new page for each hour of the day, so that all students starting classes at the same hour are listed on the same page. Include the hour that each page represents in the heading for that page.

a.  Create the print chart.
b.  Create the hierarchy chart.
c.  Create the flowchart.
d.  Create the pseudocode.

6.  The Stanton Insurance Agency needs a report summarizing the counts of life, health, and other types of insurance policies it sells. Input records contain policy number, name of insured, policy value, and type of policy, and have been sorted in alphabetical order by type of policy. At the end of the report, display a count of all the policies.

a.  Create the print chart.
b.  Create the hierarchy chart.
c.  Create the flowchart.
d.  Create the pseudocode.

7.  If a university is organized into colleges (such as Liberal Arts), divisions (such as Languages), and departments (such as French), what would constitute the major, intermediate, and minor control breaks in a report that prints all classes offered by the university?

8.   A zoo keeps track of the expense of feeding the animals it houses. Each record holds one animal's ID number, name, species (elephant, rhinoceros, tiger, lion, and so on), zoo residence (pachyderm house, large cat house, and so on), and weekly food budget. The records take the following form:

```
ANIMAL FEED RECORDS
File name: ANIMFOOD
Sorted by: Species within house
FIELD DESCRIPTION        POSITIONS      DATA TYPE      DECIMALS      EXAMPLE
Animal ID                1-4            Numeric        0             4116
Animal Name              5-29           Character                    Elmo
Species                  30-45          Character                    Elephant
House                    46-55          Character                    Pachyderm
Weekly Food              56-59          Numeric        0             0075
 Budget in Dollars
```

Design a report that lists each animal's ID, name, and budgeted food amount. At the end of each species group, print a total budget for the species. At the end of each house (for example, the species lion, tiger, and leopard are all in the large cat house), print the house total. At the end of the report, print the grand total.

a.   Create the print chart.
b.   Create the hierarchy chart.
c.   Create the flowchart.
d.   Create the pseudocode.

9.   A soft-drink manufacturer produces several flavors of drink—for example, cola, orange, and lemon. Additionally, each flavor has several versions such as regular, diet, and caffeine-free. The manufacturer operates factories in several states.

Assume you have input records that list version, flavor, yearly production in gallons, and state (for example: Regular Cola 5000 Kansas). The records have been sorted in alphabetical order by version within flavor within state. Design the report that lists each version and flavor, with minor total production figures for each flavor and major total production figures for each state.

a.   Create the print chart.
b.   Create the hierarchy chart.
c.   Create the flowchart.
d.   Create the pseudocode.

10. An art shop owner maintains records for each item in the shop, including the title of the work, the artist who made the item, the medium (for example, watercolor, oil, or clay), and the monetary value. The records are sorted by artist within medium. Design a report that lists all items in the store, with a minor total value following each artist's work, and a major total value following each medium. Allow only 40 detail lines per page.

   a. Create the print chart.
   b. Create the hierarchy chart.
   c. Create the flowchart.
   d. Create the pseudocode.

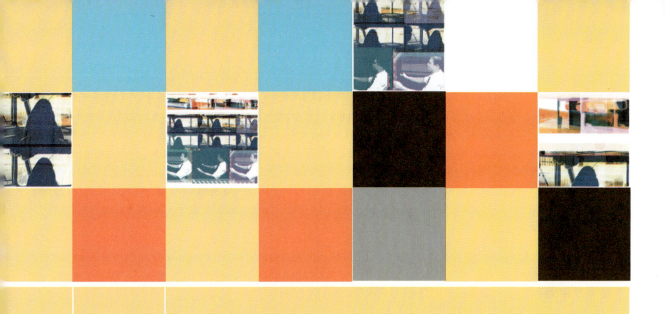

# 8 ARRAYS

## After studying Chapter 8, you should be able to:

- ☐ Understand how arrays are used
- ☐ Understand how arrays occupy computer memory
- ☐ Manipulate an array to replace nested decisions
- ☐ Declare and initialize an array
- ☐ Understand the difference between run-time and compile-time arrays
- ☐ Load array values from a file
- ☐ Search an array for an exact match
- ☐ Use parallel arrays
- ☐ Force subscripts to remain within array bounds
- ☐ Improve search efficiency by using an early exit
- ☐ Search an array for a range match

## UNDERSTANDING ARRAYS

An **array** is a series or list of variables in computer memory, all of which have the same name but are differentiated with special numbers called subscripts. A **subscript** is a number that indicates the position of a particular item within an array. Whenever you require multiple storage locations for objects, you are using a real-life counterpart of a programming array. For example, if you store important papers in a series of file folders and label each folder with a consecutive letter of the alphabet, then you are using the equivalent of an array. If you store mementos in a series of stacked shoeboxes, each labeled with a year, or if you sort mail into slots, each labeled with a name, then you are also using a real-life equivalent of a programming array.

When you look down the left side of a tax table to find your income level before looking to the right to find your income tax obligation, you are using an array. Similarly, if you look down the left side of a train schedule to find your station before looking to the right to find the train's arrival time, you also are using an array.

Each of these real-life arrays helps you organize real-life objects. You *could* store all your papers or mementos in one huge cardboard box, or find your tax rate or train's arrival time if both were printed randomly in one large book. However, using an organized storage and display system makes your life easier in each case. Using a programming array accomplishes the same results for your data.

**TIP** □ □ □ □ | Some programmers refer to an array as a *table* or a *matrix*.

## HOW ARRAYS OCCUPY COMPUTER MEMORY

When you declare an array, you declare a programming structure that contains multiple variables. Each variable within an array has the same name and the same data type; each separate array variable is one **element** of the array. Each array element occupies an area in memory next to, or contiguous to, the others, as shown in Figure 8-1. You indicate the number of elements an array will hold—the **size of the array**—when you declare the array along with your other variables.

**FIGURE 8-1:** APPEARANCE OF A THREE-ELEMENT ARRAY AND A SINGLE VARIABLE IN COMPUTER MEMORY

All array elements have the same group name, but each individual element also has a unique subscript indicating how far away it is from the first element. Therefore, any array's subscripts are always a sequence of integers such as 1 through 5 or 1 through 10. Depending on the syntax rules of the programming language you use, you place the subscript within either parentheses or square brackets following the group name; when writing pseudocode or drawing a flowchart, you can use either form of notation. This text uses square brackets to hold array element subscripts so that you don't mistake array names for method names. For example, Figure 8-1 shows how a single variable and an array are stored in computer memory. The single variable named `aNumber` holds the value 15. The array named `someVals` contains three elements, so the elements are `someVals[1]`, `someVals[2]`, and `someVals[3]`. The value stored in `someVals[1]` is 25, `someVals[2]` holds 36, and `someVals[3]` holds 47.

 In general, older programming languages such as COBOL and RPG use parentheses to hold their array subscripts. Newer languages such as C#, C++, and Java use square brackets.

 In some languages (for example, Java, C#, and C++), the first array element's subscript is 0; in others (for example, Visual Basic, COBOL, and RPG), it is 1. In Pascal, you can identify the starting number as any value you want. In all languages, however, the subscript values must be integers (whole numbers) and sequential.

You are never required to use arrays within your programs, but learning to use arrays correctly can make many programming tasks far more efficient and professional. When you understand how to use arrays, you will be able to provide elegant solutions to problems that otherwise would require tedious programming steps.

 When you describe people or events as "elegant," you mean they possess a refined gracefulness. Similarly, programmers use the term "elegant" to describe programs that are well-designed and easy to understand and maintain.

## MANIPULATING AN ARRAY TO REPLACE NESTED DECISIONS

Consider a program that keeps statistics for a recycling drive competition at a high school. The school is holding a competition between the freshman, sophomore, junior, and senior classes to see which class can collect the greatest number of aluminum cans. Each time a student brings in some cans, a clerk adds a record to a file in the following format, shown in Figure 8-2.

**FIGURE 8-2:** FILE DESCRIPTION FOR RECYCLING RECORDS

```
File name: STURECORDS
FIELD DESCRIPTION      POSITIONS      DATA TYPE      DECIMALS
Student class          1              Numeric        0
Cans collected         2-4            Numeric        0
```

For example, if a junior brings in 25 cans, one record is created with a 3 (for junior) in the class field and a 25 in the cans collected field. If a freshman brings in 10 cans, a record with 1 and 10 is created. If a second junior then brings in

20 more cans, the third record will contain a 3 and a 20. The contents of the data file appear as a series of numbers, as follows:

```
3 25
1 10
3 20
... and so on.
```

At the end of the recycling competition, after all the records have been collected, the file might contain hundreds of records, each holding a one-digit number representing a class and up to a three-digit number representing cans. You want to write a program that summarizes the total number of cans brought in by each class. The print chart for this report appears in Figure 8-3.

**FIGURE 8-3:** PRINT CHART FOR THE CAN-RECYCLING REPORT

| | | |
|---|---|---|
| | Can Competition Report | |
| | Class | Cans |
| | 1 | 99999 |
| | 2 | 99999 |
| | 3 | 99999 |
| | 4 | 99999 |

If all the records were sorted in order by the student's class, this report could be a control break report. You would simply read each record for the first (freshman) class, accumulating the number of collected cans in a variable. When you read the first record from a different class, you would print out the total for the previous class, reset the total to zero, and update the control break field before continuing.

**TIP** ▫ ▫ ▫ ▫ | You learned about control break logic in Chapter 7.

Assume, however, that the records have not been sorted. Without using an array, could you write a program that would accumulate the four class can-recycling totals? Of course you could. The program would have the same mainline logic as most of the other programs you have seen, as flowcharted in Figure 8-4.

**TIP** ▫ ▫ ▫ ▫ | The program shown in Figures 8-4 through 8-7 accomplishes its purpose, but is cumbersome. Follow its logic here, so that you understand how the program works. Later in this chapter, you will see how to write the can-recycling program much more efficiently using arrays.

**FIGURE 8-4:** FLOWCHART AND PSUEDOCODE FOR MAINLINE LOGIC OF THE CAN-RECYCLING PROGRAM

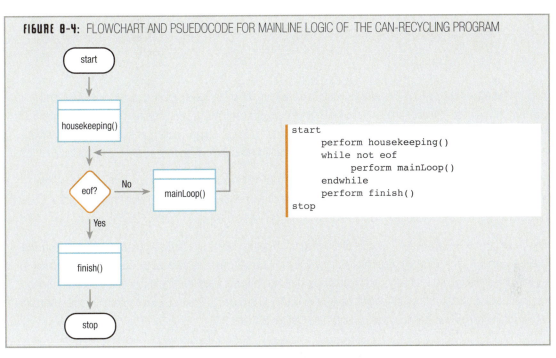

```
start
      perform housekeeping()
      while not eof
            perform mainLoop()
      endwhile
      perform finish()
stop
```

In the `housekeeping()` module of the can-recycling program (Figure 8-5), you declare variables including `stuClass` and `stuCans`. Then, you open the files and read the first record into memory. The headings *could* print in `housekeeping()`, or—because no other printing takes place in this program until the `finish()` module—you can choose to wait and print the headings there.

**FIGURE 8-5:** THE `housekeeping()` MODULE FOR THE CAN-RECYCLING PROGRAM

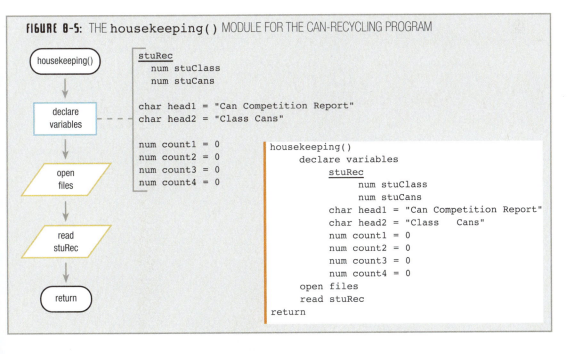

```
stuRec
   num stuClass
   num stuCans

char head1 = "Can Competition Report"
char head2 = "Class Cans"

num count1 = 0
num count2 = 0
num count3 = 0
num count4 = 0
```

```
housekeeping()
      declare variables
            stuRec
                  num stuClass
                  num stuCans
            char head1 = "Can Competition Report"
            char head2 = "Class    Cans"
            num count1 = 0
            num count2 = 0
            num count3 = 0
            num count4 = 0
      open files
      read stuRec
return
```

TIP ◻ ◻ ◻ ◻ In Figure 8-5, the variable list is identical for the flowchart and the pseudocode. It is included twice in this figure and in the next few for clarity because arrays are a new and complicated topic. In later examples in this book, the duplication of the variable list will be eliminated.

Within the `housekeeping()` module, you can declare four variables, `count1`, `count2`, `count3`, and `count4`; the purpose of these variables is to keep running counts of collected-can totals for the four different classes. Each of these four counter variables needs to be initialized to zero. You can tell by looking at the planned output that you need two heading lines, so `head1` is defined as "Can Competition Report" and `head2` as "Class   Cans".

Eventually, four summary lines will be printed on the report, each with a class number and a count of cans for that class. These lines cannot be printed until the `finish()` module, however, because you won't have a complete count of each class's cans until all input records have been read.

The logic within the `mainLoop()` module of the program requires adding a record's `stuCans` value to `count1`, `count2`, `count3`, or `count4`, depending on the `stuClass`. After one student's `stuCans` value has been added to one of the four accumulators, you read the next record, and if it is not `eof`, you repeat the decision-making and accumulating process. When all records have been read, you proceed to the `finish()` module, where you print the four summary lines with the four class counts. See Figures 8-6 and 8-7.

**FIGURE 8-6:** THE `mainLoop()` MODULE FOR THE RECYCLING PROGRAM

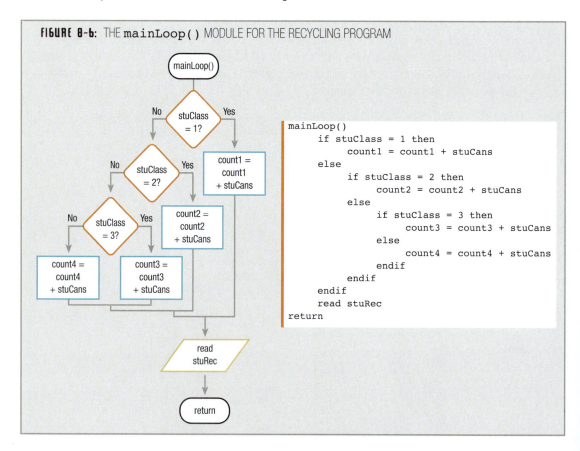

**FIGURE 8-7:** THE `finish()` MODULE FOR THE RECYCLING PROGRAM

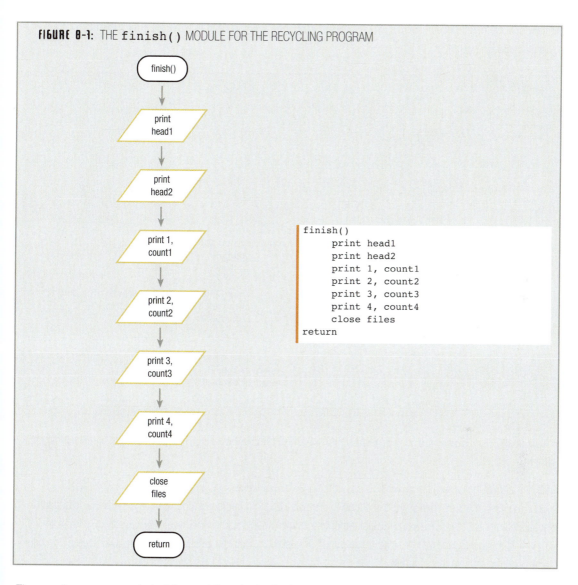

```
finish()
     print head1
     print head2
     print 1, count1
     print 2, count2
     print 3, count3
     print 4, count4
     close files
return
```

The recycling program works just fine, and there is absolutely nothing wrong with it logically. But what if the recycling drive is held at an elementary school with eight classes, in a school district with 12 grade levels, or in a company with 30 departments? With any of these scenarios, the basic logic of the program would remain the same; however, you would need to declare many additional accumulator variables. You also would need many additional decisions within the `mainLoop()` module and many additional print statements within the `finish()` module in order to complete the processing.

Using an array provides an alternative approach to this programming problem, which greatly reduces the number of statements you need. When you declare an array, you provide a group name for a number of associated variables in memory. For example, the four can-collection count accumulators can be redefined as a single array named `count`.

The individual elements become `count[1]`, `count[2]`, `count[3]`, and `count[4]`, as shown in the new `housekeeping()` module in Figure 8-8.

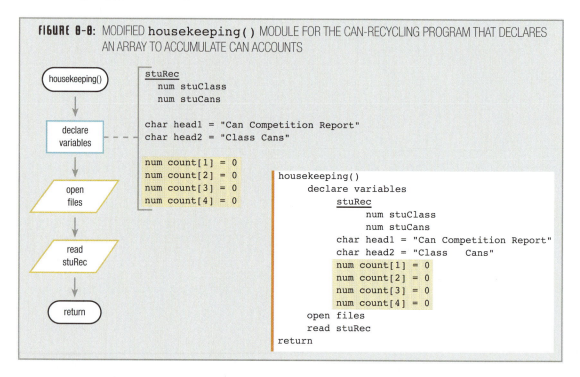

**FIGURE 8-8:** MODIFIED `housekeeping()` MODULE FOR THE CAN-RECYCLING PROGRAM THAT DECLARES AN ARRAY TO ACCUMULATE CAN ACCOUNTS

With the change to `housekeeping()` shown in Figure 8-8, the `mainLoop()` changes to the version shown in Figure 8-9.

Figure 8-9 shows that when the `stuClass` is 1, the `stuCans` value is added to `count[1]`; when the `stuClass` is 4, the `stuCans` value is added to `count[4]`. In other words, the value in `stuCans` is added to one of the elements of the `count` array instead of to a single variable named `count1`, `count2`, `count3`, or `count4`. Is this a big improvement over the original? Of course, it isn't. You still have not taken advantage of the benefits of using the array in this program.

**FIGURE 8-9:** MODIFIED `mainLoop()` MODULE THAT USES COUNT ARRAY

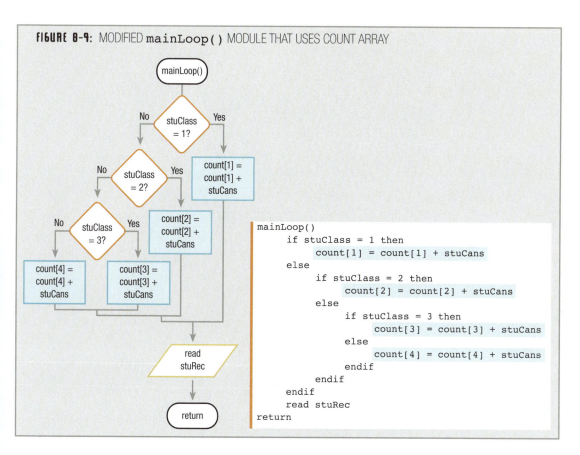

```
mainLoop()
    if stuClass = 1 then
        count[1] = count[1] + stuCans
    else
        if stuClass = 2 then
            count[2] = count[2] + stuCans
        else
            if stuClass = 3 then
                count[3] = count[3] + stuCans
            else
                count[4] = count[4] + stuCans
            endif
        endif
    endif
    read stuRec
return
```

The true benefit of using an array lies in your ability to use a variable as a subscript to the array, instead of using a constant such as 1 or 4. Notice in the `mainLoop()` in Figure 8-9 that within each decision, the value you are comparing to `stuClass` and the constant you are using as a subscript in the resulting "Yes" process are always identical. That is, when the `stuClass` is 1, the subscript used to add `stuCans` to the `count` array is 1; when the `stuClass` is 2, the subscript used for the `count` array is 2, and so on. Therefore, why not just use `stuClass` as a subscript? You can rewrite the `mainLoop()`, as shown in Figure 8-10.

FIGURE 8-10: MODIFIED `mainLoop()` USING VARIABLE `stuClass` AS A SUBSCRIPT TO THE COUNT ARRAY

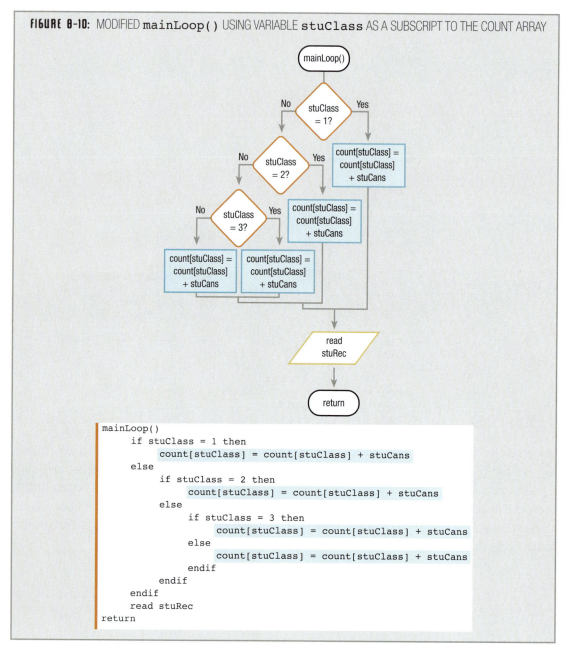

```
mainLoop()
    if stuClass = 1 then
        count[stuClass] = count[stuClass] + stuCans
    else
        if stuClass = 2 then
            count[stuClass] = count[stuClass] + stuCans
        else
            if stuClass = 3 then
                count[stuClass] = count[stuClass] + stuCans
            else
                count[stuClass] = count[stuClass] + stuCans
            endif
        endif
    endif
    read stuRec
return
```

Of course, the code segment in Figure 8-10 looks no more efficient than the one in Figure 8-9. However, notice that in Figure 8-10 the process that occurs after each decision is exactly the same. In each case, no matter what the value of `stuClass`, you always `add stuCans to count[stuClass]`. If you are always going to take the same action no matter what the answer to a question is, why ask the question? Instead, you can write the `mainLoop()` module, as shown in Figure 8-11.

**FIGURE 8-11:** MODIFIED `mainLoop()` MODULE, ELIMINATING NESTED DECISIONS

```
mainLoop()
    count[stuClass] = count[stuClass] + stuCans
    read stuRec
return
```

The two steps in Figure 8-11 represent the *entire* `mainLoop()` module! When `stuClass` is 2, `stuCans` is added to `count[2]`; when `stuClass` is 4, `stuCans` is added to `count[4]`, and so on. *Now*, you have a big improvement to the previous `mainLoop()` from Figure 8-9. What's more, this `mainLoop()` does not change whether there are 8, 30, or any other number of classes and `count` array elements, as long as the classes are numbered sequentially. To use more than four accumulators, you would declare additional `count` elements in the `housekeeping()` module, but the `mainLoop()` logic would remain the same as it is in Figure 8-11.

The `finish()` module originally shown in Figure 8-7 can also be improved. Instead of four separate print statements, you can use a variable to control a printing loop, as shown in Figure 8-12. Because the `finish()` module follows the `eof` condition, all input records have been used, and `stuClass` is not currently holding any needed information. In `finish()`, you can set `stuClass` to 1, then print `stuClass` and `count[stuClass]`. Then add 1 to `stuClass` and use the same set of instructions again. You can use `stuClass` as a loop control variable to print the four individual `count` values. The improvement in this `finish()` module over the one shown in Figure 8-7 is not as dramatic as the improvement in the `mainLoop()`, but in a program with more `count` elements, the only change to the `finish()` module would be in the constant value you use to control the loop. Twelve or 30 `count` values can print as easily as four if they are stored in an array.

**TIP** ▢ ▢ ▢ ▢ In the `finish()` module in Figure 8-12, instead of reusing `stuClass` as a subscript, many programmers prefer to declare a separate numeric work variable to initialize to 1, use it as a subscript to the array while printing, and increment it during each cycle through the loop. Their reasoning is that `stuClass` is part of the input record and should be used only to hold actual data being input—not used as a work variable in the program. Use this approach if it makes more sense to you. You might be required to use this technique if the input data are accessed from databases containing an input field that is no longer available after the input has reached the `eof` condition.

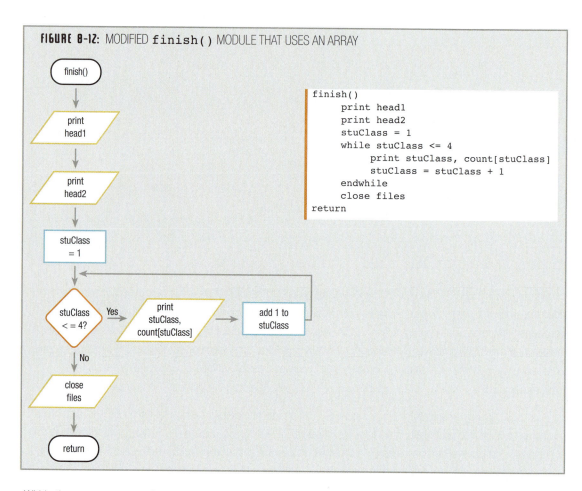

**FIGURE 8-12:** MODIFIED `finish()` MODULE THAT USES AN ARRAY

```
finish()
     print head1
     print head2
     stuClass = 1
     while stuClass <= 4
          print stuClass, count[stuClass]
          stuClass = stuClass + 1
     endwhile
     close files
return
```

Within the `finish()` module in Figure 8-12, the `stuClass` variable is handy to use as a subscript, but any variable could have been used as long as it was:

- Numeric with no decimal places
- Initialized to 1
- Incremented by 1 each time the logic passed through the loop

In other words, nothing is linking `stuClass` to the `count` array per se; within the `finish()` module, you can simply use the `stuClass` variable as a subscript to indicate each successive element within the `count` array.

The can-recycling program *worked* when the `mainLoop()` contained a long series of decisions and the `finish()` module contained a long series of print statements, but the program is easier to write when you employ arrays. Additionally, the program is more efficient, easier for other programmers to understand, and easier to maintain. Arrays are never mandatory, but often they can drastically cut down on your programming time and make a program easier to understand.

## ARRAY DECLARATION AND INITIALIZATION

In the can-recycling program, the four `count` array elements were declared and initialized to 0s in the `housekeeping()` module. The `count` values need to start at 0 so they can be added to, during the course of the program. Originally (see Figure 8-8), you provided initialization in the `housekeeping()` module as:

```
num count[1] = 0
num count[2] = 0
num count[3] = 0
num count[4] = 0
```

Separately declaring and initializing each `count` element is acceptable only if there are a small number of `count`s. If the can-recycling program were updated to keep track of recycling in a company with 30 departments, you would have to initialize 30 separate fields. It would be too tedious to write 30 separate declaration statements.

Programming languages do not require the programmer to name each of the 30 `count`s: `count[1]`, `count[2]`, and so on. Instead, you can make a declaration such as one of those in Figure 8-13.

---

**FIGURE 8-13:** DECLARING A 30-ELEMENT ARRAY NAMED **count** IN SEVERAL COMMON LANGUAGES

| Declaration | Programming Language |
|---|---|
| DIM COUNT(30) | BASIC, Visual Basic |
| int count[30]; | C#, C++ |
| int[] count = new int[30]; | Java |
| COUNT OCCURS 30 TIMES PICTURE 9999. | COBOL |
| array count [1..30] of integer; | Pascal |

---

 C, C++, Pascal, and Java programmers typically use lowercase variable names. COBOL and BASIC programmers often use all uppercase. Visual Basic programmers are likely to begin with an uppercase letter.

 The terms `int` and `integer` in the code samples within Figure 8-13 both indicate that the `count` array will hold whole-number values. The value 9999 in the COBOL example indicates that each `count` will be a four-digit integer. These terms are more specific than the `num` identifier this book uses to declare all numeric variables.

All the declarations in Figure 8-13 have two things in common: They name the `count` array and indicate that there will be 30 separate numeric elements. For flowcharting or pseudocode purposes, a statement such as `num count[30]` indicates the same thing.

Declaring a numeric array does not necessarily set its individual elements to zero (although it does in some programming languages, such as BASIC, Visual Basic, and Java). Most programming languages allow the equivalent of `num count[30] all set to 0`; you should use a statement like this when you want to initialize an array in your flowcharts or pseudocode. Explicitly initializing all variables is a good programming practice; assuming anything about noninitialized variable values is a dangerous practice. Array elements are no exception to this rule.

Alternately, to start all array elements with the same initial value, you can use an initialization loop within the `housekeeping()` module. An **initialization loop** is a loop structure that provides initial values for every element in any array. To create an initialization loop, you must use a numeric field as a subscript. For example, if you declare a field named `sub`, and initialize `sub` to 1, then you can use a loop like the one shown in the `housekeeping()` module in Figure 8-14 to set all the array elements to zero.

**FIGURE 8-14:** A `housekeeping()` MODULE DEMONSTRATING ONE METHOD OF INITIALIZING ARRAY ELEMENTS

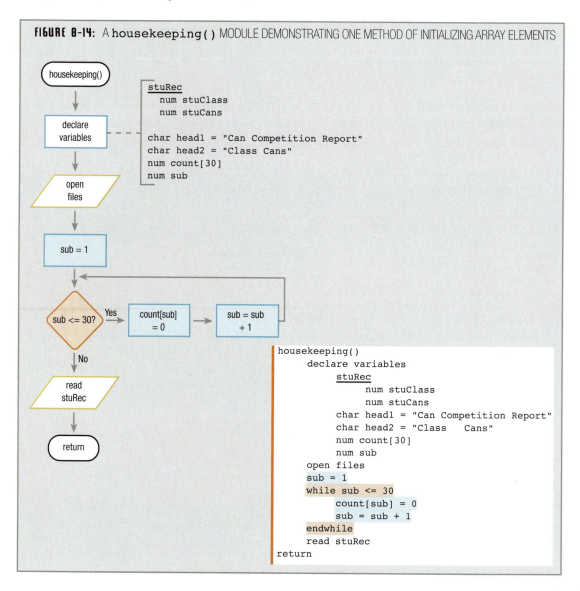

```
housekeeping()
    declare variables
        stuRec
            num stuClass
            num stuCans
        char head1 = "Can Competition Report"
        char head2 = "Class    Cans"
        num count[30]
        num sub
    open files
    sub = 1
    while sub <= 30
        count[sub] = 0
        sub = sub + 1
    endwhile
    read stuRec
return
```

# RUN-TIME AND COMPILE-TIME ARRAYS

The array that you used to accumulate class counts in the can-recycling program is a **run-time array** or **execution-time array**, because the values that you want to use—the final can counts—are created during an actual run, or execution, of the program. In other words, if the freshman class is going to collect 1,000 cans, you don't know that fact at the beginning of the program. Instead, that value is accumulated during the execution of the program and not known until the end.

Some arrays are not run-time, but rather **compile-time arrays**. Recall from Chapter 1 that compiling is the act of translating a high-level language into machine code (1s and 0s). A compile-time array is one whose final desired values are fixed at the beginning of the program.

For example, let's say you own an apartment building with five floors, and you have records for all your tenants with the information shown in Figure 8-15. The combination of each tenant's floor number and apartment letter provides you with a specific apartment—for example, apartment 3B.

---

**FIGURE 8-15:** TENANT FILE DESCRIPTION

```
File name: TENANTS
FIELD DESCRIPTION        POSITIONS        DATA TYPE        DECIMALS
Tenant name              1-40             Character
Floor number             41               Numeric          0
Apartment letter         42               Character
```

---

Every month, you print a rent bill for each tenant. Your rent charges are based on the floor of the building, as shown in Figure 8-16.

---

**FIGURE 8-16:** RENTS BY FLOOR

| Floor | Rent in $ |
|-------|-----------|
| 1 | 350 |
| 2 | 400 |
| 3 | 475 |
| 4 | 600 |
| 5 | 1000 (the penthouse!) |

---

To create a computer program that prints each tenant's name and rent due, you could use five decisions concerning the floor number. However, it is more efficient to use a compile-time array to hold the five rent figures. The array is a compile-time array because you set its values once at the beginning of the program, and they never change.

 TIP

Remember that another name for an array is a *table*. If you can use paper and pencil to list items like tenants' rent values in a table format, then using an array is an appropriate programming option.

The mainline logic for this program is shown in Figure 8-17. The housekeeping module is named `prep()`. When you declare variables within the `prep()` module, you create an array for the five rent figures and set `num rent[1] = 350`, `num rent[2] = 400`, and so on. The rent amounts are **hard coded** into the array; that is, they are explicitly assigned to the array elements. The `prep()` module is shown in Figure 8-18.

**FIGURE 8-17:** FLOWCHART AND PSEUDOCODE FOR MAINLINE LOGIC OF RENT PROGRAM

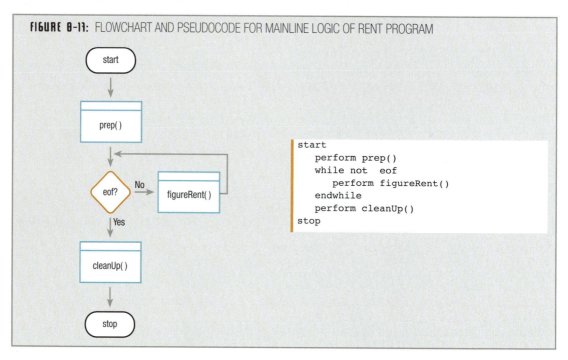

```
start
    perform prep()
    while not  eof
        perform figureRent()
    endwhile
    perform cleanUp()
stop
```

**FIGURE 8-18:** FLOWCHART AND PSEUDOCODE FOR `prep()` MODULE OF RENT PROGRAM

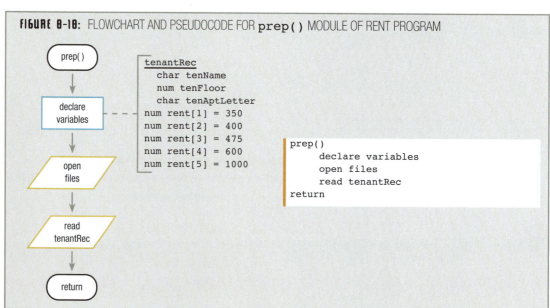

```
tenantRec
    char tenName
    num tenFloor
    char tenAptLetter
num rent[1] = 350
num rent[2] = 400
num rent[3] = 475
num rent[4] = 600
num rent[5] = 1000
```

```
prep()
    declare variables
    open files
    read tenantRec
return
```

TIP ▫ ▫ ▫ ▫ As an alternative to defining `rent[1]`, `rent[2]`, and so on as in Figure 8-18, most programming languages allow a more concise version that takes the general form num `rent[5] = 350, 400, 475, 600, 1000`. When you use this form of array initialization, the first value you list is assigned to the first array element, and the subsequent values are assigned in order. Most programming languages allow you to assign fewer values than there are array elements declared, but none allow you to assign more values.

At the end of the **prep()** module, you read a first record into memory. When the logic enters **figureRent()** (the main loop), you can print three items: "Dear", **tenName**, and ", Here is your monthly rent bill" (the quote begins with a comma that follows the recipient's name). Then, you must print the rent amount. Instead of making a series of selections such as `if tenFloor = 1 then print rent[1]` and `if tenFloor = 2 then print rent[2]`, you want to take advantage of the **rent** array. The solution is to create a **figureRent()** module that looks like Figure 8-19. You use the **tenFloor** variable as a subscript to access the correct **rent** array element. When deciding which variable to use as a subscript with an array, ask yourself, "Of all the values available in the array, what does the correct selection depend on?" When printing a **rent** value, the rent you use depends on the floor on which the tenant lives, so the correct action is `print rent[tenFloor]`.

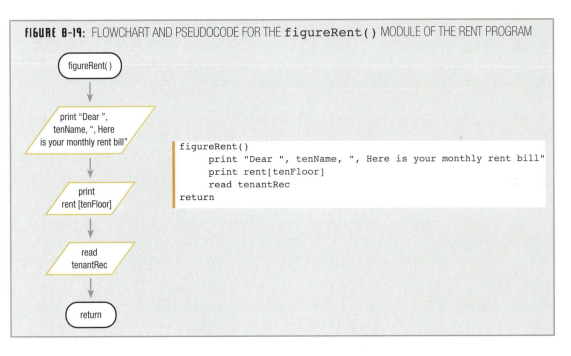

**FIGURE 8-19:** FLOWCHART AND PSEUDOCODE FOR THE `figureRent()` MODULE OF THE RENT PROGRAM

```
figureRent()
    print "Dear ", tenName, ", Here is your monthly rent bill"
    print rent[tenFloor]
    read tenantRec
return
```

TIP ▫ ▫ ▫ ▫ Every programming language provides ways to space your output for easy reading. For example, a common technique to separate "Dear" from the tenant's name is to include a space after the *r* in *Dear*, as in `print "Dear ", tenName`.

The `cleanUp()` module for this program is very simple—just close the files. See Figure 8-20.

FIGURE 8-20: THE `cleanUp()` MODULE FOR THE RENT PROGRAM

```
cleanUp()
    close files
return
```

Without a `rent` array, the `figureRent()` module would have to contain four decisions and five different resulting actions. With the `rent` array there are no decisions. Each tenant's rent is simply based on the `rent` element that corresponds to the `tenFloor` because the floor number indicates the positional value of the corresponding rent. Arrays can really lighten the work load required to write a program.

## LOADING AN ARRAY FROM A FILE

Writing the rent program from the previous section requires you to set values for five `rent` array elements within the `prep()` module. If you write the rent program for a skyscraper, you may have to initialize 100 array elements. Additionally, when the building management changes the rent amounts, you must alter the array element values within the program to reflect the new rent charges. If the rent values change frequently, it is inconvenient to have hard-coded values in your program. Instead, you can write your program so that it loads the array rent amounts from a file. The array of rent values is an example of a run-time array—an array that gets its values during the execution of the program.

A file that contains all the rent amounts can be updated by apartment building management as frequently as needed. Suppose you periodically receive a file named RENTFILE that is created by the building management and always contains the current rent values. You can write the rent program so that it accepts all records from this input file within the `prep()` module. Figure 8-21 shows how this is accomplished.

In the `prep()` module in Figure 8-21, you set the variable `count` to 1 and read a `rentRec` record from the `RENTFILE`. Each record in the `RENTFILE` contains just one field—a numeric `rentAmt` value. For this program, assume that the rent records in the `RENTFILE` are stored in order by floor. When you read in the first `rentAmt`, you store it in the first element of the `rent` array. You increase the `count` to 2, read the second record, and, assuming it's not `eof`, you store the second rent in the second element of the `rent` array. After the `RENTFILE` is exhausted, you begin to read the file containing the `tenantRec` records, and then the program proceeds as usual.

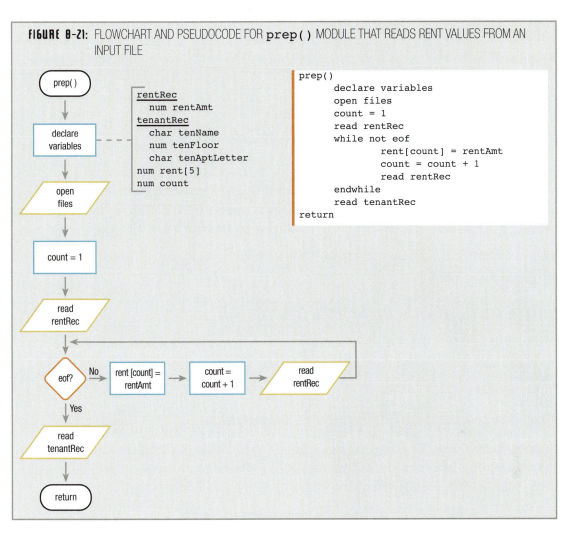

**FIGURE 8-21:** FLOWCHART AND PSEUDOCODE FOR `prep()` MODULE THAT READS RENT VALUES FROM AN INPUT FILE

```
prep()
        declare variables
        open files
        count = 1
        read rentRec
        while not eof
                rent[count] = rentAmt
                count = count + 1
                read rentRec
        endwhile
        read tenantRec
return
```

> **TIP** ☐ ☐ ☐ ☐    You could choose to close the RENTFILE at the end of the `prep()` module. Unlike the tenant file and the printer, it will not be used again in the program. Alternately, you can wait, and close all the files at the end of the program.

When you use this method—reading the rents from an input file instead of hard coding them into the program—clerical employees can update the `rentRec` values in the **RENTFILE**. Your program takes care of loading the rents into the program array from the most recent copy of the **RENTFILE**, ensuring that each rent is always accurate and up-to-date. Using this technique, you avoid the necessity of changing code within the program with each rent update.

> **TIP** ☐ ☐ ☐ ☐    Another way to organize the RENTFILE is to include two fields within each record—for example, `rentFloor` and `rentAmt`. Then, the records would not have to be read into your program in floor-number order. Instead, you could use the `rentFloor` variable as a subscript to indicate which position in the array to use to store the `rentAmt`.

TIP ▫ ▫ ▫ ▫ You might question how the program knows which file's `eof` condition is tested when a program uses two or more input files. In some programming languages, the `eof` condition is tested on the file most recently read. In many programming languages, you have to provide more specific information along with the `eof` question, perhaps `rentRec eof?` or `tenantRec eof?`.

## SEARCHING FOR AN EXACT MATCH IN AN ARRAY

In both the can-recycling program and the rent program that you've seen in this chapter, the fields that the arrays depend on conveniently hold small whole numbers. The classes in the high school are 1 through 4, and the floors of the building are 1 through 5. Unfortunately, real life doesn't always happen in small integers. Sometimes, you don't have a variable that conveniently holds an array position; sometimes, you have to search through an array to find a value you need.

Consider a mail-order business in which orders come in with a customer name, address, item number ordered, and quantity ordered, as shown in Figure 8-22.

**FIGURE 8-22:** MAIL-ORDER CUSTOMER FILE DESCRIPTION

```
File name: CUSTREC
FIELD DESCRIPTION        POSITIONS       DATA TYPE       DECIMALS
Customer name            1-20            Character
Address                  21-40           Character
Item number              41-43           Numeric         0
Quantity                 44-45           Numeric         0
```

The item numbers are three-digit numbers, but perhaps they are not consecutive 001 through 999. Instead, over the years, items have been deleted and new items have been added. For example, there might no longer be an item with number 005 or 129. Sometimes, there might be a hundred-number gap or more between items.

For example, let's say that this season you are down to the items shown in Figure 8-23.

When a customer orders an item, you want to determine whether the customer has ordered a valid item number. You could use a series of six decisions to determine whether the ordered item is valid; in turn, you would compare whether each customer's item number is equal to one of the six allowed values. However, a superior approach is to create an array that holds the list of valid item numbers. Then, you can search through the array for an exact match to the ordered item. If you search through the entire array without finding a match for the item the customer ordered, you can print an error message, for example: "No such item."

Suppose you create an array with the six elements shown in Figure 8-24. If a customer orders item 307, a clerical worker can tell whether it is valid by looking down the list and verifying that 307 is a member of the list. In a similar fashion, you can use a loop to test each `validItem` against the ordered item number.

| FIGURE 8-23: AVAILABLE ITEMS IN MAIL-ORDER COMPANY |
| --- |

```
ITEM NUMBER
106
108
307
405
457
688
```

| FIGURE 8-24: ARRAY OF VALID ITEM NUMBERS |
| --- |

```
num validItem[1] = 106
num validItem[2] = 108
num validItem[3] = 307
num validItem[4] = 405
num validItem[5] = 457
num validItem[6] = 688
```

The technique for verifying that an item number exists involves setting a subscript to 1 and setting a flag variable to indicate that you have not yet determined whether the customer's order is valid. A **flag** is a variable that you set to indicate whether some event has occurred; frequently, it holds a True or False value. For example, you can set a character variable named `foundIt` to "N", indicating "No". Then you compare the customer's ordered item number to the first item in the array. If the customer-ordered item matches the first item in the array, you can set the flag variable to "Y", or any other value that is not "N". If the items do not match, you increase the subscript and continue to look down the list of numbers stored in the array. If you check all six valid item numbers and the customer item matches none of them, then the flag variable `foundIt` still holds the value "N". If the flag variable is "N" after you have looked through the entire list, you can issue an error message indicating that no match was ever found. Assuming you declare the customer item as `custItemNo` and the subscript as `x`, then Figure 8-25 shows a flowchart segment and the pseudocode that accomplishes the item verification.

**FIGURE 8-25:** FLOWCHART AND PSEUDOCODE SEGMENTS FOR FINDING AN EXACT MATCH TO A CUSTOMER ITEM NUMBER

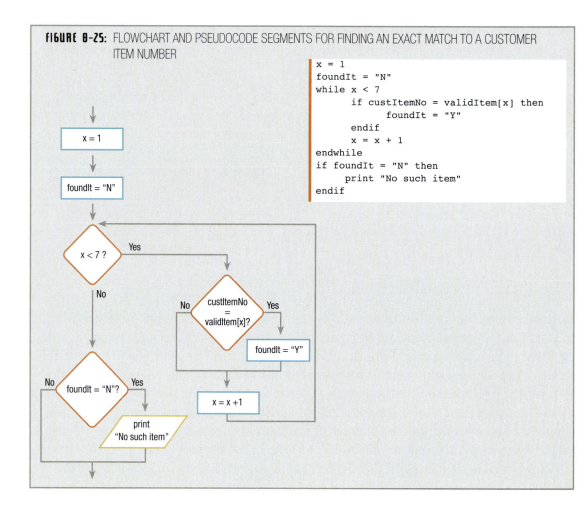

```
x = 1
foundIt = "N"
while x < 7
        if custItemNo = validItem[x] then
                foundIt = "Y"
        endif
        x = x + 1
endwhile
if foundIt = "N" then
        print "No such item"
endif
```

## USING PARALLEL ARRAYS

In a mail-order company, when you read in a customer's order, you usually want to accomplish more than simply verifying that the item exists. You want to determine the price of the ordered item, multiply that price by the quantity ordered, and print a bill. Suppose you have prices for six available items, as shown in Figure 8-26.

**FIGURE 8-26:** AVAILABLE ITEMS WITH PRICES FOR MAIL-ORDER COMPANY

| ITEM NUMBER | ITEM PRICE |
|---|---|
| 106 | 0.59 |
| 108 | 0.99 |
| 307 | 4.50 |
| 405 | 15.99 |
| 457 | 17.50 |
| 688 | 39.00 |

You *could* write a program in which you read in a customer order record and then use the customer's item number as a subscript to pull a price from an array. To use this method, you need an array with at least 688 elements. If a customer orders item 405, the price is found at `validItem[custItemNo]`, which is `validItem[405]`, or the 405th element of the array. Such an array would need 688 elements (because the highest item number is 688), but because you sell only six items, you would waste 682 of the memory positions. Instead of reserving a large quantity of memory that remains unused, you can set up this program to use two arrays.

Consider the mainline logic in Figure 8-27 and the `ready()` routine in Figure 8-28. Two arrays are set up within the `ready()` module. One contains six elements named `validItem`; all six elements are valid item numbers. The other array also has six elements. These are named `validItemPrice`; all six elements are prices. Each price in this `validItemPrice` array is conveniently and purposely in the same position as the corresponding item number in the other `validItem` array. Two corresponding arrays such as these are **parallel arrays** because each element in one array is associated with the element in the same relative position in the other array.

FIGURE 8-27: MAINLINE LOGIC FOR THE PRICE PROGRAM

```
start
        perform ready()
        while not eof
                perform getPrice()
        endwhile
        perform finish()
stop
```

**FIGURE 8-28:** THE `ready()` MODULE FOR THE PRICE PROGRAM

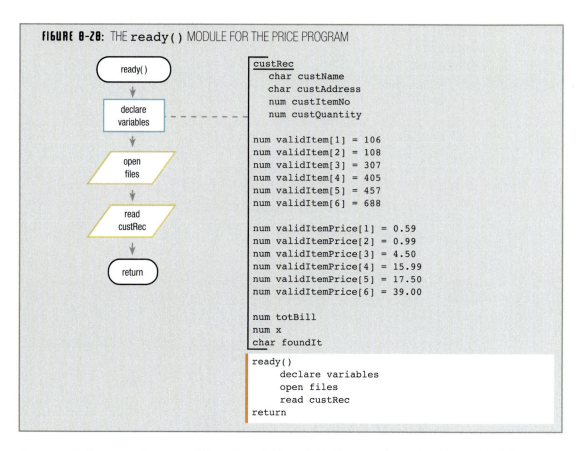

You can write the `getPrice()` module as shown in Figure 8-29. The general procedure is to read each item number, look through each of the `validItem` values separately, and when a match for the `custItemNo` on the input record is found, pull the corresponding parallel price out of the list of `validItemPrice` values.

**TIP** ☐ ☐ ☐ ☐   In this book, you have repeatedly seen the flowchart decision that asks the `eof` question phrased as a positive question so the program continues while the answer is No, and the pseudocode decision that asks the `eof` question in a negative form (`while not eof`) so that the program continues while the condition is true. Figure 8-29 follows the same convention—the flowchart compares the customer item number to a valid item using a positive question so the loop continues while the answer is No, whereas the pseudocode asks if the customer number is *not* equal to a valid item number, continuing while the answer is Yes. The logic is the same either way.

You must create a variable to use as a subscript for the arrays. If you name the subscript `x` (see the declaration of `x` in the variable list in Figure 8-28), then you can start by setting `x` equal to 1. Then, if `custItemNo` is the same as `validItem[x]`, you can use the corresponding price from the other table, `validItemPrice[x]`, to calculate the customer's bill.

TIP □ □ □ □     Some programmers object to using a cryptic variable name such as **x** because it is not descriptive. These programmers would prefer a name like `priceIndex`. Others approve of short names like x when the variable is used only in a limited area of a program, as it is used here, to step through an array. There are many style issues like this on which programmers disagree. As a programmer, it is your responsibility to find out what conventions are used among your peers in your organization.

**FIGURE 8-29:** THE `getPrice()` MODULE FOR THE PRICE PROGRAM

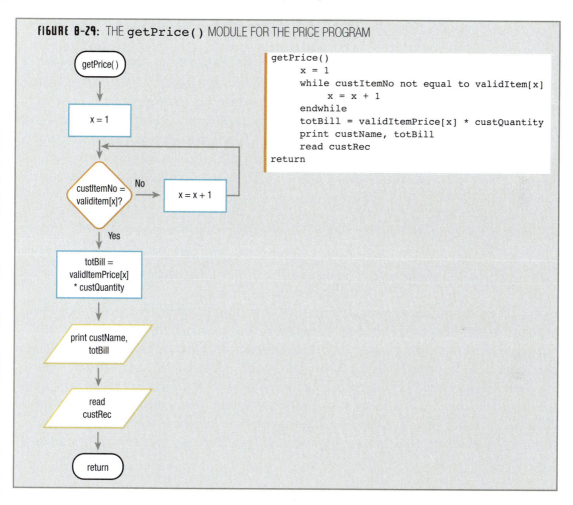

```
getPrice()
    x = 1
    while custItemNo not equal to validItem[x]
        x = x + 1
    endwhile
    totBill = validItemPrice[x] * custQuantity
    print custName, totBill
    read custRec
return
```

Within the `getPrice()` module, the variable used as a subscript, **x**, is set to 1. If `custItemNo` is *not* the same as `validItem[x]`, then add 1 to **x**. Because **x** now holds the value 2, you next compare the customer's requested item number to `validItem[2]`. The value of **x** keeps increasing, and eventually a match between `custItemNo` and some `validItem[x]` should be found.

After you find a match for the `custItemNo` in the `validItem` array, you know that the price of that item is in the same position in the other array, `validItemPrice`. When `validItem[x]` is the correct item, `validItemPrice[x]` must be the correct price.

Suppose that a customer orders item 457, and walk through the flowchart yourself to see if you come up with the correct price.

## REMAINING WITHIN ARRAY BOUNDS

The getPrice() module in Figure 8-29 is not perfect. The logic makes one dangerous assumption: that every customer will order a valid item number. If a customer is looking at an old catalog and orders item 107, the program will never find a match. The value of x will just continue to increase until it reaches a value higher than the number of elements in the array. At that point, one of two things happens. When you use a subscript value that is higher than the number of elements in an array, some programming languages stop execution of the program and issue an error message. Other programming languages do not issue an error message but continue to search through computer memory beyond the end of the array. Either way, the program doesn't end elegantly. When you use a subscript that is not within the range of acceptable subscripts, your subscript is said to be **out of bounds**. Ordering a wrong item number is a frequent error; a good program should be able to handle the mistake and not allow the subscript to go out of bounds.

You can improve the price-finding program by adding a flag variable and a test to the getPrice() module. You can set the flag when you find a valid item in the validItem array, and after searching the array, check whether the flag has been altered. See Figure 8-30.

In the ready() module, you can declare a variable named foundIt that acts as a flag. When you enter the getPrice() module, you can set foundIt equal to "No". Then, after setting x to 1, check to see if x is still less than or equal to 6. If it is, compare the custItemNo to validItem[x]. If they are equal, you know the position of the item's price, and you can use the price to print the customer's bill and set the foundIt flag to "Yes". If the custItemNo is not equal to validItem[x], you increase x by 1 and continue to search through the array. When x is 7, you shouldn't look through the array anymore; you've gone through all six legitimate items, and you've reached the end. If foundIt doesn't have a "Yes" in it at this point, it means you never found a match for the ordered item number; you never took the Yes path leading from the custItemNo = validItem[x]? question. If foundIt does not have "Yes" stored in it, you should print an error message; the customer has ordered a nonexistent item.

**FIGURE 8-30:** THE `getPrice()` MODULE USING THE `foundIt` FLAG

```
getPrice()
     foundIt = "No"
     x = 1
     while x <= 6
          if custItemNo = validItem[x] then
               totBill = validItemPrice[x] * custQuantity
               print custName, totBill
               foundIt = "Yes"
               x = x + 1
          else
               x = x + 1
          endif
     endwhile
     if foundIt not equal to "Yes" then
          print "Error"
     endif
     read custRec
return
```

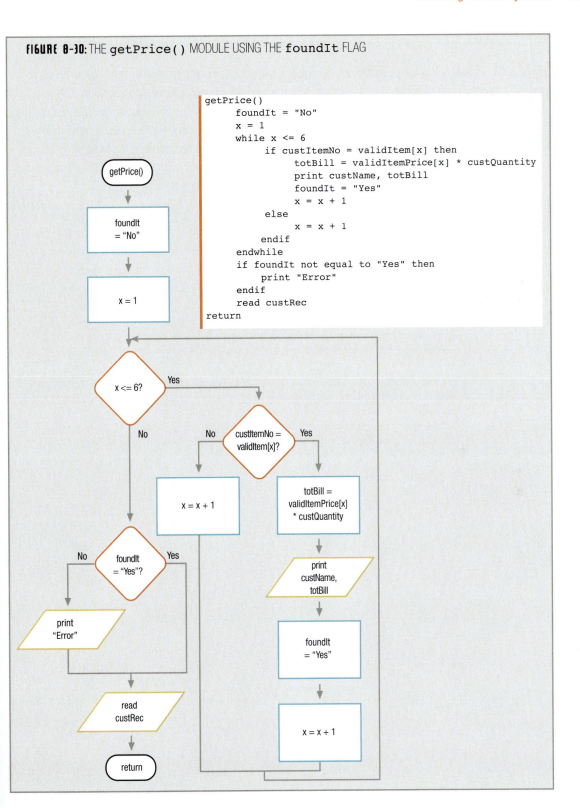

## IMPROVING SEARCH EFFICIENCY USING AN EARLY EXIT

The mail-order program is still a little inefficient. The problem is that if lots of customers order item 106 or 108, their price is found on the first or second pass through the loop. The program continues searching through the item array, however, until `x` exceeds the value 6. One way to stop the search once the item has been found, and `foundIt` is set to "Yes", is to force `x` to 7 immediately. Then, when the program loops back to check whether `x` is greater than 6 yet, the loop will be exited and the program won't bother checking any of the higher item numbers. Leaving a loop as soon as a match is found is called an **early exit**; it improves the program's efficiency. The larger the array, the more beneficial it becomes to exit the searching loop as soon as you find what you're looking for.

Figure 8-31 shows the final version of the price program. Notice the improvement to the `getPrice()` module. You search the `validItem` array, element by element. If an item number is not matched in a given location, the subscript is increased and the next location is checked. As soon as an item number is located in the array, you print a line, turn on the flag, and force the subscript to a high number (seven) so the program will not check the item number array any further.

TIP □ □ □ □   Notice that the price program is most efficient when the most frequently ordered items are stored at the beginning of the array. When you use this technique, only the seldom-ordered items require many cycles through the searching loop before finding a match.

TIP □ □ □ □   You can make programs that contain arrays more flexible by declaring a variable to hold the size of the array. Then, whenever you need to refer to the size of the array within the program—for example, when you loop through the array during a search operation—you can use the variable name instead of a hard-coded value like 6. If the program must be altered later to accommodate more or fewer array elements, you need to make only one change—you change the value of the array-size variable where it is declared.

**FIGURE 8-31:** THE FINAL VERSION OF THE PRICE PROGRAM THAT EFFICIENTLY SEARCHES FOR PRICES BASED ON THE ITEM A CUSTOMER ORDERS

```
start
    perform ready()
    while not eof
        perform getPrice()
    endwhile
    perform finish()
stop

ready()
    declare variables
    open files
    read custRec
return

getPrice()
    foundIt = "No"
    x = 1
    while x <= 6
        if custItemNo = validItem[x] then
            totBill = validItemPrice[x] * custQuantity
            print custName, totBill
            foundIt = "Yes"
            x = x + 1
        else
            x = x + 1
        endif
    endwhile
    if foundIt not equal to "Yes" then
        print "Error"
    endif
    read custRec
return

finish()
    close files
return
```

## SEARCHING AN ARRAY FOR A RANGE MATCH

Customer item numbers need to match numbers in a table exactly in order to determine the correct price of an item. Sometimes, however, programmers want to work with ranges of values in arrays. A **range of values** is any set of contiguous values, for example 1 though 5.

Recall the customer file description from earlier in this chapter, shown again in Figure 8-32.

**FIGURE 8-32:** CUSTOMER FILE DESCRIPTION

File name: CUSTREC

| FIELD DESCRIPTION | POSITIONS | DATA TYPE | DECIMALS |
|---|---|---|---|
| Customer name | 1 | Character | |
| Address | 21-40 | Character | |
| Item number | 41-43 | Numeric | 0 |
| Quantity | 44-45 | Numeric | 0 |

Suppose the company decides to offer quantity discounts, as shown in Figure 8-33.

**FIGURE 8-33:** DISCOUNTS ON ORDERS BY QUANTITY

| Number of items ordered | Discount % |
|---|---|
| 1-9 | 0 |
| 10-24 | 10 |
| 25-48 | 15 |
| 49 or more | 25 |

You want to be able to read in a record and determine a discount percentage based on the value in the quantity field. One ill-advised approach might be to set up an array with as many elements as any customer might ever order, and store the appropriate discount for each possible number, as shown in Figure 8-34.

**FIGURE 8-34:** USABLE—BUT INEFFICIENT—DISCOUNT ARRAY

```
num discount[1] = 0
num discount[2] = 0
.
.
.
num discount[9] = 0
num discount[10] = 10
.
.
.
num discount[48] = 15
num discount[49] = 25
num discount[50] = 25
.
.
.
```

This approach has three drawbacks:

- It requires a very large array that uses a lot of memory.

- You must store the same value repeatedly. For example, each of the first nine elements receives the same value, 0, and each of the next 15 elements receives the same value, 10.

- Where do you stop adding array elements? Is a customer order quantity of 75 items enough? What if a customer orders 100 or 1,000 items? No matter how many elements you place in the array, there's always a chance that a customer will order more.

A better approach is to create just four discount array elements, one for each of the possible discount rates, as shown in Figure 8-35.

**FIGURE 8-35:** SUPERIOR DISCOUNT ARRAY

```
num discount[1] = 0
num discount[2] = 10
num discount[3] = 15
num discount[4] = 25
```

With the new four-element `discount` array, you need a parallel array to search through, to find the appropriate level for the discount. At first, beginning programmers might consider creating an array named `discountRange` and testing whether the quantity ordered equals one of the four stored values. For example:

```
num discountRange[1] = 1 through 9
num discountRange[2] = 10 through 24
num discountRange[3] = 25 through 48
num discountRange[4] = 49 and higher
```

However, you cannot create an array like the previous one. Each element in any array is simply a single variable. A variable like `payRate` can hold 6 or 12, but it can't hold every value 6 *through* 12. Similarly, the `discountRange[1]` variable can hold a 1, 2, 9, or any other single value, but it can't hold 1 *through* 9; there is no such numeric value.

One solution is to create an array that holds only the low-end value of each range, as Figure 8-36 shows.

**FIGURE 8-36:** THE `discountRange` ARRAY USING THE LOW END OF EACH DISCOUNT RANGE

```
num discountRange[1] =  1
num discountRange[2] = 10
num discountRange[3] = 25
num discountRange[4] = 49
```

Using such an array, you can compare each `custQuantity` value with each `discountRange` value in turn. You can start with the *last* range limit (`discountRange[4]`). If the `custQuantity` is at least that value, 49, the customer gets the highest discount rate (`discount[4]`). If the `custQuantity` is not at least `discountRange[4]`, then you check to see if it is at least `discountRange[3]`, or 25. If so, the customer receives `discount[3]`, and so on. If you declare a variable named `rate` to hold the correct discount rate, and another variable named `sub` to use as a subscript, then you can use the `determineDiscount()` module shown in Figure 8-37. This `determineDiscount()` module uses a loop to find the appropriate discount rate for an order, then calculates and prints a customer bill.

**FIGURE 8-37:** FLOWCHART AND PSEUDOCODE FOR DISCOUNT DETERMINATION

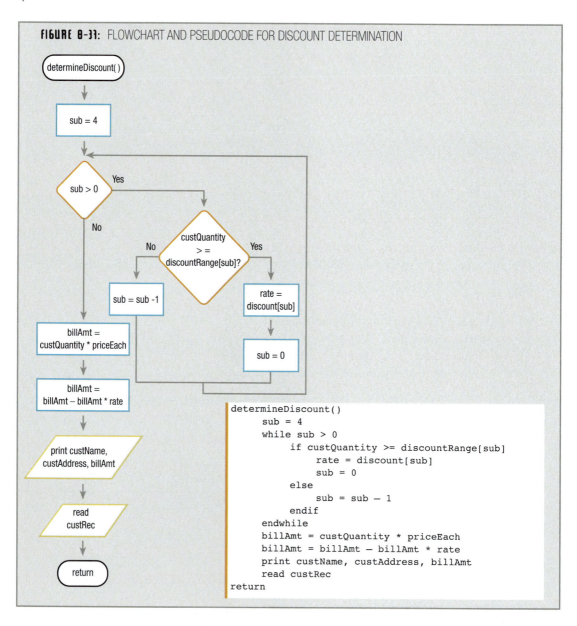

```
determineDiscount()
    sub = 4
    while sub > 0
        if custQuantity >= discountRange[sub]
            rate = discount[sub]
            sub = 0
        else
            sub = sub - 1
        endif
    endwhile
    billAmt = custQuantity * priceEach
    billAmt = billAmt - billAmt * rate
    print custName, custAddress, billAmt
    read custRec
return
```

**TIP** ☐ ☐ ☐ ☐  An alternative approach is to store the high end of every range in an array. Then, you start with the *lowest* element and check for values *less than or equal to* each array element value.

When using an array to store range limits, you use a loop to make a series of comparisons that would otherwise require many separate decisions. Your program is written using fewer instructions than would be required if you did not use an array, and modifications to your program will be easier to make in the future.

## CHAPTER SUMMARY

☐ An array is a series or list of variables in computer memory, all of which have the same name but are differentiated with special numbers called subscripts.

☐ When you declare an array, you declare a programming structure that contains multiple elements, each of which has the same name and the same data type. Each array element has a unique integer subscript indicating how far away the individual element is from the first element.

☐ You often can use a variable as a subscript to an array, replacing multiple nested decisions.

☐ You can declare and initialize all of the elements in an array using a single statement that provides a type, a name, and a quantity of elements for the array. You also can initialize array values within an initialization loop.

☐ An array whose values are determined during the execution of a program is a run-time array, or execution-time array. An array whose final desired values are fixed at the beginning of the program is a compile-time array.

☐ You can load an array from a file. This step is often performed in a program's housekeeping module.

☐ Searching through an array to find a value you need involves initializing a subscript, using a loop to test each array element, and setting a flag when a match is found.

☐ In parallel arrays, each element in one array is associated with the element in the same relative position in the other array.

☐ Your programs should ensure that subscript values do not go out of bounds, that is, take on a value out of the range of legal subscripts.

☐ When you need to compare a value to a range of values in an array, you can store either the low- or high-end value of each range for comparison.

## KEY TERMS

An **array** is a series or list of variables in computer memory, all of which have the same name but are differentiated with special numbers called subscripts.

A **subscript** is a number that indicates the position of a particular item within an array.

Each separate array variable is one **element** of the array.

The **size of an array** is the number of elements it can hold.

An **initialization loop** is a loop structure that provides initial values for every element in any array.

A run-time array, or execution-time array, receives its final values during an actual run, or execution, of a program.

A compile-time array is one whose final desired values are fixed at the beginning of the program.

Hard-coded values are explicitly assigned.

A flag is a variable that you set to indicate whether some event has occurred.

Parallel arrays are two or more arrays in which each element in one array is associated with the element in the same relative position in the other array or arrays.

When you use a subscript that is not within the range of acceptable subscripts, your subscript is said to be out of bounds.

Leaving a loop as soon as a match is found is called an early exit.

A range of values is any set of contiguous values.

## REVIEW QUESTIONS

1. **A subscript is a(n) _____.**

   a. element in an array
   b. alternate name for an array
   c. number that indicates the position of a particular item within an array
   d. number that represents the highest value stored within an array

2. **Each variable in an array must have the same _____ as the others.**

   a. subscript
   b. data type
   c. value
   d. memory location

3. **Each variable in an array is called a(n) _____.**

   a. element
   b. subscript
   c. component
   d. data type

4. **The subscripts of any array are always _____.**

   a. characters
   b. fractions
   c. integers
   d. strings of characters

5.  Suppose you have an array named `number`, and two of its elements are `number[1]` and `number[4]`. You know that _____.

    a.  the two elements hold the same value
    b.  the two elements are at the same memory location
    c.  the array holds exactly four elements
    d.  there are exactly two elements between those two elements

6.  Suppose you want to write a program that reads customer records and prints a summary of the number of customers who owe more than $1,000 each, in each of 12 sales regions. Customer fields include `name`, `zipCode`, `balanceDue`, and `regionNumber`. At some point during record processing, you would add 1 to an array element whose subscript would be represented by _____.

    a.  `name`
    b.  `zipCode`
    c.  `balanceDue`
    d.  `regionNumber`

7.  Arrays are most useful when you use a _____ as a subscript.

    a.  numeric constant
    b.  character
    c.  variable
    d.  file name

8.  Suppose you create a program containing a seven-element array that contains the names of the days of the week. In the `housekeeping()` module, you display the day names using a subscript named `dayNum`. In the same program, you display the same array values again in the `finish()` module. In the `finish()` module, you _____ as a subscript to the array.

    a.  must use `dayNum`
    b.  can use `dayNum`, but can also use another variable
    c.  must not use `dayNum`
    d.  must use a numeric constant

9.  Declaring a numeric array sets its individual elements' values to _____.

    a.  zero in every programming language
    b.  zero in some programming languages
    c.  consecutive digits in every programming language
    d.  consecutive digits in some programming languages

10. A(n) _____ array is one in which the values stored in the array are created during the actual execution of the program.

    a.  run-time
    b.  compile-time
    c.  exact-time
    d.  code-time

11. **A compile-time array is one whose final desired values are set _____.**

   a. at the beginning of the program

   b. during the execution of the program

   c. by the end of the program

   d. to zero

12. **When you create an array of values that you explicitly set upon creation, using numeric constants, the values are said to be _____.**

   a. postcoded

   b. precoded

   c. soft coded

   d. hard coded

13. **Many arrays contain values that change periodically. For example, a bank program that uses an array containing mortgage rates for various terms might change several times a day. The newest values are most likely _____.**

   a. typed into the program by a programmer who then recompiles the program before it is used

   b. calculated by the program, based on historical trends

   c. read into the program from a file that contains the current rates

   d. typed in by a clerk each time the program is executed for a customer

14. **A _____ is a variable that you set to indicate a True or False state.**

   a. subscript

   b. flag

   c. counter

   d. banner

15. **Two arrays in which each element in one array is associated with the element in the same relative position in the other array are _____ arrays.**

   a. cohesive

   b. perpendicular

   c. hidden

   d. parallel

16. **A subscript for a 10-element array is out of bounds when it _____.**

   a. is lower than 1

   b. is higher than 10

   c. both of these

   d. neither of these

17. **If you perform an early exit from a loop while searching through an array for a match, you _____.**

   a. quit searching as soon as you find a match

   b. quit searching before you find a match

   c. set a flag as soon as you find a match, but keep searching for additional matches

   d. repeat a search only if the first search was unsuccessful

18. In programming terminology, the values 0.25 through 0.40 represent a(n) _____ of values.
    a. assortment
    b. range
    c. diversity
    d. collection

19. Each element in a five-element array can hold _____ value(s).
    a. one
    b. five
    c. at least five
    d. an unlimited number of

20. After the annual dog show in which the Barkley Dog Training Academy awards points to each participant, the Academy assigns a status to each dog based on the following criteria:

    | Points Earned | Level of Achievement |
    |---|---|
    | 0–5 | Good |
    | 6–7 | Excellent |
    | 8–9 | Superior |
    | 10 | Unbelievable |

    The Academy needs a program that compares a dog's points earned with the grading scale, in order to award a certificate acknowledging the appropriate level of achievement. Of the following, which set of values would be most useful for the contents of an array used in the program?
    a. 0, 6, 9, 10
    b. 5, 7, 8, 10
    c. 5, 7, 9, 10
    d. any of these

## EXERCISES

1. The city of Cary is holding a special census. The census takers collect one record for each citizen, as follows:

```
CENSUS FILE DESCRIPTION
File name: CENSUS
Not sorted
FIELD DESCRIPTION     POSITIONS     DATA TYPE     DECIMALS
Age                   1-3           Numeric       0
Gender                4             Character
Marital Status        5             Character
Voting District       6-7           Numeric       0
```

The voting district field contains a number from 1 through 22.

Design the logic of a program that would produce a count of the number of citizens residing in each of the 22 voting districts.

a. Create the print chart.
b. Create the hierarchy chart.
c. Draw the flowchart.
d. Write the pseudocode.

2. The Midville Park District maintains records containing information about players on its soccer teams. Each record contains a player's first name, last name, and team number. The teams are:

```
Soccer Teams
Team Number          Team Name
1                    Goal Getters
2                    The Force
3                    Top Guns
4                    Shooting Stars
5                    Midfield Monsters
```

Design the logic for a report that lists all players along with their team numbers and team names.

a. Create the print chart.
b. Create the hierarchy chart.
c. Draw the flowchart.
d. Write the pseudocode.

3. **Create the logic for a program that produces a count of the number of players registered for each team listed in Exercise 2.**

   a. Create the print chart.
   b. Create the hierarchy chart.
   c. Draw the flowchart.
   d. Write the pseudocode.

4. **An elementary school contains 30 classrooms numbered 1 through 30. Each classroom can contain any number of students up to 35. Each student takes an achievement test at the end of the school year and receives a score from 0 through 100. One record is created for each student in the school; each record contains a student ID, classroom number, and score on the achievement test. Design the logic for a program that lists the total points scored for each of the 30 classrooms.**

   a. Create the print chart.
   b. Create the hierarchy chart.
   c. Draw the flowchart.
   d. Write the pseudocode.

5. **Modify Exercise 4 so that each classroom's average of the test scores prints, rather than each classroom's total.**

6. **The school in Exercises 4 and 5 maintains a file containing the teacher's name for each classroom. Each record in this file contains a room number 1 through 30, and the last name of the teacher. Modify Exercise 5 so that the correct teacher's name appears on the list with his or her class's average.**

7. **A fast-food restaurant sells the following products:**

   ```
   Fast-Food Items
   Product              Price
   Cheeseburger         2.49
   Pepsi                1.00
   Chips                 .59
   ```

   **Design the logic for a program that reads in a record containing a customer number and item name, then prints either the correct price or the message "Sorry, we do not carry that" as output.**

   a. Draw the flowchart.
   b. Write the pseudocode.

8. **Each week, the home office for a fast-food restaurant franchise distributes a file containing new prices for the items it carries. The file contains the item name and current price. Design the logic for a program that loads the current values into arrays. Then, the program reads in a customer record containing a customer number and item name, and prints either the correct price or the message "Sorry, we do not carry that" as output.**

   a. Draw the flowchart.
   b. Write the pseudocode.

9. The city of Redgranite is holding a special census. The census takers collect one record for each citizen as follows:

```
CENSUS FILE DESCRIPTION
File name: CENSUS
Not sorted
```

| FIELD DESCRIPTION | POSITIONS | DATA TYPE | DECIMALS |
|---|---|---|---|
| Age | 1-3 | Numeric | 0 |
| Gender | 4 | Character | |
| Marital Status | 5 | Character | |
| Voting District | 6-7 | Numeric | 0 |

Design the logic of a program that produces a count of the number of citizens in each of the following age groups: under 18, 18 through 30, 31 through 45, 46 through 64, and 65 and older.

    a. Create the print chart.
    b. Create the hierarchy chart.
    c. Draw the flowchart.
    d. Write the pseudocode.

10. A company desires a breakdown of payroll by department. Input records are as follows:

```
PAYROLL FILE DESCRIPTION
File name: PAY
```

| FIELD DESCRIPTION | POSITIONS | DATA TYPE | DECIMALS | EXAMPLE |
|---|---|---|---|---|
| Employee Last Name | 1-20 | Character | | Dykeman |
| First Name | 21-30 | Character | | Ellen |
| Department | 31 | Numeric | 0 | 3 |
| Hourly Salary | 32-36 | Numeric | 2 | 12.50 |
| Hours Worked | 37-38 | Numeric | 0 | 40 |

Input records are organized in alphabetical order by employee, *not* in department number order.

The output is a list of the seven departments in the company (numbered 1 through 7) and the total gross payroll (rate times hours) for each department.

    a. Create the print chart.
    b. Create the hierarchy chart.
    c. Draw the flowchart.
    d. Write the pseudocode.

11. Modify Exercise 10 so that the report lists department names as well as numbers. The department names are:

```
Department Names and Numbers
Department Number    Department Name
1                    Personnel
2                    Marketing
3                    Manufacturing
4                    Computer Services
5                    Sales
6                    Accounting
7                    Shipping
```

12. Modify the report created in Exercise 11 so that it prints a line of information for each employee before printing the department summary at the end of the report. Each detail line must contain the employee's name, department number, department name, hourly wage, hours worked, gross pay, and withholding tax.

Withholding taxes are based on the following percentages of gross pay:

```
Withholding Taxes
Weekly Salary        Withholding %
0.00-200.00          10
200.01-350.00        14
350.01-500.00        18
500.01-up            22
```

13. The Perfect Party Catering Company keeps records concerning the events it caters as follows:

```
EVENT FILE DESCRIPTION
File name: CATER
```

| FIELD DESCRIPTION | POSITIONS | DATA TYPE | DECIMALS | EXAMPLES |
|---|---|---|---|---|
| Event Number | 1-5 | Numeric | 0 | 15621 |
| Host Name | 6-25 | Character | | Profeta |
| Month | 26-27 | Numeric | 0 | 10 |
| Day | 28-29 | Numeric | 0 | 15 |
| Year | 30-33 | Numeric | 0 | 2003 |
| Meal Selection | 34 | Numeric | 0 | 4 |
| Number of Guests | 35-40 | Numeric | 0 | 150 |

Additionally, a meal file contains the meal selection codes (such as 4), name of entree (such as "Roast beef"), and current price per guest (such as 19.50). Assume there are eight numbered meal records in the file.

Design the logic for a program that produces a report that lists each event number, host name, date, meal, guests, gross total price for the party, and price for the party after discount. Print the month *name*—for example, "October"—rather than "10". Print the meal selection—for example, "Roast beef"—rather than "4". The gross total price for the party is the price per guest for the meal times the number of guests. The final price includes a discount based on the following table:

```
Discounts for Large Parties
Number of Guests        Discount
1-25                    $0
26-50                   $75
51-100                  $125
101-250                 $200
251 and over            $300
```

a. Create the print chart.
b. Create the hierarchy chart.
c. Draw the flowchart.
d. Write the pseudocode.

14. *Daily Life Magazine* wants an analysis of the demographic characteristics of its readers. The Marketing Department has collected reader survey records in the following format:

```
Magazine Reader FILE DESCRIPTION
File name: MAGREADERS
Not sorted
```

| FIELD DESCRIPTION | POSITIONS | DATA TYPE | DECIMALS | EXAMPLE |
|---|---|---|---|---|
| Age | 1-3 | Numeric | 0 | 38 |
| Gender | 4 | Character | | F |
| Marital Status | 5 | Character | | M |
| Annual Income | 6-11 | Numeric | 0 | 45000 |

a. Create the logic for a program that would produce a count of readers by age groups as follows: under 20, 20–29, 30–39, 40–49, and 50 and older.
b. Create the logic for a program that would produce a count of readers by gender within age group—that is, under 20 females, under 20 males, and so on.
c. Create the logic for a program that would produce a count of readers by income groups as follows: under $20,000, $20,000–$24,999, $25,000–$34,999, $35,000–$49,999, and $50,000 and up.

15. **Glen Ross Vacation Property Sales employs seven salespeople as follows:**

```
Salespeople
ID Number    Name
103          Darwin
104          Kravitz
201          Shulstad
319          Fortune
367          Wickert
388          Miller
435          Vick
```

When a salesperson makes a sale, a record is created including the date, time, and dollar amount of the sale, as follows: The time is expressed in hours and minutes, based on a 24-hour clock. The sale amount is expressed in whole dollars.

```
SALE FILE DESCRIPTION
File name: SALES
```

| FIELD DESCRIPTION | POSITIONS | DATA TYPE | DECIMALS | EXAMPLES |
|---|---|---|---|---|
| Salesperson | 1–3 | Numeric | 0 | 319 |
| Month | 4–5 | Numeric | 0 | 02 |
| Day | 6–7 | Numeric | 0 | 21 |
| Year | 8–11 | Numeric | 0 | 2003 |
| Time | 12–15 | Numeric | 0 | 1315 |
| Sale Amount | 16–22 | Numeric | 0 | 95900 |

Salespeople earn a commission that differs for each sale, based on the following rate schedule:

```
Commission Rates
Sale Amount          Rate
$0-$50,000           .04
$51,000-$125,000     .05
$126,000-$200,000    .06
$201,000 and up      .07
```

Design the print chart, hierarchy chart, and either the flowchart or pseudocode that produces each of the following reports:

a. A report listing each salesperson number, name, total sales, and total commissions
b. A report listing each month of the year as both a number and a word (for example, "01 January"), and the total sales for the month for all salespeople
c. A report listing total sales as well as total commissions earned by all salespeople for each of the following time frames, based on hour of the day: 00–05, 06–12, 13–18, and 19–23

# APPENDIX A

## SOLVING DIFFICULT STRUCTURING PROBLEMS

In Chapter 2, you learned that you can solve any logical problem using only the three standard structures—sequence, selection, and looping. Often it is a simple matter to modify an unstructured program to make it adhere to structured rules. Sometimes, however, it is a challenge to structure a more complicated program. Still, no matter how complicated, large, or poorly structured a problem is, the same tasks can *always* be accomplished in a structured manner.

Consider the flowchart segment in Figure A-1. Is it structured?

**FIGURE A-1:** UNSTRUCTURED FLOWCHART SEGMENT

No, it's not. To straighten out the flowchart segment, making it structured, you can use the "spaghetti" method. Using this method, you untangle each path of the flowchart as if you were attempting to untangle strands of spaghetti in a bowl. The objective is to create a new flowchart segment that performs exactly the same tasks as the first, but using only the three structures—sequence, selection, and loop.

To begin to untangle the unstructured flowchart segment, you start at the beginning with the decision labeled A, shown in Figure A-2. This step must represent the beginning of either a selection or a loop, because a sequence would not contain a decision.

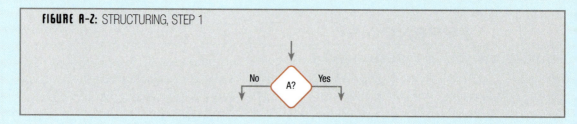

**FIGURE A-2:** STRUCTURING, STEP 1

If you follow the logic on the No, or left, side of the question in the original flowchart, you can pull up on the left branch of the decision. You encounter process E, followed by G, followed by the end, as shown in Figure A-3. Compare the "No" actions after Decision A in the first flowchart (Figure A-1), with the actions after Decision A in Figure A-3; they are identical.

**FIGURE A-3:** STRUCTURING, STEP 2

Now continue on the right, or Yes, side of Decision A in Figure A-1. When you follow the flowline, you encounter a decision symbol, labeled B. Pull on B's left side, and a process, D, comes up next. See Figure A-4.

**FIGURE A-4:** STRUCTURING, STEP 3

After Step D in the original diagram, a decision labeled F comes up. Pull on its left, or No, side and get a process, G, and then the end. When you pull on F's right, or Yes, side in the original flowchart, you simply reach the end, as shown in Figure A-5. Notice in Figure A-5 that the G process now appears in two locations. When you improve unstructured flowcharts so that they become structured, you often must repeat steps. This eliminates crossed lines and difficult-to-follow spaghetti logic.

**FIGURE A-5:** STRUCTURING, STEP 4

The biggest problem in structuring the original flowchart segment from Figure A-1 follows the right, or Yes, side of the B decision. When the answer to B is Yes, you encounter process C, as shown in both Figures A-1 and A-6. The structure that begins with Decision C looks like a loop because it doubles back, up to Decision A. However, the rules of a structured loop say that it must have the appearance shown in Figure A-7: a question, followed by a structure, returning right back to the question. In Figure A-1, if the path coming out of C returned right to B, there would be no problem; it would be a simple, structured loop. However, as it is, Question A must be repeated. The spaghetti technique says if things are tangled up, start repeating them. So repeat an A decision after C, as Figure A-6 shows.

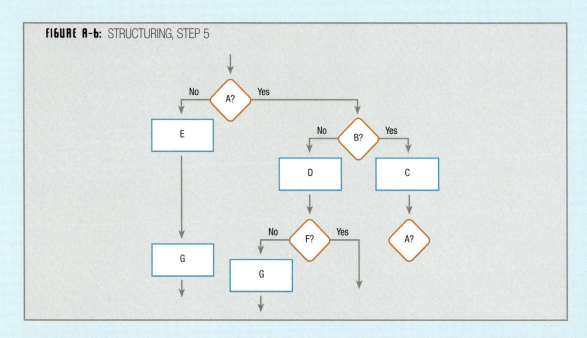

**FIGURE A-6:** STRUCTURING, STEP 5

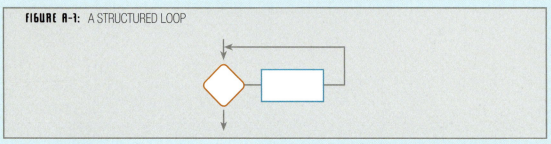

**FIGURE A-7:** A STRUCTURED LOOP

In the original flowchart segment in Figure A-1, when A is Yes, Question B always follows. So, in Figure A-8, after A is Yes, B is Yes, Step C executes, and A is asked again, when A is Yes, B repeats. In the original, when B is Yes, C executes, so in Figure A-8, on the right side of B, C repeats. After C, A occurs. On the right side of A, B occurs. On the right side of B, C occurs. After C, A should occur again, and so on. Soon you should realize that, in order to follow the steps in the same order as in the original flowchart segment, you will repeat these same steps forever. See Figure A-8.

**FIGURE A-8:** STRUCTURING, STEP 6, WHICH NEVER ENDS

If you continue with Figure A-8, you will never be able to end; every C is always followed by another A, B, and C. Sometimes, in order to make a program segment structured, you have to add an extra flag variable to get out of an infinite mess. A flag is a variable that you set to indicate a true or false state. Typically, a variable is called a flag when its only purpose is to tell you whether some event has occurred. You can create a flag variable named `shouldRepeat` and set the value of `shouldRepeat` to "Yes" or "No," depending on whether it is appropriate to repeat Decision A. When A is No, the `shouldRepeat` flag should be set to "No" because, in this situation, you never want to repeat Question A again. See Figure A-9.

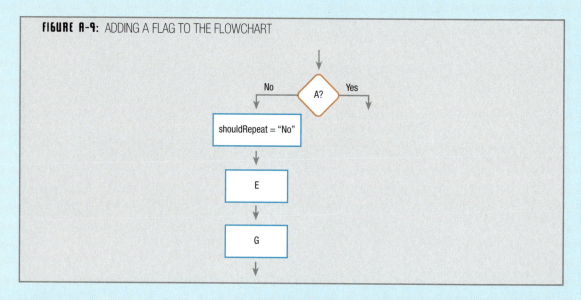

**FIGURE A-9:** ADDING A FLAG TO THE FLOWCHART

Similarly, after A is Yes, but when B is No, you never want to repeat Question A again, either. Figure A-10 shows that you set `shouldRepeat` to "No" when the answer to B is No. Then you continue with D and the F decision that executes G when F is No.

**FIGURE A-10:** ADDING A FLAG TO A SECOND PATH IN THE FLOWCHART

However, in the original flowchart segment in Figure A-1, when the B decision result is Yes, you *do* want to repeat A. So when B is Yes, perform the process for C and set the `shouldRepeat` flag equal to "Yes", as shown in Figure A-11.

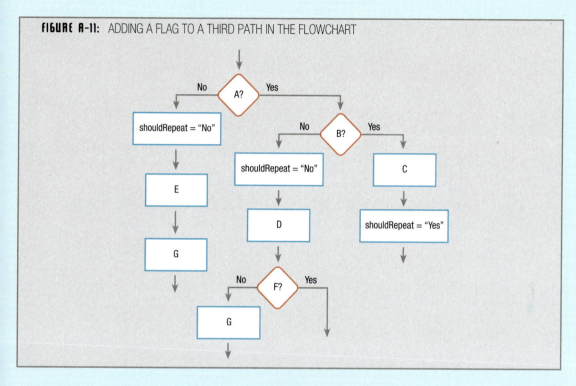

**FIGURE A-11:** ADDING A FLAG TO A THIRD PATH IN THE FLOWCHART

Now all paths of the flowchart can join together at the bottom with one final question: Is `shouldRepeat` equal to "Yes"? If it isn't, exit; but if it is, extend the flowline to go back to repeat Question A. See Figure A-12. Take a moment to verify that the steps that would execute following Figure A-12 are the same steps that would execute following Figure A-1.

- When A is No, E and G always execute.
- When A is Yes and B is No, D and decision F always execute.
- When A is yes and B is Yes, C always executes and A repeats.

**TIP** ☐ ☐ ☐ ☐   Figure A-12 contains three nested selection structures. In Figure A-12, notice how the F decision begins a complete selection structure whose Yes and No paths join together when the structure ends. This F selection structure is within one path of the B decision structure; the B decision begins a complete selection structure, the Yes and No paths of which join together at the bottom. Likewise, the B selection structure resides entirely within one path of the A selection structure.

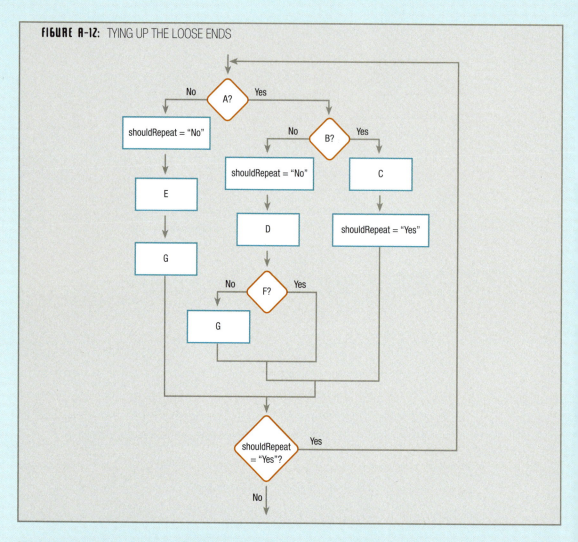

**FIGURE A-12:** TYING UP THE LOOSE ENDS

The flowchart segment in Figure A-12 performs identically to the original spaghetti version in Figure A-1. However, is this new flowchart segment structured? There are so many steps in the diagram, it is hard to tell. You may be able to see the structure more clearly if you create a module named `aThroughG()`. If you create the module shown in Figure A-13, then the original flowchart segment can be drawn as in Figure A-14.

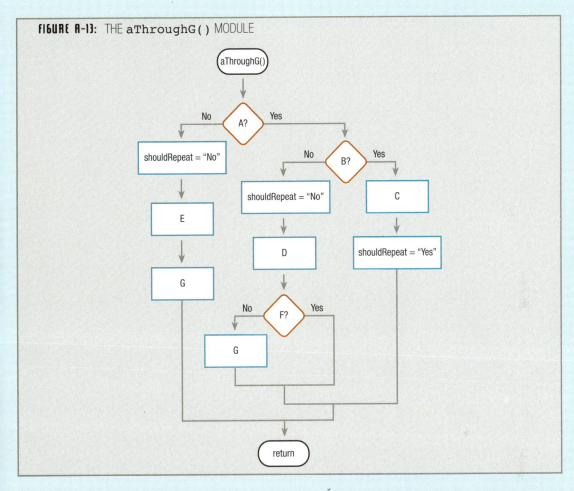

**FIGURE A-13:** THE `aThroughG()` MODULE

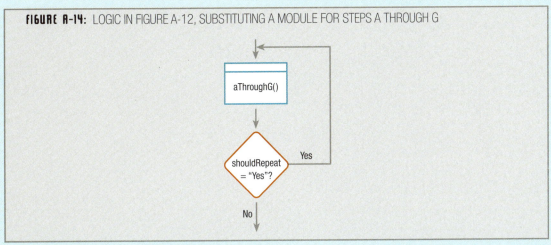

**FIGURE A-14:** LOGIC IN FIGURE A-12, SUBSTITUTING A MODULE FOR STEPS A THROUGH G

Now you can see that the completed flowchart segment in Figure A-14 is a `do until` loop. If you prefer to use a `while` loop, you can redraw Figure A-14 to perform a sequence followed by a `while` loop, as shown in Figure A-15.

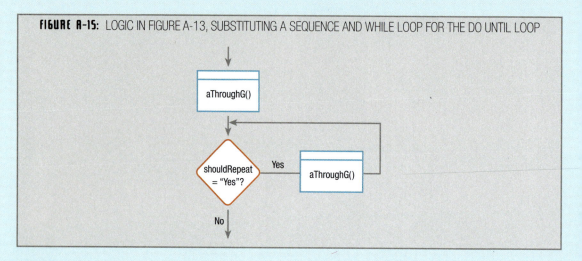

**FIGURE A-15:** LOGIC IN FIGURE A-13, SUBSTITUTING A SEQUENCE AND WHILE LOOP FOR THE DO UNTIL LOOP

It has taken some effort, but any logical problem can be made to conform to structured rules. It may take extra steps, including repeating specific steps and using some flag variables, but every logical problem can be solved using the three structures: sequence, selection, and loop.

# APPENDIX B

## UNDERSTANDING NUMBERING SYSTEMS AND COMPUTER CODES

The numbering system with which you are most familiar is the decimal system—the system based on ten digits, 0 through 9. When you use the decimal system, there are no other symbols available; if you want to express a value larger than 9, you must resort to using multiple digits from the same pool of ten, placing them in columns.

When you use the decimal system, you analyze a multicolumn number by mentally assigning place values to each column. The value of the rightmost column is 1, the value of next column to the left is 10, the next column is 100, and so on, multiplying the column value by 10 as you move to the left. There is no limit to the number of columns you can use; you simply keep adding columns to the left as you need to express higher values. For example, Figure B-1 shows how the value 305 is represented in the decimal system. You simply sum the value of the digit in each column after it has been multiplied by the value of its column.

**FIGURE B-1:** REPRESENTING 305 IN THE DECIMAL SYSTEM

| Column value: | 100 | 10 | 1 |
|---|---|---|---|
| Number: | 3 | 0 | 5 |
| Evaluation: | 3*100 | +0*10 | +5*1 |

The **binary numbering system** works in the same way as the decimal numbering system, except that it uses only two digits, 0 and 1. When you use the binary system, if you want to express a value greater than 1, you must resort to using multiple columns, because no single symbol is available that represents any value other than 0 or 1. However, instead of each new column to the left being 10 times greater than the previous column, when you use the binary system, each new column is only two times the value of the previous column. For example, Figure B-2 shows how the number 9 is represented in the binary system, and Figure B-3 shows how the value 305 is represented. Notice that in both figures that show binary numbers, as well as in the decimal system, it is perfectly acceptable—and often necessary—to write a number containing 0 as some of the digits. As with the decimal system, when you use the binary system, there is no limit to the number of columns you can use—you use as many as it takes to express a value.

**FIGURE B-2:** REPRESENTING 9 IN THE BINARY SYSTEM

| Column value: | 8 | 4 | 2 | 1 |
|---|---|---|---|---|
| Number: | 1 | 0 | 0 | 1 |

```
Conversion to decimal:   1*8 = 8
                        +0*4 = 0
                        +0*2 = 0
                        +1*1 = 1
                        ─────────
             Total:        9
```

**FIGURE B-3:** REPRESENTING 305 IN THE BINARY SYSTEM

| Column value: | 256 | 128 | 64 | 32 | 16 | 8 | 4 | 2 | 1 |
|---|---|---|---|---|---|---|---|---|---|
| Number: | 1 | 0 | 0 | 1 | 1 | 0 | 0 | 0 | 1 |

```
Conversion to decimal:          1* 256 = 256
                             +  0* 128 =   0
                             +  0*  64 =   0
                             +  1*  32 =  32
                             +  1*  16 =  16
                             +  0*   8 =   0
                             +  0*   4 =   0
                             +  0*   2 =   0
                             +  1*   1 =   1
                                        _____
                        Total:             305
```

**TIP** ▫ ▫ ▫ ▫  Mathematicians call decimal numbers **base 10 numbers** and binary numbers **base 2 numbers**.

Every computer stores every piece of data it ever uses as a set of 0s and 1s. Each 0 or 1 is known as a **bit**, which is short for **b**inary dig**it**. Every computer uses 0s and 1s because all values in a computer are stored as electronic signals that are either on or off. This two-state system is most easily represented using just two digits.

Every computer uses a set of binary digits to represent every character it can store. If computers used only one binary digit to represent characters, then only two different characters could be represented, because the single bit could be only 0 or 1. If they used only two digits, then only four characters could be represented—one that used each of the four codes 00, 01, 10, and 11, which in decimal values are 0, 1, 2, and 3, respectively. Many computers use sets of eight binary digits to represent each character they store, because using eight binary digits provides 256 different combinations. One combination can represent an "A", another a "B", and still others "a" and "b", and so on. Two hundred fifty-six combinations are enough so that each capital letter, small letter, digit, and punctuation mark used in English has its own code; even a space has a code. For example, in some computers 01000001 represents the character "A". The binary number 01000001 has a decimal value of 65, but this numeric value is not important to ordinary computer users; it is simply a code that stands for "A". The code that uses 01000001 to mean "A" is the **American Standard Code for Information Interchange**, or **ASCII**.

**TIP** ▫ ▫ ▫ ▫  A set of eight bits is called a **byte**. Half a byte, or four bits, is a **nibble**.

The ASCII code is not the only computer code; it is typical, and is the one used in most personal computers. The **Extended Binary Coded Decimal Interchange Code**, or **EBCDIC**, is an eight-bit code that is used in IBM mainframe computers. In these computers, the principle is the same—every character is stored as a series of binary digits. The only difference is that the actual values used are different. For example, in EBCDIC, an "A" is 11000001, or 193. Another code used by languages such as Java and C# is Unicode; with this code, 16 bits are used to represent each character. The character "A" in Unicode has the same decimal value as the ASCII "A", 65, but it is stored as 0000000001000001. Using 16 bits provides many more possible combinations than using only eight—65,536 to be exact. With Unicode, not only are there enough available codes for all English letters and digits, but also for characters from many international alphabets.

Ordinary computer users seldom think about the numeric codes behind the letters, numbers, and punctuation marks they enter from their keyboards or see displayed on a monitor. However, they see the consequence of the values behind letters when they see data sorted in alphabetical order. When you sort a list of names, "Andrea" comes before "Brian," and "Caroline" comes after "Brian" because the numeric code for "A" is lower than the code for "B", and the numeric code for "C" is higher than the code for "B" no matter whether you are using ASCII, EBCDIC, or Unicode.

Table B-1 shows the decimal and binary values behind the most commonly used characters in the ASCII character set— the letters, numbers, and punctuation marks you can enter from your keyboard using a single key press.

TIP ▫ ▫ ▫ ▫   Most of the values not included in Table B-1 have a purpose. For example, the decimal value 7 represents a bell—a dinging sound your computer can make, often used to notify you of an error or some other unusual condition.

TIP ▫ ▫ ▫ ▫   Each binary number in Table B-1 is shown containing two sets of four digits; this convention makes the long eight-digit numbers easier to read.

**TABLE B-1:** DECIMAL AND BINARY VALUES FOR COMMON ASCII CHARACTERS

| Decimal number | Binary number | ASCII character | |
|---|---|---|---|
| 32 | 0010 0000 | | Space |
| 33 | 0010 0001 | ! | Exclamation point |
| 34 | 0010 0010 | " | Quotation mark, or double quote |
| 35 | 0010 0011 | # | Number sign, also called an octothorpe or a pound sign |
| 36 | 0010 0100 | $ | Dollar sign |
| 37 | 0010 0101 | % | Percent |
| 38 | 0010 0110 | & | Ampersand |
| 39 | 0010 0111 | ' | Apostrophe, single quote |
| 40 | 0010 1000 | ( | Left parenthesis |
| 41 | 0010 1001 | ) | Right parenthesis |
| 42 | 0010 1010 | * | Asterisk |
| 43 | 0010 1011 | + | Plus sign |
| 44 | 0010 1100 | , | Comma |
| 45 | 0010 1101 | - | Hyphen or minus sign |
| 46 | 0010 1110 | . | Period or decimal point |
| 47 | 0010 1111 | / | Slash or front slash |

**TABLE B-1:** DECIMAL AND BINARY VALUES FOR COMMON ASCII CHARACTERS (CONTINUED)

| Decimal number | Binary number | ASCII character | |
|---|---|---|---|
| 48 | 0011 0000 | 0 | |
| 49 | 0011 0001 | 1 | |
| 50 | 0011 0010 | 2 | |
| 51 | 0011 0011 | 3 | |
| 52 | 0011 0100 | 4 | |
| 53 | 0011 0101 | 5 | |
| 54 | 0011 0110 | 6 | |
| 55 | 0011 0111 | 7 | |
| 56 | 0011 1000 | 8 | |
| 57 | 0011 1001 | 9 | |
| 58 | 0011 1010 | : | Colon |
| 59 | 0011 1011 | ; | Semicolon |
| 60 | 0011 1100 | < | Less-than sign |
| 61 | 0011 1101 | = | Equal sign |
| 62 | 0011 1110 | > | Greater-than sign |
| 63 | 0011 1111 | ? | Question mark |
| 64 | 0100 0000 | @ | At sign |
| 65 | 0100 0001 | A | |
| 66 | 0100 0010 | B | |
| 67 | 0100 0011 | C | |
| 68 | 0100 0100 | D | |
| 69 | 0100 0101 | E | |
| 70 | 0100 0110 | F | |
| 71 | 0100 0111 | G | |
| 72 | 0100 1000 | H | |
| 73 | 0100 1001 | I | |
| 74 | 0100 1010 | J | |
| 75 | 0100 1011 | K | |
| 76 | 0100 1100 | L | |
| 77 | 0100 1101 | M | |
| 78 | 0100 1110 | N | |
| 79 | 0100 1111 | O | |

**TABLE B-1:** DECIMAL AND BINARY VALUES FOR COMMON ASCII CHARACTERS (CONTINUED)

| Decimal number | Binary number | ASCII character | |
|---|---|---|---|
| 80 | 0101 0000 | P | |
| 81 | 0101 0001 | Q | |
| 82 | 0101 0010 | R | |
| 83 | 0101 0011 | S | |
| 84 | 0101 0100 | T | |
| 85 | 0101 0101 | U | |
| 86 | 0101 0110 | V | |
| 87 | 0101 0111 | W | |
| 88 | 0101 1000 | X | |
| 89 | 0101 1001 | Y | |
| 90 | 0101 1010 | Z | |
| 91 | 0101 1011 | [ | Opening or left bracket |
| 92 | 0101 1100 | \ | Backslash |
| 93 | 0101 1101 | ] | Closing or right bracket |
| 94 | 0101 1110 | ^ | Caret |
| 95 | 0101 1111 | _ | Underline or underscore |
| 96 | 0110 0000 | ` | Grave accent |
| 97 | 0110 0001 | a | |
| 98 | 0110 0010 | b | |
| 99 | 0110 0011 | c | |
| 100 | 0110 0100 | d | |
| 101 | 0110 0101 | e | |
| 102 | 0110 0110 | f | |
| 103 | 0110 0111 | g | |
| 104 | 0110 1000 | h | |
| 105 | 0110 1001 | i | |
| 106 | 0110 1010 | j | |
| 107 | 0110 1011 | k | |
| 108 | 0110 1100 | l | |
| 109 | 0110 1101 | m | |
| 110 | 0110 1110 | n | |
| 111 | 0110 1111 | o | |

**TABLE B-1:** DECIMAL AND BINARY VALUES FOR COMMON ASCII CHARACTERS (CONTINUED)

| Decimal number | Binary number | ASCII character | |
|---|---|---|---|
| 112 | 0111 0000 | p | |
| 113 | 0111 0001 | q | |
| 114 | 0111 0010 | r | |
| 115 | 0111 0011 | s | |
| 116 | 0111 0100 | t | |
| 117 | 0111 0101 | u | |
| 118 | 0111 0110 | v | |
| 119 | 0111 0111 | w | |
| 120 | 0111 1000 | x | |
| 121 | 0111 1001 | y | |
| 122 | 0111 1010 | z | |
| 123 | 0111 1011 | { | Opening or left brace |
| 124 | 0111 1100 | I | Vertical line or pipe |
| 125 | 0111 1101 | } | Closing or right brace |
| 126 | 0111 1110 | ~ | Tilde |

# APPENDIX C

## USING A LARGE DECISION TABLE

In Chapter 5, you learned to use a simple decision table, but real-life problems often require many decisions. A complicated decision process is represented in the following situation. Suppose your employer sends you a memo outlining a year-end bonus plan with complicated rules. Appendix C walks you through the process of solving this problem by using a large decision table.

```
To: Programming staff
From: The boss
I need a report listing every employee and the
bonus I plan to give him or her. Everybody gets
at least $100. All the employees in Department 2
get $200, unless they have more than 5 dependents.
Anybody with more than 5 dependents gets $1000
unless they're in Department 2. Nobody with an ID
number greater than 800 gets more than $100 even
if they're in Department 2 or have more than 5
dependents.
P.S. I need this by 5 o'clock.
```

Drawing the flowchart or writing the pseudocode for the `mainLoop()` for this task may seem daunting. You can use a decision table to help you manage all the decisions, and you can begin to create one by listing all the possible decisions you need to make to determine an employee's bonus. They are:

- $empDept = 2$?
- $empDepend > 5$?
- $empIdNum > 800$?

Next, determine how many possible Boolean value combinations exist for the conditions. In this case, there are eight possible combinations, shown in Figure C-1. An employee can be in Department 2, have over five dependents, and have an ID number greater than 800. Another employee can be in Department 2, have over five dependents, but have an ID number that is 800 or less. Because each condition has two outcomes and there are three conditions, there are 2 * 2 * 2 , or eight possibilities. Four conditions would produce 16 possible outcome combinations, five would produce 32, and so on.

**FIGURE C-1:** POSSIBLE OUTCOMES OF BONUS CONDITIONS

| Condition | Outcome | | | | | | | |
|---|---|---|---|---|---|---|---|---|
| empDept = 2 | T | T | T | T | F | F | F | F |
| empDepend > 5 | T | T | F | F | T | T | F | F |
| empIdNum > 800 | T | F | T | F | T | F | T | F |

**TIP** □ □ □ □

In Figure C-1, notice how the pattern of Ts and Fs varies in each row. The bottom row contains one T and F, repeating four times, the second row contains two of each, repeating twice, and the top row contains four of each without repeating. If a fourth decision was required, you would place an identical grid of Ts and Fs to the right of this one, then add a new top row containing eight Ts (covering all eight columns you see currently) followed by eight Fs (covering the new copy of the grid to the right).

Next, list the possible outcome values for the bonus amounts. If you declare a numeric variable named **bonus** by placing the statement **num bonus** in your list of variables at the beginning of the program, then the possible outcomes can be expressed as:

- bonus = 100
- bonus = 200
- bonus = 1000

Finally, choose one required outcome for each possible combination of conditions. For example, the first possible outcome is a $100 bonus. As Figure C-2 shows, you place Xs in the **bonus = 100** row each time **empIdNum > 800** is true, no matter what other conditions exist, because the memo from the boss said, "Nobody with an ID number greater than 800 gets more than $100, even if they're in Department 2 or have more than 5 dependents."

**FIGURE C-2:** DECISION TABLE FOR BONUSES, PART 1

| Condition | Outcome | | | | | | | |
|---|---|---|---|---|---|---|---|---|
| empDept = 2 | T | T | T | T | F | F | F | F |
| empDepend > 5 | T | T | F | F | T | T | F | F |
| empIdNum > 800 | T | F | T | F | T | F | T | F |
| bonus = 100 | X | | X | | X | | X | |
| bonus = 200 | | | | | | | | |
| bonus = 1000 | | | | | | | | |

Next, place an X in the **bonus = 1000** row under all remaining columns (that is, those without a selected outcome) in which **empDepend > 5** is true *unless* the **empDept = 2** condition is true, because the memo stated, "Anybody with more than 5 dependents gets $1000 unless they're in Department 2." The first four columns of the decision table do not qualify, because the **empDept** value is 2; only the sixth column in Figure C-3 meets the criteria for the $1000 bonus.

**FIGURE C-3:** DECISION TABLE FOR BONUSES, PART 2

| Condition | Outcome | | | | | | | |
|---|---|---|---|---|---|---|---|---|
| empDept = 2 | T | T | T | T | F | F | F | F |
| empDepend > 5 | T | T | F | F | T | T | F | F |
| empIdNum > 800 | T | F | T | F | T | F | T | F |
| bonus = 100 | X | | X | | X | | X | |
| bonus = 200 | | | | | | | | |
| bonus = 1000 | | | | | | X | | |

Place Xs in the `bonus = 200` row for any remaining columns in which `empDept = 2` is true and `empDepend > 5` is false, because "All the employees in Department 2 get $200, unless they have more than 5 dependents." Column 4 in Figure C-4 satisfies these criteria.

**FIGURE C-4:** DECISION TABLE FOR BONUSES, PART 3

| Condition | Outcome | | | | | | | |
|---|---|---|---|---|---|---|---|---|
| empDept = 2 | T | T | T | T | F | F | F | F |
| empDepend > 5 | T | T | F | F | T | T | F | F |
| empIdNum > 800 | T | F | T | F | T | F | T | F |
| bonus = 100 | X | | X | | X | | X | |
| bonus = 200 | | | | X | | | | |
| bonus = 1000 | | | | | | X | | |

Finally, fill any unmarked columns with an X in the `bonus = 100` row because, according to the memo, "Everybody gets at least $100." The only columns remaining are the second column and the last column on the right. See Figure C-5.

**FIGURE C-5:** DECISION TABLE FOR BONUSES, PART 4

| Condition | Outcome | | | | | | | |
|---|---|---|---|---|---|---|---|---|
| empDept = 2 | T | T | T | T | F | F | F | F |
| empDepend > 5 | T | T | F | F | T | T | F | F |
| empIdNum > 800 | T | F | T | F | T | F | T | F |
| bonus = 100 | X | X | X | | X | | X | X |
| bonus = 200 | | | | X | | | | |
| bonus = 1000 | | | | | | X | | |

The decision table is complete. When you count the Xs, you'll find there are eight possible outcomes. Take a moment and confirm that each bonus is the appropriate value based on the specifications in the original memo from the boss. Now you can start to plan the logic. If you choose to use a flowchart, you start by drawing the path to the first outcome, which occurs when `empDept = 2`, `empDepend > 5`, and `empIdNum > 800` are all true, and which corresponds to the first column in the decision table. See Figure C-6.

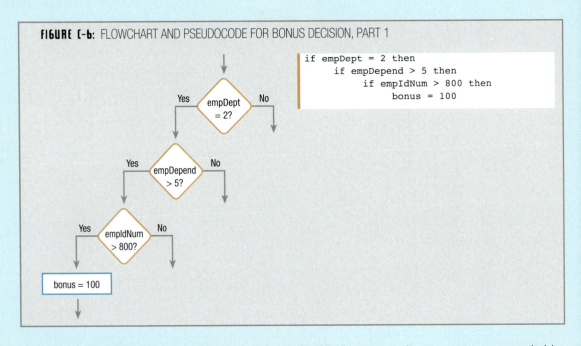

**FIGURE C-6:** FLOWCHART AND PSEUDOCODE FOR BONUS DECISION, PART 1

```
if empDept = 2 then
    if empDepend > 5 then
        if empIdNum > 800 then
            bonus = 100
```

To continue creating the diagram started in Figure C-6, add the "false" outcome to the `empIdNum > 800` decision; this corresponds to the second column in the decision table. When an employee's department is 2, dependents greater than 5, and ID number not greater than 800, the employee's bonus should be $100. See Figure C-7.

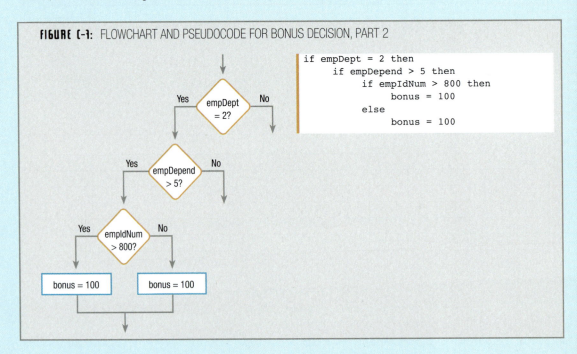

**FIGURE C-7:** FLOWCHART AND PSEUDOCODE FOR BONUS DECISION, PART 2

```
if empDept = 2 then
    if empDepend > 5 then
        if empIdNum > 800 then
            bonus = 100
        else
            bonus = 100
```

Continue the diagram in Figure C-7 by adding the "false" outcome when the `empDepend > 5` decision is No and the `empIdNum > 800` decision is Yes, which is represented by the third column in the decision table. In this case, the bonus is again $100. See Figure C-8.

**FIGURE C-8:** FLOWCHART AND PSEUDOCODE FOR BONUS DECISION, PART 3

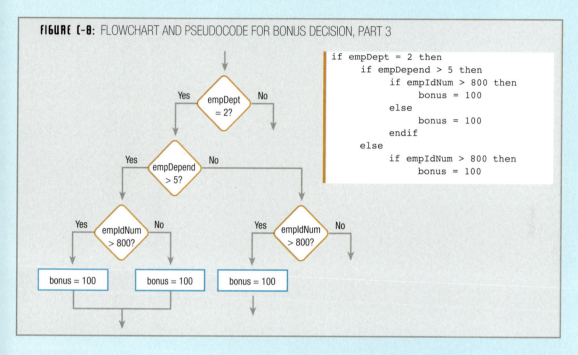

```
if empDept = 2 then
        if empDepend > 5 then
                if empIdNum > 800 then
                        bonus = 100
                else
                        bonus = 100
                endif
        else
                if empIdNum > 800 then
                        bonus = 100
```

Continue adding decisions until you have drawn all eight possible outcomes, as shown in Figure C-9.

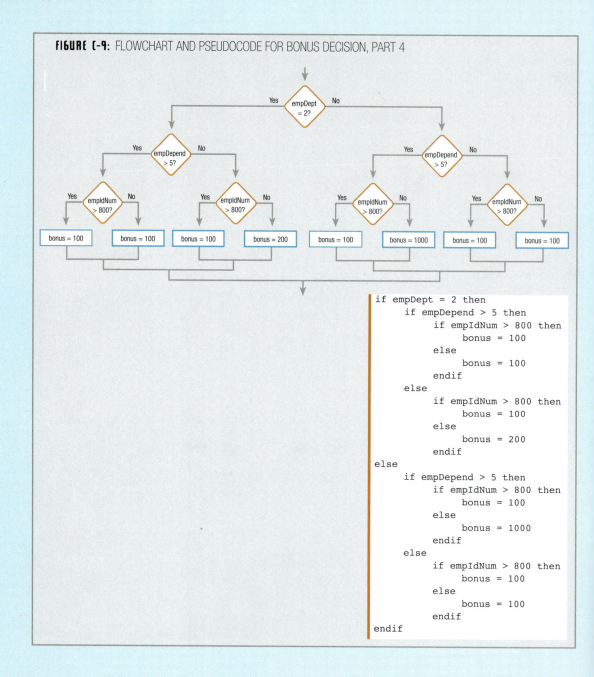

FIGURE C-9: FLOWCHART AND PSEUDOCODE FOR BONUS DECISION, PART 4

```
if empDept = 2 then
      if empDepend > 5 then
            if empIdNum > 800 then
                  bonus = 100
            else
                  bonus = 100
            endif
      else
            if empIdNum > 800 then
                  bonus = 100
            else
                  bonus = 200
            endif
else
      if empDepend > 5 then
            if empIdNum > 800 then
                  bonus = 100
            else
                  bonus = 1000
            endif
      else
            if empIdNum > 800 then
                  bonus = 100
            else
                  bonus = 100
            endif
endif
```

The logic shown in Figure C-9 correctly assigns a bonus to any employee, no matter what combination of characteristics the employee's record holds. However, you can eliminate many of the decisions shown in Figure C-9; you can eliminate any decision that doesn't make a difference. For example, if you look at the far left side of Figure C-9, you see that when `empDept` is 2 and `empDepend` is greater than 5, the outcome of `empIdNum > 800` does not matter; the `bonus` value is 100 either way. You might as well eliminate the selection. Similarly, on the far right, the question `empIdNum` makes no difference. Finally, many programmers prefer the True, or Yes, side of a flowchart decision always to appear on the right side. The result is Figure C-10.

FIGURE C-10: COMPLETE FLOWCHART AND PSEUDOCODE FOR BONUS DECISION

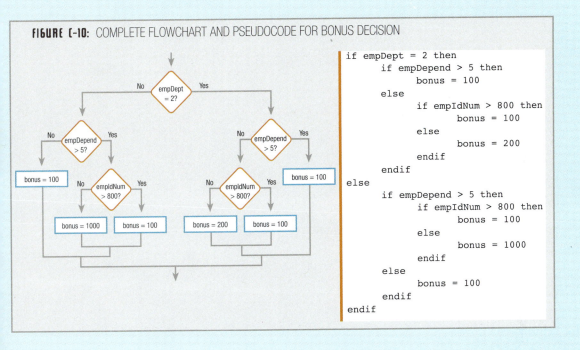

```
if empDept = 2 then
        if empDepend > 5 then
                bonus = 100
        else
                if empIdNum > 800 then
                        bonus = 100
                else
                        bonus = 200
                endif
        endif
else
        if empDepend > 5 then
                if empIdNum > 800 then
                        bonus = 100
                else
                        bonus = 1000
                endif
        else
                bonus = 100
        endif
endif
```

# GLOSSARY

**abstraction**—The process of paying attention to important properties while ignoring nonessential details.

**accumulator**—A variable that you use to gather or accumulate values.

**algorithm**—The sequence of steps necessary to solve any problem.

**AND decision**—A decision in which two conditions must both be true for an action to take place.

**annotation symbol** or **annotation box**—A flowchart symbol that represents an attached box containing notes.

**array**—A series or list of variables in computer memory, all of which have the same name but are differentiated with special numbers called subscripts.

**assignment operator**—The equal sign; it always requires the name of a memory location on its left side.

**assignment statement**—A programming statement that stores the result of any calculation performed on its right side to the named location on its left side.

**assumed data**—Data that does not exist explicitly.

**binary selection** or **binary decision**—A selection or decision structure that has an action associated with each of two possible outcomes. It is also called an if-then-else structure.

**block**—A group of statements that execute as a single unit.

**Boolean expression**—An expression that represents only one of two states, usually expressed as true or false.

**byte**—A unit of computer storage that can contain any of 256 combinations of 0s and 1s that often represent a character.

**calling program**—A program that calls a module.

**camel casing**—The format for naming variables in which multiple-word variable names are run together, and each new word within the variable name begins with an uppercase letter.

**cascading if statement**—A decision "inside of" another decision.

**case structure**—A structure that provides a convenient alternative to using a series of decisions when you must make choices based on the value stored in a single variable.

**central processing unit (CPU)**—The piece of hardware that processes data.

**character**—A letter, number, or special symbol such as "A", "7", and "$". *See also* data hierarchy.

**character constant**—In most programming languages, a character constant holds a single character. In this book, "character constant" is used synonymously with "string constant" to mean one or more characters enclosed within quotation marks. If a working program contains the statement lastName = "Lincoln" then "Lincoln" is a character or string constant.

**character variable**—In most programming languages, a variable that holds a single character value. If a working program contains the statement lastName = "Lincoln" then lastName is a character or string variable. In this book, "character variable" is used synonymously with "string variable" and "text variable".

**client**—A person who requests a program and who will actually use the output of a program. Also called a user.

**coding**—To write statements in a programming language.

**compiler**—Software that translates a high-level language into machine language and tells you if you have used a programming language incorrectly. Similar to an interpreter. However, a compiler translates all the statements in a program prior to executing any statements.

**compile-time array**—An array whose final desired values are fixed at the beginning of the program.

**connector**—A flowchart symbol used when limited page size forces you to continue the flowchart on the following page.

**constant output**—Output that does not change based on any conditions.

**control break**—A temporary detour in the logic of a program.

**control break field**—A variable that holds the value that signals a break in a program.

**control break program**—A program in which a change in the value of a variable initiates special actions or causes special or unusual processing to occur.

**control break report**—A report that lists items in groups. Frequently, each group is followed by a subtotal.

**conversion**—The entire set of actions an organization must take to switch over to using a new program or set of programs.

**counter**—Any numeric variable you use to count the number of times an event has occurred.

**data dictionary**—A list of every variable name used in a program, along with its type, size, and description.

**data hierarchy**—The representation of the relationship of databases, files, records, fields, and characters.

**database**—A logical container that holds a group of files, often called tables, that together serve the information needs of an organization.

**dead path**—A logical path that can never be traveled. Also called an unreachable path.

**decision**—Testing a value.

**decision structure**—A programming structure in which you ask a question, and depending on the answer, you take one of two courses of action. Then, no matter which path you follow, you continue on with the next event. Also called a selection structure.

**decision symbol**—A diamond shape that represents a decision in a flowchart.

**decision table**—A problem-analysis tool that consists of four parts: conditions, possible combinations of Boolean values for the conditions, possible actions based on the conditions, and the specific actions that correspond to each Boolean value of each condition.

**declaration**—A statement that names a variable and tells the computer which type of data to expect.

**declaring a variable**—To provide a name for the memory location where the computer will store the variable value and notifying the computer what type of data to expect. In contrast, when defining a variable, an initial value for the variable is also supplied.

**decrementing**—To decrease a variable by one.

**default value**—A value assigned after all test conditions are found to be false.

**defining a variable**—To provide a variable with a value, as well as a name and a type, when you create it. In contrast, when you are simply declaring a variable, the variable is not initialized.

**definite loop**—A loop for which you definitely know the repetition factor.

**detail line**—On a report, a line that contains data details. Most reports contain many detail lines.

**do until loop**—A structure in which you ensure that a procedure executes at least once; then, depending on the answer to the controlling question, the loop may or may not execute additional times.

**do while**—A loop in which a process continues while some condition continues to be true.

**documentation**—All of the supporting material that goes with a program.

**dual-alternative if**—A structure that defines one action to be taken when the tested condition is true and another action to be taken when it is false. Also called a dual-alternative selection, or an if-then-else structure.

**dual-alternative selection**—A selection structure that has an action associated with each of two possible outcomes. Also called a dual-alternative if or an if-then-else structure.

**dummy value**—A preselected value that stops the execution of a program. *See also* sentinel value.

**early exit**—Leaving a loop before all scheduled repetitions, for example, as soon as a match is found.

**else clause**—Part of a decision that holds the action or actions that execute only when the Boolean expression in the decision is false.

**end user**—A person who uses computer programs. Also called a user.

**end-of-job routine**—The steps you take at the end of the program to finish the application.

**eof**—An end-of-data file marker, short for "end of file."

**executing**—To have a computer use a written and compiled program. *See also* running a program.

**execution-time array**—An array that receives its final values during an actual run, or execution, of a program.

**external program documentation**—The supporting paperwork that programmers develop before they write a program.

**external storage**—Permanent storage outside the main memory of the computer, on a device such as a floppy disk, hard disk, or magnetic tape.

**field**—A single data item such as lastName, streetAddress, or annualSalary. *See also* data hierarchy.

**file**—A group of records that go together for some logical reason. *See also* data hierarchy.

**file description**—A document that describes the data contained in a file.

**flag**—A variable that you set to indicate whether some event has occurred.

**floating-point**—A value that is a fractional numeric variable and contains a decimal point.

**flowchart**—A pictorial representation of the logical steps it takes to solve a problem.

**flowline**—A line or arrow that connects the steps in a flowchart.

**footer**—A message that prints at the end of a page or other section of a report.

**footer line**—The end-of-job message line. Also called footer.

**for loop**—A structure that can be used to code definite loops. It contains a loop control variable that it automatically initializes, evaluates, and increments.

**for statement**—A statement that can be used to code definite for loops.

**function**—A small program unit that you can use together to make a program. Also called modules, subroutines, procedures, or methods.

**functional cohesion**—A quality of a module that determines the degree to which all the module statements contribute to the same task.

**functional decomposition**—The act of reducing a large program into more manageable modules.

**garbage**—The unknown value of an undefined variable.

**global variable**—A variable given a type and name once, and then used in all modules of the program.

**group name**—A name for a collection of associated variables.

**GUI**—Short for graphical user interface; an environment that uses screens to display program output. Users interact with GUI programs with a device like a mouse.

**hard copy**—A printed copy.

**hard-coded value**—A value that is explicitly assigned or used in a program.

**hardware**—The equipment of a computer system.

**heading line**—On a report, a line that contains the title and any column headings; usually appears only once per page.

**hierarchy chart**—A diagram that illustrates modules' relationships.

**high-level programming language**—A programming language that is English-like, as opposed to a low-level programming language.

**housekeeping**—A module that includes steps you must perform at the beginning of a program to get ready for the rest of the program.

**Hungarian notation**—A variable-naming convention in which a variable's data type or other information is stored as part of the name.

**identifier**—A variable name.

**if clause**—Part of a decision holds the action that results when a Boolean expression in a decision is true.

**if-then-else**—Another name for a dual-alternative selection structure or dual-alternative if structure.

**implied data**—Data that does not exist explicitly.

**incrementing**—To add 1 to a variable.

**indeterminate loop**—A loop for which you cannot predetermine the number of executions. Also called an indefinite loop.

**infinite loop**—A loop that never stops executing; a repeating flow of logic without an ending.

**initialization loop**—A loop structure that provides initial values for every element in any array.

**initializing**—To provide a variable with a value when you create it, which is part of defining a variable.

**inner loop**—A loop that is contained within another loop. *See also* outer loop.

**input device**—A hardware device such as a keyboard or mouse; through these devices, data enter the computer system.

**input symbol**—Represented as a parallelogram in flowcharts.

**integer**—A value that is a whole number, numeric variable.

**internal program documentation**—The documentation within a program.

**internal storage**—Temporary storage within the computer; also called memory, main memory, or primary memory.

**interpreter**—Software that translates a high-level language into machine language and tells you if you have used a programming language incorrectly. Similar to a compiler. However, an interpreter translates one statement at a time, executing each statement as soon as it is translated.

**iteration**—Repetition; another name for a loop structure. *See also* loop structure.

**line counter**—A variable that keeps track of the number of printed lines on a page.

**local variable**—A variable declared within the module that uses it.

**logic**—Instructions given to the computer in a specific sequence, without leaving any instructions out or adding extraneous instructions.

**logical AND operator**—A symbol that you use to combine decisions so that two (or more) conditions must be true for an action to occur.

**logical comparison operator**—The symbol that expresses Boolean comparisons. Examples include =, >, <, >=, <=, and <>.

**logical error**—An error that occurs when incorrect instructions are performed, or when instructions are performed in the wrong order.

**logical OR operator**—A symbol that you use to combine decisions when any one can be true for an action to occur.

**loop**—A structure that repeats actions while some condition continues.

**loop body**—The set of statements that execute within a loop.

**loop control variable**—A variable that determines whether a loop will continue.

**loop structure**—A structure in which you ask a question; if the answer requires an action, you perform the action and ask the original question again.

**low-level detail**—A small, nonabstract step.

**low-level programming language**—A programming language not far removed from machine language, as opposed to a high-level programming language.

**lozenge**—A four-sided shape where the top and bottom sides are parallel straight lines and the left and right sides are convex curves; terminal symbols, or start/stop symbols, in flowcharts are lozenges.

**machine language**—A computer's on-off circuitry language; the low-level language made up of 1s and 0s that the computer understands.

**main loop**—The part of a program that contains the steps that are repeated for every record.

**main program**—The program that runs from start to stop and calls other modules.

**mainline logic**—The overall logic of the main program from beginning to end.

**major-level break**—A break caused by a change in the value of a higher-level field.

**method**—A small program unit that you can use together to make a program. Also called modules, subroutines, functions, or procedures.

**minor-level break**—A break caused by a change in the value of a lower-level field.

**mnemonic**—A memory device; variable identifiers act as mnemonics for hard-to-remember memory addresses.

**modularization**—The process of breaking a program into modules.

**module**—A small program unit that you can use together to make a program. Programmers also refer to modules as subroutines, procedures, functions, or methods.

**multiple-level control break**—A break in which the normal flow of control breaks away for special processing in response to more than just one change in condition.

**nested decision** or **nested if**—A decision "inside of" another decision.

**nesting**—To place a structure within another structure.

**nesting loop**—A loop within a loop.

**null case**—The branch of a decision in which no action is taken.

**numeric constant**—A specific numeric value.

**numeric variable**—A variable that holds numeric values.

**object-oriented programming**—A programming technique that focuses on objects, or "things," and describes their features, or attributes, and their behaviors.

**opening a file**—To tell the computer where the input is coming from—for example, a specific disk drive, CD, or tape drive.

**OR decision**—A decision that contains two (or more) decisions; if at least one condition is met, the resulting action takes place.

**out of bounds**—A subscript that is not within the range of acceptable subscripts.

**outer loop**—A loop that contains another loop. *See also* inner loop.

**output device**—A computer device such as a printer or monitor that lets people can view, interpret, and work with information produced by a computer.

**output symbol**—Represented as a parallelogram in flowcharts.

**parallel arrays**—Two or more arrays in which each element in one array is associated with the element in the same relative position in the other array or arrays.

**precedence**—The quality of an operation that means it is evaluated before others.

**prefix**—A set of characters used at the beginning of related variable names.

**priming input** or **priming read**—The first read or data input statement in a program.

**print chart** or **print layout** or **printer spacing chart**—A tool for planning program output. Also called a print layout.

**procedural program**—A program in which one procedure follows another from the beginning until the end.

**procedural programming**—A programming technique that focuses on the procedures that programmers create.

**procedure**—A small program unit that you can use together to make a program. Also called modules, subroutines, functions, or methods.

**processing**—To organize data items, check them for accuracy, or perform mathematical operations on them.

**processing symbol**—Represented as a rectangle in flowcharts.

**program comment**—A nonexecuting statement that programmers place within their code to explain program statements in English.

**program documentation**—The set of instructions that programmers use when they begin to plan the logic of a program.

**programming language**—A language such as Visual Basic, Pascal, COBOL, RPG, C#, C++, Java, or Fortran, used to write programs.

**prompt**—A message that appears on a monitor, asking the user for a response.

**pseudocode**—An English-like representation of the logical steps it takes to solve a problem.

**query**—A question that pulls related data items together from a database in a format that enhances efficient management decision making.

**range**—A series of values that encompasses every value between a high an low limit.

**range check**—A test that compares a variable to a series of values between limits.

**range of values**—A set of contiguous values.

**record**—A group of fields that go together for some logical reason. *See also* data hierarchy.

**reliability**—The feature of modular programs that assures you that a module has been tested and proven to function correctly.

**repetition**—Another name for a loop structure. *See also* loop structure.

**reusability**—The feature of modular programs that allows individual modules to be used in a variety of applications.

**rolling up the totals**—The process of adding a total to a higher-level total.

**running**—To have a computer use a written and compiled program. *See also* executing a program.

**run-time array**—An array that receives its final values during an actual run, or execution, of a program.

**saving**—To store a program on some nonvolatile medium.

**selection structure**—A programming structure in which you ask a question, and depending on the answer, you take one of two courses of action. Then, no matter which path you follow, you continue on with the next event. Also called a decision structure.

**self-documenting program**—A program that describes itself to the reader through the use of comments.

**sentinel value**—A limit, or ending value.

**sequence structure**—A programming structure in which you perform an action or event, and then you perform the next action in order. A sequence can contain any number of events, but there is no chance to branch off and skip any of the events.

**single-alternative if** or **single-alternative selection**—A selection structure where action is required for only one outcome of the question. You call this form of the selection structure an if-then, because no "else" action is necessary. *See also* unary selection.

**single-level control break**—A break in the logic of a program based on the value of a single variable.

**size (of an array)**—The number of elements it can hold.

**soft copy**—A screen copy.

**software**—Programs written by programmers that tell the computer what to do.

**sort**—To take records that are not in order and rearrange them so that they are in order based on some field.

**spaghetti code**—Snarled, unstructured program logic.

**stacking**—To attach structures end-to-end.

**standard input device**—The default device from which input comes, most often the keyboard.

**standard output device**—The default device to which output is sent, usually the monitor.

**string constant**—One or more characters enclosed within quotation marks. If a working program contains the statement lastName = "Lincoln" then "Lincoln" is a character or string constant. In this book, "string constant" is used synonymously with "character constant."

**string variable**—A variable that holds character values. If a working program contains the statement lastName = "Lincoln" then lastName is a character or string variable. In this book, "string variable" is used synonymously with "character variable" and "text variable."

**structure**—A basic unit of programming logic; each structure is a sequence, selection, or loop.

**subroutine**—A small program unit that you can use together to make a program. Also called modules, procedures, functions, or methods.

**subscript**—A number that indicates the position of a particular item within an array.

**summary line**—On a report, a line that contains end-of-report information. *See also* total line.

**summary report**—A report that does not include any information about individual records, but instead includes group totals.

**syntax**—The rules of a language.

**syntax error**—An error in language or grammar.

**terminal symbol**—Represents the end of the flowchart; its shape is a lozenge. Also called a start/stop symbol.

**text variable**—A variable that holds character values. If a working program contains the statement lastName = "Lincoln" then lastName is a text variable. *See also* string variable.

**total line**—On a report, a line that contains end-of-report information. *See also* summary line.

**trivial Boolean expression**—A Boolean expression that always evaluates to the same result.

**unary selection**—A selection structure where action is required for only one outcome of the question. You call this form of the selection structure an if-then, because no "else" action is necessary. *See also* single-alternative if or single-alternative selection.

**user**—A person who uses computer programs. Also called an end-user.

**user documentation**—All the manuals or other instructional materials that nontechnical people use, as well as the operating instructions that computer operators and data-entry personnel need.

**variable**—A memory location, whose contents can vary, or differ, over time.

**volatile**—The characteristic of internal memory, which loses its contents every time the computer loses power.

**while statement**—A statement that can be used to code any loop.

**work field** or **work variable**—A variable you use to temporarily hold a calculation.

\* sign, 21
= sign
  assignment operator, 21, 22, 28
  equivalency operator, 152–156
  varied language uses, 21, 22,
    152–153
\> operator, 152, 153, 154, 156
\>= operator, 153, 154, 156
< operator, 152, 153, 154, 156
<= operator, 153, 156
<> operator, 155, 156
!= operator, 155
≠ operator, 155
ll symbol, 173
# sign, 135

## A

abstraction
  defined, 74, 101
  example, 74–75
  high-level programming language, 75
  low-level details vs., 75, 101
accumulators, 230–232
  defined, 230–231, 234
  example programs, 230–232, 288–291
  initializing, 231
  resetting, 232
addresses (memory)
  arrays, 286–287
  assigning, 5, 16, 22, 118, 120
  content-based calculations, 22
  historical perspective, 24
  mnemonics, 16, 28
  module locations, 79
  stacks, 79
algorithms, 6, 27
American Standard Code for Information
  Interchange. *See* ASCII (American
  Standard Code for Information
  Interchange)
AND decisions, 156–166, 190
  combining decisions, 163–164,
    178–180
  common errors, 164–166, 169–170
  defined, 156, 191
  efficient use, 161–163

  examples, 157–161, 163–164,
    169–170
  logical AND operator, 163–164, 191
  nested decisions, 156, 161–163, 191
  precedence, 178–180, 191
  prioritizing order, 161–163
  program example. *See* insurance plan
    program
  range comparisons, 165–166
  using "or" erroneously, 169–170
annotation symbol (box)
  defined, 83, 102
  example, 123
apartment rent program, 299–304
  `cleanUp()` module, 301–302
  compile-time arrays, 299–302
  `figureRent()` module, 301, 302
  file description, 299
  hard-coded values, 300, 319
  loading arrays from files, 302–304, 318
  mainline logic, 300
  `prep()` (housekeeping) module,
    300–301, 302–303
  reading records, 301
application software, 2
arithmetic operation statements, 13
  combining steps, 130–131
  multiplication symbols, 21
arrays, 285–319
  advantages, 286, 293
  alternative names, 286
  assessing applicability, 299
  boundaries, 310–311
  compile-time array, 299–302, 318, 319
  declaring elements, 297, 318
  defined, 286, 318
  elements, 286, 297, 318
  exact matches, 304–306
  flags. *See* flags
  hard-coded values, 300, 319
  increasing flexibility, 312
  initializing variables, 297, 298, 318
  loading, from files, 302–304, 318
  non-array programs vs., 287–291
  out of bounds, 310–311, 318, 319
  overview, 286
  parallel array, 306–310, 318, 319

program/module examples. *See*
  apartment rent program; mail-order
  programs; recycling statistics
  program
  range match searches, 314–317,
    318, 319
  replacing nested decisions, 291–296
  run-time (execution) array, 299, 318, 319
  search efficiency, 312–313
  size, 286, 318
  subscripts. *See* subscripts
  summary, 318
ASCII (American Standard Code for
  Information Interchange), 95
  character chart, B-3–6
  coding scheme, B-2–3
  EBCDIC vs., 95, B-2–3
  Unicode vs., 95, B-2–3
assignment operator, 21, 28
assignment statements, 21–22
  defined, 21, 28
  legal/illegal examples, 24
  syntax, 21–22, 26
assumed data, 95, 96, 102
asterisk (\*) sign, 21
averaging program, 79–85
  declaring variables, 83–84
  hierarchy chart, 84–85
  modularizing example, 79–80
  modules calling modules, 81–82

## B

base 16, 5
binary decisions, 18, 28, 150, 191.
  *See also* dual-alternative selections
  (if-then-else)
binary digits. *See* bits
binary numbering systems
  ASCII, 95, B-2, B-3–6
  bits, 10, B-2
  decimal vs., B-1
  EBCDIC, 95, B-2–3
  representation scheme, B-1–2
  types, 95, B-2–3
  Unicode, 95, B-2–3
bits, 10, B-2

blocks, 42, 65
`bookListLoop()` module, 257, 258
bookstore file program
  `bookListLoop()` module, 257, 258, 259
  `categoryChange()` module, 259–260, 261
  `closedown()` module, 257, 258
  control break totals, 256–261
  file description, 257
  reading records, 259
bookstore sales report
  `cityBreak()` module, 262–264, 265–267
  `closedown()` module, 261, 266–267
  control break modules, 262–264, 265–267
  `housekeeping()` module, 262, 263
  `mainloop()` module, 264, 265
  major-level break, 264
  minor-level break, 264
  multiple-level control breaks, 261–267
  presorting records, 261–262
  reading records, 261–262
  `stateBreak()` module, 262–264, 265–267
Boole, George, 152
Boolean expressions. *See also* dual-alternative selections (if-then-else); single-alternative selections (if-then)
  comparison operators. *See* logical comparison operators
  defined, 152, 191
  evaluating, 150–152, 190
  operator precedence, 178–180
  outcome possibilities, 185–186
  structuring unstructured code, 55–58, A-1–10
  trivial, 152, 156, 191
  universality, 152
bytes
  coding schemes, 95, B-1–6
  defined, 95, 102

## C

C#. *See* programming languages
C++. *See* programming languages

calling programs
  conventions, 78–79
  defined, 78, 102
  flowchart example, 80
  flowchart symbol, 78
  logic flow, 79
  main programs as, 79–80
  multiple modules, 78–79
  multiple-use modules, 86
  pseudocode example, 79, 80
camel casing, 16, 28
cascading if statements, 156, 191
case structure, 59–60, 180–182, 190
  computer processing vs., 60
  defined, 59, 65
  example, 59–60, 180–182
  flowcharts, 59, 60, 181, 182
  pseudocode, 59, 60, 181, 182
  when to use, 60, 180, 191
`categoryChange()` module, 259–260, 261
central processing unit (CPU), 2, 27
`char` variables, 82–83
character constants, 23, 28. *See also* constants
character variables
  defined, 23–24, 28
  single vs. string, 83
  this book, 82–83
characters
  ASCII chart, B-3–6
  byte position allocation, 95
  data hierarchy position, 10, 11
  defined, 10, 27
  foreign alphabet characters, 10
  repeated, 96
  specific, languages supporting, 83
`cityBreak()` module, 262–264, 265–267
clarity, 50
classes, 121
`cleanUp()` module, 301–302
client. *See* user
`closedown()` modules
  bookstore file program, 257, 258
  bookstore sales report, 261, 266–267
COBOL. *See* programming languages
coding programs
  defined, 7, 27
  language selection, 7
  overview, 7
  planning logic concurrently, 7

coding schemes, 95, B-1–6
  ASCII, 95, B-2, B-3–6
  binary vs. decimal, B-1–2
  EBCDIC, 95, B-2–3
  types, 95, B-2–3
  Unicode, 95, B-2–3
column headings, 122. *See also* heading lines
combining steps, 130–131
comments. *See* program comments
compact disc drives, 4
compact discs, 2
comparison operators (symbols). *See* specific operators; logical comparison operators
compile-time arrays
  defined, 299, 318, 319
  example, 299–302
compilers. *See also* translating programs
  defined, 3, 27
  identifying errors, 7–8
  interpreters vs., 3
  mechanics, 7–8
compiling code, 7–8
  illustrated, 8
  multiple times, 8
  overview, 7–8
  syntax error corrections, 7–8
complete program exercise. *See* inventory report program
computer components, 2–3, 4–5, 26
computer operations, 2–5, 26
confusing code. *See* spaghetti code
connector symbols, 20–21, 26, 28
constant output
  defined, 89, 102
  report layouts, 89, 90, 91, 92–93
constants
  appropriate use, 139–140
  character constant, 23, 28
  legal/illegal examples, 24
  literal constant, 23
  named constant, 22
  numeric constant, 23, 28
  output. *See* constant output
control break fields
  defined, 248, 274
  initializing variables, 248–249
  reading records process, 248–252

control break modules
in footers, 254–256
in headings, 252–253
control break programs, 246, 274
control break reports
common traits, 246
defined, 246, 274
generating, 246
program examples. *See* bookstore file
program; bookstore sales report;
employees by department report
control breaks, 245–274. *See also*
multiple-level control breaks;
page breaks
defined, 246, 273, 274
intermediate-level, 264
major-level, 264, 274
minor-level, 264, 274
overview, 246, 273
presorting records, 246, 261–262, 274
program examples. *See* bookstore file
program; bookstore sales report;
employees by department report
remembering previous record. *See*
control break fields
required tasks, 259, 262, 273
single-level, 246–252, 274
starting new pages, 246–252
summary, 273
with totals, 256–261
conversion, 9, 27
copy statements, 135
counters, 207–211
defined, 208, 234
example, 207–211
incrementing, 208, 234
CPU. *See* central processing unit (CPU)
customer report program, 267–272
complete program, 272
`getReady()` module, 268, 269
line-counter variable, 268, 270, 271
mainline logic, 268, 269
page breaks, 267–272
print chart, 268
`produceReport()` module, 268,
269, 270
`startNewPage()` module,
270–271

**D**

data, 2, 27
field positions, 95–99
programmer-required, 97
types, 22–24
data dictionary, 83, 102
data hierarchy, 10–11, 26
databases, 10, 27
defined, 10, 27
example, 11
fields, 10, 11, 27
file descriptions, 96–97
files. *See* files
illustrated, 11
records, 10, 27
tables, 10
data position allocation, 95
implied data, 95, 96, 102
input vs. output, 97
"packed" vs. "unpacked" storage, 95
data structure, 121
databases
data hierarchy position, 10–11
defined, 10, 27
dead path. *See* unreachable paths
decimal points
implied data, 95, 96, 102
printed reports, 96
storage convention, 95, 96, 101
decimal system
ASCII values, B-3–6
binary system vs., B-1–2
decision structures. *See* dual-alternative
selections (if-then-else); selection
structures; single-alternative selections
(if-then)
decision tables, 182–189, 190
components, 182
defined, 182, 191
large, example, C-1–7
outcome possibilities, 185–186, C-1–3
program examples. *See* payroll bonus
program; residence hall selection
program
when to use, 182, 188
decisions, 149–191. *See also* AND
decisions; Boolean expressions; OR
decisions; range checks
binary decisions, 18
combining, 163–164, 172–174,
178–180

comparison operators. *See* logical
comparison operators
defined, 18, 28
flowchart symbols, 18, 28
good vs. bad questions, 18
numerous, example, C-1–7
precedence, 178–180, 191
program example. *See* insurance plan
program
sentinel values. *See* sentinel values
structuring unstructured code, 55–58,
A-1–10
summary, 190
declaring variables (declarations), 82–84,
118–123
arrays, 297, 318
assigning values, 21–22, 121
camel casing, 16, 28
data dictionary, 83, 102
defined, 23, 28, 29, 82, 101, 102
defining vs., 121
distinguishing data types, 22–24, 26,
82–83, 118–119, 129–130
examples, 83, 84, 118–123
file descriptions, 95–96
flowchart example, 83, 84
group names, 120–121, 142
heading lines, 122
Hungarian notation, 119, 142
initializing vs., 121
inventory report program, 118–123
legal/illegal assignments, 24
memory addresses, 5, 16, 22, 24, 79,
118, 120
naming variables, 16–18, 26, 29, 96,
118–119, 137–138, 208, 309
prefixes, 119, 141
pseudocode example, 83, 84
reusing names, 96, 119
temporary placeholders, 131, 139
unknown values, 121
decrementing variables, 213–214,
233, 234
default case, 60
default values
defined, 175, 191
range check example, 175–176
defining variables. *See* declaring variables
(declarations); initializing variables
definite loops, 218, 234
design importance, 134, 141

desk-checking, 140, 142
detail lines
    constants, 89, 91
    defined, 89, 102
    print chart, 89–91
    printed reports, 93
`determineDiscount()` module,
    316
diamond shapes, 18, 26, 28
disk drives, 4
do until loops, 60–63, 219–223, 233
    converting, to do while loops, A-10
    defined, 61, 65
    do while loops vs., 63, 64, A-10
    examples, 61–63, 220–223
    when to use, 219–220
do while loops. *See* loop structures (do
    while loops)
documentation, 86–100, 101
    categories, 86, 102
    completing, 99–100
    defined, 86, 102
    end user documentation, 86
    input documentation, 94–99
    output documentation. *See* report layouts
    program documentation, 86–87, 102
    user documentation, 99–100, 102
double-sided decisions. *See* dual-
    alternative selections (if-then-else)
dual-alternative selections (if-then-else)
    defined, 39, 64, 150, 191
    else clauses, 151, 191
    examples, 39, 151
    if clauses, 151, 191
    illustrated, 150
dummy values, 19, 28

**E**

early exits
    defined, 312, 319
    example, 312–313
EBCDIC (Extended Binary Coded Decimal
    Interchange Code), 95, B-2–3
efficiency, 50
elegant programs, 287
elements
    declaring, 297, 318
    defined, 286, 318
else clauses, 151, 191. *See also* dual-
    alternative selections (if-then-else)
employee/supervisor list program, 174–178

employees by department report, 246–256
    control data in footer, 254–256
    control data in heading, 252–253
    file description, 247
    `finish()` modules, 251–252, 256
    `housekeeping()` modules,
        248–249, 252–253, 256
    mainline logic, 248
    `mainloop()` module, 249–250
    `newpage()` modules, 250–251,
        252–253, 254–255
    print charts, 247, 252, 254
    reading records, 247
    single-level control break, 246–252
end-of-job routine, 132–134, 141. *See
    also* `finish()` modules
    defined, 117, 141
    flowchart example, 132
    footers, 132, 142
    inventory report program, 132–134
    pseudocode example, 132
    subroutines, 132
end-structure statements, 41
end users. *See* users
`endif` statements, 41, 42, 43, 52
ending programs, 19. *See also* end-of-
    job routine; `finish()` modules
`endwhile` statements, 41, 43
entry points, 43–44
eof (end of file)
    defined, 19, 28
    illustrated, 20
`eof` question, 45, 46, 48, 49
    controlling main loop, 129,
        131–132, 141
    placement, 125
    testing condition, 124, 125, 131–132
    `while not eof` vs., 308
equal (=) sign
    assignment operator, 21, 22, 28
    equivalency operator, 152–156
    varied language uses, 21, 22, 152–153
equivalency operator, 152–156
errors
    AND decisions, 164–166, 169–170
    compilers identifying, 3, 7–8
    initializing variables, 214, 216–217
    looping, 214–217, 233
    OR decisions, 167–170
    range checks, 176–178
    syntax, 3, 7–8

evolution, of programming, 24–25
executing programs, 3, 27
execution-time arrays, 299, 318, 319
exit points, 43–44
Extended Binary Coded Decimal
    Interchange Code (EBCDIC), 95, B-2–3
external program documentation, 87, 102
external storage
    defined, 4, 27
    devices, 4
    nonvolatile, 5
    saving programs, 5

**F**

fields
    data hierarchy position, 10–11
    defined, 10, 27
`figureRent()` module, 301, 302
file descriptions, 94–99
    data field positions, 95, 97
    data hierarchy, 96–97
    decimal point representation, 95, 96
    defined, 94, 102
    examples, 95, 98, 114, 135, 157, 183
    field names. *See* declaring variables
        (declarations)
    generating output, 97–99
    implied data, 95, 96, 102
    insufficient, 98–99
    inventory report program, 114
    leading zeros, 95, 96
    output format vs., 97
    variables. *See* variables
files
    data hierarchy position, 10–11
    defined, 10, 27
    disk storage illustration, 119–120
    field position allocation, 97
    loading arrays from, 302–304, 318
    opening, 123–124, 142
    programmer-required data, 97
    record volume, 10
    repeated characters, 96
`finish()` modules. *See also*
    end-of-job routine
    employees by department report,
        251–252, 256
    `eof` engaging, 124
    inventory report program, 132, 133, 134
    label-making programs, 207, 209,
        211, 219

payroll report program, 226, 227
recycling statistics program, 290–291, 295–296
flags
adding to flowcharts, A-5–7
controlling out of bounds, 310–311
defined, 305, 319, A-5
floating-point (fractional) numeric variables, 23, 29
flowcharts, 6, 26
annotation symbol (box), 83, 102, 123
calling module symbol, 78, 101
connector symbol, 20–21, 26, 28
decision symbols, 18, 28
defined, 12, 28
diamond shapes, 18, 26, 28
example, 14
flowlines, 13, 28
infinite, 15
input symbols, 12, 28
lozenge shape, 14
multiple values, 13
open file command, 124
output symbols, 13, 28
parallelograms, 12, 13, 26, 28, 124
processing symbols, 13, 28
pseudocode vs., 14
reading convention, 13
rectangles, 13, 26, 28, 78, 101
steps following, 14
structured. *See* structures
terminal symbols, 14, 28
unstructured, example, 47
untangling, 55–58
flowlines
defined, 13, 28
untangling flowcharts, 55–58
font (file names), 16, 28
footers (footer lines)
control breaks within, 254–256
defined, 132, 142, 254, 274
`for` statements (`for` loops), 217–219, 233, 234
foreign alphabet characters, 10
formatting
heading lines, 122–123
subscripts, 286–287, 293–294, 296
variable names. *See* naming variables

Fortran. *See* programming languages
fractional (floating-point) numeric variables, 23, 29
functional cohesion, 82, 102
functional decomposition, 117, 141
functions. *See* modules

## G

garbage, 121, 142
`getPrice()` module, 308–310, 311, 312
`getReady()` modules
customer report program, 268, 269
residence hall selection program, 184, 185, 189
global variables, 83, 102
"go to" statements, 49
good habits, 140
graphical user interface (GUI) environment
defined, 93, 102
report layouts, 93–94
greater than (>) operator, 152, 153, 154, 156
greater than or equal to (>=) operator, 153, 154, 156
group names, 120–121
defined, 120, 142
example, 120–121
limitations, 121
GUI. *See* graphical user interface (GUI) environment

## H

habits, good programming, 140
hard-coded values, 300, 319
hard copy, 94, 102
hard drives, 5
hardware
defined, 2, 26
varied systems, 4
heading lines
constants, 89, 90
control breaks. *See* control breaks
declaring variables for, 122
defined, 89, 102
formatting, 122–123
print chart, 89
printed reports, 93
printing, 124
variables, 90

hexadecimal notation, 5
hierarchy. *See* data hierarchy
hierarchy charts
creating, 84–86
defined, 84, 102
examples, 85–86, 118
features, 84, 86
inventory report program, 118
high-level programming languages
abstraction, 75
advantages, 75, 101
defined, 7, 27
`housekeep()` module, 207, 208–209, 214, 217, 219
housekeeping, 118–128
declaring variables. *See* declaring variables (declarations)
defined, 117, 141
one-time-only tasks, 118, 124
opening files, 123–124, 142
printing headings, 124
reading first input record. *See* priming read (input)
tasks, 118, 141
`housekeeping()` modules
AND decision example, 159
array examples, 292, 297, 298, 300–301, 302–303
bookstore sales report, 262, 263
control break examples, 248–249, 252–253, 262–263
counter control example, 207, 208–209
employees by department report, 248–249, 252–253, 256
`eof` immediately following, 117, 125
insurance plan program, 159
inventory report program, 123, 127–128
last task of, 124
line break examples, 138–139
nesting loop example, 226–228
payroll report program, 226–228
reading first input record, 125
Hungarian notation, 119, 142

## I

identifiers
camel casing, 16, 28
defined, 16, 28, 137, 142
examples, 18
font format, 16, 28

meanings, 16, 17
mnemonics, 16, 28
naming, 16–18, 26, 29, 96, 118–119, 137–138, 208, 309
if clauses, 151, 191
if-then. *See* single-alternative selections (if-then)
if-then-else. *See* dual-alternative selections (if-then-else)
implementation hiding
    defined, 136, 142
    protecting source code, 136
implied data, 95, 96, 102
import statements, 135
included statements, 135
incrementing variables, 208, 234
indeterminate (indefinite) loops, 218, 234
infinite loops, 18–19
    defined, 18, 28, 234
    ending, 18–19
initialization loops
    defined, 298, 318
    early exits, 312–313, 319
    example, 298
    subscripts, 298
initializing variables
    arrays, 297, 298, 318
    control breaks, 248–249
    declaring vs., 121
    defined, 121, 142
    errors, 214, 216–217
    loop control, 206, 214, 216–217
inner loops, 224, 234
input
    correct vs. faulty logic, 125–126
    devices, 2, 4, 27, 123, 142
    flowchart symbols, 12, 28
    ignoring extraneous data, 98, 115
    opening files, 123–124, 142
    operations, 4
    reading first record. *See* priming read (input)
    standard device, 123, 142
input documentation, 94–99. *See also* file description
    data field positions, 95–99
    interactively supplied, 94
insurance plan program, 156–168, 170–174
    AND logic, 156–166
    avoiding errors, 164–166, 167–170

combining decisions, 163–164, 172–174
efficiency techniques, 161–163, 170–172
file description, 157
`housekeeping()` module, 159
mainline logic, 158
`mainloop()` modules, 159–160, 161–162, 166–168, 170–172
nested AND decisions, 161–163
OR logic, 166–174
print chart, 158
integer numeric variables, 23, 28
intermediate-level breaks, 264
internal memory. *See* memory
internal program documentation, 87, 102
internal storage. *See* memory
interpreters.
    compilers vs., 3
    defined, 3, 27
    identifying errors, 7–8
    mechanics, 7–8
inventory report program, 113–142
    declaring variables, 118–123
    end-of-job routine, 132–134
    file description, 114
    `finishUp()` modules, 132, 133, 134
    flowchart (complete), 133–134
    `housekeeping()` module, 123, 127–128
    mainline logic, 114–118
    `mainloop()` module, 129–132
    opening files, 123–124, 142
    overview, 116–118
    printing headings, 124
    procedural program overview, 116–118
    pseudocode (complete), 133–134
    reading first input record, 124–128
    report layout, 114–115
    understanding requirements, 115
iteration. *See* loop structure

**J**

Java. *See* programming languages

**L**

label-making programs, 207–223
    avoiding errors, 214–217
    counter looping, 207–211

decrementing looping, 213–214
do until loops, 219–223
file descriptions, 207, 211
`finishUp()` modules, 207, 209, 211, 219
`for` loops, 217–219
`housekeep()` modules, 207, 208–209, 214, 217, 219
mainline logic, 207
`mainLoop()` modules, 207, 209–211, 212–213, 215–216, 217–218, 219
variable sentinel value looping, 211–213
languages. *See also* programming languages
    machine language, 3, 27
    translation software. *See* compilers
leading zeros
    in files, 95, 96, 101
    printed reports, 96
less than (<) operator, 152, 153, 154, 156
less than or equal to (<=) operator, 153, 156
let statements, 22
letters, 10
line breaks, 138–139
line-counter variables
    defined, 268, 274
    page breaks with, 267–272
loading programs, 4
local variables
    declaring, 83, 102
    defined, 83
logic
    defined, 3, 27
    errors. *See* logical errors
    syntax vs., 3
logical AND operator. *See also* AND decisions
    defined, 163, 191
    errors, 165–166
    example, 163–164
logical comparison operators, 152–156, 190. *See also* specific operators
    defined, 152, 191
    loop control errors, 215
    multiple uses, same results, 153–155
    possible comparisons, 152–155
    precedence, 178–180, 191
    summary, 156

logical errors
  defined, 8, 27
  locating, 3, 8–9
  testing programs, 8–9
logical OR operator. *See also* OR decisions
  defined, 172–173, 191
  example, 173–174
  symbols, 173
long statements, clarifying, 139
loop body, 206, 233
loop control
  altering variables, 206, 214
  counters, 207–211, 234
  decrementing variables, 213–214,
    233, 234
  definite loops, 218, 234
  errors, 214–217, 233
  `for` statements (`for` loops), 217–219,
    233, 234
  indeterminate (indefinite) loops, 218, 234
  initializing variables, 206, 214, 216–217
  requirements, 206
  sentinel values, 19, 206, 211–213, 233
  statement misplacement, 215–216
  variables, 204–206, 214–215, 233
  `while` statements, 218, 219, 234
  wrong comparison, 215
loop structures (do while loops), 203–234
  accumulators, 230–232, 234, 288–291
  advantages, 204
  alternative names, 40, 64
  assessing, 46
  body, 233
  common characteristics, 223–224, 233
  common errors, 214–217, 233
  comparison operators. *See* logical
    comparison operators
  controlling. *See* loop control
  defined, 39–40, 64, 204, 233
  definite loop, 218, 234
  distinguishing, 63
  do until loop vs., 63, 64, A-10
  flowcharts, 43, 44, 61, 62, 63
  for statements, 234
  indeterminate (indefinite) loop, 218, 234
  inner loop, 224, 234
  last element, 48
  nesting. *See* nesting loops
  outer loop, 224, 234
  program examples. *See* label-making
    programs; payroll report program
  pseudocode, 43, 61, 62, 63

  reasons for, 50–52
  recognizing, 54
  requirements, 206
  subroutines, 205–206
  summary, 233
  types, 63, 65
  unstructured vs., 47, 62–63, 223–224
  `while` statements, 218, 219, 234
loops
  infinite loop, 18–19, 28, 234
  unstructured, 62–63
low-level details, 75, 101
low-level machine language, 7, 27
lozenge, 14

## M

machine language
  components, 7
  defined, 3, 27
  low-level language, 7, 27
  translating programs, 7–8
magnetic disks, 2
mail-order programs, 304–317
  array exact matches, 304–306
  available items, 305, 306
  `determineDiscount()` module,
    316
  discounts program, 314–317
  early exit, 312–313
  file descriptions, 304, 314
  finding range matches, 314–317
  flag variables, 305, 310–311
  `getPrice()` module, 308–310,
    311, 312, 313
  improving search efficiency, 312–313
  mainline logic, 307
  matching item numbers, 304–306
  parallel arrays, 306–310
  pricing program, 306–313
  `ready()` module, 307, 308, 310
  staying within array bounds, 310–312
  valid item numbers, 305
main loop, 129–132. *See also*
  `mainloop()` modules
  controlling, with `eof` decision, 129,
    131–132, 141
  declaring new variables, 129–130
  defined, 117, 141, 204, 233
  ending, 132
  reading subsequent records, 131–132
main memory. *See* memory

main programs
  calling programs, example, 79–80
  defined, 79, 102
mainline logic, 114–118. *See also* end-of-
  job routine; housekeeping; main loop
  AND decision example, 158
  apartment rent program, 300
  array examples, 300, 307
  compile-time array example, 300
  control break examples, 248, 269
  counter control example, 207
  customer report program, 268, 269
  decision table example, 184
  defined, 117, 141
  design preparation, 114–115, 134, 141
  distinct parts, 117
  employees by department report, 248
  insurance plan program, 158
  inventory report program, 114–118
  label-making program, 207
  nesting loop example, 227
  overview, 183
  parallel array example, 307
  payroll report program, 226, 227
  recycling statistics program, 288–289
  residence hall selection program,
    183–184
`mainloop()` modules. *See also* main
  loop
  AND decision example, 159–160
  array examples, 290, 291,
    292–295, 296
  bookstore sales report, 264, 265
  bypassing, 124
  control break examples, 248, 249–250,
    251, 264, 265
  counter control example, 209–210
  employees by department report,
    249–250
  engaging, 124
  flowcharts, 131, 160, 171, 172,
    210, 212
  insurance plan program, 159–160,
    161–162, 166–168, 170–172
  inventory report program, 129–132
  label-making programs, 207, 209–211,
    212–213, 215–216, 217–218, 219
  nested AND decisions, 161–162
  nesting loop example, 228–230
  OR logic, 166–168, 170–172
  payroll report program, 228–230

pseudocode, 131, 160–161, 171, 172, 210, 212

recycling statistics program, 290, 291, 292–295, 296

sentinel value example, 212

maintaining programs, 10

maintenance, 50

major-level breaks, 264, 274

matches, array, 304–306

mathematical operations

  combining steps, 130–131

  expressing, 22, 129

  multiplication symbols, 21

  temporary variables, 131, 139

matrix. *See* arrays

memory

  addresses, 5, 16, 22, 24, 79, 118, 120

  array storage, 286–287

  defined, 4, 27

  external storage vs., 4, 5, 27

  mnemonics, 16, 28

  stacks, 79

methods. *See* modules

minor-level breaks, 264, 274

mistakes. *See* errors

mnemonics, 16, 28

modularity. *See* modules

modularization, 74, 101. *See also specific modules*; modules

modules, 74–82. *See also specific modules*

  abstraction, 74–75, 101

  accessing, 135–136

  addresses, 79

  advantages, 74–77, 101, 135–136

  alternative names, 74

  arbitrary rules, 82

  calling, 102. *See* calling programs

  constants in. *See* constants

  defined, 50, 74, 101

  designing clear statements, 138–140

  features, 74–77

  flowcharts, 80, 81–82

  functional cohesion, 82, 102

  functional decomposition, 117, 141

  hierarchy charts. *See* hierarchy charts

  identifying structures, 76–77

  implementation hiding, 136, 142

  line break clarity, 138–139

  main programs calling, 78–80

  modularizing programs, 77–80

modules calling, 81–82

multiple programmers using, 75, 135–136

multiple-use module, 86

naming, 77–78, 101, 137–138

protecting source code, 136

pseudocode, 80, 81–82

reliability, 75–76, 101

reusability, 75–76, 101

storing components separately, 135–136

subdividing, 82

temporary variables, 131, 139

movie patron discounts program, 168–170, 179–180

multiple-level control breaks, 261–267, 273. *See also* control breaks

  checklist, 267

  defined, 261, 274

  example, 261–267

  major-level breaks, 264, 274

  minor-level breaks, 264, 274

  presorting records, 246, 261–262, 274

  required tasks, 262

multiple programmers

  coordinating names, 309

  sharing modules, 75, 135–136

multiplication signs, 21

**N**

named constants, 22

naming. *See also* declaring variables (declarations)

  conventions, coordinating, 309

  modules, 77–78, 101, 137–138

  self-documenting programs, 137

  variables, 16–18, 26, 29, 96, 118–119, 137–138, 208, 309

negative comparisons, 154–155

nested AND decisions (nested ifs), 161–163

  arrays replacing, 291–296

  cascading if statements, 156, 191

  defined, 156, 191

  prioritizing decision order, 161–163

  series of, 156, 191

nesting loops, 224–230, 233

  defined, 224, 234

  example, 224–230

  inner loops, 224, 234

  outer loops, 224, 234

payroll report program, 224–230

  unlimited quantity, 230

nesting structures, 41–43

  defined, 41, 65

  examples, 42–43, 52–53

  flowchart, 42

  pseudocode, 42, 52–53

`newpage()` modules, 250–251, 252–253, 254–255

not equal to operators, 154–155, 156

null case, 39, 64

`num` variables, 82–83

numbers, 10

numeric constants, 23, 28

numeric data entry conventions, 23

numeric variables

  decimal points, 95, 96, 101

  defined, 23, 28

  leading zeros, 95, 96, 101

  legal/illegal examples, 24

  this book, 82–83

**O**

object-oriented programming

  defined, 25, 29, 117

  procedural programming vs., 26, 117

opening files, 123–124

  defined, 123, 142

  flowchart symbol, 124

  standard output device vs., 123

OR decisions, 166–173, 190

  combining decisions, 172–174, 178–180

  common errors, 167–170

  defined, 166, 191

  efficient use, 170–172

  examples, 166–167, 170–172

  logical OR operator, 173–174, 191

  maintaining structure, 167–168

  precedence, 178–180, 191

  prioritizing decision order, 170–172

  using "and" erroneously, 168–169

out of bounds, 310–311, 318, 319

outcome possibilities, 185–186, C-1–3

outer loops, 224, 234

output. *See also* report layouts

  devices, 2, 4, 27, 123, 142

  documentation, 87–94

  example, 4

  input generating, 97–99

inventory report program, 115
opening files, 123–124
spacing, 301
standard device, 123, 142
symbols, 13, 28

**P**

"packed" storage, 95
page breaks, 267–272, 273. See also
control breaks
control break fields, 248–252, 274
line-count-based, 267–272
multiple-level. See multiple-level
control breaks
single-level control break, 246–252
page numbers, 90–91
parallel arrays
defined, 307, 318, 319
example, 306–310
parallelograms, 12, 13, 26, 28, 124
Pascal. See programming languages
payroll bonus program, C-1–7
complete flowchart/pseudocode, C-7
decision flowcharts/pseudocode, C-4–6
decision tables, C-1–7
outcome possibilities, C-1–3
payroll report program, 224–230
`finish()` module, 226, 227
`housekeeping()` module,
226–228
mainline logic, 226, 227
`mainloop()` module, 228–230
nesting loops, 224–230
print chart, 225
planning logic. See also flowcharts;
pseudocode
coding concurrently, 7
design importance, 134, 141
difficulty degree, 7
overview, 6–7
tools, 6
pound (#) sign, 135
pre-processor directives, 135
precedence (operators), 178–180, 191
prefixes, 119, 141
`prep()` (housekeeping) module,
300–301, 302–303
primary memory. See memory

priming read (input), 44–50, 64
defined, 44, 65
empty, default, 124
housekeeping task of, 124–128
inventory report program, 124–128
logic flow, 124–126
purpose, 48
print chart (layout). See printer
spacing charts
printer spacing charts. See also report
layouts
defined, 87, 102
examples, 88–89, 90–93, 158, 183,
225, 230
summary report example, 230
printing
decimal points, 96
heading lines, 124
output spacing, 301
repeating messages, 205–206
reports. See printer spacing charts;
report layouts
statement, calculating within, 130–131
totals, 257, 258
prioritizing decision order
nested AND decisions (nested ifs),
161–163
OR decisions, 170–172
problems. See understanding problems
procedural programming
defined, 25, 29
object-oriented programming vs.,
26, 117
procedural programs, 116–118. See also
end-of-job routine; housekeeping; main
loop; mainline logic
defined, 116–117, 141
major modules, 117
object-oriented vs., 117
procedures. See modules
processing
defined, 2, 4, 27
example, 4
types, 4
processing symbols, 13, 28
`processRequest()` module, 184,
187, 188
`produceReport()` module, 268,
269, 270

production stage, 9
professionalism, 50
program comments
defined, 87, 102
inserting, 87
programming language examples, 87
program design, 134, 141
program documentation
categories, 87
defined, 86, 102
external, 87
internal, 87
programmer job. See programming
process
programming evolution, 24–25
programming languages
defined, 2, 27
formatting subscripts, 286–287,
293–294, 296
high-level, 7, 27, 75, 101
logic. See logic
programming comment examples, 87
selecting, 7
syntax. See syntax
translating, 3
varied operator expressions, 21, 22,
152–153, 155
programming process, 5–10, 26
coding programs, 7
design importance, 134, 141
desk-checking logic, 140
good habits, 140
maintenance stage, 10
planning logic, 6–7
production stage, 9
required data, 97
steps, 5–6
testing programs, 8–9
translating programs, 7–8
understanding problem, 6
prompts, 79, 102
pseudocode, 6
advantages, 12
conventions, 12
defined, 12, 28
ending, 12
examples, 12, 14
flowcharts vs., 14
infinite, 15

multiple values, 13
stacking structures, 41
starting, 12
steps following, 14
structured, examples, 41–43, 45–50, 51–52

## Q

queries, 10–11, 28
questions, unnecessary, 177–178
quotation marks, 23, 28

## R

range checks, 174–178, 190
common errors, 176–178
default values, 175–176, 191
defined, 174, 191
employee/supervisor list program, 174–178
example, 174–176
unnecessary questions, 177–178
unreachable paths, 176–177, 191
range of values
defined, 314, 319
search example, 314–317
storing, 318
ranges
AND decision comparisons, 165–166
defined, 165, 191
selections within, 174–178
reading records
apartment rent program, 301
bookstore file program, 259
bookstore sales report, 261–262
control break fields, 248–252
employees by department report, 247
first record. See priming read (input)
inventory report program, 124–128
ready() module, 307, 308, 310
real estate report, 230–232
recognizing structures, 52–59
records
data hierarchy position, 10–11, 96–97
defined, 10, 27
file description, 96
presorting, 246, 261–262, 274
reading. See priming read (input); reading records
remembering previous, 248, 274

rectangles, 13, 26, 28, 78, 101
recycling statistics program, 287–296
arrays replacing nested decisions, 291–296
file description, 287
finish() modules, 290–291, 295–296
housekeeping() modules, 289–290, 292; 297
mainline logic, 288–289
mainloop() modules, 290, 291, 292–295, 296
nesting decisions, 287–291
print chart, 288
reliability
defined, 101
modules, 75–76, 101
reusability increasing, 75–76
repetition. See loop structure
report layouts, 87–94. See also reports
components, 102
constant data, 89, 90, 91, 92–93
control break examples, 247, 252, 254, 257
designing, 87–94
detail lines, 89–91, 102
heading lines, 89, 90, 102
inventory report program, 114–115
line-counter variables, 267–268
page numbers, 90–91
print charts. See printer spacing charts
printed reports, 93, 94
screens (GUI), 93–94
summary report examples, 93, 230
total (summary) lines, 91–93, 256–261
variable information, 89–90, 91–92, 93
reports. See also bookstore sales report; customer report program; employees by department report; inventory report program; payroll report program
line counters, 274
nesting loop example, 224–230
page breaks. See page breaks
starting new pages, 246–252
summary report, 93, 230–232, 234, 261, 274
totals, 256–261
understanding requirements, 115
user collaboration, 115

residence hall selection program, 182–189
file description, 183
flowchart (complete), 189
getReady() module, 184, 185, 189
mainline logic, 183–184
possible outcomes, 185–186
print chart, 183
processRequest() module, 184, 187, 188
pseudocode (complete), 189
reusability
advantages, 75–76
defined, 101
examples, 75
multi-programmer access, 75
rolling up totals, 259, 274
RPG. See programming languages
run-time arrays, 299, 318, 319
running programs, 3, 27

## S

saving programs
nonvolatile media, 5, 27
periodically, 5
screen layouts. See graphical user interface (GUI) environment
selection structures. See also dual-alternative selections (if-then-else); single-alternative selections (if-then)
alternative name, 38
assessing, 46
defined, 38, 64
examples, 38–39
flowcharts, 38, 42, 43, 44
nesting, 42–43
reasons for, 50–52
recognizing, 54
reorganizing into, 58
self-documenting programs, 137, 142, 226, 234
sentinel values, 19
defined, 206, 233
looping with, 211–213
variable, 211–213, 233
sequence structures
assessing, 45–46
defined, 38, 64
event quantity, 38, 64
flowcharts, 38, 41, 42, 43, 44
nesting, 42–43

pseudocode, 41, 42, 43
reasons for, 50–52
recognizing, 54, 55–56
single-alternative selections (if-then)
defined, 39, 64, 150, 191
examples, 39, 151–152
illustrated, 150
single-level control break
defined, 247, 274
example, 246–252
presorting records, 246, 274
remembering previous record, 248, 274
single-sided decisions. *See* single-
alternative selections (if-then)
snarled statements. *See* spaghetti code
soft copy, 94, 102
software
application software, 2
defined, 2, 26
system software, 2
sorting records, 246, 261–262, 274
source code
defined, 136, 142
protecting, 136
spaces, eliminating, 4, 17
spaghetti bowl method
defined, 55, 64
examples, 55–58, A-1–10
spaghetti code, 36–37
defined, 36, 64
example, 36–37
flowcharts, 37
structuring, 55–58, A-1–10
special symbols, 10
stacking structures
defined, 40, 65
example, 40–41
flowchart, 41
pseudocode, 41
stacks, 79
standard input device, 123, 142
standard output device, 123, 142
`startNewPage()` module,
270–271
`stateBreak()` module, 262–264,
265–267
statements. *See also specific statement
types*
accessing modules, 135
constants use, 139–140

designing clear, 138–140
long, clarifying, 139
storage. *See also* memory
byte position allocation, 95
categories, 4
data file illustration, 119–120
decimal points, 95, 96, 101
devices, 4
external storage, 4, 5, 27
hardware, 2, 26
input, 95–99
internal storage, 4, 27
loading programs, 4
"packed" vs. "unpacked", 95
range of values, 318
size, 119
volatility, 4–5, 27
storing program components, 135–136
string constants, 23, 28. *See also*
constants
string variables. *See* character variables
structured programs
assessing validity, 45–50
characteristics, 44
priming read. *See* priming read (input)
structuring spaghetti code, 55–58,
A-1–10
unstructured vs., 45, 47, 55–58,
62–63, A-1–10
structures, 35–65. *See also specific
structures*
blocks, 42, 65
characteristics, 44
combining, 40–44, 52–53
defined, 37–38, 64
difficult problems, A-1–10
entry points, 43–44
exit points, 43–44
identifying, 45–50, 76–77
nesting, 41–43, 52–53, 65
reasons for, 50–52
recognizing, 52–59
spaghetti code and, 36–37, 55–58,
A-1–10
stacking, 40–41, 65
summary overview, 64
types, 38, 43–44
variable groups as, 121
subroutines. *See* modules
subscripts. *See also* arrays

assigning, 286–287, 293–294, 296
defined, 286, 318
for initialization loops, 298
formatting, 286–287, 293–294, 296
numeric fields, 298
out of bounds, 310–311, 318, 319
selecting variables, 301, 308–309
subtotals, 259
summary lines. *See also* totals
defined, 91, 102
examples, 92–93
printed reports, 93
summary reports, 230–232. *See also*
totals
accumulators, 230–232, 233, 234
defined, 230, 234, 261, 274
examples, 93, 230–232
syntax
defined, 2, 27
logic vs., 3
variables, 23
syntax errors
correcting, 3, 7–8
defined, 7, 27
identifying, 7–8
system software, 2

**T**

tables, 10. *See also* arrays
tapes, 2
temporary variables, 131, 139
terminal symbols, 14, 28
testing programs, 8–9
logical errors, 8–9
selecting data, 9
testing values. *See* AND decisions;
Boolean expressions; decisions; OR
decisions; range checks
text variables. *See* character variables
then and only then test, 160
total lines. *See also* summary reports
control breaks, 256–261
defined, 91, 102
examples, 92–93
totals
accumulators, 230–232, 233, 234
printing, 257, 258
rolling up, 259
subtotals and, 259

translating programs, 7–8
  illustrated, 8
  overview, 7–8
  syntax error corrections, 3, 7–8
trivial Boolean expressions, 152, 156, 191
true/false evaluations. *See* Boolean
  expressions; dual-alternative selections
  (if-then-else); single-alternative
  selections (if-then)

**U**

unary selections. *See* single-alternative
selections (if-then)
understanding problems, 6
Unicode, 95, B-2–3
unnecessary questions, 177–178
"unpacked" storage, 95
unreachable paths, 176–177, 191
unstructured flow chart
  examples, 45, 47, A-1
  untangling, 55–58, A-1–10
unstructured loops, 47, 62–63, 223–224
user documentation, 86
  areas addressed, 100
  defined, 99, 102
  formats, 99

users
  defined, 86, 102, 115, 141
  report collaboration, 115

**V**

variables. *See also* declaring variables
(declarations)
  accumulators, 230–232, 234, 288–291
  adding new, 129–130
  advantages, 16
  arrays. *See* arrays
  assigning values, 21–22, 121
  character variable, 23–24, 28
  counters, 207–211, 234
  data dictionary, 83, 102
  decrementing, 213–214, 233, 234
  defined, 16, 28
  exactness, 83
  flags, 305, 310–311, 319, A-5–7
  floating-point variable, 23, 29
  global variable, 83, 102
  grouping, 120–121, 142
  identifiers, 16–18, 29
  incrementing, 208, 234
  initializing. *See* initializing variables
  integer variable, 23, 28

  line-counter variable, 267–272, 274
  local variable, 83, 102
  numeric variable, 23, 28, 82–83
  sentinel values, 206, 211–213, 233
  specific numeric types, 83
  statement sequence rules, 22
  string variable, 23, 28
  temporary, 131, 139
  text variable, 23, 28
  types, 23
  work variable (field), 131, 142
Visual Basic. *See* programming languages
volatility, 4–5, 27

**W**

while loops. *See* loop structures (do
while loops)
`while not eof`, 308
`while` statements, 218, 219, 234
work variable (field), 131, 142

**Y**

yes-or-no decisions. *See* binary decisions